Created and Directed by Hans Höfer

INSIGHT GUIDES

NATIVE AMERICA

Edited by John Gattuso
Photography by John Running, Monty Roessel
and others

Editorial Director Brian Bell

APA PUBLICATIONS

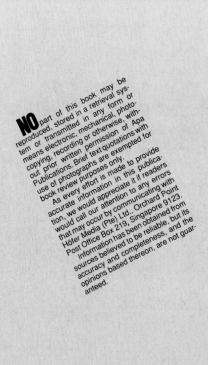
NATIVE AMERICA

First Edition (3rd Reprint)
© 1992 APA PUBLICATIONS (HK) LTD
All Rights Reserved
Printed in Singapore by Höfer Press Pte. Ltd

ABOUT THIS BOOK

In *Insight Guide: Native America*, Apa Publications takes you into the heart of Indian Country. This is a cultural journey, a passage of discovery into American Indian history, cultures and communities. Project Editor **John Gattuso** (a contributor to several Apa guides) put together a team of writers and photographers from every corner of the US. They include journalists, poets, scholars, lawyers and tribal officials. Many are Native Americans, bringing readers a rare inside view of their people and cultures. All have a deep commitment to Native American life.

The Writing Team

Gattuso's first recruit was **Roger Clawson**, an award-winning journalist formerly with the *Billings Gazette*. He grew up among Montana's Crow and Cheyenne Indians and was recently awarded an Alicia Patterson Foundation grant to conduct research on Indian alcohol issues. He has brought his considerable expertise to several chapters on the tribes of the Northern Plains, including the Blackfeet, Northern Cheyenne and Crow.

Another journalist, **Mark Trahant**, wrote about his own people, the Shoshone-Bannock, as well as current issues in Native American life and politics. Trahant is publisher of the *Navajo Nation Today*, and writes a syndicated column on national Indian affairs.

George Hardeen, who wrote on the Navajos and Havasupais, is a freelance writer living on the Navajo Reservation. He is a regular contributor to the *New York Times*, *Los Angeles Times* and National Public Radio.

Journalist **Marjane Ambler**, author of "Wind River," specializes in Indian and environmental issues. Her book, *Breaking the Iron Bonds: Indian Control of Energy Development*, was published in 1990.

Betty Reid, a member of the Navajo Tribe, wrote "Between Two Worlds," a moving account of life between Indian and Anglo cultures. Reid covers Indian affairs for the *Gallup Independent*. She won a Native American Press Association award in 1990.

Native American religions was covered by **Sam Gill**, a professor of religious studies at the University of Colorado, Boulder. Gill is the author of a number of works on Native American cultures.

Edith Wolff, author of "Tribes of Puget Sound," has worked with Native Americans all her adult life as a teacher, newspaper editor and attorney. She currently lives in Seattle, where she specializes in Indian law.

"Warm Springs" was penned by **Elizabeth Woody**, a member of the Warm Springs Tribe and co-founder of the Northwest Native American Writers Association. She has published an award-winning collection of poems, *Hand Into Stone*.

Gloria Bird, a member of the Colville Indian Tribe, is also a founding member of the same writers' association. Her poetry has been widely published.

Joan Baeza, who covered Arizona's Apaches, was formerly the editor of the *Fort Apache Scout*, the newspaper of the White Mountain Apache Tribe. Her work has appeared in many Southwestern publications.

"Hopi Homeland" was contributed by **Abbot Sekaquaptewa**, former Hopi tribal chairman and publisher of *Quatoqti*, a newspaper for Native Americans. He is chairman emeritus of Futures For Children, a self-help community development organi-

Gattuso   *Clawson*   *Trahant*   *Sekaquaptewa*

zation with programs in the American Southwest and Latin America.

Ofelia Zepeda, who wrote "Desert People," is an assistant professor of linguistics and director of American Indian Studies at the University of Arizona, Tucson. She is a member of the Tohono O'odham Nation.

The chapter on powwows was written by **George Horse Capture**, formerly the curator of the Plains Indian Museum, Buffalo Bill Historical Center. A Gros Ventre Indian, he now lives on the Fort Belknap Reservation.

The chapter on art was tackled by **Nancy Shanaman**, a writer and filmmaker specializing in Native American culture. Archaeology was covered by **Linda Gregonis**, coauthor of *The Hohokam Indians of the Tucson Basin* and editor of *Kiva*, an archaeological quarterly. **Dolan Eargle**, who wrote about the native peoples of California, is the author of *The Earth Is Our Mother: A Guide to the Indians of California*. He serves as an advisory member of the Esselen tribal council. "Travel Tips" was researched and organized by **Thomas Jardim**, presently a law student.

The Native Image

Most of the book's stunning images are the work of two men: John Running and Monty Roessel. **John Running** has taken pictures all over the world and is especially well-known for his work with Native Americans. His publications include *Dancer*, a book on ballet; and *Honor Dance*, a book of Native American photographs. Running lives and works in Flagstaff, Arizona.

Monty Roessel's most recent work has appeared in national magazines as well as in two books of photography, *Baseball In America* and *Beyond the Mythic West*. A member of the Navajo Tribe, he is managing editor of the *Navajo Nation Today*.

Additional illustration was provided by a number of talented photographers. Both **Alan Manley** and **Steve Bruno** publish regularly in *Arizona Highways*. **Larry Mayer**, a *Billings Gazette* staffer, contributes to major national magazines. Part-time photographer **Richard Baldes** is a biologist for the US Fish and Wildlife Service. **Lee Brumbaugh** is a PhD candidate in anthropology at the University of California, Berkeley, and a staff member of the California Indian Project. **Kenny Blackbird**, an Assiniboine/Sioux, is a photojournalism student at the University of Montana. **Sandra Tatum**, formerly a *Los Angeles Times* staff photographer, freelances from Corrales, New Mexico. **Jan Wigen** is director of development at the Museum of Native American Cultures in Spokane, Washington. **Stewart Nicholas**, **Bennet Cosay** and **Vennie White** are photographers with the *Fort Apache Scout*. And **Tom Root** runs a photography studio in Plymouth, Ohio.

Special thanks go to **Edward Jardim**, whose sharp eye oversaw the final preparation of the text. The book was proofread and indexed by **Dorothy Stannard**. Thanks also to **Brother C. M. Simon**, SJ, at the Heritage Center in Pine Ridge, South Dakota; the **Eight Northern Indian Pueblos Council**; the **North American Indian Heritage Center**; the **Indian Pueblo Cultural Center**; and all the tribal councils and cultural centers that offered help and information. And most important, a warm thank you to all the Native American people who let the writers and photographers share their lives and cultures. Without their kindness, patience and generosity, this book would not exist.

Horse Capture   *Shanaman*   *Running*   *Roessel*

History and Culture

Places

Maps

WHERE IS NATIVE AMERICA?

Native America is not so much a geographical destination as a cultural one. To find it, you have to experience it.

In a sense, Native America *is* America. Before Christopher Columbus stumbled on San Salvador Island in 1492, Indian people had been the sole human inhabitants of the continent for at least 15,000 years. They migrated from Asia across the Bering Land Bridge and slowly occupied every mountain range, desert, forest and prairie in North America. As they spread out, they grew more diverse, adapting to many environments, speaking hundreds of languages, creating vastly different ways of life. They hunted game, gathered a bounty of wild foods, and raised corn in rich bottomlands and parched deserts. They built powerful confederacies and great civilizations, and developed beautiful and compelling traditions of artistic and religious expression.

With this ancient tenure behind them, it's not difficult to understand why Native Americans feel spiritually rooted to the land. Even today, there are Indians who can trace the migration of their ancestors for thousands of years. They can point to mountains, rivers and canyons and say, "This is where our people came from." They can point to the ruins of ancient villages and say, "These are the footprints of our ancestors."

In 1854, at a treaty council in Washington Territory, the distinguished Duwamish chief, Sealth, spoke of Native America as ancestral and holy ground, filled with the spirits of the people who came before him: "Every part of this soil is sacred in the estimation of my people. Every hillside, every valley, every plain and grove, has been hallowed by some sad or happy event in days long vanished. The very dust upon which you now stand responds more lovingly to their footsteps than to yours, because it is rich with the blood of our ancestors…

"Even the little children who lived here

and rejoiced here for a brief season will love these somber solitudes and at eventide they greet shadowy returning spirits. And when the last red man shall have perished, and the memory of my tribe shall have become a myth among the white men, these shores will swarm with the invisible dead of my tribe, and when your children's children think themselves alone in the field, the store, the shop, upon the highway, or in the silence of the pathless woods, they will not be alone. At night when the streets of your cities and

villages are silent and you think them deserted, they will throng with the returning hosts that once filled and still love this beautiful land. The white man will never be alone."

Many years later, Chief Joseph of the Nez Perce expressed his people's attachment to the land in even more fundamental terms: "The earth and myself are of one mind," he said. "The measure of the land and the measure of our bodies are the same."

And so, if you find yourself in North America, you have, in some respects, already arrived in Native America. But to say that you have found Native America, that you

Preceding pages: powwow outfit; dancer at Rocky Boys Powwow, Montana; tepees; fancy dancer at Blackfeet Powwow; Navajo cowgirl; Ak Chin fireman. Left, powwow lunch. Above, Navajo woman with silver and turquoise jewelry.

have experienced it, is something else again.

Discovering Native America requires more than a physical journey, even if that journey takes you across the stunning landscapes of "Indian Country." To find Native America, you have to glimpse the world of Native American people, their history and traditions, thoughts and beliefs, visions and realities. You have to give a piece of yourself over to the insistent beat of a powwow camp; surrender to the prayerful rhythms of a kachina dance; experience the beauty of Pueblo pottery or Shoshone beadwork; grasp the subtle wisdom of a Navajo coyote story; feel the timeless presence of ancient cliff-dwellings, temple mounds, historic battle-

fields and massacre sites; hike the grasslands, canyons, deserts and forests of Indian Country; and try to understand a people who regard the earth as their mother and the sky as their father.

How this book is organized: *Insight Guide: Native America* is a guide to the communities, cultures and history of American Indian people in the US. It is a window into another way of life, an invitation to the traveler not only to experience new and different places, but to experience familiar places in a new and different way.

This book takes you to Indian Country – the communities, ceremonies, powwows,

historic places, trading posts, art shows, archaeological sites and special events. It gives information on more than 200 Indian tribes and reservations, many located in areas of extraordinary natural beauty such as the Black Hills, Great Smoky Mountains, Olympic Peninsula and Yosemite Valley.

In the first section, *Insight Guide: Native America* tackles topics of broad cultural and historical interest. Where did Native Americans come from? How did they get where they are today? How do Indian people relate to traditional and mainstream cultures? What are Native American religions all about? What are the issues that impact their lives? Because these are such wide-ranging questions, the writers have tried to inform by example, letting specific experiences suggest a larger body of issues.

Next follows the "Features" section, articles on topics of special interest, including American Indian art, powwows and archaeological sites.

The main part of this book, "Places," is the travel guide proper. "Places" is divided into seven broadly defined culture areas – the Great Plains, Northwest, Southwest, Northeastern Woodlands, Great Southeast, Oklahoma (formerly Indian Territory) and California – each representing a major geographical region in which Indian tribes shared various environmental adaptations and cultural traits.

Again, because there is so much to cover in so little space, the writers have stayed within reasonable geographic limits. Although the destinations occasionally spill over international boundaries, the focus remains on the continental US. This is, admittedly, a somewhat arbitrary restriction, especially when you consider that Indian people ranged over North America long before modern political boundaries were established. But then, one cannot overstate the impact that colonialism and nation-building had on native populations. And from a strictly travel-oriented perspective, it seems wise to limit the scope of a book that already covers so vast an area.

In addition, not every Indian reservation and community is covered in the main body of the text. A selection of the most rewarding and important areas is presented at length in "Places." Smaller or less accessible reservations, communities and events are covered in "Travel Tips" at the end of the book. Essentially, "Travel Tips" covers the nuts and bolts of getting around in Indian Country as well as information about museums, galleries, tribal governments, shopping, and other practical matters.

Minding manners: Before setting out on your journey, you should keep in mind that travel in Indian Country is unlike travel elsewhere in the US. Aside from practical concerns – the availability of tourist facilities, the condition of backcountry roads, obtaining tribal permits, etc. – it's essential for travelers to be aware of the troubled history of Indian-white relations and its impact on Indian communities today. For many communities, years

and people by turning them into curiosities.

Given this range of opinion, it is vitally important that travelers make every effort to be well-behaved, informed, and sensitive to their surroundings. Advice about specific people, places and events is offered in the corresponding parts of this book, but there are a number of general considerations that ought to be kept in mind as well. Here, then, are a few essential guidelines:

1) Be respectful! If there is a golden rule of traveling in Indian Country, this is it. And although it sounds like simple advice, it is too often neglected. What's more, "respect" is a culturally relative concept. Behavior that is appropriate in a Western context may be

of oppression and exploitation still weigh heavily on day-to-day life.

While many tribes are working hard to attract and accommodate visitors, some Indian people remain ambivalent about the presence of outsiders. Those in favor of tourism usually argue that it is both a reliable source of income and an inducement to cultural and environmental protection. There are others, however, who feel that tourism compromises the integrity of Indian communities, that it demeans traditional cultures

inappropriate, or offensive, to Native Americans. A little investigation into local standards goes a long way.

2) Native American villages are living, working communities; the privacy of the residents and the integrity of the structures must be respected at all times. The term "living museum" is often applied to Indian communities (especially the pueblos of New Mexico and Arizona), as if these villages are some kind of elaborate display. Indian people are full of stories about rude tourists who enter their homes uninvited, or who knock on the door and ask to be shown around.

Above all, do not enter any areas that are

Left, dancer at Santa Clara Pueblo's feast day.
Above, Quileute fisherman with catch of the day.

marked off-limits. These may include religious buildings (churches or kivas), dance plazas, sacred sites, or wilderness areas. Ignoring these restrictions may result in fines or ejection.

3) Similarly, ceremonies, powwows, dances and other events are held *by* Indian people *for* Indian people. They are not shows or exhibitions performed for the benefit of tourists (although these are occasionally given at museums, cultural centers, parks, etc.). In many cases, these events are of a religious nature and should be accorded the same deference as a church service or other ceremony, even if community members behave informally. Indian people tend to be uncom-

crowd. Don't block anyone's view. And, at ceremonial events, don't speak loudly or applaud. Religious matters are often held in the strictest secrecy, and it is extremely rude to talk about them or ask probing questions. If you are already familiar with a dance or ceremony, this is not the time to regale your friends with your knowledge. If you absolutely must ask a question about what you are seeing, remember it until later and then ask someone privately. If the answer is elusive, don't push it. Chances are they genuinely don't know or would rather not discuss it.

5) While hospitality and generosity are highly valued by Indian people, don't expect them to go out of their way to be your "Indian

fortable with photography, and this is especially true on ceremonial occasions.

As a general rule, do not attempt to photograph, videotape or sketch any religious event unless you are granted permission by the appropriate authorities. On some reservations, photography of any sort requires a special permit and fee. If you plan to photograph a person, you must ask permission first. A gratuity of $2 or $3 is sometimes appropriate as a sign of appreciation.

4) Try to be unobtrusive. If you are visiting an Indian community or event, keep a low profile. Be patient, considerate and accommodating. Don't push to the front of the

friend." Worse, don't expect them to act deferentially because you are spending a few dollars on Indian goods.

The Indian style of interaction tends to be conservative. Making eye contact with a stranger, being overly demonstrative, or talking about personal matters, is often considered an invasion of privacy. If an Indian person fails to shake your hand or look you in the eye, he is probably being polite. In general, personal assertiveness is not highly valued.

English is spoken by the vast majority of Indian people. Many also speak a tribal language and perhaps Spanish or French as

26

well. If you meet someone who doesn't speak your language, try to find a translator.

6) Finally, while traveling on Indian reservations, obey all tribal laws and regulations. It is advisable to contact tribal councils before your arrival and ask about any rules or prohibitions you need to be aware of. Again, these may include restrictions on photography, travel, fishing, hunting, hiking and – this is important – carrying or consuming alcohol. On some occasions, an entire reservation may be closed. At least one, Santa Ana Pueblo in New Mexico, is open to visitors only one day a year. Before attending a ceremony or dance, confirm that visitors are welcome. If you are asked to leave an event

The last word of this introduction goes to Chief Joseph of the Nez Perce, who, after leading his people in a heroic flight from US soldiers, was never allowed to return to his homeland. Still, after years of exile, he was able to talk of peace: "Too many misrepresentations have been made, too many misunderstandings have come up between the white men about the Indians. If the white man wants to live in peace with the Indian he can live in peace. There need be no trouble. Treat all men alike. Give them the same law. Give them an even chance to live and grow. All men were made by the same Great Spirit Chief. They are all brothers. The earth is the mother of all people, and all people should

or Indian land, do so quickly, quietly and without complaint.

Building bridges: Exploring Native America is more than travel. It is an opportunity to engage in cultural exchange, to build bridges of understanding. It is a chance to be enriched by the teachings of a culture which, despite years of hardship and suffering, continues to speak so poignantly to the problems of the "civilized" world. Most of all, it is an opportunity to establish mutual respect, to celebrate difference, and reaffirm unity.

<u>**Left**</u>, preparing for Crow Fair powwow. <u>**Above**</u>, young Navajo woman in Pendleton blanket.

have equal rights upon it… We shall all be alike – brothers of one father and one mother, with one mother, with one sky above us and one country around us, and one government for all. Then the Great Spirit Chief who rules above will smile upon this land, and send rain to wash out the bloody spots made by brothers' hands from the face of the earth. For this time the Indian race are waiting and praying. I hope that no more groans of wounded men and women will ever go to the ear of the Great Spirit Chief above, and that all people may be one people.

"*In-mut-too-yah-lat-lat* (Chief Joseph) has spoken for his people."

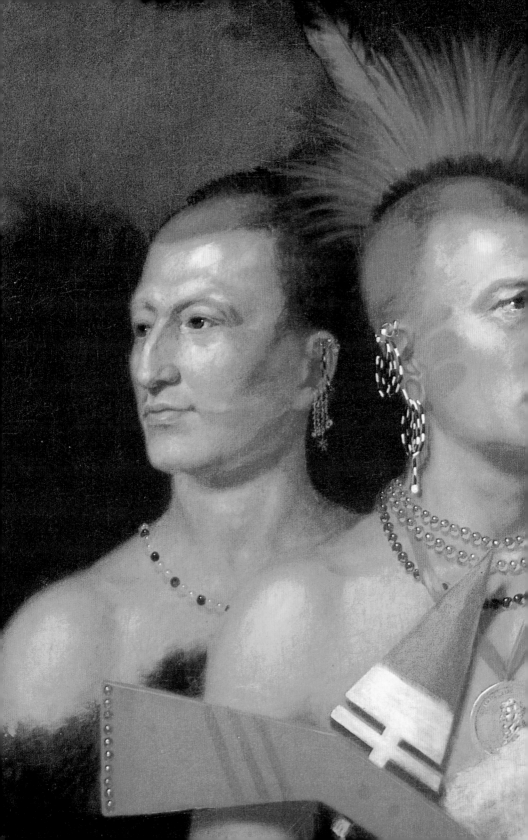

They came from Asia more than 20,000 years ago, small bands of Ice Age hunters following game across the Siberian tundra, moving east toward the rising sun, unaware that they were entering a new land, a continent never before seen by human eyes.

They traveled across the Bering Land Bridge, a mass of dry land that stretched between Siberia and Alaska during the late Pleistocene – or Ice Age – when much of the earth's water was locked up in glaciers. As passageways opened in the great walls of ice, these early Indians pushed south and east into the heart of North America.

These Paleoindians were a simple people, hunter-gatherers who stalked game with wooden spears, wore animal skins, and lived in caves or crude lean-tos. The land they discovered was moist and lush and teeming with game: cave bears, giant sloths, ancient elk and horses. In later years they developed stone spearheads of the simple Sandia type – rough, symmetrical flaked points – and then, by 8000 BC, the more sophisticated Clovis and Folsom points – with fluting on both sides and finely worked edges.

Although their weapons were primitive, they were ingenious hunters able to take down the largest and most ferocious game. Mammoths were chased into swamps where they were mired and easily killed. Entire herds of bighorn bison were stampeded over cliffs or into corrals. Some archaeologists believe that prehistoric hunters may have contributed to the widespread extinction of giant Pleistocene mammals.

Agricultural revolution: By 10,000 BC, the Ice Age was coming to a close, and North America was undergoing major climatic changes. Indian cultures were changing, too – from the big-game hunting of the Paleo-Indians to the broad-based economies of the Archaic period.

For the most part, the Archaic period saw the refinement of hunting-and-gathering in order to meet the demands of emerging

ecological zones. The ways of life of the Archaic Indians became more specialized; their tools grew more sophisticated, their traditions more distinct. In the Southwest, for example, a foraging people known broadly as the Cochise Culture (7000–1000 BC) adapted to the harsh conditions of the high desert, subsisting on small game, seeds and nuts, and living in seasonal pit houses.

In the Northwest, along the cold rivers of the Columbia Plateau, hunting and foraging was supplemented by a growing reliance on

fishing, typical of later Northwestern cultures. In the lush forests of the Great Lakes region, the hunters and fishers of the Old Copper Culture (4000–1500 BC) became the only Archaic Indians north of Mexico to utilize copper in tool making. On the rocky coast of New England and Canada, the so-called Red Paint People (3000–500 BC) left behind elaborate burial sites clearly indicative of a complex ceremonial life.

But by far the most important development of the Archaic period was the domestication of plants. By 2500 BC, early varieties of maize (Indian corn) were being cultivated in the Valley of Mexico, probably as

Preceding pages: Pawnee warriors, by Charles Bird King. Left, Anasazi ruins at Chaco Canyon, New Mexico. Above, petroglyphs near Galisteo, also in New Mexico.

a supplement to a largely hunting-and-gathering economy. Gradually, agriculture expanded, opening the door to an entirely new level of social organization. By 1200 BC, the first of Mesoamerica's classic cultures, the Olmecs, was establishing large, socially stratified towns and laying foundations in art, religion and agriculture from which the great civilizations of the Mayas, Toltecs and Aztecs would later emerge.

North of Mexico, the development of agriculture had its greatest impact on the American Southwest, where desert farmers like the Hohokam and Mogollon (AD 500–1500) represented a northern branch of Mesoamerican influence. To the north, the cliff-dwelling Anasazi constructed the Southwest's classic pueblos.

The major sites of all three cultures – Anasazi, Mogollon and Hohokam – were abandoned in the 14th century, probably as a result of drought, overpopulation and the arrival of Athabascan raiders (Apaches and Navajos) who migrated into the region from the arctic north. It is thought that the Anasazi and Mogollon settled in the pueblos of New Mexico and Arizona, and the Hohokam scattered into the small farming villages of the O'odham in southern Arizona's deserts.

Agriculture also spread to the Temple Mound civilization of the Mississippi Valley (AD 700–1600), which followed on the heels of the earlier mound-building Hopewell and Adena cultures. The Temple Mound Builders reached the height of their influence between AD 1000 and 1500, spreading from the Gulf Coast to the Great Lakes and from the Allegheny Mountains to the edge of the Great Plains. The civilization collapsed some time in the late 1500s, possibly as a result of an advance wave of European disease.

It's impossible to know with certainty the total number of Indians living in North America before the arrival of Europeans, but a reasonable estimate puts the figure at about 15 million, the vast majority concentrated in Mesoamerica. North of Mexico, the population was quite sparse – perhaps between 1.5 and 2 million – but even here cultural variety was enormous, with some 300 languages spoken by as many as 250 tribes.

Right, Bighorn petroglyphs well preserved at Death Valley in California.

The Spanish came first. In 1492, Christopher Columbus landed on San Salvador Island and, believing he was somewhere in the East Indies, named the inhabitants *Indios*. "They are the best people in the world and the most peaceable," he wrote of the indigenous people, a branch of the Arawaks. "I do not believe that in all the world there are better men, any more than there are better lands… They are to such a degree lacking in artifice and so generous with what they possess, that no man would believe it unless he had seen such a thing."

Back in Spain, there were more than a few questions about exactly what type of creatures these *Indios* were. "Peaceable" and "generous" were all well and good, but did they have souls? Could they reason? Were they really human?

The debate was finally resolved in 1512, when Pope Julius II proclaimed the *Indios* descendants of Adam and Eve. They were humans just like the rest of us, Julius declared, although clearly in need of a good dose of Catholicism, which, in the name of expanding the empire, the Spanish were only too happy to provide.

By the time the news of their humanity reached San Salvador, however, there were hardly any *Indios* left to celebrate. Within 10 years of Columbus's discovery, the *Indios* had been virtually wiped out – victims of disease, slavery, torture, war. Within a single generation, the Spanish had destroyed them. Thousands of people, gone forever, and much of the Caribbean soon to follow. After 20,000 years of isolation, the long dawn of Native American life was over.

The impact of European contact on Native Americans is difficult, if not impossible, to imagine. Epidemics alone wiped out 25 to 50 percent of the population, warfare another 10 percent. In places like the Caribbean and Central America, only about one person in 10 survived, possibly less. In the US, a pre-contact population of approximately 1.5 million (a very rough estimate) dropped to

less than 250,000 between 1890 and 1910.

More difficult to measure was the cultural devastation. Some tribes, like the Pequot of New England and the Yana and Maidu of California, were hunted down like wild animals and virtually exterminated. Others, like the Mandan and Pawnee of the Northern Plains, were decimated by smallpox, measles, cholera, syphilis and other European diseases. Survivors saw their cultures stripped away or brutally suppressed.

For the Europeans, on the other hand,

colonizing this "New World" promised to be a money-making venture, and, by the mid-1700s, no less than six foreign powers (Spain, France, England, Holland, Sweden and Russia) had staked a claim to some part of North America. Europe was in the throes of empire-building during this period, and tended to look on Indians as either assets to be exploited or liabilities to be removed. Europeans were also on a religious mission and, to one extent or another, felt an obligation to Christianize their poor pagan brothers. Then as now, religion and politics made a potent combination. In the twisted rhetoric of conquest, "saving" the Indians

Left, Wampanoag leader Metacom, known to the English as King Philip. Above, Pocahontas begs her father, King Powhatan, to spare John Smith.

was usually equated with subjugating them.

Conquistadores, Voyageurs, Planters: After decimating much of the Caribbean, the Spanish pushed into Mexico, where Hernando Cortés and his conquistadores laid waste to the Aztec empire, killing thousands, including Montezuma himself, who received Cortés as a god.

While still gorging themselves on Aztec gold, the Spanish moved north into the rugged canyon-country of the American Southwest, where they helped themselves to the land and labor of the village-dwelling Pueblo Indians. They also established a colonial toehold in Florida, and, by the late 1700s, a chain of Catholic missions

the Hurons, Nipissings, Ottawas and Micmacs, in particular. By the early 1700s, voyageurs had paddled down the Mississippi River into Caddo territory and west along the Missouri, Red and Platte rivers into the territory of the Wichitas, Quapaws and Comanches. In 1718, the French founded New Orleans, and 10 years later, after years of conflict, they crushed the Natchez, last surviving vestige of the once powerful Temple Mound civilization.

The English had a hand in the fur trade as well, although to a lesser extent than the French. Most English fur-trading was inherited from the Dutch, who had established a trading network with the powerful Iroquois

stretched along the California coast.

While the Spanish were pushing north from Mexico, the French were taking their first steps into the lush woodlands of the Great Lakes region. Unlike the Spanish, who were primarily interested in ranching and mining, the French were lured by the fur trade. Rather than armored conquistadores, the French sent voyageurs – independent traders who paddled the lakes and rivers in Indian canoes, learned Indian languages, and married Indian women.

In the early years, between 1550 and 1650, trade was limited to the tribes in the St Lawrence River and Great Lakes region –

tribes (Mohawks, Oneidas, Cayugas, Onondagas, Senecas) on the upper Hudson River.

For the most part, however, English colonists were more interested in farming than trading. Unlike the French, who relied on Indian trade, or the Spanish, who wanted to transform natives into serfs, the English had little use for the Indians themselves. The English wanted land, and whether they bought it, swindled it, or stole it, there was never any question that Indians should be pushed aside.

At first, relations were cordial if not exactly friendly. During the first wretched years at both Plymouth and Jamestown, alliances were made with local tribes in order to keep the peace. Famous "Indian helpers" like Squanto, Massasoit Samoset and Pocahontas acted as go-betweens, exchanging food and instruction for English trade goods. But as the settlements grew larger and the colonists became hungrier for land, conflict erupted. Squabbles turned into skirmishes, skirmishes into war. Whether it was the Indians or the whites who attacked first, the cause of violence, and the results, were usually the same.

In Jamestown, an uncertain peace lasted some 15 years between the English and the Powhatan Confederacy, thanks to the moderating influence of Wahunsonacook,

exception of a few small villages, the Powhatans were nearly wiped out.

The story was much the same in New England. In 1636, just 16 years after the Pilgrims landed at Plymouth, the Puritans established their might by slaughtering the Pequots, the region's most powerful Indian tribe. "It was a fearful sight to see them frying in the fire," a Puritan leader wrote after burning a Pequot village and killing 600 Indians. "But the victory seemed a sweet sacrifice and they gave praise thereof to God…" Indian survivors were hunted down and killed; some were sold into slavery. The Pequots never recovered.

War broke out again about 50 years later

known to the English as King Powhatan. In order to seal the peace, Wahunsonacook's daughter, Pocahontas, was married to a colonist named John Rolfe. Wedding vows could not hold back the enormous tide of resentment, however, and in 1622, after the death of Wahunsonacook, the Powhatans rose up against the settlers. The attack proved too little, too late. The English countered, killing 1,000 Indians in a single raid. The Indian confederacy was shattered, and with the

Left, Canyon de Chelly rock paintings recount the arrival of the Spanish. **Above**, George Catlin's impression of a Mandan bull dance.

when the Wampanoag chief Metacom – dubbed King Philip by the English – organized an alliance with the Narragansets and Nipmucs. A generation earlier, Metacom's father, Chief Massasoit, took pity on the starving Pilgrims and offered them food, land and protection. But by the time Massasoit died, 42 years later, the Wampanoags had nothing left to give. Metacom's attack devastated villages throughout New England. But again, retribution was quick and merciless. The Puritans launched a campaign of extermination against the Indians, virtually wiping out the Wampanoags and their allies. Hundreds of Indians were massacred, and hundreds more were sold to slavers. In Plymouth, Metacom's head was stuck on a pike, where it stayed for 20 years.

By the late 1600s, whites were not only fighting Indians, they were also fighting each other. The English and French were particularly fond of butting heads, and during the 80-year conflict known as the French and Indian Wars, colonial administrators turned to the Indians to tip the scales of military power.

The Europeans were especially interested in wooing the formidable Iroquois League, located strategically on the current New York-Ontario border. In general, the Iroquois aligned themselves with the Eng-

chose the losing side. The war was especially devastating for the Iroquois League, which split its allegiance – the Mohawks, Cayugas, Senecas and Onondagas joining the British, the Oneidas and Tuscaroras joining the Americans. In some battles, Iroquois fought Iroquois, with tragic results. By the end of the war, the Six Nations were crippled. Their homeland was trampled and their villages were destroyed. Some sought refuge in Canada; others moved onto reservations in New York.

The Trail of Tears: After the Revolution, the Indian frontier was pushed back to the Great Lakes region, where native tribes and their displaced eastern neighbors joined together

lish, while the Abnakis, Shawnees, Chippewas and Ottawas sided with the French. But even in victory, the Indians lost more than they won. For more than three generations, soldiers and warriors overran their fields, burned their villages, and killed their young men. Even the Iroquois, who were pivotal in England's ultimate victory, were all but forgotten by their former allies after the wars were over.

With the outbreak of the American Revolution, Indians were dragged into a white-against-white conflict once again. This time, most tribes – including the Shawnees, Delawares and Wyandots –

to hold back the advance of white settlers. As early as 1760, a charismatic Ottawa chief named Pontiac forged an army of warriors from several tribes in order to strike against the English. Nine English forts were captured by the Indians and some 1,000 settlers killed, but Pontiac was unable to sustain the siege, and his loose confederacy of warriors was driven back and scattered.

About 25 years later, Little Turtle of the Miamis created an alliance of Shawnees, Chippewas, Delawares and Potawatomis, among others, and won several humiliating

Above, Catlin's *Grand Pawnee Chief, Keokuk.*

TECUMSEH

Tecumseh has been called the greatest Indian leader of all time. He was a Shawnee chief and warrior, a strategist and statesman. He was a visionary who dreamed of creating a single Indian nation from the Great Lakes to the Gulf of Mexico. He was a patriot who believed that Indian land belonged to all Indian people and could not be sold by any one tribe or individual.

To his American adversaries, Tecumseh was known as "one of those uncommon geniuses which springs up occasionally to produce revolutions and overturn the established order of things." Among his own people, the Shawnees, he was called Tekamti, the "Shooting Star."

Tecumseh grew up surrounded by war. During his early years, between 1780 and 1800, the tribes of the Great Lakes country were under increasing pressure to give up territory to advancing settlers. Frontier violence was rife in this period. Tecumseh's father and brother had both been killed while battling whites, and Tecumseh himself was little more than a boy when he first joined the fight against the "Long Knives."

By 1805, Tecumseh had assumed a position of influence among the Shawnees, and his vision of intertribal unity was already taking shape. He saw how treaties divided and weakened Indian people and how Indian territory was being carved up piece by piece and ceded to whites. He believed that all native people had a claim to the land regardless of tribe or status.

TECUMTHA.

"The way, the only way to stop this evil," he said, "is for the red men to unite in claiming a common and equal right in the land, as it was at first, and should be now – for it was never divided, but belongs to all. No tribe has the right to sell, even to each other, much less to strangers, who demand all, and will take no less… Sell a country! Why not sell the air, the great sea, as well as the earth? Did not the Great Spirit make them all for the use of his children?"

The only hope for Indians, Tecumseh believed, was a united Indian front, a confederacy of tribes that could withstand America's military power. In 1808, Tecumseh and his brother, a religious leader named Tenskwatawa (or the Prophet) established a town, Tippecanoe, where Indian people of all tribes could return to a traditional way of life uninfluenced by white society. Meanwhile, Tecumseh traveled from tribe to tribe recruiting warriors and preaching unity.

"Where today are the Pequot?" he asked at one speech. "Where are the Narraganset, the Mohican, the Pocanet, and other powerful tribes of our people? They have vanished before the avarice and oppression of the white man, as snow before the summer sun… Will we let ourselves be destroyed in our turn, without making an effort worthy of our race? Shall we, without a struggle, give up our homes, our lands, bequeathed to us by the Great Spirit? The graves of our dead and everything that is dear and sacred to us?… I know you will say with me, Never! Never!"

But before Tecumseh's plan could be brought together, his Indian confederacy suffered a major setback. While Tecumseh was drumming up support among the southern tribes, territorial governor William Henry Harrison marched on Tippecanoe with 1,000 men, hoping to draw the Indians into a confrontation. Tecumseh's brother, promising the warriors that his medicine would protect them, ordered a raid on Harrison's camp. The soldiers rallied, beat the Indians back, and then marched to Tippecanoe and burned it to the ground.

Tecumseh's confederacy was shattered, but his dream was still alive. Eight months after the Battle of Tippecanoe, at the outbreak of the War of 1812, Tecumseh and his warriors joined the British Army in the hope of striking against the Americans and winning back the Ohio Valley. The British made him a brigadier general, and he led his troops brilliantly in several campaigns. His allies could not withstand American might, however, and while covering a British retreat back to Canada, Tecumseh was killed.

Hostilities in the region continued for another 20 years; Tecumseh's dream of an Indian confederacy never materialized. Tecumseh's people, the Shawnees, were eventually removed to Indian Territory, now Oklahoma, where many live today.

engagements against American troops. They were no match for the full force of the American Army, however, and with little choice, Little Turtle signed a treaty ceding the coveted Ohio Valley.

And then in 1811, a brilliant Shawnee chief named Tecumseh led a confederacy of tribes against the Americans, ultimately joining the British in the War of 1812. But again, despite a few initial victories, the effort was repelled. Tecumseh's warriors were overrun while defending a British retreat. Tecumseh himself was shot several times and killed.

After two smaller uprisings, one by the Kickapoos and one by the Winnebagos, the

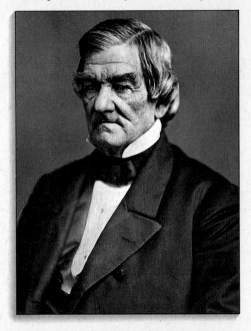

struggle for the Old Northwest came to a bloody end in the early 1830s when 300 "hostiles" led by the Sauk chief Black Hawk were slaughtered while retreating across the Mississippi River.

At roughly the same time, the Indian frontier was also being challenged in the Southeast. The major players here were the so-called Five Civilized Tribes – the Cherokees, Choctaws, Chickasaws, Creeks and Seminoles – and a hardbitten, backwoods Indian-fighter known to the Indians as Sharp Knife and to the Americans as Andrew Jackson.

Jackson first slung his saber against Indi-ans during the Creek War of 1813, and then again in 1818 against the Seminoles of Florida. Both encounters ended with huge cessions of Indian land.

In 1828, Jackson was elected president and immediately set to work clearing the Indians out of the South once and for all. In 1830, he signed the Indian Removal Act, which called for the relocation of Indian tribes to a permanent Indian Territory west of the Mississippi River. The land was to be theirs "as long as the grass shall grow and the rivers run," Jackson promised. But the Indians had heard this sort of talk before.

The Choctaws were the first to go, leaving behind their Mississippi lands to the squatters and speculators who forced them out of their homes while the government turned a blind eye. As they walked away, the Indians touched trees, rocks, water and leaves as if to say goodbye. A quarter of the Choctaws died during the bitterly cold journey.

Some time later, after a trumped-up rebellion, the Creeks were swept out of Alabama at gunpoint. Many of the Indians were marched in chains. Nearly 3,500 died along the way. The Chickasaws were shipped out of Tennessee in 1837, and were immediately cut down by an outbreak of cholera.

Deep in the Florida swamps, several bands of Seminoles maintained a bloody resistance until 1848. Only a few hundred remained after the government finally gave up trying to root them out.

With nowhere else to turn, the Cherokees took their case to the US Supreme Court. Chief Justice John Marshall affirmed the sovereignty of the Cherokee Nation and prohibited outsiders from entering their territory. But "Sharp Knife" Jackson would not be swayed. "John Marshall has made his decision," he reportedly said, "now let him enforce it."

In 1838, the US Army was called in to corral the Cherokees and force them out of their Georgia homeland. Of the 18,000 Cherokees who walked the 800-mile "Trail of Tears" to Indian Territory, 4,000 died. A few escaped to the mountains of North Carolina, where their descendants still live on the Qualla Reservation.

Left, John Ross, leader of the Cherokee Nation during the Trail of Tears. Right, Hopi man on kiva ladder, *circa* 1897.

The 50 years following the Trail of Tears saw the pace of western expansion quicken. These were the years of the so-called "Great Indian Wars," a period of wagon trains, gold strikes, cavalry and cowboys – the very staple of Wild West mythology. Searching for cheap land and a fresh start, and often lured by the discovery of gold, thousands of American settlers struck out across the Great Plains looking for their piece of paradise. Although many western tribes had been in contact with whites for as much as 250 years (the Spanish in the Southwest, the French on the edges of the Great Plains, the Russians along the Northwest coast), they had never seen whites come in such vast numbers or with so voracious an appetite for land.

The catch-all rationalization behind this Great American Land Grab was a concept commonly known as manifest destiny, a belief that white Americans were fated to snatch up the entire continent. The roots of this sort of thinking went at least as far back as the Pilgrims, who praised God for clearing out the Indians around Plymouth with a terrible epidemic prior to their arrival. More than 200 years later, an American official resorted to the same rationalization when he attributed the near-extinction of California Indians to the "great cause of civilization, which, in the natural course of things, must exterminate Indians."

By the time the Cherokees had settled into exile in Indian Territory, conflicts between western tribes and Americans were already starting to erupt. As early as 1835, Comanche and Kiowa raiders were harassing travelers on the Staked Plains of Texas. In 1847, a group of rebels from Taos Pueblo killed the governor of New Mexico Territory and 20 Anglo settlers. In California, public funds were disbursed to freelance Indian-hunters. And in the Northwest – a region of Indian-white peace since the Lewis and Clark expedition of 1804 – the Cayuse War of 1847 triggered a series of small wars involving the Yakima, Coeur d'Alene, Palouse, Northern Paiute, Spokane, Walla

Walla and Umatilla tribes that lasted for more than 10 years.

As always, violence was preceded by years of bad blood. Whites invaded hunting grounds, peddled liquor, harassed and kidnapped Indian women and children. Indians raided homesteads and ranches, stole livestock, and attacked travelers. By the time soldiers were called out, both sides were so poisoned with resentment that almost nothing could hold back the bloodshed. All too often it was the ambitious officer, hotheaded

warrior, or unscrupulous trader who drew first blood, and the innocents who suffered the consequences.

Apache raiders: Among the first tribes to feel the brunt of the new American presence in the West were the Apaches, particularly the Chiricahua band of Apaches, who made their homes around the mountains of the same name in southeastern Arizona. Unlike the nearby Pueblo Indians, the Apaches had remained largely unfettered by Spanish domination. They were a wild and free-ranging people, predominantly hunter-gatherers, who had honed their considerable fighting skills for 200 years against the

Left, Juan, a young Apache, *circa* 1904. **Right**, Manuelito, Navajo leader during the Long Walk.

Spanish, and against the Pueblo Indians for 400 years before that.

Relations between Apaches and whites had never been good. The age-old practice of kidnapping and enslaving Apache children had survived well into the era of American rule, as did the Apaches' taste for revenge. Despite a few initial friendly overtures between Apaches and Americans, neither side trusted the other. Violence broke out in 1861, when an American military officer wrongly accused a Chiricahua leader, Cochise, of kidnapping a rancher's son. The bungled arrest led to bloodshed on both sides, setting off a typical cycle of revenge.

For the next 10 years, Cochise and his

flected, "that they carry their lives on their fingernails?" Growing old and weary of fighting, Cochise requested a reservation in the Chiricahua Mountains. After much negotiation, the request was finally granted. Cochise died there in 1874.

But two years later, the Chiricahuas were again forced to leave their homeland. The government wanted them to go to the San Carlos Reservation where other western Apaches were confined. A few Chiricahuas complied for the sake of peace. Others, like Victorio, Nana and Geronimo, fled to the mountains and for the next 10 years fought an intermittent war of resistance. One by one, they surrendered or were killed.

Mimbreño Apache ally, Mangas Colorado, plagued the frontier with deadly hit-and-run tactics. In response, the Americans launched an all-out war of extermination, encouraging soldiers and citizens to kill Apaches however they saw fit. In some parts of Arizona, a fresh Apache scalp fetched a handsome $250 reward.

The madness came to a head in 1871 with the massacre of 85 Apaches by a mob of Tucson vigilantes. The victims were neither Chiricahuas nor Mimbreños, but Aravapais – a peaceful band of Apaches that had settled near a military fort for protection. "Why is it that the Apaches wait to die," Cochise re-

Geronimo was the last. By the time he surrendered in 1886, the entire country knew his name, and many people, including the president, wanted him hanged. Instead, he and the Chiricahuas were shipped to Fort Marion in Florida as prisoners of war. In 1894 the surviving Chiricahuas were allowed to go to Fort Sill Indian Territory (now Oklahoma. Geronimo died there in 1909, still a prisoner of war.

Navajo wealth: While Cochise was terrorizing the border country, a second Southwestern tribe – the Navajos – was also being pursued by the American military.

The Navajos and Apaches are both of

Athabascan stock, their common ancestors having migrated into the Southwest from western Canada about 600 years earlier. Culturally, however, the two groups were miles apart. The Navajos – or, as they call themselves, the Dine (the People) – had long since followed a different path, borrowing liberally from the Pueblo Indians and Spanish. They took up sheepherding, weaving, and various elements of Pueblo religion, creating a way of life that was distinctly their own.

Like their Apache cousins, the Navajos had a fiercesome reputation as warriors. They were like "wolves that run through the mountains," an American general said, and needed to be removed by force. It hadn't escaped the general's attention that the Navajos were likely to be sitting on a fortune in mineral wealth.

In 1863, the US Army commissioned Christopher "Kit" Carson to round up the Navajos and ship them to a camp in eastern New Mexico at a place called Bosque Redondo. Carson was a former mountain man, trader and Indian fighter. He knew the Navajos, their willingness to fight, and the sheer impossibility of defeating them on their own rugged terrain. He chose, instead, to starve them out. Under Carson's orders, the Navajos' sheep and horses were seized or killed; crops were burned; hogans destroyed; even the beloved peach orchards of Canyon de Chelly were cut down.

The Navajos were slowly starved into surrendering. By 1865, more than 8,000 had been sent on the "Long Walk" – 300 miles to Bosque Redondo. Some 400 died along the way. There the Navajos suffered more hardships: scarce supplies, undrinkable water, poor soil, disease, crop failure. Finally, in 1868, after conditions at the Bosque were publicly condemned, the Navajos were allowed to go home.

Fire on the plains: The crimson flower of war was blooming on the Great Plains, too. Gold strikes in Colorado, California, Montana and the Black Hills sent white people sweeping across the plains like a prairie fire, engulfing the Plains tribes and igniting their passion for war. "When the white man

comes into my country he leaves a trail of blood behind him," Chief Red Cloud once told a council of military men. For the major tribes of the Great Plains – the Sioux, Cheyennes, Crows, Blackfeet, Arapahos, Comanches and Kiowas – these trails were many, tangled and bloody indeed.

The Plains Indians hold a special place in the American imagination. The mounted Plains warrior – eagle feathers streaming in his hair, bow and arrow in his hand – has become a Wild West icon, the essential American Indian. And yet, ironically, the horse-and-buffalo culture that blossomed on the Great Plains in the 19th century was impossible before European contact. Until

the Spanish brought their herds to the New World, wild horses hadn't roamed American soil since the Ice Age. By the time Indian–white hostilities broke out in the mid-1800s, most Plains tribes had only been mounted for 80 or 90 years. In only three or four generations, the Plains Indian tribes had created a culture of raw and vital beauty.

By the late 1850s, white encroachment had already triggered a number of bloody engagements on the Great Plains, and several tribes, including the Santee Sioux of Minnesota – easternmost branch of the great Sioux tribe – had made enormous land cessions to the US government. The Santees

Left, Geronimo (lower row, fourth from left) and Chiricahua prisoners, 1886. **Right**, Cheyenne chiefs Little Wolf (standing) and Dull Knife.

felt swindled by their treaty, and after 10 miserable years of reservation life they had nothing to show but hunger, hopelessness and an explosive hatred of whites. In 1862, under the leadership of Chief Little Crow, they rampaged across the countryside, killing 800 settlers and soldiers before the army drove them back. More than 35 Santees were hanged and 250 imprisoned. Little Crow escaped, only to be shot by a white settler a few months later.

Two years after the Santee uprising, violence broke out again, this time in the Colorado hunting range of the Southern Cheyenne and Arapaho tribes. Gold had been discovered in the Rocky Mountains just

outside of Denver and with thousands of whites flooding the area, authorities were pressured to open Indian land to settlement. In 1864, a campaign was launched to harass the Cheyennes and Arapahos into submission. Villages were burned to the ground, skirmishes were fought, Indian raids were answered with cavalry and cannon, but with little apparent success.

Itching for a decisive victory, and dead-set on killing Indians, an American commander, Col. John Chivington, set his men on a peaceful group of Cheyennes camped at Sand Creek near Fort Lyon in southern Colorado. The camp was led by Chief Black

Kettle, a long-time advocate of peace who had brought his people to the fort in order to protect them from the hostilities. When Chivington's soldiers appeared around the camp, Black Kettle flew an American flag and a white flag over his tepee, confident that the bluecoats wouldn't attack their steadfast friend. But Chivington's orders had been brutally clear: "Kill and scalp all, big and little." His "boys" were instructed to take no prisoners, not even women and children. The reason, in Chivington's own words: "Nits make lice."

By all accounts, the Sand Creek Massacre was an orgy of murder and mutilation. Of perhaps 270 Indians killed, 200 were women and children. Even Kit Carson, the man who sent the Navajos on their Long Walk, described Chivington's men as "cowards and dogs." But back in Denver, "the boys" received a hero's welcome, displaying fresh scalps like badges of honor. Terse as ever, Chivington's official report commended their behavior: "All did nobly."

Miraculously, Black Kettle survived. But still he did not make war against the whites. Hoping to spare his people further suffering, he led them into Indian Territory, thinking they would be safe. But four years later, the nightmare happened again. This time the bluecoats were led by a brash young officer named Lt-Col. George Armstrong Custer. It made no difference to Custer that Black Kettle had personally sued for peace, or that he had never led a raid against white settlers. Custer ordered his men to charge at dawn. They rode into the sleeping camp with the strains of *Garry Owen*, Custer's favorite battle theme, blaring in the background. The Indians responded as best they could, killing 20 soldiers and wounding many others, but they were badly outnumbered. The Battle of Washita, as it came to be known, claimed more than 100 Cheyenne lives. This time, Black Kettle did not survive.

While the Southern Cheyennes were losing ground on the Southern Plains, the Sioux and Northern Cheyennes, led by Red Cloud, Sitting Bull and Cheyenne chief Dull Knife, were driving soldiers out of the rich Powder River country of Montana and Dakota territories. At stake in the fighting was one of the white people's roads, the Bozeman Trail, which cut a path across the Indians' best hunting ground toward the goldfields of

Montana. After two years of hard fighting, the Americans pulled out. In 1868, Red Cloud signed a treaty guaranteeing the Powder River country, including the sacred Black Hills, to the Indians. The treaty provided that "No white person shall be permitted to settle upon… any portion of the territory, or without the consent of the Indians to pass through the same."

Red Cloud promised never to lift his hand against whites again. He retired to the agency named after him, and kept his word to the day he died. He was the only Indian leader in the American West to have won a war against the US.

The treaty lasted for eight years. Almost Horse, the Sioux, Cheyennes and Arapahos frustrated the soldiers again and again. A major campaign was launched against the Indians, with Custer commanding the Seventh Calvary. On June 25, 1876, he located a large Indian camp on the Little Bighorn River and ordered an immediate attack. Custer rode into the valley and never returned. In the battle remembered as "Custer's Last Stand," the dashing young officer and his elite corps of Indian-fighters were wiped out to the man.

But the engagements that followed were bitter defeats for the Indians. In the hard winter of 1877 the flush of victory at the Battle of the Little Bighorn was worn away

from the day it was signed, rumors of gold in the Black Hills proved too enticing for prospectors to ignore. In 1874, the US Army dispatched its own gold-hunting expedition under the command of Lt-Col. Custer. It was to be Custer's last transgression against Indian people.

The army's brazen disregard for the treaty brought war back to the Great Plains, and under the leadership of Sitting Bull, Gall and a brilliant young warrior named Crazy

Left, Sioux delegation, 1875, with Chief Red Cloud standing on right. **Above**, Wovoka, the Paiute prophet (sitting), with Arapahos.

by constant harassment, heavy losses, chronic hunger and biting cold. By the following spring, even the young mystic, Crazy Horse, was ready to surrender, as were Dull Knife and Little Wolf of the Cheyennes. Seeing the hopelessness of life in the US, Sitting Bull escaped to Canada with his band of Hunkpapa Sioux.

The final days: Elsewhere in the West, other tribes were coming to the end of years of struggle. On the Southern Plains of Texas and Oklahoma, the Comanches, led by Quanah Parker, and the Kiowas, led by chiefs Setangya (or Satank) and Satanta, were meeting bitter defeat in their efforts to save the southern buffalo herd from the onslaught of professional hunters. In 1872, Captain Jack and the Modocs made a last desperate attempt to save themselves in the rugged lava beds of northern California. In the Northwest, Nez Perce Chief Joseph led his people on a four-month flight through Idaho and Montana territories only to be captured by the army a mere 30 miles from Canada, where he hoped to take refuge with Sitting Bull.

Despite years of peace with whites, the Utes were driven out of Colorado and confined to several reservations in Utah. And in a desperate attempt to return to their northern homeland, Cheyenne chiefs Dull Knife and

swept away and the Indian dead would return to earth. Reservation officials were frightened by the ecstatic dancing, and, fearing a new uprising, ordered the capture of all off-reservation bands.

Among the "hostile" groups was a ragged band of Miniconjou Sioux led by Chief Big Foot. Big Foot's people were met by an army unit and ordered to make camp at Wounded Knee Creek on the Pine Ridge Indian Reservation. The soldiers set up their own camp around the Indians, positioning artillery on an overlooking bluff. The following morning, a small group of soldiers entered the camp and began rifling through tepees looking for weapons.

Little Wolf fled Indian Territory with nearly 300 followers, but were hunted down and captured.

The final blow in the wars for the west came in 1890 as the last of the Sioux "hostiles" were being confined to reservations. By this time both Crazy Horse and Sitting Bull, the two most compelling Sioux leaders, had been killed – cut down by guards while under arrest. Demoralized and desperate, many Sioux sought refuge in a new religious movement known as the Ghost Dance. Founded by a Paiute prophet named Wovoka, the Ghost Dance promised the dawning of a new age when whites would be

What happened next is not entirely clear, but somewhere, somehow, a shot was fired into the line of soldiers guarding the Sioux men. And that's when the killing started. The artillery opened up on the camp, cutting down anything that moved. Soldiers swept in and murdered the survivors, chasing them into ravines and gullies. By the end of the day, nearly 300 Indians and 25 soldiers lay dead on the ground. It was the last tragic episode of a courageous but desperate struggle. The Indian wars were over.

Above, Chief Big Foot lying dead at Wounded Knee Massacre site. **Right**, Sitting Bull.

SITTING BULL

In the summer of 1876, just two weeks before the defeat of Custer at the Battle of the Little Bighorn, Tatanka Yotanka – known to whites as Sitting Bull – had a vision. The implacable chief was at the Sioux and Cheyenne sun dance on Rosebud Creek in Montana Territory. He sacrificed 100 pieces of flesh from his arms, and then danced until he fell unconscious. When he awoke, he told what he had seen: white soldiers falling from the sky into the Indian camp. "I give you these," a voice spoke to him, "because they have no ears." It was a prophesy of Indian victory.

In the last turbulent years of the Plains Indian Wars, Sitting Bull was widely recognized as a pillar of defiance. As a military leader, medicine man, oracle, and Hunkpapa Sioux chief, he stood steadfast against white incursion into the buffalo country of Wyoming, Montana and the Dakotas. He scorned Indian leaders who accepted reservations, believing himself and his people to be the last true Indians.

Months before Sitting Bull's vision, Custer had discovered gold in the Black Hills, and the government pressured the Indians to sell. But Sitting Bull refused. He said the hills were sacred ground, that they did not have a

price. "If the whites try to take them, I will fight," he warned. But the treaty-makers would not listen; they had no ears for his talk. Instead, they threatened to attack his people, to force them onto reservations.

A few days after the sun dance, Sitting Bull's warriors intercepted a column of soldiers marching directly toward their camp. In a day of frenzied battle, the Indians beat the bluecoats back. The Battle of the Rosebud was a significant victory for the Indians, but Sitting Bull still felt that his vision had not been fully realized.

The triumph he had been waiting for came soon enough. On June 25, 1876, Custer and the Seventh Calvary attacked at the Little Bighorn River. When the smoke cleared, more than 200 soldiers lay dead on the ground. Sitting Bull's vision had finally been fulfilled.

After the Custer fight, Sitting Bull escaped to Canada rather than be confined to an Indian agency. When a commission was sent to coax him back, offering to pardon his "crimes" in return for surrender, he angrily turned them down. "What have we done that you should want us to stop?" he asked. "We have done nothing. It is all the people on the other side who started us to making trouble… Look at me. I have ears, I have eyes to see with. If you think me a fool, you are a bigger fool than I am… You come here to tell us lies, but we don't want to hear them… This country is my country now, and I intend to stay here and raise people up to fill it…"

But the Canadians would not grant Sitting Bull a reservation. With the buffalo dwindling and his people homesick, even Sitting Bull realized that he had come to the end of the road. After difficult years in Canada, Sitting Bull relented. "My followers are weary of cold and hunger. They wish to see their brothers and their old home, therefore I bow my head."

As a reservation chief, Sitting Bull remained a commanding presence, feared for his influence over the explosive Sioux. Beyond the reservation, his name had become a household word. He received mail from well-wishers all over the country, and even spent a summer touring with Buffalo Bill Cody's Wild West Show. A circus horse and sombrero, both gifts from Cody, were among his most prized possessions.

When the Ghost Dance broke out in 1890, Sitting Bull was identified as one of the "fomenters of disturbances" and was killed during an arrest. Ironically, the old chief had always been skeptical about the new religion.

Today, Sitting Bull remains a symbol of integrity and will, a man who never ceased struggling for control over his own destiny, and who never apologized for who he was. "If the Great Spirit had desired me to be a white man he would have made me so in the first place," Sitting Bull said while still in Canada. "He put in your heart certain wishes and plans, in my heart he put other and different desires. Each man is good in his sight. It is not necessary for eagles to be crows. Now we are poor but we are free. No white man controls our footsteps. If we must die, we die defending our rights."

The Indian wars were over, but the struggle for Indian land and culture continued. Whites had defeated Indian tribes on the field of battle, and now they attacked them in Congress and courtrooms. Indians not only had to contend with the hardships of reservation life, but with ever-shifting federal policy and the intrigues of local developers. By the turn of the century, it was commonly assumed that Native Americans were destined for extinction, that the "vanishing Red Man" would fade into obscurity. According to many policymakers, the most efficient and "humane" way to finish the job of "Indian removal" was to dismantle tribal society and eradicate traditional cultures.

Just as some tribes were beginning to come to terms with their new way of life, it became clear that even on reservations Indians were not safe from land-hungry whites. In an attempt to speed up the assimilation of Indians into mainstream society, Congress passed the General Allotment Act of 1887, which divided tribal lands into parcels and deeded them directly to individual Indians. The idea behind the new law was to encourage Indians to take up farming and learn the virtues of private property. Any land that was left over after allotment was thrown open to settlers.

Within a few years Indian-held land was cut by more than half, from about 150 million acres to 60 million. A second battery of laws dismantled Indian Territory, wresting land from Indian control and dissolving tribal governments – again, under the guise of promoting assimilation. Ultimately, in 1907, Indian Territory became the state of Oklahoma, and reservations were abolished within its boundaries.

In the 1950s an equally disastrous policy was put into action by the federal government. It was called "termination," and its purpose, like allotment's, was to force Indians into mainstream American life. Essentially, the termination policy annulled the special re-

lationship between Indian tribes and the federal government, leaving tribal assets in private hands where they were easily exploited by outside interests.

A secondary goal of the termination policy was to encourage relocation to cities. Today, more than one-third of America's native population resides at least part-time in urban areas. In all, 61 tribes were terminated. Only a handful have been restored to their former status. Fewer yet have regained their land.

In addition to allotment and termination,

federal Indian policy has undergone a number of changes, with little discernible direction. During the 1980s the federal government promoted tribal self-determination – a concept favored by most Indian leaders – but then cut funding for social programs by 40 percent. More recently, Indian policy has been guided by the so-called "new federalism," which stresses tribal decision-making over federal intervention.

Some Indian people see it as a step in the right direction. Others are concerned that the federal government is trying to wiggle out of its legal obligations to Indian tribes. In the meantime, little seems to have changed at the

Preceding pages: native village, Alert Bay, British Columbia, *circa* 1888. **Left**, Navajos protesting against the Navajo–Hopi relocation. **Right**, Cheyenne tepee draped with flag.

Bureau of Indian Affairs, the federal government's administrative arm. It is still considered one of the most poorly run and inefficient branches of government.

While trying to sort out the tangle of Indian policies, tribes were also faced with the enduring hardships of reservation life. From the very beginning, hunger, illness, alcoholism, poor education, unemployment and a prevailing sense of hopelessness plagued reservation life. While the Indian population steadily grew – from an all-time low of about 250,000 in 1900 to more than 1.5 million today – opportunities seemed to shrink. To this day, many tribes have not recovered. The statistics tell a story of despair, poverty

Lake to Taos Pueblo and some 20,000 acres to the Yakima Tribe in Washington.

In the meanwhile, hundreds of land claims are still being disputed in both the US and Canada, most notably the Sioux claim on the Black Hills of South Dakota. In Arizona, the longstanding land dispute between the Navajos and Hopis has resulted in the relocation of thousands of Navajos.

During the late 1960s, a generation of Indian activists took their grievances directly to the government and the American people. In 1968, the American Indian Movement (AIM) was created in Minneapolis and quickly gained a reputation for its militant tactics. In 1969, Indian activists attracted national

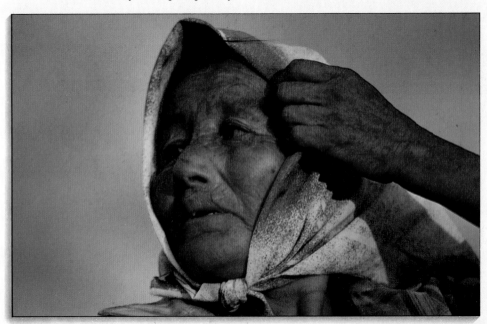

and ineffective bureaucracy. Compared to other ethnic groups in the US, Indian people have the highest unemployment, the lowest per capita income, and the shortest life span.

Fighting back: The response from Indian leaders has been vehement, if not always unified. In the early 1900s a number of intertribal organizations sprang up dedicated to keeping Indian issues on the federal agenda. The National Congress of American Indians was established in 1944, for example, and continues to be a major player in Washington. After years of petitioning the courts, a number of land claims have been granted Indian tribes, including the return of Blue

attention by occupying the abandoned prison on Alcatraz Island. Other groups staged dramatic protests at Mount Rushmore, Ellis Island, and Washington, DC, among other places. In 1972, a protest march known as the Trail of Broken Treaties Caravan culminated with the occupation of Bureau of Indian Affairs offices in Washington, DC. A year later, AIM members occupied the Pine Ridge Indian Reservation, site of the Wounded Knee Massacre. Two activists were killed and a number of federal agents wounded.

More recently, demonstrations on the Mohawk reservations of Ontario and New York turned into a two-month standoff between armed members of the Mohawk Warrior Society and Canadian police. The incident was spurred by the proposed development of land claimed by the tribe, but quickly exploded into an international debate over Indian rights.

Indian rights are being tested in a number of other places as well. In Montana, Washington, and especially Wisconsin, the right to fish and hunt in the traditional manner – a right retained by treaty – is being attacked as "treaty abuse." Protests staged by non-Indians have degenerated into violence and intimidation. A 1990 US Supreme Court decision has questioned the legality of the religious use of peyote, a hallucinogenic cactus taken

There is a story that people in the Southwest tell about a Hopi elder who was asked if it was possible for traditional Hopi ways to survive the influences of modern American lfe. "The Navajos came a long time ago and raided Hopi villages," the old man is supposed to have said. "But the Navajos went away, and the Hopis are still here. Then the Spanish came with their horses, guns and Bible. The Spanish disappeared, and the Hopis are still here. Now the Americans come with electricity, automobiles and television. And perhaps, one day, they too will go away. And the Hopis will still be here."

In her history of the Indians of the US, Angie Debo quotes Pleasant Porter, a Creek

as a sacrament by members of the Native American Church. The legal status of peyote use is being left to the states. And after years of petitioning lawmakers, Indian people are finally making headway in their attempts to recover sacred artifacts and skeletal remains from museum collections.

Strength to endure: In the end, Native Americans will endure. Time and again, through centuries of war, epidemics and hunger, they have proven their resiliency, their ability to adapt.

<u>Left</u>, Navajo farmer. <u>Above</u>, banner recalls the Wounded Knee occupation of 1973.

leader, who, in 1900, assured his people: "The vitality of our race still persists... We are the original discoverers of this continent, and the conquerors of it from the animal kingdom, and on it first taught the arts of war and peace, and first planted the institutions of virtue, truth and liberty. The European nations found us here and were made aware that it was possible for men to exist and subsist here. We have given to the European people on this continent our thought forces... We have made ourselves an indestructible element in their national history... The race that has rendered this service to the other nations of mankind cannot utterly perish."

BETWEEN TWO WORLDS

Each morning a young Navajo mother wakes up at 4.30 a.m., walks to her daughter's door and listens to the child breathe in her sleep. She makes her way towards the front door where a bag filled with corn pollen lies on her desk. Ordinarily, her grandmother carried this sacramental pollen in a buckskin pouch or a small bag made from an old flour sack.

She picks up a handful of pollen, walks out the door, and inhales the clean, crisp air in the quiet darkness. She looks to the east, where the ridges of a jagged sandstone formation are outlined by a familiar layer of white spilling over the horizon. Dawn.

She raises her right hand and releases the pollen, feeling the grains brush past her index finger and thumb. She prays: "To the Holy People who talk at dawn, to Father Sun, to Grandmother Darkness, to Mother Earth, Father Sky, give me health, strength, prosperity as my day begins." She prays in Navajo, asking for blessings in the form of *hozjo* for herself, her daughter and her people. She finishes her prayer with "*hozjonashadoo*," beauty all around.

As a child, she lived with her relatives in the dry western region of the Navajo Indian Reservation known as Bodaway. Caring for their sheep herds, she and her family covered miles of open, semi-arid desert gently broken by looming purple buttes and red mesas. The dawn ritual was always a part of that life. As a girl, she wondered why the Holy People refused to come to life and judge her prayers. She remembers hanging onto her mother's skirt fearing that she prayed improperly.

Today, she still thinks about Navajo gods lurking in the heavens just past Gallup, New Mexico, near one of the four sacred mountains, Mount Taylor. Sometimes there are questions: Do the talking dawn gods understand her thoughts in the English language? Do they exist at all?

Checking once more on her sleeping seven-year-old daughter snug tightly in a Mickey Mouse comforter, she is tempted to awaken the child and ask her to pray. "The Holy People wouldn't understand her English," she tells herself. "She is growing up in a modern world."

Unlike her mother, who spent most of her childhood living in a traditional Navajo hogan, the sleeping child is growing up in a two-bedroom house with all the modern conveniences: running water, electricity, color television, video recorder. Her daughter's ties to the traditional culture are limited to a few weekends a year helping her grandmother herd sheep near a place known

as "Where-the-Mesas-Meet." The elder is troubled that her grandaughter doesn't speak Navajo and that she wasn't raised in the wilderness. The child's mother thinks that her generation may be the last to speak both English and Navajo, the last to identify with the rituals, prayers, songs and life-style passed on by the elders.

Whenever the child tries to talk with her grandmother, the elderly woman folds her ears with her fingers to show failed communication. Understanding the situation, the child's mother interprets the little girl's chatter as though she were building a bridge between two islands, spanning the gap be-

Preceding pages: Blackfeet Chief Wildshoe and family in automobile. Left and right, Navajo Indian girls, then and now.

tween two cultures. Like many Indian people, she is caught between two worlds – Navajo and Anglo. She finds herself riding the fence, switching back and forth, never able to bring them fully together.

Hard lessons: She lights the butane stove and the tea kettle whistles to life. She picks a spoon out of an old brown pot she uses to carry her silverware, and recalls that her grandmother, Long Reed, used to keep her kitchen utensils in a similar coffeepot. Long Reed lit her fires in the half-bellied water barrels using paper brought home from school. To the old woman, the writing on the paper held no meaning.

The sleeping child's day won't begin until

part in a ritual of another sort, pledging allegiance to the American flag. "One nation under God, indivisible, with liberty and justice for all," the child recites with her classmates, her right hand over her heart.

In the early 1960s, Grandmother Long Reed spoke out against her grandchildren acquiring a modern education: "You are Navajo. Why do you need to become *bilagaana* (white)?" she asked her grandchildren when they brought lessons home for summer vacation. She felt that laws mandating that all Indian children receive an English education were too severe. At the time, many Indian children were forced to attend boarding schools, many of them miles away

6.45 a.m., an hour before school starts. Grandmother Long Reed would probably scold her for allowing the child to sleep so late. Her grandmother was an uneducated woman. For her family, she desired a future of caring for the sheep, learning how to weave rugs, respecting the elders, and raising a family off the land. She taught her grandchildren to do strenuous chores, to tend sheep, haul water, chop wood, and cook at an early age. She stressed daily adherence to the centuries-old tradition of the Navajo people, -focused on strong ties to family and land, and walking the "path of the corn pollen."

An hour later, the child is in school taking

from their homes. It was the policy of these government-run schools to sever children's ties with their families in order to assimilate them into mainstream American society – to weed out the Indian and make the children act like *bilagaana*.

She remembers the day she enrolled at boarding school. She was dressed like Grandmother Long Reed in a calico skirt, a velveteen blouse, a pair of well-oiled work boots her father picked out of the missionary's box. Her long black hair was arranged in the traditional way, tied with white yarn. Carrying a light-blue suitcase for which her mother pawned a beautiful turquoise pendant, and

and excited about meeting new friends, she entered the dormitory.

A dorm aide guided her to the shower stalls. She removed the saftey pin on her skirt. She took off the velveteen blouse, pulled off her shoes, and undid her hair bun. Earlier that morning, before her grandmother took out the sheep, the willowy old woman washed the little girl's hair in yucca root and brushed out the strands with dried tall grass.

Gently folding the girl's hair four times and forming a bun, grandmother told her a story: "Your thoughts are derived from your hair. It is made of showers of black rain. My mother used to say, the Holy People made hair-yarn from lightning. Your mind is your

military boot camp, the children would always live in two worlds. Instead of waking with family to the aroma of freshly brewed coffee, she woke with other children to rigid lessons about the modern world. While her family ate on the earthen floor of a hogan, the government taught her to eat at a table. While her mother and father slept on sheepskins, she was required to sleep in a bed.

From the very beginning, speaking Navajo was forbidden. Non-Indian teachers had the children memorize the Pledge of Allegiance before they understood what the flag was. To the little girl, standing up and mumbling English words to a red-white-and-blue cloth seemed meaningless, and slightly ridiculous.

hair. You take care of it."

Her thick black hair tumbled free as the yarn fell to the floor. The smell of sheep camp, the sweet scent of the female rains of August, the aroma of fry bread and mutton roasting on an open fire, the herbal water sprinkled earlier that day by a medicine man – all washed into the sewer pipes on the shower's concrete floor.

The school may have tried to take the Navajo out of her, but it failed. Although training at the school was as rigorous as

Left, gathering wood for cooking. **Above**, modern education stresses cultural identity.

"English, English, English," the dorm aides said if they found clusters of little girls talking to each other in Navajo. Many were punished for speaking their language by scrubbing toilets or by being put in isolation. Others lapsed into silence until they learned to communicate in English.

Like most children, she and her friends resisted assimilation and continued to speak Navajo whenever they could. At night, when the dorm aides went home, the darkened barracks exploded with Navajo chatter.

Practicing traditional Navajo religion was also forbidden at the school. The government saw to it that the children were enrolled with various religious organizations. As a child, the mother joined the Presbyterian Church, not knowing who this new God was. "Think about him as though he is one of your grandmother's gods," a dorm aide told her when she asked why she had to pray to him.

Back at the sheep camp, she tried to educate her mother about the god in the black Bible. Her mother forbade her to raise the subject. "The elders say First Man and First Woman created the Navajo people and gave them a religion," she remembers her mother saying. "You are a Dine [one of the People]. That God was made for the Anglo people." At one time, the child developed a routine of worshipping with the Presbyterians during the week and saying prayers to the Holy People when she went home.

Eventually, tribal leaders intervened and the policy of forced assimilation was abandoned. New programs designed to retain Indian identity were put in place. But for the children who were already told that they had to assimilate, the new policy only caused more confusion.

Racing with coyote: Despite the efforts of the government to Americanize her, she left boarding school still understanding more Navajo than English. Later, in high school and college, she struggled to understand Shakespeare, Melville and Poe, and to write and think quickly in her second language. Once she tried to make an English teacher understand her struggle to balance two languages, two cultures. He suggested she see a psychologist or speech therapist. In history class, she learned about the "winning of the West" and how the white man brought "progress" to the wilderness. She learned about American "heroes" like Andrew Jackson, George Armstrong Custer, and even Kit Carson, who rounded up the Navajos and sent them on their tragic Long Walk.

Today, depending on where she's living, the modern and traditional worlds tend to overlap, forcing her to accommodate both as best she can. But for certain issues, like religion, no shades of gray exist. Her people's teachings stay firmly in her mind.

Grandmother Long Reed and her father once told her about an omen involving the mythological trickster, Coyote. During the creation of the world, Coyote proclaimed himself a sender of messages. Coyote said: "If I appear across your path, I'm usually asking for corn pollen and a prayer. If you don't offer corn pollen to me, I could be sending you a good or bad message."

Recently, while she was driving down a washboard road near Navajo Mountain, a gray coyote darted out from a field of sage. She was already late for an appointment, and, panicking, she floored the gas pedal, hoping to race ahead of the coyote before it crossed her path. "If Coyote doesn't cross my path," she reasoned, "a prayer won't be needed."

But Coyote won. A plume of dust rose behind the truck as she skidded to a stop. She quickly searched her computer bag for corn pollen. She thought of how she dealt with similar situations when she was living in the city. Unlike in the reservation, where animals enjoy open space, city people keep coyotes penned up in zoos.

A Navajo friend once told her that the whole belief sounded trivial, a silly superstition. He wouldn't stop to make an offering to Coyote, he said. It wasn't any different than praying to a black cat if it crossed your path. But to her, Coyote was an important figure, a part of her childhood experience of Navajo religion.

As an adult, she told her daughter stories about Coyote's exploits during the emergence of the world and how the Holy People dealt with the disorder he created. The stories were a source of identity and strength. Her father used to say: "In the beginning, every being had a place in the emerging world. Then Coyote came, acting in outrageous and disrespectful ways. People didn't understand why he did these things."

Coyote brought chaos, confusion. He made the world complex. Like many Indian people, she often found herself living in Coyote's world, grappling with the ambiguities and contradictions of two overlapping cultures. Try as she might to reconcile these worlds, to achieve *hozjo* – balance, harmony, beauty – Coyote was never far behind.

And that is where many Indian people find themselves: caught between two worlds, struggling every day to make them work together. Whether Navajo, Hopi, Crow, Lakota, Cherokee, Mohawk, Chippewa, Miwok or any other tribe, Indian people are, to one degree or another, racing with Coyote.

Right, Navajo great-grandmother.

High atop the mesas that rise majestically from the northern Arizona desert lie the villages of the Hopi. From a distance, the old stone houses are scarcely distinguishable from the reddish-brown sandstone on which they are built. Like a layer of rock weathered by the ages, the Hopi pueblos recall an ancient time, a time remembered in myths and songs when the earth was newly created, and when people walked with spirits.

On many a hot spring and summer day, the Hopis go to the village plaza, an arena formed by a rectangle of lumpy stone houses, to see the kachinas dance. In the houses skirting the plaza, women are busy in their kitchens baking bread, stirring stew, preparing to feed family and friends. The inviting smells of home-cooked food and juniper smoke waft into the warm air.

At the approaching sounds of the kachinas – clack! jingle! clack! jingle! – the women spill from their houses to watch these stunning masked figures, spiritual messengers, enter from a corridor between two pueblos. Many of the young people and non-Indian guests climb wooden ladders to gain a rooftop vantage of the dancers.

Among the hundreds of distinct kachinas, the *angak' china*, or long-hair kachina, appears. Filing into the plaza are many identically costumed figures, varying only in size from the slim hard bodies of the young men to the massive barrel-chested torsos of the middle-aged.

Clay markings: Their outfits are spectacular. Every one has a turquoise face set on a long mane of black hair hanging from the crown of the head midway down the chest and back. On top of the head is a tuft of yellow downy feathers from which rises a long brilliant macaw feather. Clay markings painted with fingers adorn the naked upper body. A white woven kilt hangs from the waist, which billows with spruce boughs secured by a belt. Turquoise moccasins are worn on the feet. A tortoise-shell rattle clacks on the right calf and a band of sleigh bells jingles on the left. Turquoise bracelets,

necklaces and bow guards provide further decoration.

The colorful *angak' china* file into the dusty brown plaza, their arms loaded with corn stalks and cattails, fruit and bread, kachina dolls and miniature bows and arrows. They pile the gifts in the center, then align themselves about one end of the plaza. A hush falls over the crowd. Even the young people watch with anticipation.

The head kachina lifts and asserts his right heel. His tortoise-shell rattle comes to life

and sets the rhythm – Clack! Clack! – and the other *angak' china* take up the beat. The song, sonorous yet beautifully melodic, wells up to fill the plaza. As the dance progresses, the sleigh bells alternate with the shell rattle. Clack! Jingle! Clack! Jingle!

The kachinas dance three sets, distributing gifts to the Hopi people between each one. They then return to their secret resting place below the mesa edge, filing out of the plaza much as they came in. Again and again throughout the day, the kachinas come to dance, sing, and bear gifts. They bring rain. They bring corn. They bring life. Experiencing this ancient Hopi ritual leaves no doubt.

<u>Left</u>, buffalo dancer, Santa Clara Pueblo. <u>Right</u>, dancing at San Ildefonso feast day.

Living faith: People often think of Native American religions as a thing of the past, a sort of ancient relic that has survived only in bits and pieces. They look upon Indian beliefs as remnants of a bygone era, scraps of archaic wisdom, timeless and unchanging. And although it is true that the roots of Indian traditions sink deep into the past, it is a mistake to think that native religions are somehow frozen in time or that they do not speak to modern concerns.

Like all aspects of human culture, Native American religions change over time. And that change has certainly not been more tumultuous or dramatic than in the last 400 years, since the arrival of Europeans. One

need only experience Indian religions to understand their vitality, timeliness and potential for growth. In fact, it is this very ability to grow and adapt to radically different situations that has enabled them to survive.

Today, as in the past, Native American religions are more than a collection of old ceremonies, prayers and rituals. They are a living faith, a way of seeing and understanding the world. For many Indian people, religion touches all aspects of human experience, from the spiritual to the mundane.

Another common misconception about Native American religions is that they are all

more or less alike. We see references to such things as medicine men, peace pipes, peyote, vision quests and kachinas, and we tend to lump them all together into a single, vaguely animistic belief system. But this, too, is more romance than reality. It is a distortion that obscures the differences and variety among the hundreds of distinct cultures native to North America.

Native American religious practices vary extensively from the grand masked ceremonial dances related to the agricultural cycle in the American Southwest to individual quests for power in the Great Plains; from brief but intense healing rituals performed by entranced shamans in California to the healing ceremonials of the Navajos involving hundreds of songs and many hours of prayer; from the dramatic self-sacrifice of the Plains Indians' sun dance to the masked False Face ceremonies of the Iroquois; from the feasts, giveaways and masked dramas of the Northwest coast to the community fasts and purges in preparation for the Green Corn Dance in the Southeast.

The life cycle of all Native Americans is a religious journey, a lifelong rite of passage marked by key transitions – birth, naming, puberty, marriage, death – all effected through religious practice. These beliefs and practices are performed with wide variation among hundreds of distinct tribes, each with its own language, history and character. Their complexity and richness is living testimony to the creative powers of Indian cultures.

Crisis and change: The arrival of Europeans in North America heralded a period of crisis and change for Native Americans, and like other aspects of Indian cultures, their religious lives were deeply affected. In response to the flood of missionaries, settlers and soldiers, Native Americans sought new means of religious expression, new ways of understanding a changing world.

Ironically, some of these new religions drew on the Christian faith of the invaders – like Smohalla's Dreamer Cult, which spread among Northwest tribes in the 1850s. Others, like the Iroquois religious revival of Handsome Lake, were staunchly non-Christian. These movements may not have succeeded in removing the Indians' oppressive situation, or even in significantly changing it, but they gave Native American people a way of finding religious significance even in their experience of suffering and loss.

Among the most widespread of these crisis cults was the Ghost Dance movement, which swept across the Northern Plains in the late 1880s just as the Plains Indian wars were entering their final, tragic chapter.

The 1880s saw the culmination of almost a century of American contact. After years of ranging freely across the prairie, many Plains Indian tribes were confined to reservations, where they were riddled with poverty, disease and hunger. Most tribes experienced a total transformation of their way of life. Many faced possible extinction.

In this milieu of crisis, wave upon wave of dances and uphold right living by not drinking alcohol, fighting or quarreling. The message spread rapidly, and the movement was widely practiced by the tribes of the Great Plains and Northwest.

At the height of the Ghost Dance, dancers would fall into a trance. Upon reviving, they told of their visions, often of visiting the Indian dead. Among the Lakota (or Sioux), the Ghost Dance took on a particularly martial aspect. They believed that whites would be destroyed by the cataclysm and Indians would inherit the earth, that the buffalo and antelope would return to the plains, and the ancestors would be restored to life. The most radical followers fashioned long white "ghost

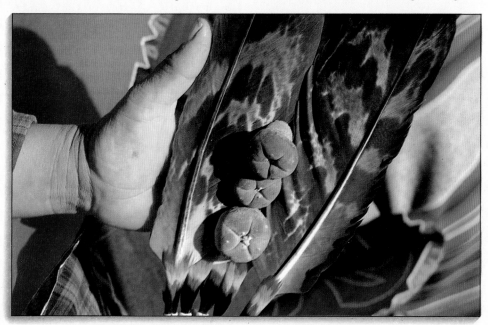

prophetic movements washed over the tribes. When the Ghost Dance movement was introduced in 1889, they immediately latched onto its message of hope.

The Ghost Dance was started in January 1889 by a Paiute man named Wovoka. Wovoka had a vision in which he visited the spirit world to receive a millennial message, instructions to prepare the people for the imminent end of the world. According to the message, Indian people should perform trance

Left, pollen is sprinkled on a girl's face during Apache puberty rite, Sunrise Ceremony. <u>Above</u>, peyote, sacrament of the Native American Church.

shirts," believing that they were invulnerable to the white soldiers' bullets.

But this last spark of hope was short-lived. The Ghost Dance was crushed on December 29, 1890, at Wounded Knee, South Dakota, when US troops massacred hundreds of Lakota men, women and children. Today, the Ghost Dance persists in a number of tribal communities, although with far less emphasis on the destruction of the world.

The peyote way: In the wake of the Ghost Dance, other religious movements crossed tribal boundaries and were taken up by Indian people throughout North America. Among the most influential of these pan-

Indian movements was, and continues to be, the peyote religion of the Native American Church. Although peyotism is not necessarily a reaction to the crisis of Indian-white contact, the rise of the peyote religion corresponds with a growing sense among Native Americans that they share a religious identity distinct from mainstream Americans.

The peyote religion was introduced to North America from Mexico late in the 19th century and was carried by itinerant leaders, or road chiefs, to the tribes of the Great Plains, Northwest, Southwest and beyond. Although there is a good deal of variation between the ceremonies of one road chief and another, all peyote meetings involve the

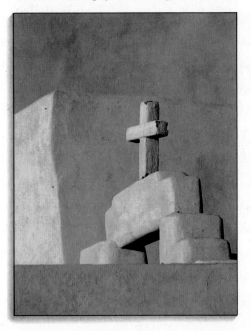

sacramental use of dried buttons cut from the peyote cactus, which, when eaten, have hallucinogenic properties. Peyote meetings are usually held in a tepee, the participants sitting in a circle around an earthen, crescent-shaped altar with a large button known as "father peyote" on it. Meetings usually start in the evening and continue until dawn, and involve song, prayer and meditation.

From the very beginning, peyotists were entangled in legal battles over their right to use a hallucinogen for religious purposes. In 1918, peyotists in Oklahoma formally established the Native American Church, hoping to put these questions to rest once and for all.

But the struggle over legality continues to the present day. A 1990 US Supreme Court decision allowed the state of Oregon (and by implication all states) the right to challenge the legal status of sacramental peyote-use. It is absolutely essential, however, that the ceremonies of the Native American Church not be mistaken for bizarre or promiscuous rituals. In fact, members of the Native American Church are characteristically conservative and strongly community-oriented. Their use of peyote is sacramental, for healing and spiritual insight.

Native American Christianity: No discussion of Native American religions is complete without including the pervasive and longstanding influence of Christianity. Throughout North America, Christian missionaries were among the first outsiders to settle and live with Native American people. Many Native American communities were at least nominally Christianized soon after their earliest contact with whites.

Christianity doesn't fit the popular image of Native American religion, but it has long been important to many native people all over the Americas. Native American Christianity differs greatly from tribe to tribe, being reinterpreted in terms of the history and traditions of each tribal community. Unlike Christians in Europe or America, Native Americans usually hold that Christianity need not be practiced to the exclusion of other religions. In fact, many Native Americans practice Christianity in addition to their traditional religions. Others have even added a third form of religious practice such as the Native American Church.

The distinctive reinterpretation of Christianity is nowhere more evident than among the Yaqui people now living in Arizona and northern Mexico. Their principal religious festival centers upon the dramatic re-enactment of the crucifixion of Christ. Yet, in every respect, this festival bears a distinctively Yaqui religious ethos.

The dramatic theme of this passion play is enhanced with masked figures and black-clad troupes who portray the forces of evil. On Holy Saturday, these evil forces try to overthrow the good spirits and recapture the body of Christ, which they have crucified yet lost. Throwing flower petals, which represent the transformed blood of Christ, at these evil characters, the women and children repel them. When evil has finally been suppressed, the entire Yaqui village explodes in celebration. The fiesta includes the ancient deer dancers, the masked pascola dancers, and a dancing matachine troupe.

Like so many native people, the Yaquis have accepted and transformed Christianity, moulding it into an Indian religion.

American Indian spirituality: Perhaps the most visible form of contemporary Native American religion is a loosely defined movement that can be termed American Indian Spirituality. Mindful of the historical plight of Native Americans and the wisdom and richness of their traditions, American Indian Spirituality draws on some very general re-

Spirituality is the Northern Plains, and much of its inspiration comes from popular books like *Black Elk Speaks* and *The Sacred Pipe*, both featuring the recollections of Black Elk, a Lakota medicine man.

In large part, the attraction of American Indian Spirituality is its inherent critique of mainstream American culture. It presents an alternative to the Western tradition and suggests that we learn from ancient Indian teachings. What attracts many people to Native American religions is their openness, vitality and capacity to change.

Today, some Native Americans continue their ancient religious traditions exclusively, but these are exceptional. Many have com-

ligious themes in order to forge a common intertribal spiritual identity. It poses a Native American religion that exemplifies harmonious living and spiritual interconnectedness with the natural world. Politically, it stands in firm opposition to environmental exploitation and other forms of Western materialism. It also has a strong appeal to non-Indians and is one of the mainstays of the New Age movement and other forms of "pop spirituality."

The historical center of American Indian

Left, mission church, Laguna Pueblo. **Above**, Lakota *hunkalowanpi* ceremony, *circa* 1907.

plemented these traditions with the practice of Christianity. For some, the older traditions are wholly supplanted by Christianity, the Native American Church or a modern pan-Indian spirituality. Frequently all these religious forms are practiced without contradiction in a single community, in a single family, and, not so rarely, even practiced faithfully by an individual.

In whatever form Indian spirituality is expressed, it plays a critical role in the cohesiveness, strength and continuity of Native American communities. Perhaps now more than ever, religion is the cornerstone of American Indian identity.

The defendant sits in a tiny courtroom in southern Arizona, waiting in a legal never-never world. He is accused of beating his wife. The charge is usually filed as misdemeanor assault.

Tohono O'odham Tribal Judge Ned Norris says he has seen this man several times during the past year. The man has been brought to court nearly a dozen times for assault, public intoxication and drunken driving. But the man won't be charged with a criminal offense this day. He'll walk out of the court free. And he will remain free – free to commit additional misdemeanors without fear of prosecution.

According to legal guidelines, most issued by the US Supreme Court, tribal governments have criminal jurisdiction only over their own members. It doesn't matter that the man has committed the crime on the Tohono O'odham Reservation. Nor does it matter that he is married to an O'odham woman and lives on the reservation.

What does matter is that even a simple assault is not simple when it occurs on one of America's 300-plus Indian reservations. Like so many difficult issues facing Indians today – employment, health care, education, resource management, housing – crime has become snarled in a policy-maze of court rulings, legislation and treaties.

At the root of the problem is a deep-seated confusion about the status of Indian tribes and their relationship to the US government. Federal Indian policy has undergone so many changes over the past 200 years, and is now so completely snarled in bureaucratic red tape, that it is virtually impossible to unravel. Simply put, federal Indian policy is a mess. As Senator Daniel K. Inouye, chairman of the Senate Select Committee on Indian Affairs, noted, "You could talk to 10 people, and I suppose they'd give you 10 policies."

Two centuries of confusion: In the past 200 years, the US government's policy on Indian tribes has wavered between separation and assimilation. The question is: should Indian tribes be allowed to govern themselves as

domestic nations within the US, or should Indian people be absorbed into mainstream American society – another spice in the "melting pot" without any special status?

Clearly, there are arguments to be made for both positions – and for reasonable compromises. The problem has always been the use of these policies to advance white rather than Indian interests.

It all began in 1790, when Secretary of War Henry Knox proposed that tribes be treated as foreign nations. His intention was to negotiate land cessions on a government-to-government basis, and then make the Indians good neighbors by "civilizing" them. Knox wanted to supply the tribes with hoes, plows and spinning wheels, and send missionaries into their lands with Bibles, federal laws and strange ideas about private property.

Needless to say, the policy was a failure. But the Knox policy did produce more than 200 treaties between Indian tribes and the US government. Once these treaties were ratified, the Constitution called them the "supreme law of the land." The government gave its word that Indian land, hunting rights, and other benefits were guaranteed forever.

But the treaties were subjected to shifts in political will. In the late 1800s, a new federal law, the Allotment Act, broke up Indian land into 360-acre squares so that Indians could become farmers. The new policy promised assimilation by agriculture. By some miracle, Indians were supposed to become civilized by the mere act of cultivating their plots. Plains Indians, who had wandered the Great Plains for generations, were told to stay put on a square piece of ground.

The idea was to dissolve tribal governments just as soon as all the land was transferred to individual Indians. It was no coincidence, of course, that any leftover land was thrown open to homesteaders. The effects of allotment were devastating: 65 percent of all Indian lands were lost.

In the 1930s, John Collier, head of the Bureau of Indian Affairs, reversed the allotment policy and tried to re-establish tribal rights. Collier tried to create modern tribal governments, with three branches, by federal order. What Collier didn't appreciate was that a single form of government, ignoring differences in culture and language, was simply not workable for all Indian tribes.

The assimilation camp took control again, this time in the form of "termination." Between the 1940s and 1960s, Congress pressured tribes to give up their unique status. It was a get-rid-of-the-Indians-quick policy. Tribal members would be paid a lump sum of money and their rights would vanish. No more Indians. No more treaties. No more problems. More than a dozen tribes were "terminated" during this period.

In 1970, the termination era was officially repudiated by President Richard Nixon in a special message to Congress. Nixon's speech

try see new federalism as an elaborate dodge. By slashing funds and cutting programs, they say, the federal government is trying to get out of the "Indian business" altogether.

Bureaucratic roadblocks: Confusion about federal Indian policy is surpassed only by the tangled bureaucracy that is supposed to implement it. Originally created by the War Department, the mission of the Bureau of Indian Affairs (BIA) is to protect the interests of Indian tribes. But many Indian leaders and government officials view the BIA as the most inefficient agency in Washington. Waste and mismanagement have penetrated the agency so deeply, in fact, many believe "it routinely works against the interests of America's 1.4

opened the US government's policy of self-determination – better known in the Reagan and Bush administrations as "new federalism." This policy recognizes that tribal governments know best how to solve their problems; it reaffirms government-to-government relations between tribes and Washington; and, perhaps most importantly, it promises to channel money directly to tribal authorities rather than pass it through an intervening and voracious federal bureaucracy.

Opinions about new federalism have been mixed. Members of the administration say that it's basically sound, promising results if given more time. But many in Indian Coun-

million Indians."

In the 1980s, for example, the BIA watched silently as more than a billion dollars worth of Indian-owned gas, coal and oil revenues were lost or stolen. In some areas, the BIA used an "honor system," allowing the oil companies to keep track of the oil they pumped off reservation lands.

The bureau's handling of taxpayer funds wasn't much better. Dozens of audits by the General Accounting Office have shown that the bureau's accounting system is so bad that it often doesn't know how much money it has to spend on its own programs. One federal administrator said that of every dollar appropriated for Indian people, only one dime actually reaches the tribes. The rest is absorbed by the BIA itself.

Keeping the culture alive: Outside the political arena, Indian people are also fighting to keep their cultures alive. In some cases, this literally means saving a tribe's connection to the past by retrieving artifacts and skeletal remains that were taken by anthropologists or private collectors. At times, US Army doctors shipped the battlefield remains of Indian combatants to eastern hospitals for study. More than a century later, dozens of museums still hold their remains as well as extensive collections of pipes, medicine bundles and other religious objects that are often held sacred by Indian people. "The unspoken message to Indian people is that the profession of archaeology is more important than the practice of our religion," said Suzanne Shown Harjo, executive director of the Morning Star Foundation and member of the Cheyenne and Arapaho tribes.

The battle over Indian religious freedom has raged for more than two centuries. In 1990, for example, the US Supreme Court ruled that the sacramental use of peyote (a hallucinogenic cactus) by members of the Native American Church is not constitutionally protected. Under current federal law, it is civil to consume wine as a sacrament, yet it remains uncivil, and in some cases illegal, for Indian people to use peyote.

Success stories: But despite long years of adversity and a mountain of bureaucratic and legal obstacles, Indian people are coming up with their own solutions. *"Wa wo ici ya,"* says the motto of a tribal college in South Dakota. "We can do it ourselves."

The Quinault Nation of Washington state almost didn't make it into this century. In 1887, Congress ignored promises made to the Quinault and began to break up reservation land and sell it to white settlers. Years later, timber companies under the supervision of the BIA clear-cut the tribe's virgin forest, virtually destroying its most valuable resource. Even the salmon, plentiful only two decades ago, can no longer be relied upon as a major source of food and income.

But tribal president Joe DeLaCruz believes the tribe can return to its former great-

ness. He is working as a partner with the federal government and the private sector to restore the tribe's natural resources.

The Quinault Nation is also one of the tribes testing the promise of the new federalism policy. DeLaCruz will receive money directly from Washington for any program the tribe says is important. The money will not go through the BIA or any other federal agency. The theory here is that local governments know their own needs and are best-suited to use the funds effectively.

"When I came home in 1967, the fisheries were pretty much down, the timber industry was in decline, the mills that people had normally worked in were all shut down, and

it was pretty depressed," DeLaCruz said.

The only way to rebuild the reservation economy is for the tribe to call the shots, he said. And Washington has granted the Quinault's request. The next decade will challenge the capabilities of local government, which tribal leaders say will work if, and only if, the federal government really supports the tribal decision-making process.

There are other clues that tribal governments may be able to solve many of their own problems. Several tribes have succeeded in creating jobs and industries without federal help. The Mississippi Choctaw Tribe is a great example. Phillip Martin, the tribe's

Left, Puyallups protest for tribal rights. **Right,** Navajo coal miner.

chief, saw an opportunity to create jobs. So he sold the business community on the idea that his reservation was an ideal place to insert greetings into holiday cards or assemble automotive parts. Some 1,400 people are now employed by tribal ventures on that reservation.

The Cree Indians in Quebec have merged traditional tasks with modern technology. Recently the tribe formed a joint venture with Yamaha to produce boats for northern climates. The tribe also purchased Air Ontario and renamed it Air Creebec. The former chairman is now president of the airline.

The power of the individual is at work, too. Every weekend, just outside the Navajo capital in Window Rock, Arizona, dozens and sometimes hundreds of Indians open arts and crafts booths, T-shirt stalls, and tent-cafés selling mutton stew, fry bread and other odds and ends. This instant flea market is not designed for the outside world. It's Indian people selling to each other.

Another reservation in Arizona boasts zero-unemployment. There are countless news stories about reservations where more than 80 percent can't find jobs, but few about the tribe with jobs for every tribal member. Every able-bodied man and woman living on the Ak Chin Reservation is guaranteed a job on the successful tribal farm.

The farm started with one person: Wilbur Carlyle. Carlyle began a farm in 1954. But he knew that the future of farming was more corporate than family-oriented, so he decided that the Ak Chin Indian community ought to be corporate farmers.

The BIA immediately nixed the idea. The local official found all sorts of reasons why it wouldn't work: It had never been done before; farming is risky; and, better yet, the tribe could be guaranteed a profit of $10,000 a year by leasing its land to non-Indians.

Carlyle's answer to the BIA was blunt: "To hell with it. It's our land and we'll farm it." Instead of turning to the BIA for help, the community went to a local cotton gin, borrowed money, and a few years later was showing a profit. In 1963, after profits began rolling in, the local BIA agency declared Ak Chin a success story – a BIA success story.

The tribe has been careful to return its profits to the farming operation. Recent profits have exceeded $1.5 milion a year. Today, Ak Chin not only owns the farms, but when the local cotton gin ran into financial troubles, they bought it too.

Meeting the challenge: The 1990s promise to challenge tribal leaders again. The population growth of Indian Country is exploding at a Third World rate. The Navajo Nation is expected to top 300,000 people before the year 2000. Tribal leaders with the help of the federal government must find ways of creating jobs for new people on the same reservation land base.

One solution that is being explored by a number of tribes is new working partnerships between the tribes and state governments. Indian leaders have recognized that Indians are neighbors in a larger community

– and that many problems are best solved by the community as a whole. Tribes are also beginning to change the nature of their use of natural resources. Some tribes, with shrewd forward planning, have started using revenue from mineral extraction as a large savings account in order to plan for the day when coal mines or gas fields are empty.

But in the end, Indian Country's biggest problem – its growing population – is also its most valuable asset: a new generation of Indian youth who are better educated and prepared to be the tribal leaders of the future.

Above, the Navajo Nation's future.

INDIANS AND ALCOHOL

Vernon Kills On Top's new home is his sanctuary. Within the quiet refuge of death row at Montana State Prison, he will outlive many of his friends. "This is a safe place," Kills On Top, a Cheyenne, said recently. "My friends are out there dying." Kills On Top awaits execution for the murder of a white man. While he waits in the safety of his cell, alcohol, the leading killer in Indian Country, stalks his friends. "They'll die in car wrecks and alley fights. Some will kill themselves and others will kill their livers. Alcohol will get them all."

Cultural trauma and poverty render Indians vulnerable to alcohol addiction. Almost entirely without alcohol before the coming of Europeans, Indians are still developing the social restraints that moderate alcohol use in other cultures. The US Indian Health Service (IHS) estimates that significant drinking problems are experienced by 50 percent of the population on some reservations and calls alcohol abuse its number one problem. Of the 10 leading causes of death among Indians, alcohol is directly implicated in four: cirrhosis, homicide, suicide and accidents.

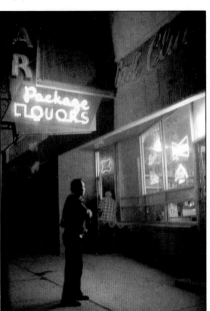

Indian alcoholism is not a new problem. In 1786 Bernardo de Galvex, viceroy of New Spain, urged that liquor be heavily traded among Apaches and other tribes in order to make them easier to manipulate. Laws forbidding the sale of alcohol to Indians were passed in Connecticut in 1645. In 1832, the US Congress passed a law prohibiting the sale of alcohol to all Indians; the legislation remained in force until 1953. The law was based on the faulty notion that Indians can't hold their liquor, a myth that gained credibility when early researchers demonstrated through biased experiments that Indians were unable to metabolize alcohol as quickly as whites. This myth was put to rest in the mid-1970s by careful scientific studies that found no difference in the ability to metabolize alcohol.

Today, alcohol threatens the next generation. When a pregnant woman drinks, the baby in her womb shares its mother's intoxication. Alcohol cripples fetal development, resulting in a condition called Fetal Alcohol Syndrome (FAS). Small and usually mentally retarded, FAS babies enter the world with a host of medical problems. Those that do not die in infancy are doomed to be wards of the state. It has been estimated that, among some Indian populations, one in 10 babies show the effects of maternal alcoholism.

Indians who consider themselves warriors in the fight against alcohol say, "It's a war we must win for ourselves." And encouraging evidence that Indians are winning comes from all quarters of Indian Country. Pilots flying into the Alaskan bush are warned that their planes may be confiscated if they are carrying liquor to certain native villages. Kotzebue, one of the larger Native American communities in Alaska, outlawed the sale of alcohol and noted a 40 percent decrease in assaults, sexual assaults, homicide and suicide. The Cheyenne River Sioux voted to rid their reservation of drugs and alcohol by the year 2000. The reservation hamlets of Green Grass, Cherry Creek and White Horse, South Dakota, have declared themselves drug and alcohol free. And more radically, several Plains tribes are considering laws which will enable them to lock up pregnant women whose drinking threatens the lives of their unborn children. "We are almost certain a law protecting babies carried by Indian mothers could stand a court test," one tribal attorney said.

Minto tribal judge Geraldine Charlie tells the story of a rowdy drunk who was brought before her tribal court in Alaska. He arrived angry. He clenched his fists and muttered threats as the judge fined him $300. But, before he was allowed to leave, the judge demanded his attention. One of the oldest of the community's elders, the judge said: "You must understand. You embarrassed your family. You shamed your village. The fine is necessary to make you understand what you are doing with your life. We love you. We want to help you."

The man fell silent. His eyes moistened. Then he asked to speak. He said he had been arrested and dragged before dozens of judges, but never treated like this. He praised the court, thanked the judge and cried. In the three years that have passed, he has not appeared in tribal court again.

Just below the ancient, wind-weathered stone houses of Old Walpi sprawls the modern village of Polacca on the Hopi Indian Reservation. Inside a small frame house, a Hopi potter sits cross-legged on the floor. She is rubbing a red clay pot with a small black rock, smoothing out the coils. The rock is rounded and shiny from generations of use. As she polishes the pot, she hums an old Hopi song taught to her by her grandmother.

The woman's hands follow centuries of tradition. Although she works in a modern house with electricity, television and running water, she makes her pottery much as Anasazi potters did 1,000 years before. And like those ancient earthen vessels, her work sings of beauty and harmony. It is an affirmation of Hopi life, a visible connection between the red clay of Mother Earth and the traditions of her people.

In some respects, talking about "American Indian art" is a contradiction in terms. In the traditional Indian view, art is so deeply interconnected with other aspects of tribal life, it simply doesn't exist as a discrete category. A word for "art" doesn't even exist in many Indian languages; neither does a word for "religion." As author Peter Mathiessen has noted: "Among Indians, the concept of Indian art separate from nature, of which life is a part, is as unnatural as the idea of a life separated from religion."

All this category-blending may seem a bit tricky for those of us raised on the good old Western analytical tradition. We usually like to see everything fit into tidy conceptual boxes. But that's the challenge of Native American art: to break out of our old frames of reference and approach it on its own terms. The aim is to gain a greater appreciation of American Indian art by adopting an Indian perspective, to see art – and, through it, the rest of the world – as American Indians do.

But that's easier said than done. Aside from the philosophical debate this sort of

cultural leap-frogging stirs up, there are a number of strictly practical concerns that stand in the way of understanding Indian art from an Indian point of view. Most of the Indian art you're likely to see, for example, will be in museums, galleries or gift shops, where it's virtually impossible to get a feeling for the object's place in a broader cultural framework. What's worse, in many museums, Indian work is exhibited in the "Primitive Art" section, as though it were somehow less advanced on the evolutionary

ladder than the Van Goghs and Renoirs, or merely an amusing bit of exotica.

Clearly, the best way to understand Indian art is to see it in the appropriate cultural context, even if the work in question was made strictly as a commodity, which, today, at least, is often the case. Whether you go to a Corn Dance at Santo Domingo Pueblo, a trading post on the Navajo Reservation, a pawn shop in South Dakota, or a powwow in Oklahoma, Indian art comes alive only when it's used in ways for which it was intended.

The artist and society: While you're browsing the museums and galleries, it's helpful to keep in mind that there are fun-

Preceding pages: rawhide pouch (*parfleche*) with Arapaho design. Left, beadwork cradleboard. Right, Navajo wearing squash blossom necklace.

damental differences between the Indian and Western traditions. In the West, for example, the artist is often perceived as an individualist and innovator – a lone wolf lurking on the fringes of society in order to critique it. The more "different" an artist's work, the more creative he or she is thought to be. The final product is a thing of beauty, yes, but also a commodity, a decoration, a self-contained object that can stand alone in a display case.

In traditional Native American cultures, on the other hand, the individuality of the artist – and the work of art – is usually de-emphasized. Indian artists tend to be guided by an ethic of tribal conformity, of working within the constraints of tradition rather than

cause symbols are not used only as a representation of spiritual power but as a channel through which spiritual power travels and a sign that this power is manifest within a person or object. A bear-claw necklace may not only be a personal adornment, for example, but a sign of a hunter's prowess, and what's more, an indication that the grizzly's power has passed to the person wearing it.

The Ghost shirts made by some Plains Indians during the Ghost Dance movement of the late 1800s are an even more striking example. The shirts were decorated with vision-images that came to the followers after hours, and sometimes days, of dancing. The shirts were thought to be a manifestation

purposely trying to break out of them. What's more, traditional Indian art is rarely created as an end in itself. It is the process of creation – often inspired by a spiritual experience – that is considered most important. The object's value depends more on an ability to evoke this inner spirituality than on its superficial appearance alone.

Indian art, then, forges a physical link between the mundane and spiritual worlds. And perhaps more than anything else, it is the symbols that an artist uses to create this link that expresses the true power of his or her "vision." Here again is an important difference with the Western tradition, be-

of the dancer's spiritual power, and those who wore them were believed to be invulnerable to the white man's bullets.

In other cases – Navajo sand paintings, for example – the work of art is a symbolic reconstruction of universal order which, when created within the proper ritual context, has power to restore order in the world. Sand paintings are part of many Navajo healing ceremonies. They are made by medicine men by sprinkling colored sand on the floor of a ceremonial hogan. The designs are thought to be passed down from the Holy People and are associated with specific episodes in the Navajo creation story. When the sand painting is complete, the patient sits on it and receives a mystical transference of healing power from the Holy People. If the ceremony is done correctly, the patient is restored to a state of *hojho*, or harmony and well-being. Although permanent sand paintings can now be bought from Navajo artists, ceremonial sand paintings are always destroyed at the end of a ritual. The permanent works aren't exact replicas, but they do use many of the same symbols, and of course are not meant to contain spiritual power.

Artwork, especially masks, can also be used in the attainment of spiritual insight. The best examples here are probably Hopi kachina masks worn by dancers not so much

masks are carved from the living wood of basswood trees and are fed and talked to like a revered member of the family. When they end up in a museum behind a glass case, it's felt that they can't breathe.

Clearly, most of the Indian art now available for sale isn't invested with the same sort of spiritual power. Ceremonial art is generally made and used privately, beyond the gaze of tourists and collectors. Still, there's usually a strong element of tradition even in works that are made explicitly for the marketplace. And with the explosive growth of the Indian art market over the past 30 years, this can make things considerably more complicated for both artists and consumers.

as a costume or disguise but as a way of assuming the personality of the spirit they are meant to impersonate. By looking through the eyes of the mask, the dancer sees the world from an alternate point of view. "When he dons the mask," a Hopi dancer explains, "he loses his identity and actually becomes what he is representing."

Among the Iroquois, the grotesque masks of the False Face Society are thought to be living spiritual entities. Inspired by dreams, and associated with healing powers, the

Today, for example, Native American artists must decide for themselves exactly where they stand on the issue of individualism and tribal conformity – or whether art forms previously restricted to ceremonial life ought to be made for the consumer market. Although there are arguments – and staunch purists – on either side of the questions, these are not exactly black-or-white issues. In fact, the majority of artists probably follow a middle course, expressing personal vision within the broadly drawn boundaries of tribal culture and religion.

Famed Hopi artist Fred Kabotie led the way in this fusion of Western and Native

Left, Navajo weaver working at traditional loom.
Above, images of the Holy People on Navajo rug.

American approaches with his realistic paintings of Hopi ceremonial dancers. More recently, a similar integration is being created in the painted abstractions of Jaune Quick To See Smith, the innovative ceramic masks of Lillian Pitt, the fiery paintings of John Nieto, Alan Houser's monumental sculptures, R.C. Gorman's large curvaceous women, and Jesse Monongye's modern Hopi jewelry worked in non-traditional gold settings. The poetry and paintings of Michael Kabotie, the sheet-steel sculptures of Bob Hazous, and the fine art kachinas of Neil David Sr also draw elements from both Western and Indian traditions. And several artists have turned to an ironic, and occa-

to the home of an artist or craftsperson. Of course, the work of widely known artists can be found at galleries in regional art centers like Santa Fe, Sedona, Phoenix, Jackson, Los Angeles, Vancouver and New York.

The Great Plains: Plains Indian art evolved in conjunction with the nomadic horse-and-buffalo culture that swept onto the prairie in the late 18th century. Objects crafted by the central Plains tribes – the Sioux, Cheyenne and Arapaho, for example – are typical. Clothing and household items were fashioned from buckskin and rawhide, and every part of the animal – usually buffalo or deer – was utilized. Clothes were finely beaded, conveying prestige on both the creator and

sionally sardonic, representation of life caught between two cultures – the coyote symbolism of Harry Fonseca and the clay figures of Nora Narajo-Morse, for example.

Regional styles: While much Indian art is bound by a common set of philosophical underpinnings, regional styles are quite pronounced, and depending where you are in Indian Country, you are likely to see very different types of work. Aside from the usual museums and galleries, the best places to start looking for Indian art are tribal museums, gift shops and trading posts.

If in doubt, ask for directions and information. It's not unusual to be shown directly

wearers. Many objects were decorated with colorful quillwork, beadwork and feathers.

On the Northern Plains, a floral beadwork style was popular, while a geometric pattern was more common on the Southern Plains. Today, beadwork is found on moccasins, medallions, earrings, bracelets, belts, vests and buckskin dresses as well as souvenir items like key chains.

To see exquisite beading, featherwork and headdresses, go to a powwow. They are held all over the country and usually include arts and crafts booths. Powwows are also a wonderful place to see Indian art in motion, as it was meant to be seen.

Even before the wide commercialization of Plains Indian art, painting was an important medium. Women painted geometric designs on clothing and parfleches while men painted war and hunting exploits on tepees and buffalo robes. Today, updated versions can be found on canvas and paper.

There are any number of other local specialties you're likely to find in the region, including hand-carved catlinite "peace pipes," Osage ribbon work, and the beautiful star quilts so prevalent at trading posts in the Dakotas. It's said that the quilting style – strikingly similar to Pennsylvania Dutch quilts – was learned by students at the Carlisle Indian School in Pennsylvania.

in bright colors, the Bella Coola being renowned for a unique shade of blue.

Basketry is highly developed in the Northwest, with extremely tight weaves and characteristic sea-inspired designs, including killer whales and canoes. Gray and white Cowitchen sweaters are also woven here, usually with oil-impregnated wool. Heavy and almost waterproof, they are a perfect defense against damp winter nights.

Elsewhere on the coast, Tlingit and Tsimshian people are famous for their goat hair and cedar-bark Chilkat blankets. And black stone totem poles and other carved items can be purchased from the Haida.

The Southwest: If you are serious about

The Pacific Northwest: The pervasive influence of forest and sea is obvious in the native art of the Pacific Northwest. Most of the work is made from wood – totem poles, longhouses, masks, rattles, even cedar-bark clothing and hats. Genealogies, sometimes going all the way back to mythical animal ancestors, are often the subject of totem poles and painted longhouses. Their distinctive semi-abstract designs, usually of conventionalized animal forms, tend to occupy every available space and are often painted

Left, colorful featherwork worn by powwow dancers. **Above**, Skokomish carver and his work.

Indian art, the Southwest is a gold mine. But be forewarned: there is so much to see and buy here it will take the better part of a lifetime to cover it all.

Let's start with the Hopi. Kachina dolls, silver jewelry, baskets, pottery and intricate masks are all fashioned for the non-Indian trade, and each Hopi mesa has its own specialty. Third Mesa carvers are famous for kachina dolls, while craftsmen from First Mesa are renowned for pottery, growing out of a turn-of-the-century revival begun by Nampeyo. The Hopis also make two types of baskets – a patterned wicker basket made on Third Mesa and a coiled yucca basket made on Second Mesa. At the Hopi Arts and Crafts Center, visitors can see a large collection of silver overlay jewelry, a signature technique using thin strips of cut-out silver overlaid on a blackened silver base.

Surrounding the Hopi Reservation is the much larger Navajo Reservation. During the mid-1800s, Navajos began working with silver, and today Navajo jewelry – usually crafted with turquoise, coral, jet and shell – is probably the one art form most commonly identified with the Southwest. Although much jewelry is now made as a commodity, it was originally invested with a spiritual intent. Navajos still judge jewelry in a somewhat different way than non-Navajos,

looking for movement within a harmonious whole, vibrancy, and a pleasing appearance from various angles.

Navajos adopted weaving from their Pueblo neighbors and by the early 1800s were producing extraordinary blankets and rugs, although as sheepherders they wove wool rather than cotton. A number of weavers on the reservation still do all the shearing, carding, spinning and dyeing by hand. The vast majority, however, buy their wool from trading posts and invest their time and energy in rug design. As a result, some of the best rugs ever woven are being produced at this time, and the collectors' market has

literally gone through the roof. Again, Navajos judge their work from a unique point of view, valuing designs with a balanced tension and resonance of color.

At nearby trading posts, travelers will also find distinctive brown pottery, which is just now hitting the commercial market after years of complex taboo restrictions. Other Navajo crafts include sash belts, velvet blouses, cedarberry necklaces and hard-soled moccasins.

Trading posts also carry work from other tribes, including exquisite Apache, Papago and Pima baskets, ranging in size from several feet wide to two-inch miniatures.

Moving east, the Pueblos of New Mexico are renowned for jewelry, pottery and other crafts, both traditional and highly contemporary. Pottery is perhaps the biggest draw. San Ildefonso and Santa Clara are famous for burnished red and black pottery – a style revived in the early 1900s by Maria Martinez and her husband Julian. Maria's grandson, Tony Da, carries on the tradition at San Ildefonso, as does the Tafoya family, among many other skilled potters, at Santa Clara.

Taos and Picuris produce a tan pottery glittering with natural mica. Acoma and Zia make whiteware with animal and plant designs, primarily in black and red. Acoma is especially noteworthy for its thin-walled jars painted in a style reminiscent of ancient Anasazi and Mimbres designs. Lucy Lewis, and the Lewis sisters, were instrumental in reviving the style and bringing it to the commercial market. Cochiti has become famous for clay storyteller figures developed by Helen Cordero. At Jemez, storyteller and nativity figures are popular.

Although pottery has also enjoyed a resurgence at Zuni Pueblo, jewelry is the main attraction. The Zuni took up silversmithing shortly after the Navajo and have specialized in channel and inlay work, creating mosaic-like pieces of extraordinary refinement. There are several well-stocked trading posts at Zuni, including the tribally owned arts and craft shop. Jewelry is made at a number of other pueblos, too, including Santo Domingo, which is known for exquisite turquoise necklaces and finely crafted shell strands called *heishi*.

Elsewhere in the United States, California tribes, including the Pomo, Maidu, Hoopa and Washo, excelled in basket-making.

Pomo work was perhaps the most skillful, ranging from baskets several feet in diameter to incredibly tiny miniatures. Although the tradition was nearly lost during the mass annihilation of the mid-1800s, there are a number of basket-weavers still doing excellent work today.

The eastern tribes also lost much of their artistic traditions during the long years of struggle against white encroachment, but in recent years several artists have staged a revival of old-time styles. Iroquois False Face masks and shell wampum belts are still available among the Iroquois of New York and Ontario, as are hand-carved Cherokee Booger masks and the brilliant patchwork

more slippery, who is an Indian and who isn't? Is tribal membership sufficient? An arbitrary level of "blood quantum"? How about an artist raised within an Indian culture without Indian blood? A person of Indian descent who was raised in an entirely mainstream environment? Are we to believe that superior work by non-Indians is of less value than inferior work by Indians? And what of Indian people of one tribe who adopt the artistic traditions of another?

Further controversy surrounds the objects themselves. Is artwork simply a commodity to be bought and sold? How do we judge replicas of ceremonial objects such as Zuni fetishes, Navajo sand paintings, or, even

clothing of the Florida Seminoles.

A few considerations: While you're shopping for Indian art, it's important to be mindful of a few difficult issues, especially concerning authenticity. In the last few years, Indian artists have grown increasingly vexed over non-Indian people selling their work as Indian art, which, in strictly stylistic terms at least, it might very well be.

Of course, that still begs the question of authenticity. Can work made by non-Indians be properly labeled as Indian art? And, even

more perplexing, Navajo replicas of Hopi kachina dolls? Does creative replication contribute to the trivialization of tribal values? Or do we simply accept that tourist dollars are adequate compensation for the erosion of cultural integrity?

Obviously these aren't easy questions. Although laws are now hitting the books prohibiting non-Indians from selling their work as Indian art, there are still an awful lot of gray areas here, and it's up to the consumers and the artists to sort their way through them all. In the end, the best advice is to buy what you like, but know exactly what you're buying.

Left, Arapaho-style beaded moccasins. **Above**, Ak Chin butterfly baskets.

As you speed across the highways of the Northern Plains, colorful place names conjure images of the old West: Cheyenne, Wolf Point, Medicine Bow, Absaroka. The names are imprints left by the ancient native people. Even the highways – many built on prehistoric trails – recall an earlier time when the plains were trampled by hundreds of thousands of bison hunted by Arapaho, Cheyenne, Sioux, Blackfeet, Gros Ventre, Shoshone and others – all patriot warriors who fought a valiant but losing struggle against white invaders.

One hundred years ago, it was commonly believed that Indian people would disappear. But the myth of the "vanishing Indian" proved untrue. In spite of their tragic history after the arrival of white people, there are still more than 300 distinct Indian tribes in the US, with a population exceeding 1.5 million – a far cry from the 250,000 survivors at the turn of the century.

Today, a cultural renaissance is blooming across Indian Country, gathering force for the last 15 years. Indian people are rediscovering traditions that were nearly lost during the years of war and hardship. Indian pride is being reasserted in schools, businesses and tribal governments, atop the buttes where vision quests are held, on the prairies where sun dance lodges are erected. And, perhaps most important for the traveler seeking a first-hand experience of Indian culture, at the celebration of life and culture known as powwow.

Said to be a Narraganset word meaning "medicine man," powwow now refers to a celebratory gathering of dancers, singers, craftsmen, families, friends and communities. In short, a celebration of Indian life and tradition. Powwows occur in many Indian communities at least once a year, sometimes more. A point of pride, the events are well attended by local Indian people as well as by Indian visitors from every corner of the US and Canada. In cities, powwows take place in huge gymnasiums or in grassy parks. But in Indian Country they are usually held outdoors, either at prepared powwow grounds or on the open prairie.

The powwow camp: The first sight of a powwow camp is always stirring – a bustling nest of activity framed by a great halo of dust. Most powwow camps are formed in a circle with a permanent arbor at the center. Shelters radiate from all directions, crisscrossed with meandering automobile paths and alive with the sounds of playing children, whinnying horses, radios, and the talk of old friends. The camp is in constant motion as cars come in and out of access roads, and visitors set up their temporary residences. In addition to the fancy motor homes and simple green pup tents, there are often a number of traditional painted tepees. The arbor is the nucleus of the gathering. It is usually circular or rectangular, open at the center, with seating around the edge shaded by a roof of pine boughs thrown over the frame. The announcer's stand is to the west, adjacent to the entrance.

Circling the arbor is a dirt midway about 25 feet (8 meters) wide. Along the walkway are booths and stands of various types selling Indian tacos, fry bread, hamburgers, tanned deerskins, newly made beadwork, jewelry and a thousand other treasures.

Grand entry: Everything is ready for the main event. It all starts with the grand entry, the most colorful and moving part of the entire powwow. It is here that the various categories of dancers enter the arena attired in their traditional finery, dancing in time to Indian songs that may be hundreds of years old. The first drum sounds, and from that moment on the camp moves to the steady pulse and cascading melodies of Plains Indian music, much of it sung by men in a powerful, piercing falsetto.

The grand entry is a key to understanding the various dance styles you're likely to see at a powwow, and the order in which participants enter is a useful way of judging their relative importance. Leading everyone and everything into the arena is the honor guard, usually bearing two flags: the Feathered Staff, representing traditional Indian values, and the Stars and Stripes, representing the US. The flags are carried only by veterans. As patriots who have always

Preceding pages: fancy dancer. **Left,** traditional dancers wear crowns of feathers

fought to protect their country, Indians consider it a high honor to bear the flags.

After the flags come the honored guests. These individuals are tribal or national leaders, Indian or non-Indian politicians, and other prominent people. Among this group are the "royalty," young ladies chosen to represent their communities at powwows and other social events throughout Indian Country. The "princess" titles – "Miss Northern Cheyenne Powwow," for example – are a recent addition to the powwow scene, but they offer exceptional young ladies an opportunity to learn and travel.

Next in line are the dancers, with the traditionals first. These dancers are closer to

The fancy dancers are next, bedecked with vividly colored, chicken hackle feathers that form bustles worn between the shoulders and below the small of the back. They are the most energetic and creative of the male dancers, leaping into the air, sending their bodies into wild spins.

Next to enter the arena, keeping in perfect time to the singing, in all their dignity, are the traditional female dancers. They are recognized as the strength and foundation of the Indian people. Strong and determined, they have passed on the Indian system of values and customs over the years, even through the tough times. Today, they are usually dressed in beaded wool or deerskin dresses and

the old ways than most, as demonstrated by their dignified attire and maturity. Black-tipped golden eagle feathers form the foundation of their outfits, and the stately dancers prefer conservative, time-honored steps.

Following the traditionals are the grass dancers – relative newcomers, although they are descended from the earlier Northern Plains grass dancers. They are readily distinguished by the absence of a feathered bustle and by the long, brilliantly colored yarn fringes on their outfits. Even their dancing is different; their movements are smoother and use the shoulders more than the other styles.

moccasins, carrying a beaded bag and, in some tribes, an eagle-wing fan. A quilled wheel or feather may decorate their hair.

Still dancing to the same, driving grand entry song, the female jingle dress dancers usually follow. This style, too, is a new arrival on the Plains. Said to have originated in the dream of a Chippewa holy man more than 70 years ago, the form-fitting dresses are made of cloth and decorated with tin cones shaped from the tops of chewing-tobacco containers, similar in style to the earlier elk tooth and cowrie shell dresses. The dress's shape causes the dancer to move differently, with a more up-and-down step, and best of all, the cones make noise – a clacking sound much like native dewclaw hoof "bells." So, with a feather fan in one hand and a scarf or bag in the other, and crested with a French braid and white plume, these beautiful dancers enter the arena.

The girl fancy dancers are next in line. They are a counterpart to the male category and they wear equally brilliant colors. The girls' costumes seem to be more creative; a greater variety of colors and materials make up their attire, and the yokes of their dresses are usually decorated with designs, symbols, and other visuals sewn in beads or sequins. Shawls are draped about their shoulders and held outstretched like wings. Soaring, glid-

from all over the country to gather as a distinct people, to gain strength from their cultural diversity and reaffirm their commitment to common values. Powwow gives Indian people a place that is rich with tradition and bright with hope for the future, a place where they are no longer a minority in their own land. Powwow also gives them an opportunity to look back on the events of the preceding year, to recognize achievements, acknowledge milestones, and reflect on personal losses. "Honor dances" are often held for exceptional members of the community, a returning veteran, perhaps, or a tribal leader. "Giveaways" are held, too, in which a family gives blankets, shawls, bustles,

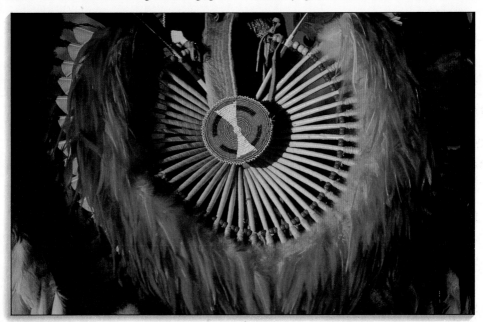

ing and banking, barely touching the earth, the graceful birds descend.

Finally, the future of the Indian people enters the arena, dressed in their finest, proudly taking part. Divided by age and dance style, the youngsters are miniatures of the adults, some wearing traditional outfits while others exhibit the attire of other categories. Now everyone is in the arena – dancing hard together, shaking the earth!

But there is more to powwow than singing and dancing. Powwow is a time for tribes

headdresses and other gifts in honor of their child receiving an Indian name, having a person "dance Indian" for the first time, acknowledging the end of a year's mourning for the passing of a relative, and, more recently, to honor a family member for receiving a college degree.

A good day to live: Traditional dancers love to powwow and to take part in the incomparable energy of the grand entry. Outfitted from head to foot, with a headdress, breastplate, feather bustle, quilled armbands, a red wool britchcloth, blue wool leggings, and beaded moccasins, all highlighted by ringing brass bells, they come to dance. Most don't

Left, bone necklace, blanket and shawl. **Above**, feathers and beadwork adorn dancer's bustle.

compete in the contests but come to enjoy themselves and to be with friends, relatives and familiar customs.

When the master of ceremonies announces that a grand entry will soon take place, the dancers begin to gather at the entrance. With much bustle, bells, laughter, apparent confusion, and beauty, the lead singer of the host drum starts the song and the grand entry begins. As the drum establishes the strong pulsating rhythm, the honor guard leads the proud procession holding their banners high. The traditional category enters, excited and proud. Positioning the head, body and arms at a cocky angle, the dancers enter, one after another, strutting, twisting,

leaning, perhaps mimicking a prairie bird or reliving the old warrior ways, but always following the heavy, persistent beat as their moccasins pound the earth.

For the participants, this is a time of warriors, of Indians, of pride in their people. They are there in the middle of the prairie, dancing. They are dressed like the old ones, moving together in the grand entry, united by the cadence, becoming one in celebration of Indian traditions. They see friends and relatives as they dance, shaking their hands as they pass each other – looking good.

As the tempo quickens, they dance harder. The sweat begins to trickle and they feel it

purging their bodies. The voices and unifying rhythm are overwhelming. It's an experience, the dancers say, of incomparable joy.

Traveling the powwow circuit: Although powwows were originally a Plains Indian phenomenon, they are now held throughout the country, from the Pacific Northwest to the Atlantic (*see Travel Tips*). Some dancers spend much of their summers traveling from one powwow to another. The general schedule is usually as follows: during the preceding week, people begin to arrive and set up camp; by Friday the grounds are full, and at about 7 p.m. the first grand entry begins.

The dancing lasts until the early morning and the camp sleeps late the next day. Just before noon things are astir again, and the next grand entry usually happens in the early afternoon. These first entries are for children, who dress and compete in the same manner as adults. The biggest grand entry is on Saturday about 7 p.m. By now those participants who have jobs during the week have arrived and the powwow has attained its maximum size. Most celebrations have other grand entries about 1 p.m. and 7 p.m. on Sunday. Sometime during the night the winners of the various contests are determined, announced and awarded cash prizes.

In general, powwows are open to outsiders, and there are often dances that spectators are invited to join. It's a great opportunity to experience Native American culture firsthand, but as always, there are a few rules that should be kept in mind at all times.

First, unless otherwise indicated, alcohol is strictly forbidden on the powwow grounds. Second, Indian people tend to be conservative when it comes to dress, so think twice about wearing shorts or a halter top, even if it's hot. Third, some photography is usually allowed, but there may be restrictions or an additional fee. In either case, you must first ask permission of the powwow organizers and from anyone whom you plan to photograph. Fourth, participate in dancing only if you have made prior arrangements or are invited by the master of ceremonies. And finally, as with all Indian events, approach powwows with a good heart. Respect the dancers, singers and other spectators, and they will respect you.

Left, jingle dress dancer. Right, grass dancer's colorful outfit.

Stuck in the mud at the marsh's edge, the mammoth was belly deep in muck. Exhausted from the struggle to free itself, the animal lay silently, watching as its companions slowly wandered off. Hunters waited for the herd to move on. When all was quiet, they walked over to the mired beast and finished the job they had begun days earlier when they first struck the giant animal with their spears.

The hunters were jubilant; the long pursuit of the wounded mammoth had been rewarded. As one man left to bring the rest of their band to the kill, others began butchering. After several days of chopping and sundrying the meat, the band carried their larder to a better campsite.

Ten thousand years later, while looking at some property in southeastern Arizona, rancher Ed Lehner walked down an eroded arroyo. There he saw bones sticking out of the bank. Realizing their importance, he contacted local archaeologists, who began to excavate the site. They soon found the stone spear points that had been left among the ribs of the butchered mammoth – evidence of Paleoindians.

Today, travelers interested in Native American archaeology can visit hundreds of sites in the United States – each one a window on the ancient lifeways and cultures of American Indians.

Winds of change: Near the end of the Ice Age, between 12,000 and 15,000 years ago, the nomadic Paleoindians traveled into North America from Siberia across what is now the Bering Strait, which at the time was a bridge of dry land. Moving south in an ice-free corridor between two continental glaciers, Paleoindian bands scattered into a world that was empty of people but rich in game and edible plants.

They followed mammoth and caribou along the edge of the glaciers in New England and hunted vast herds of bison on the well-watered Great Plains. From southern Colorado to southeastern California, the

people camped beside shallow lakes such as those near Great Sand Dunes National Monument in Colorado and marshes like the ones at the Lehner and Murray Springs sites in Arizona. North, in the Great Basin, they hunted waterfowl on the edges of lakes Lahontan and Bonneville, which covered most of northern Nevada and Utah. Emerging from the forests on the Atlantic Coast, Paleoindians captured sea turtles along shorelines that now lie below sea level.

Evidence of their travels can be found in the distinctive spear points they made, which archaeologists can sometimes trace back to a particular source such as the Alibates Flint Quarries National Monument in Western Texas. The Paleoindians moved south into Mexico, Central and South America as well, and by 10,000 years ago were living throughout the western hemisphere.

Glaciers go back: During the Ice Age, the climate in North America was cooler and wetter than now, but changed less from season to season. The climate shifted about 10,000 years ago when the glaciers began to recede. Seasonal temperature extremes became the norm, and precipitation varied from year to year. As a result, plants and animals that once were distributed widely across North America became restricted in their ranges or slowly became extinct.

Mammoths were among the animals to disappear. Some archaeologists believe that people contributed to their extinction by persistent hunting. Although it is possible that a Paleoindian killed the last mammoth, it is unlikely that people were entirely responsible for the demise of the great beasts. Many animals, including some not hunted by humans, such as dire wolves, giant armadillos and ground sloths, became extinct around the same time.

As mammoths became scarcer, winters more severe, and particular plants harder to find, people began to adapt by specializing in various hunting and gathering techniques. In the Great Basin, southern California and the Southwest, people camped along the slowly receding shorelines of shallow lakes, along marshy rivers and streams, or in rock shelters such as Danger Cave (State Park) in Utah.

Preceding pages: tepees at dusk at the Shoshone-Bannock Indian Festival, Fort Hall, Idaho. Left, Dinetah petroglyphs, Navajo Nation.

Rabbits, bighorn sheep, antelope and waterfowl were plentiful in the region, and people added to their diet by collecting seeds and nuts. They followed a cycle of ripening plant foods from low to high elevations or from south to north. Except for fringe areas where crops could be grown, the people of the Great Basin and the Mohave Desert of California continued to live in this way until the Europeans arrived – a stable lifestyle that lasted more than 8,000 years.

In central and northern California, acorns became an important staple, and along the coast from California to Washington, people exploited shellfish, piling leftover shells into large mounds. Along the Columbia River

the streams and marshes where Paleoindians had killed giant bison. Modern bison replaced the older, larger forms about 5,000 years ago, and people periodically left the comfort of the Rocky Mountain foothills to hunt. They stampeded the bison into gulleys or over cliffs, butchering and drying what they could and leaving the rest, which resulted in great heaps of bones such as those found at Madison Buffalo Jump State Park in Montana, which was used in historic times.

Along the Mississippi River and its tributaries, Indians made good use of forest foods such as nuts, berries, deer and other game while fishing in the resource-rich rivers. People lived for much of the year in camps

and its tributaries, people established seasonal salmon fishing camps that were revisited year after year.

On the Columbia Plateau of eastern Oregon and Washington, people lived like those in the Great Basin, traveling with the seasons from camp to camp. Then, around 7,000 years ago, Mount Mazama, a volcano in Oregon, erupted, spewing ash over much of eastern Oregon and Washington. In the nearby Fort Rock Valley, the ash caused so much damage that people all but abandoned the area for 2,000 years.

Farther east, on the Great Plains, sand dunes and thick layers of fine soil covered

such as the Eva Site in Tennessee, where freshwater mussels became an important part of the diet, and the Twin Ditch Site in Illinois, where archaeologists have found the oldest known house in the Midwest, dating to some 9,500 years ago.

North, along the shores of Lake Superior, about 5,000 years ago Indians discovered that they could mine chunks of copper and, by melting and pounding them, form tools such as chisels, awls, harpoons and knives. They traded these tools down the Mississippi and along the Great Lakes into eastern Canada and New England. The remains left by these early miners and traders are called the Old Copper Culture, and evidence of their work can be seen in Isle Royale National Park in Michigan and Copper Culture State Park in Wisconsin.

Although all people living along the Atlantic Coast developed ways of using the ocean's resources, nowhere during these early times did they use them more intensively than along the northeastern coast from Maine to Labrador. There, about 4,000 years ago, one group learned how to deep-sea fish. Popularly called the Red Paint People because they buried their dead with red ochre, they established a navigation system using large rocks and rock cairns set along the coast as markers. Information about the Red

campsite in early spring and come back a few months later to find a ripe crop. After many years of selectively sowing seeds, the people transformed *teosinte* from a wild plant into an early form of corn.

Corn, squash and beans were carried north by traders or travelers, and around 3,000 years ago, people in the American Southwest began to grow these crops. At the same time, squash was introduced into the Mississippi Valley and southeastern United States, followed by corn and beans.

Agriculture stimulated a cultural blossoming in the Mississippi and Ohio valleys, resulting in development of the so-called Mound Builder cultures. Around 2,500

Paint People can be found in the Haffenreffer Museum at Brown University in Rhode Island and at the Damariscotta River Shell Mounds in Maine.

Food to grow on: In central Mexico some 5,000 years ago, Indians lived much as they did in the American Southwest. Following a seasonal round, they gathered many different plant foods. One they were fond of was *teosinte*, a type of wild grass. They discovered, by accident or experimentation, that they could scatter *teosinte* seeds at their

years ago, the burial of people in low, simple mounds became an elaborate ceremonial complex that included the use of grave goods obtained by long-distance trade. Obsidian from Yellowstone, barracuda jaws from Florida, mica from North Carolina, and copper from Lake Superior all found their way into the stockaded villages of the Adena and Hopewell peoples in the Midwest. In some areas, people built enormous effigy mounds, the most famous of which is the Serpent Mound, located at Serpent Mound State Memorial in Locust Grove, Ohio.

Over a 1,000-year period, mound building evolved into the construction of large

Left, Serpent Mound, Idaho. Above, Tyuonyi ruins, Bandelier National Monument, New Mexico.

earthen platforms with civic and religious structures on top. The mound-building idea spread as far west as Oklahoma and to the Southeast, where people built temple mounds such as Etowah Mounds in Georgia and the mounds at Crystal River in Florida, both open to visitors. The largest group of mounds can be seen at the Mississippian Culture complex at Cahokia, Illinois, where people lived continuously for 700 years. From there, they established several outlying colonies, including one at what is now Aztalan State Park in Wisconsin.

Life was simpler in the Northeast, where people gardened, hunted in the forests and fished along the seashore. About 1,000 years

earth lodge villages may be the ancestral homes of the Mandan and Arikara tribes.

The people of the Northern Plains carried on extensive trade with the Northwest coast and Columbia Plateau. Access to the Northwest was over the Rocky Mountains, using passes such as the Lolo Trail in Idaho and Montana. Along this trail, traders carried dentalium shells from the Pacific and bison meat and robes from the Plains.

The forests of the Cascade Mountains, the fisheries along the Columbia and other rivers, and the Pacific Ocean provided ample supplies of food and shelter for the people of the Northwest coast. Living in abundance, they gradually developed a socially strati-

ago, people along the upper St Lawrence River began to build wooden palisades around their villages and started to build longhouses. These people were probably the ancestors of the Iroquois.

On the Great Plains, people continued to hunt bison and other game, but, influenced by the cultures of the Mississippi Valley and Southwest, some also farmed, using bison shoulder blades as hoes. Late in prehistory, Indians in North and South Dakota began to build earth lodges – large, semi-subterranean structures. Earth lodge villages were sometimes surrounded by ditches and placed in defensible positions on riverbanks. The

fied culture in which the accumulation of material wealth was important.

Farther south, in California, the Indians found wealth of a different kind. They developed ceremonial houses and sweat lodges such as those reconstructed at Clear Lake State Park (north of San Francisco), where they practiced a rich, shamanistic religion. Along the Colorado River, people cleared away dark, weathered rocks to expose light rock and soil in patterns, making intaglios – effigy figures of people and animals.

East of the Colorado River, in the Sonoran Desert, lived the Hohokam, a people who used irrigation canals to water their crops and were famous for their trade in shell, cotton and other goods. Influenced by cultures of northern Mexico, they built ball courts similar to those found south of the border and later constructed earthen platform mounds such as Pueblo Grande in Phoenix, which became the center for community activity.

Many distinct groups of farming people lived north and east of the Hohokam. Those known as the Sinagua were caught in the eruption of Sunset Crater in Arizona around AD 1060. Fleeing their homes as a cloud of ash and cinders rained down, they later returned to the area to discover that the volcano had provided them with richer, water-re-

ancestors of the Pueblo Indians. Experts at capturing rainfall to water their fields, these people lived and prospered in a harsh land, from the Mesa Verde in Colorado, where growing seasons were short, to Canyon de Chelly in Arizona and Lost City in Nevada, where rainfall was scarce and unreliable. They showed their architectural prowess in building roads and apartment-like towns. Along with the Hohokam, they participated in an extensive trade network – bartering for Mexican macaws and Hohokam cotton with turquoise they had mined.

Anasazi ruins are scatter-shot throughout the Southwest and may be visited at Navajo and Canyon de Chelly national monuments

taining soils. A brief land boom followed, as Indians throughout the region, including the Hohokam, moved into the Wupatki area to take advantage of the fertile fields. Remains of ancient Sinagua pueblos may now be visited at Wupatki, Montezuma Well and Montezuma Castle national monuments, all in central Arizona.

In the northern Southwest, a large swath of land, from Las Vegas, Nevada, to Las Vegas, New Mexico, was occupied by the Anasazi,

Left, Anasazi ruins at Pueblo Bonito, Chaco Canyon. **Above**, Hohokam ruins at Wupatki National Monument, Arizona.

in northern Arizona, and Bandelier National Monument, Aztec Ruins National Monument and Puye Cliffs Tribal Park in New Mexico. For sheer drama, however, you can't beat the cliff-dwellings at Mesa Verde National Park in the southwest corner of Colorado or Pueblo Bonito at Chaco Culture National Historic Park about 100 miles (160 km) south in New Mexico.

The last migration: The peopling of North America didn't happen with a single wave of Paleoindians. Instead, people migrated at several different times. The most recent Indian group to enter the continental US were the Athabaskans, some of whom traveled along the Rocky Mountains into the American Southwest, where they are known today as Navajos and Apaches.

Then there were the Vikings, who around AD 1000 lived for a short time in Vinland somewhere along the North Atlantic Coast and returned to Scandinavia with tales of *Skraelings*, natives of that mystical land. And there were occasional Chinese shipwrecks off the coast of Oregon, like one in Nehalem Bay 400 years ago.

By the 1500s, the centuries of isolation were over. Wild tales of riches and unbelievable civilizations drove the Spanish to explore – Ponce de Leon in Florida, De Soto along the Mississippi River, and Coronado

in the Southwest. North America was invaded and the lifeways of the people were changed forever.

Preservation concerns: In 1891, Baron Gustaf Eric Adolf Nordenskiold, a young Swedish scholar, went to the Mesa Verde on a short sightseeing trip that turned into a summer of excavating ruins and amassing ancient Indian artifacts. When he tried to ship the material to Sweden, angry citizens detained the collection at the railroad depot. They believed American artifacts should be kept in America, but as there were no laws protecting archaeological remains, the collection was shipped to Europe, where it still resides in the National Museum in Helsinki, Finland.

As a result of Nordenskiold's activities and other looting, the US Congress passed the 1906 Antiquities Act. The law protected archaeological resources on federal land and authorized scientific excavation of select archaeological sites. Other laws followed, including the 1979 Archaeological Resources Protection Act, which strengthened the 1906 Act. Many state and tribal laws also make it illegal to collect artifacts – both prehistoric and historic.

The preservation issue is somewhat different for Native Americans. They feel that their ancestral ground has been violated – not only by unthinking people who pocket "souvenirs," but also by archaeologists. For years, museums displayed American Indian skeletons with little regard for the feelings of Native Americans. That's starting to change. Human remains are seen in few museums today, and soon institutions will be required to return remains and artifacts to Indian groups with an ancestral claim. Mostly, the Indians are allowing archaeologists to study the remains so that the information is not lost to the scientific record. It is a good pact, and one that shows respect for all concerned.

A chance to participate: There are many opportunities to visit archaeological sites and to get involved in excavation and analysis. Nationwide groups such as Earthwatch fund archaeological digs, and groups such as the Kampsville Archaeological Center in Illinois and Crow Canyon Archaeological Center in Colorado offer interesting programs for amateurs. Local salvage projects sometimes make use of volunteers, and there are many archaeological and historical societies where amateurs can rub elbows with professionals.

Contact any State Historic Preservation Office for information. And if preservation is important to you, contact the Archaeological Conservancy in Santa Fe, New Mexico. Organized like the Nature Conservancy, the Archaeological Conservancy buys sites throughout the country, and then turns them over to managing agencies when they find the most appropriate one.

Left, ancient petroglyphs near Zuni Pueblo. **Above**, Anasazi cliff-dwelling at Mesa Verde, Colorado.

Haida
Bella Bella
Nootka
Klallam
Duwamish
Makah
Skokomish
Squamish
Quinault
Quileute
Chehalis
Puyallup

Kwakiutl

NORTHWEST

Cree

CANADA

Kootenai

Colville

Blood
Piegan

Assiniboine

Flathead

Spokane

Blackfeet

Hidatsa

Palouse

Coeur
D'Alene

Gros Ventre

Mandan

Walla
Walla

Nez Perce

Arikara

Cayuse

Crow

Sioux

Yurok

Yakima

Modoc

Shoshone

GREAT

Ponca

Pomo

Yana

Bannock

Cheyenne

Maidu

Omaha

Hupa

Shoshone

PLAINS

Miwok

Pawnee

Costano

Mono

Paiute

Ute

Arapaho

Ot

Esselen

Yokut

UNITED STATES

Kans

Salina

Serrano

OF AMERICA

C

Chumash

Cahuilla

Havasupai

Hualapai

Jicarilla
Apache

Oklaho
(Indian Ter

Mojave

Hopi

Diegueno

Navajo

Pueblo

Yuma

Pima

Zuni

Kiowa

O'odham

Chiricahua
Apache

Mescalero
Apache

Comanche

Wic

CALIFORNIA

Tonka

SOUTHWEST

Pacific

Ocean

MEXICO

Culture Areas

480 km / 300 miles

pewa

Micmac

Penobscot

Passamagguoddy

Abnaki

Ottawa

NORTHEAST Irioguois

Menominee

Huron

Nipmuc

Winnebago

Potawatomi

Narraganset

Massachuset

Neutral Pequot Wampanoag

Sauk
Fox

Kickapoo

Delaware

Montauk

a

Peoria

Miami

souri

Illinois

Powhatan

Shawnee

Quapaw

SOUTHEAST

Cherokee

Chickasaw

Catawba

Caddo

Creek

Hitchiti

Alabama

Yazoo

Choctaw

Yamasee

Atlantic

Ocean

Natchez

Mobile

kawa

Apalachee

Timucua

Calusa

Seminole

Miccosukee

Golf of Mexico

115

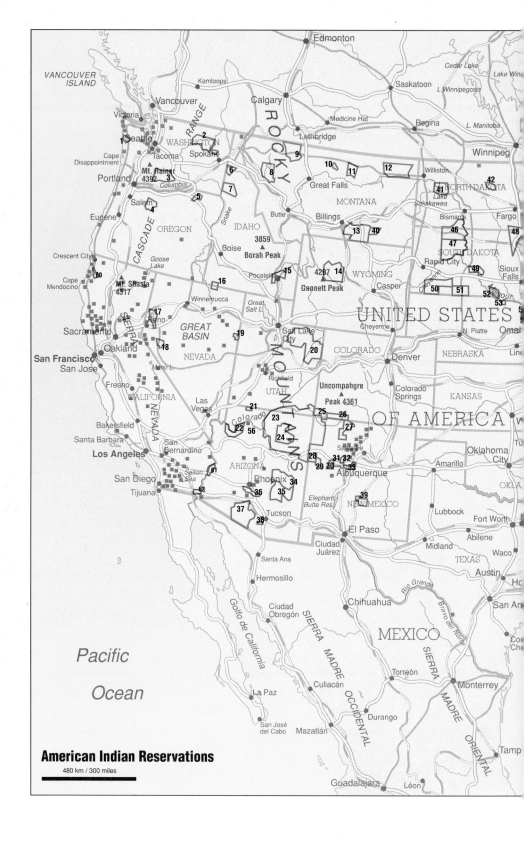

American Indian Reservations

480 km / 300 miles

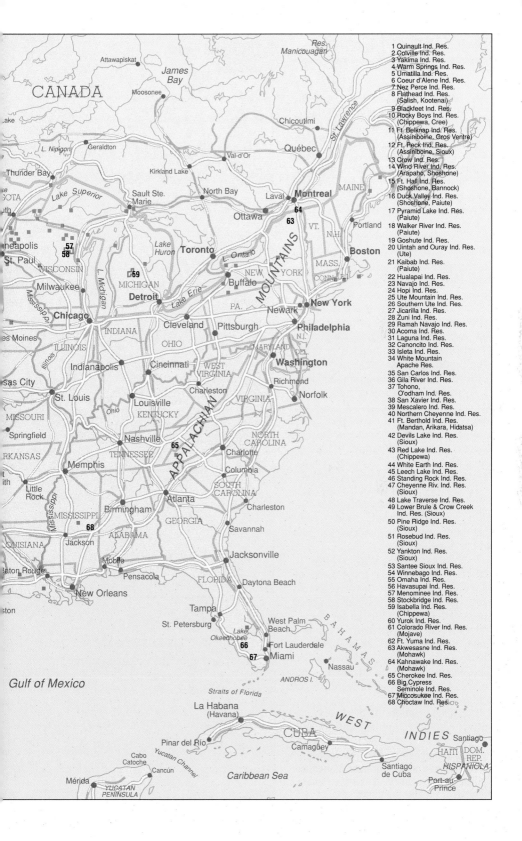

THE GREAT PLAINS

The Great Plains stretch from the Staked Plains of Texas to the glacier fields of Montana and Saskatchewan, from the Mississippi River to the Rocky Mountains. The native people who roamed this vast region of rolling prairies, wasted badlands, buttes and canyons have become an inseparable part of American history and legend.

With the introduction of the horse in the late 1700s, Plains Indian culture blossomed. Farmers once settled along fertile river valleys struck out into the boundless spaces of the Great Plains, following the great bison herds, some 15 million strong. In the mid-1800s, when whites began crossing the last of the untrammeled buffalo range, the Great Plains were dominated by tribes who became famous for their prowess as warriors and dedication to the land.

To the south, there were the Comanches, Kiowas, Southern Cheyennes and Arapahos; to the north, the Sioux, Crows, Northern Cheyennes, Assiniboines, Gros Ventres and Blackfeet. They were among the last native people to range freely across the Great Plains.

Today, Plains Indian culture is finding new strength, discovering new vitality. The drumbeat still sounds – pulsing, loud, insistent – honoring the past and inviting the future.

It finds expression at powwows, in the wild gyrations and dignified steps of fancy and traditional dancers, in the words and powerful melodies of honor songs. It comes to life at sun dance lodges, sweat lodges and on the isolated buttes where men seek visions. It takes shape in beautiful beadwork, star quilts, paintings and featherwork, and in respect for the elders and reverence for traditional lands.

The native people of the Plains are still with us. The drumbeat still sounds.

Preceding pages: Dinetah petroglyphs; Navajo woman and child near Monument Valley; Apache clown, San Juan Pueblo; nightfall at Fort Berthold powwow.

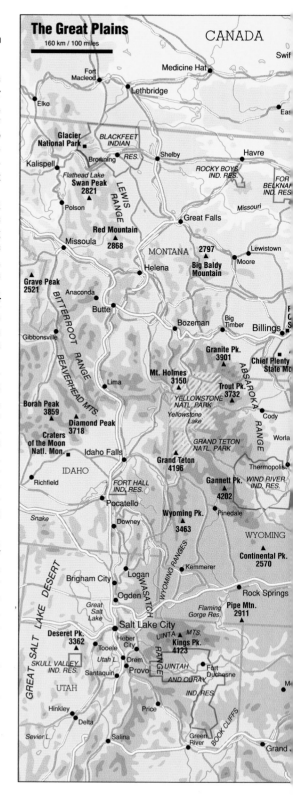

118

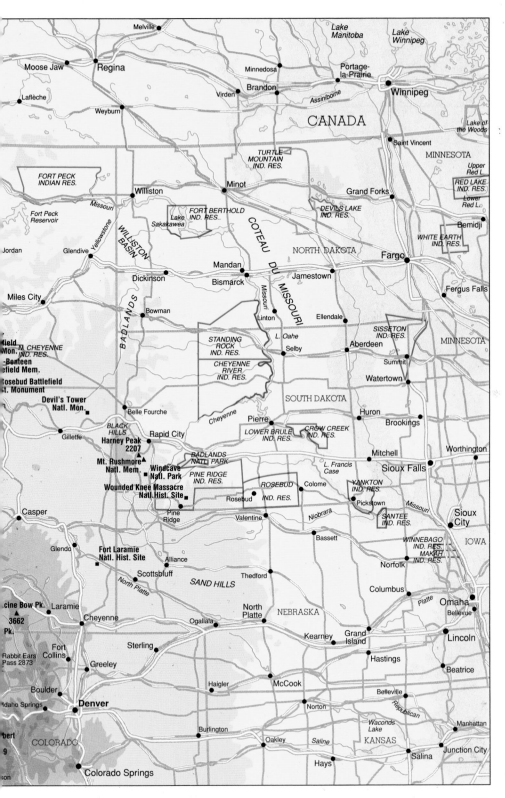

LAND OF THE SIOUX

White people know them as the Sioux, a French corruption of a Chippewa word meaning "little snake." But they know themselves best by the names of their bands – the Oglala, Hunkpapa, Miniconjou, Yankton, Sihasapa, Mdewakanton and Itazipco, among others. Or the names of the dialects they speak – Lakota, Dakota, Nakota. Together they are known as Oceti Sakowin, the Seven Fireplaces, the seven branches of the great Sioux nation.

They were the mightiest of the Plains Indian tribes. They held back the tide of western expansion for more than 50 years, won crushing victories against the US Army, and intimidated their Indian enemies. Their leaders – Red Cloud, Sitting Bull, Crazy Horse – became stock figures in the lore of the American West. Their triumphs and defeats – the Red Cloud War, the Battle of the Little Bighorn, the Wounded Knee Massacre – became chapters in American history.

To many people, they are the quintessential American Indian: the mounted buffalo hunter, war bonnet streaming in the wind, thundering across the open plains – proud, defiant, fierce.

It seems ironic now that the classic horse-and-buffalo culture of the Sioux was impossible before European contact. Until the Spanish brought their herds into New Mexico, wild horses hadn't roamed North American soil since the Ice Age. In truth, Plains tribes had only known horses for about 100 years before their land was overrun by white people. "Horse culture" blazed across the plains like wildfire, burning with fierce intensity, and then was quickly snuffed out.

Before the coming of the horse, the Sioux were a farming people living along the Minnesota and upper Mississippi rivers. They were chased out of the region by the Chippewas, who had been armed with guns by French fur-traders. Back even farther, the Sioux may have migrated from the mid-Atlantic coast, where they lived the life of the woodland Indian tribes.

Today, there are 14 Sioux Indian reservations. The largest are in North and South Dakota, once part of the Great Sioux Reservation established by the Fort Laramie Treaty of 1868. For the traveler, the best place to focus attention is in the southwest corner of this vast territory, where the Pine Ridge Indian Reservation is flanked by the beautiful Black Hills and Badlands National Park. This was among the most highly valued country in Sioux territory, and appropriately, the setting of the last tragic days of the Plains Indian wars.

Paha Sapa: It comes as no surprise that the Sioux think of the Black Hills – Paha Sapa – as sacred land. It is, perhaps, the most unlikely mountain range in North America, rising like an island of rock amid a vast expanse of prairie. And while the plains are dry, treeless and lacking in dramatic shape, the Black Hills are well-watered with streams and lakes, densely forested, and etched with deep canyons and craggy peaks. Famous Sioux mystics like Crazy Horse and Black Elk came here seeking visions, as

Left, young dancer at Rosebud Fair. Right, sunset over Dakota tepee.

do young men today. It is the holy land of the Sioux.

Under the provisions of the Fort Laramie Treaty of 1868, the Black Hills were to remain within the boundaries of the Great Sioux Reservation. "No white person shall be permitted to settle upon or occupy any portion of the territory," the treaty said, "or without the consent of the Indians to pass through the same." But when gold was discovered in the Black Hills just four years later, the government's promise proved as thin as the paper it was written on. Officially, the discovery was made by none other than Lieutenant Colonel George Armstrong Custer, already a Civil War hero and experienced Indian fighter. His trumped-up claims of gold "from the grass roots down" attracted prospectors by the hundreds, and in a very real sense brought about his own destruction.

In an effort to coerce the Indians into giving up the Black Hills, troops were sent into the unceded territory just west of the Black Hills still controlled by Sitting Bull, Gall, Crazy Horse and their Cheyenne and Arapaho allies. Custer was among the commanders. On June 25, 1876, his scouts sighted a large encampment on the Little Bighorn River. Rather than wait for reinforcements, Custer and his men rushed to the attack. They were never seen alive again.

But the Indian victory at the Little Bighorn did not save the Black Hills. If anything, it increased the pressure on the Sioux and their allies, and by July 1877 their struggle was virtually over. Sitting Bull and Gall retreated to the relative safety of Canada. Cheyenne chief Dull Knife surrendered. And perhaps most disheartening to the Sioux, Crazy Horse – the famous warrior and mystic – gave up his weapon and was later killed while in custody at Fort Robinson, Nebraska.

In the Black Hills today, the new tenants have carved an entire mountainside into a portrait of their leaders – the four presidential faces of Mount Rushmore. At least one, Theodore Roosevelt, was well-known for his belief in manifest destiny and the

Rocky spires in the sacred Black Hills.

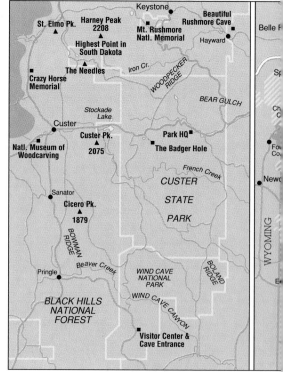

ultimate extinction of "the weaker race." An even larger sculpture is being made of Crazy Horse, although with the dynamite blasts, tons of rubble and throngs of tourists, it's difficult to determine whether he is being honored or not. Elsewhere, miners are still extracting gold from the Black Hills, and local entrepreneurs are extracting dollars from tourists.

But there are still a few spots where the Black Hills haven't lost their power. A short drive on the **Needles Highway**, **Rim Rock Drive**, **Nemo Road** or into the rugged backcountry is proof of that. Bear Butte, Harney Peak and the majestic granite mass of **Devil's Tower** – all highly sacred to the Sioux – are still an awe-inspiring presence. The rolling grasslands, bison herd and prairie dog towns at **Custer State Park** and **Wind Cave National Park** are also a peaceful refuge from the tourist traps and a potent reminder of what this country looked like before white settlement.

Ghost Dance and Wounded Knee: By the winter of 1890, the glory days of the Plains Indian tribes were already a memory. The buffalo were gone; the hunters were living on handouts; the tribes were confined to reservations. In 1881, after four difficult years in Canada, Sitting Bull and his people returned to the Standing Rock Agency. In 1889, the Great Sioux Reservation was broken up into several smaller reservations in order to open the land to settlement.

Like so many other tribes, the Sioux were a broken and desperate people. After 50 years of struggling against whites, their old way of life was clearly at an end. Many of their leaders were dead. Their people were reduced to poverty. And despite the government's promises, life on the reservations was continually dogged by chronic hunger, disease and a shortage of supplies.

And then, in 1890, a shred of hope came their way. Rumors had reached them of an Indian prophet west of the Rocky Mountains who had received a vision from the Great Spirit. He was a Paiute Indian named Wovoka. His new religion, a combination of Christian and

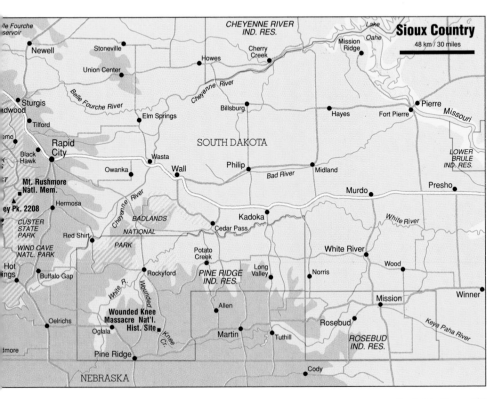

Indian beliefs, was known as the Ghost Dance.

Two Sioux medicine men traveled across the Rockies to meet this Messiah and learn his medicine. Wovoka told them that the day was quickly approaching when the world would come to an end. A great flood would cleanse the land, carrying away everything unholy. The whites would be swept away. Hunger, disease and poverty would disappear. The Indian dead would come back to life and rejoin their families. And the buffalo and antelope would return to the plains. Wovoka then taught them the sacred dance, the Ghost Dance, and promised that all who performed it would find a home in this new world.

The Ghost Dance spread like wildfire across the Northern Plains. The Sioux seized it with a fanaticism matched only by their desperation. Life on the reservations ground to a halt as the Indians took up the dance to the exclusion of everything else. Some followers danced and chanted for hours, even days, until they "died" and visions of their ances-tors filled their heads. The most radical believers painted images from these visions on white muslin "ghost shirts," which they believed were impervious to the white men's bullets.

By December 1890, Ghost Dancing had reached such a fever pitch that reservation officials were getting panicky about an uprising. "Indians are dancing in the snow and are wild and crazy," the agent at Pine Ridge Reservation wrote. "We need protection and we need it now." Reinforcements were sent to Pine Ridge, but the sight of so many soldiers scared the Indians away. Little by little, they fled into the rugged backcountry of the Badlands, where several hundred Ghost Dancers gathered on an isolated mesa called Stronghold Table, or *O-ona-gashee*, the Sheltering Place. The dancers planned to stay until the following spring, when they were sure the Messiah would come to save them.

Meanwhile, at the Standing Rock Agency, the order had gone out to arrest Sitting Bull and several other leaders. On December 15, 1890, a contingent of

Spring flowers blossom in Badlands National Park.

124

Indian police led by Lieutenant Bull Head came to take Sitting Bull away. Sitting Bull complied peacefully, but as Bull Head and another Indian policeman led the old chief out of his cabin a large group of followers surrounded them, screaming for Sitting Bull's release. A shot was fired from the crowd and Bull Head was mortally wounded. As he fell, he pulled his revolver and shot Sitting Bull in the side. From behind, another policeman, Red Tomahawk, shot Sitting Bull in the head.

Terrified by Sitting Bull's death, the Hunkpapas fled the reservation. Some joined the Ghost Dancers in the Badlands; others joined a small band of Miniconjou Sioux led by Chief Big Foot camped near the Cheyenne River.

Big Foot was also on the army's list of troublemakers, and when he heard about Sitting Bull's death, he decided to take his people south to the Pine Ridge Reservation for safety. In order to evade the soldiers sent to arrest him, Big Foot (who was deathly ill with pneumonia) led his people across the Badlands on an ancient trail, known today as Big Foot Pass. But the grueling journey was to no avail. The soldiers caught up with Big Foot's band just south of the Badlands and ordered them to make camp near a creek called Wounded Knee. There were about 350 Indians in the camp that night and some 450 soldiers surrounding them. For added protection, a battery of Hotchkiss guns was set up on a rise overlooking the Indians.

The following morning, a contingent of soldiers was sent to disarm Big Foot's people. As the soldiers ransacked tepee after tepee, the warriors became agitated. A medicine man, Yellow Bird, began dancing and chanting, chiding the warriors and reminding them that their ghost shirts were invulnerable to the bluecoats' bullets. Just then, somewhere in the camp, a shot was fired.

That was all it took to start the killing. A hale of shrapnel fell on the camp, slaughtering everything that moved, including women and children. The shooting was so frenzied that many soldiers were killed in the crossfire by

Followers of the Ghost Dance.

their own comrades. All in all, it took less than an hour. When the smoke cleared, the camp was littered with bodies. Survivors tried to run away, but the soldiers hunted them down. Bodies were found as much as 3 miles from the Indian camp.

A blizzard swept over the plains that night, and it snowed for the next two days. On New Year's Day 1891, a detachment was sent out to bury the dead. The bodies were covered with snow, frozen in positions of violent death. A pit was dug in the hard earth, and the Indian dead were tumbled in.

Walking with ghosts: Walking in that valley today, you would never think that such brutality could have touched this place. The land is as plain and silent as any other part of the Pine Ridge Reservation, a little rougher maybe, but with the same rolling hills and grassy stubble. Bluffs and hollows stretch out in every direction like the folds of a rumpled blanket, broken here and there by a crooked line of pine trees, twisting ravines or a rutted lane.

The only thing that saves the site from complete anonymity is a small church and cemetery, located about a mile from **Wounded Knee Village**. If there wasn't a hand-painted sign hammered into the ground on the roadside that said "massacre site," you would most likely drive past without blinking an eye.

There is the church, though – a log cabin with a steeple that looks like it's right out of a western movie. If you didn't already know that it was a memorial to the massacre victims, chances are you would never guess. There are no plaques, no signs, not even the church's name is clearly posted. The same is true of the cemetery, which is just a little way down the hill. There's a tall stone monument in the middle, surrounded by a chain link fence. Tattered flags representing the four corners of the Sioux universe are tied to the fenceposts, marking the cemetery as sacred ground. The date at the top of the stone is 1890. This is the common grave in which the Indian victims were buried.

Every now and then you meet old-

Wounded Knee Massacre Monument.

timers on the reservation who mention that they had a relative who camped with Big Foot, Sitting Bull or Crazy Horse. For an outsider, the names have become such a well-worn part of Western lore, they don't seem to refer to real people anymore. They are like figures from some mythical past, hopelessly removed from the here and now.

And that's how it feels at Wounded Knee. There is something vague and anonymous about the place that stands between the past and present. There is too little to grab hold of, too few details to make the horror come to life. You find yourself wanting to know specifics. Where were Big Foot's people camped? Where did the soldiers stand? What happened to the survivors?

It's maddening and comforting at the same time. There ought to be some sign, some terrible black wound in the earth to remind us of the suffering. And yet, despite the horrors committed that day, the land remains peaceful, quiet and undisturbed.

Maybe it's best that way. This isn't a tourist attraction, after all, and no plaque or monument could do more to keep vigil here than the low, lonesome sound of the wind. But as you walk away from the church into the valley on the opposite side of the road, it's difficult to ignore the feeling that we have lost something. It's as if the land has conspired to fade the memory, to cover the names, the places, the details of each life with a tide of forgetting as vast and blank as the open plains.

Grotesque shapes: In the **Badlands**, too, there are few reminders of what went before, but the landscape is so powerful it seems unnecessary to post monuments or signs. Known to the Sioux as *mako sica*, this is a country of stark and severe beauty. Ridges twist like crooked spines; rocks are bent in grotesque shapes, and grass-capped "tables" rise to dizzying heights.

In the early 19th century, French fur-traders called it *les mauvaises terres à traverser*, "the bad lands to cross," because of the maze of twisting canyons that blocked their passage to the White

roded cliffs, heep lountain able.

River basin. Many years later, American surveyors compared it to a "magnificent city of the dead, where the labour and the genius of forgotten nations had left a multitude of monuments of art and skill." Today, most of the region falls within **Badlands National Park**, which includes a designated wilderness area where antelope, deer, bighorn sheep, several prairie dog towns and a sizable buffalo herd live much as they did when the Sioux roamed this rugged territory in search of game. The southern branch of the Badlands crosses into the Pine Ridge Indian Reservation.

The Badlands may seem barren or forbidding by day, but in the evenings, when the light grows softer, the air of desolation begins to lift. As the sun goes down, delicate shadows creep along the broken ridges, softening the landscape's fractured lines. The long rays bring out the deep bruise-colors that stripe the cliffs, and where the sun's full glare reflected only gray and white, the more forgiving light of evening shows reds, yellows and burning violets.

The evening also brings a rush of life, as if the animals are reluctant to give up the day. An eagle circles over a canyon, scanning for a final meal. Turkey vultures hang on the wind without flapping a wing. Bighorn sheep clamber to higher ground. And out on the prairie, bison slowly gather in preparation for night.

Just after sunset, an afterglow of pink and blue spills over the horizon, setting off the day's final, and most dazzling, blaze of color. In the last few minutes of twilight, the land seems to glow like a fading coal. It slowly grows fainter, until finally, with nothing more than a momentary flicker, it yields to the night.

Among the many turn-outs along the park's 40-mile (64-km) loop is **Big Foot Pass**, where Chief Big Foot led his people before being ordered to Wounded Knee. It also happens to be one of the best places in the park to stop and watch the sun go down. The cliffs face west, with nothing but broken land between you and the horizon. The sun sets as it must have on the first day of creation, over an unfinished world, still imper-

Bison, staple of Plains Indian hunters, roam the Badlands

fectly shaped. Somewhere in the weathered canyons, mingled with the colors and the disturbing play of shadows, the horror of that day seems to have left its mark.

The scene is altogether different at **Window Notch**, which is a chink in the cliffs overlooking the Pine Ridge Reservation. In order to get there, you have to walk a three-quarter-mile trail across some rugged terrain. At the end, a 20-ft rope ladder leads up the side of a canyon towards the viewing area. From there, the Badlands seem to melt into the White River basin, where the rains continually wash the sediments away. The jagged peaks grow smaller and less defined, until there is nothing left but bluffs and hollows stretching out to the horizon.

The balance of beauty and desolation is probably no more precarious or spectacular than at **Sheep Mountain Table**, a high plateau on the Pine Ridge Reservation overlooking a labyrinth of barren canyons. A dirt road veers off Highway 44 and crosses the snow-white alkali flats that lead to the hill. Squat,

mushroom-shaped formations stand like guardians on either side – to warn or welcome is not entirely clear.

At the top, the table is broad and flat, and surprisingly lush. A thick growth of prairie grass covers the ground and scattered groves of juniper stand near the edge. This is one of the least-traveled parts of the Badlands, and a great place to go if you're looking for solitude. A profound sense of quiet hangs over the landscape. It's not difficult to imagine young Indians coming here and fasting, in search of visions.

Farther south on Highway 44, you can stop at the White River Visitors Center for directions to **Stronghold Table**, where Sioux Ghost Dancers gathered in the winter of 1890. The only way to get there is to take a gravel road about 7 miles off the highway, and then hike a mile or so until you reach "the narrows," the eroding land-bridge that connects the table to the "mainland." Stronghold Table is like a thumb-shaped peninsula jutting into the Badlands' wasted landscape.

The plateau itself is flat and featureless, covered with a coarse growth of prairie grass and cactus. Sitting on the cliffs, with nothing but the wind, an occasional meadowlark and a few semi-wild horses to keep you company, is like dangling your feet over the edge of the world. At times, the only thing that stirs is the wind, coursing like a restless spirit through the canyons and ravines. Its ceaseless whispering is a slender defense against the powers of silence, but it reminds you that, despite the stark surroundings, this is not a place of death.

Powwows and museums: Elsewhere on the Pine Ridge Reservation, you will find several other places of interest. The biggest community, **Pine Ridge Village**, is still the site of government bureaucracy, but offers little in the way of amenities. Problems that plague many reservation communities – alcoholism, poor housing, hopelessness – are all too apparent here. About 4 miles north of Pine Ridge Village, you can visit the **grave of Chief Red Cloud** at Holy Rosary Mission. While you're at the mission, you can also stop at the **Her-**

osebud
air.

itage Center for a look at a fine collection of Indian art and locally made handicrafts. The Heritage Center attracts Indian artists from all over the country to its national Indian art show each summer between mid-June and mid-August. It is well worth a stop while you are in the area.

Events on the reservation include the **Pine Ridge Powwow**, attended by some of the best singers and dancers in both the US and Canada. It's usually held in August at the Pine Ridge Village Powwow Grounds. The **Rosebud Fair** (and powwow), held in August, is located on the **Rosebud Reservation**, about 60 miles (100 km) from Pine Ridge Village. The **Sioux Indian Museum**, located at St Francis on the Rosebud Reservation, is also well worth a visit.

Powwows are given at the adjacent **Standing Rock** and **Cheyenne River reservations** (see *Travel Tips* for details), too, about 250 miles (400 km) directly north of Pine Ridge. Sitting Bull's Hunkpapas still live at Standing Rock, and his burial site may be visited

outside Mobridge, South Dakota. Sun dances, *yuwipis*, sweat lodges and other ceremonies should be considered off-limits to outsiders unless explicitly invited by a participant.

Off the reservation, you may want to visit the **Sioux Indian Museum** and **Prairie's Edge Gallery** in Rapid City, both of which carry high-quality arts and crafts. In addition to traditional beadwork and quillwork, you'll find an abundance of "star quilts," a style of quilting learned by Sioux women in the early 1900s at the famous Carlisle Indian School in Pennsylvania (you may notice a similarity with Pennsylvania Dutch quilting). Star quilts have become a common item at Indian giveaways. They make beautiful gifts and can be found at trading posts, galleries and pawn shops throughout the area.

Other museums with good Sioux collections include the Plains Indian Museum at the Buffalo Bill Historical Center in Cody, Wyoming, and the W.H. Over Museum at the University of South Dakota in Vermillion.

Traditions are passed to the next generation.

RED CLOUD

In the fall of 1822, a meteor passed over the Northern Plains, painting a brilliant red streak across the night sky. Several months later, a child was born to a man and woman of the Bad Face band of Oglala Sioux. Remembering the great fire that passed in the heavens, they named the child Mahpiua Luta – Red Cloud. He was to become one of the most influential leaders of the Oglala Sioux.

As a young man, Red Cloud won a reputation for daring and courage. He counted coups many times against traditional Sioux enemies, killed the leader of a rival Oglala band, and was almost killed himself during a horse-stealing raid against the hated Pawnees.

When whites began encroaching on Indian land in Wyoming and Dakota, Red Cloud led the fight to drive them out. "There are now white people all about me," the Oglala leader explained. "I have but a small spot of land left. The Great Spirit told me to keep it."

In 1866, a treaty commission was sent to Fort Laramie, Wyoming, with instructions to make peace with the "hostile" tribes and get permission to cross their territory. They were especially keen on getting Red Cloud's signature, without whose support the treaty would have meant nothing.

At stake at the Fort Laramie council was one of the white people's roads – the Bozeman Trail – which cut through the rich buffalo range of the Powder and Big Horn rivers toward the goldfields of Montana. Red Cloud and his allies had made passage on the trail perilous, and they punished the "bluecoats" who had been sent to guard it.

Red Cloud came to the council in the spring of 1866 ready to hear the commissioners' talk, only to discover that still more soldiers were being sent to fortify the road. He grabbed his rifle, stormed out of the meeting, and resumed the fight.

What happened over the next two years has come to be known as the Red Cloud War. With Cheyenne, Arapaho and Sioux warriors, Red Cloud put up a relentless barrage of raids and ambushes that made securing the road impossible. In one

demoralizing defeat – the Fetterman Massacre – a party of 81 soldiers was lured away from their fort and annihilated.

In 1868, the government called for another treaty council, but Red Cloud refused to attend. "When we see the soldiers moving away and the forts abandoned, then I will come down and talk," his message said.

The commissioners reluctantly complied. Soldiers were withdrawn from the Bozeman Trail, and Red Cloud burned the forts. In the subsequent Fort Laramie Treaty of 1868, Red Cloud agreed never to raise his hand against white people again.

As a leader in peace, Red Cloud fought hard to secure the rights of his people and to protect their remaining land. In 1870, with pressure mounting for further Sioux concessions, he traveled to Washington, DC, to meet with the Indian commissioner and with President Grant, the "Great Father."

"Whose voice was first sounded on this land?" Red Cloud asked. "The red people who had but bows and arrows. The Great Father says he is good and kind to us. I can't see it... The white children have surrounded me and have left me nothing but an island. When we first had this land we were strong, now we are melting like snow on the hillside while you are growing like spring grass."

Red Cloud's refusal to take up arms again was seen as weakness by some Sioux leaders. "The white people have put bad medicine over Red Cloud's eyes, to make him see everything and anything they please," Sitting Bull remarked. When whites invaded the sacred Black Hills in 1874, many of Red Cloud's people, including his son, left his camp to join Crazy Horse and Sitting Bull in defying the whites.

Still, the old war leader remained dedicated to peace. "I am poor and naked," he told an audience in New York City, "but I am the chief of the nation. We do not want riches, but we want to train our children right. Riches would do us no good. We could not take them with us to the other world. We do not want riches, we want peace..."

Red Cloud lived out his life on the Pine Ridge Indian Reservation in South Dakota. He died in 1909, blind and aged. His grave is at Holy Rosary Mission, 4 miles north of Pine Ridge Village.

WIND RIVER

Pink and gold sunshine still lingers on mountain peaks as appetizing aromas from two cutthroat trout sputter into the air from the frying pan. The campers gather with their Arapaho guide around the fire to sniff the dinner's progress, share fish tales, and marvel at their good fortune. All day long they saw only three other people. Although they stand near timberline, 20 miles from the nearest road, they feel just pleasantly tired; the guide's horses carried them into this wilderness on the Wind River Indian Reservation in the high country of west central Wyoming.

Tomorrow they plan a short hike to the lake where their guide promises fat golden trout. Photographers in the group are more interested in the hillside covered with early summer's flowers, phlox and sagebrush buttercups, and in the yellowbelly marmots chirping in the rocks nearby. Perhaps the guide will show them ancient pictographs chipped on rock walls by early Indians and tell them which plants his people have used for food and medicine.

Unexplored territory: Although close to the celebrated Bridger Wilderness Area, the high country of the Wind River Indian Reservation is known best by the bighorn mountain sheep and by a few, mostly local enthusiasts. The uncrowded trails, the fish and wildlife make visitors feel as if they have traveled back in time some 30 or 40 years. Not only mountain sheep but also moose, ptarmigan, deer and mountain lions still roam this untrammeled mountain range.

The Wind River plains below are, in a way, almost equally unexplored. Thousands of cars and buses cross the reservation each year on their way to Yellowstone National Park. Yet few travelers realize that by detouring less than 10 miles, they can find the grave of Lewis and Clark's famous scout, Sacajawea. Tuned to their radios or cassette players, they miss the drumbeats reverberating across the sagebrush, inviting them to watch one of the intertribal powwows held nearly every weekend somewhere on the 2½ million-acre reservation.

Sitting around the campfire in "the Winds," surrounded by so much natural beauty, it's hard to believe that this is an Indian reservation. The Shoshones and Northern Arapahos – the two tribes now occupying Wind River – have fared better than most Indian people. This is partly due to the friendliness of the Shoshone Indians and especially of Shoshone Chief Washakie toward white people. At the Fort Bridger Treaty conference in 1868, Washakie chose the Wind River Valley for his people, saying, "I am laughing because I am happy. Because my heart is good. I like the country you mentioned, then, for us, the Wind River Valley."

The Northern Arapahos joined the Shoshones on the reservation in 1877, preferring Wyoming to Indian Territory (Oklahoma), where the government wanted to send them. They were attracted to this area for many of the reasons that attract people today: Wyoming was

for the most part unsettled and free.

Most visitors agree that the tribes made a good choice. To the west, glaciated peaks in the Wind River Mountain Range glisten year-round with ice fields more than 7,000 ft above the valley. The ice and snow feed streams that slice deep canyons into the earth and slake the thirst of deer, elk, mountain sheep and people. The streams flow into the Big Wind River, which meanders diagonally toward the southeast corner of the reservation before turning northward. The Shoshones call it Warm Valley because the mountains on the west shelter the lowlands, making it one of the least windy areas in Wyoming. While the high elevation – about a mile above sea level – and the short growing season make the valley unsuitable for many crops, it is ideal for grazing cattle and horses and for growing alfalfa, barley and sugar beets.

Despite poverty and unemployment, the two tribes have put a high priority on maintaining the quality of this environment, and it has clearly paid off. In 1983, tribal leaders declared a 187,000-acre roadless area where vehicles are prohibited, the first wilderness designation in the country. That area contains some of the most pristine forests and beautiful alpine areas in the country, with more than 200 lakes. The tribes have also adopted tough environmental-protection laws. Although the tribes have developed oil and gas extensively on the reservation, they have turned their backs on more disruptive types of development, such as power plants and strip mining, focusing instead upon tourism and service businesses.

In the 1990s, the tribes hope to build a conference center and reopen a hot-springs swimming pool and bath house. They have also sanctioned the Northern American Indian Heritage Center, which through its visitors' bureau, Singing Horse Tours, promotes tourism in the Wind River area.

Traditional enemies: Shoshone and Arapaho tribal leaders meet at Fort Washakie, a town on the west side of the reservation built in 1871 as a military

Moraine Lake, one of many in the Wind River Mountains.

post. Joint decision-making is sometimes difficult since the two tribes are traditional enemies. As recently as 1874, the Shoshones joined with US soldiers to attack the Arapahos at their camp on Bates Creek, a battle that historians consider disastrous to the Arapahos' lives as a free and roaming people. Chief Washakie agreed only reluctantly to allow the Arapahos to join the Shoshones on the reservation.

Memories of those early reservation years and of personalities such as Tim McCoy, Sacajawea and Chief Washakie are still alive among the people of Wind River. In 1909, McCoy arrived on the train in Lander and soon found his way to the reservation, where he earned the respect of the Indian people by learning sign language. Other cowboys routinely offended the Arapahos and Shoshones by greeting them all with, "Hello, John, how the hell are you?" Before long, McCoy became a star of silent films, and he helped bring money into the reservation by hiring Arapahos and Shoshones, first to appear in the epic silent film *Covered Wagon* and later in the talkies. Silent-film enthusiasts may recognize settings for the Tim McCoy film *War Paint*, filmed near Fort Washakie in 1926.

McCoy describes his experiences on the reservation and traveling with Indian actors in his autobiography, *Tim McCoy Remembers the West*. After returning from London, reporters asked one of the Arapahos, Goes In Lodge, how members of the two enemy tribes were able to travel together on the same train. Goes In Lodge said: "We're not with the Shoshone. We're with him [McCoy]." One of McCoy's saddles holds a place of honor at the museum at **St Stephen's Indian Mission**, located in the southeastern corner of the reservation near Riverton, Wyoming.

The Jesuits established the St Stephen's Mission in 1884 and within a few years opened a school for Arapahos, who live primarily in communities in the eastern portion of the reservation. The school still operates today. Photographers find St Stephen's Catholic

Snow
blankets the
high country.

Church one of the reservation's best attractions, a white, high-steepled church with the brightly colored geometric designs characteristic of the Arapahos. Although the **North American Indian Heritage Center** is now housed in modest offices in one of the old mission buildings, the board of the private, nonprofit organization has ambitious plans to build a new facility with an ethnographic Indian museum and an American Indian Hall of Fame.

The Jesuits built their mission on the eastern part of the reservation because a Welsh Episcopal minister, the Rev. John Roberts, already had established the **Shoshone Episcopal Mission** near Fort Washakie on the west side. When Roberts arrived he was introduced to an aged woman whom he became convinced was Sacajawea, the legendary Shoshone guide for the Lewis and Clark expedition.

Perhaps because she did not want to emphasize her assistance to white incursion into the West, Sacajawea never boasted about her journey. She told her son, Baptiste, however, that she had carried him on her back when she led the "first Washington" across the mountains to the Great Waters toward the setting sun. Roberts said in a letter: "There is no doubt in my mind that she is the Shoshone woman who guided the Lewis and Clark Expedition... I, as well as other white men on the reservation, was reluctant to believe her story until she told of many aspects of that trip that would not have been known to anyone who had not participated in it."

While some historians question whether the old woman was really the famous guide, she is buried in the **Sacajawea Cemetery** within a mile of **Roberts' Mission**. To find them, turn west at the Hines General Store, 15 miles north of Lander. The old log buildings of Robert's Mission are located on the south side of the road and a sign for the graveyard is just beyond the mission on the north side. The cemetery will delight the photographer, especially in the early morning when the sun's rays illuminate the large stone as well as

The grave of Sacajawea, Lewis and Clark's Indian guide.

those of her son, Baptiste Charbonneau, and her nephew and adopted son, Bazil. Plastic flowers look like colorful confetti adorning the other graves, marked mostly by white, wooden crosses or white-washed stones. To the west, Indian ponies graze along the sage-covered foothills, with jagged peaks scribbled across the skyline above.

The **Chief Washakie Cemetery** is also located at Fort Washakie, in the shadow of the Wind River Mountains where the Shoshone chief often sought solace during difficult times. Washakie was buried here in 1900 with full military honors after serving nearly 60 years as a leader with rare vision. His name lives on in the name of the reservation capital, Fort Washakie, and in the name of a county north of the reservation. Also north of the reservation is Togwotee Pass, named after a lesser known Shoshone Indian who guided white expeditions into the magnificent Yellowstone country to watch the earth's innards boil, spit and cough.

To the south of the reservation lies

South Pass, the route of the Oregon Trail and home of two historic gold-mining towns, Atlantic City and South Pass City. According to the 1868 treaty, the South Pass area was orginally included in the Wind River Indian Reservation. Soon after the discovery of gold, however, more than 5,000 whites settled illegally on Indian lands. In 1874, the US government purchased the southern 700,000 acres from the Shoshones for a meager 4¢ an acre and removed this highly lucrative area from their reservation.

Most of the above sites are included on the itinerary of Singing Horse Tours, the only tour office based on the reservation. The one-day tour for motorcoach groups and independent travelers includes the missions, Washakie and Sacajawea gravesites, Bureau of Indian Affairs structures in Fort Washakie, museums in neighboring towns of Lander and Riverton, and both Shoshone and Arapaho cultural centers. Extended tours can also include the gold-mining towns, Oregon Trail sites, and pow-

The elements weather an abandoned ranch on the Wind River reservation.

wows. Although the North American Indian Heritage Center started the Singing Horse Tours only in 1989 and its guides are somewhat untested, the center provides a high-quality portfolio of literature about the reservation, full of historic photos.

Those who would rather explore on their own can purchase an audio-cassette tape for $15 with a self-guided tour from Singing Horse. The tape, well worth the price, includes historic and contemporary material with evocative sounds of thunder and drums.

Enduring traditions: Shoshone and Arapaho cultures are still very much alive, and tribal leaders are putting a good deal of energy into passing them on to the next generation. English is the *lingua franca* at Wind River, but the native languages are also spoken. The tribes have started a program to teach both the Arapaho and the Shoshone languages in school and in language camps each summer. Instructors give classes on how to decorate parfleche bags, tan skins, and make hoof bags from elk hoofs. "Entertainment committees" oversee internal social and cultural affairs, such as powwows and memorial feasts. Each tribe also holds an annual sun dance, a deeply religious ceremony that visitors are not encouraged to attend. Those who are invited cannot take photographs and must not eat or drink in front of the dancers, who undergo a devotional period of fasting for several days prior to the ceremony.

All visitors are welcome at powwows, however, and they can roam among tepees and buy jewelry and Indian tacos during breaks in the dancing. Between Memorial Day and Labor Day, eight different powwows are held on the reservation, offering thousands of dollars in prizes and attracting dancers and drum groups from throughout the country. All-Indian rodeos accompany the two biggest celebrations, the **Shoshone Indian Days** (third weekend in June) and the **Ethete Celebration** (third weekend in July). Between 500 and 1,000 dancers compete in each. During the **Big Wind Powwow** (second

Powwow color.

weekend in June), Indian riders race bareback in a rowdy exhibition reminiscent of the old rendezvous days when trappers and Indians competed in various contests. Keep in mind that alcoholic beverages are not allowed on the powwow grounds.

Excellent beadwork can be purchased at several shops on the reservation, including the **Rendezvous Gift Shop** at St Stephen's, which specializes in Arapaho work, and the **Warm Valley Arts and Crafts Shop** at Fort Washakie, which specializes in Shoshone work. Also at St Stephen's, the **Nature Window Gallery** has contemporary photographs and the **Singing Horse Gallery** specializes in craft miniatures, such as war bonnets and cradleboards, and paintings by local artists. Shoshone beadwork often features a rose pattern with soft curves, while the Arapahos favor geometric designs.

At both the arts and crafts stores and the powwow dances, visitors can see evidence of how the tribal cultures have endured despite efforts to suppress them.

Purists might reject beadwork sewn with nylon thread instead of sinew, but the artists – and the tribes – have survived by adapting. The **Warm Valley Arts and Crafts Shop**, for example, sells beaded baseball caps, cigarette lighters, photo frames, watch bands, barrettes and key chains, items foreign to the Plains Indians of the 1700s. On the other hand, horses, firearms and cut beads were once foreign until they were adopted by the tribes.

Alert observers at the powwow will see similar anachronisms, such as chewing-tobacco lids adorning the jingle dancers' dresses, singers passing bottles of Perrier, teenage girls wearing buckskin and using curling irons, moccasins and running shoes. At the same time, many of the dancers achieve an unified feather, buckskin and beaded image. They instill a love for American Indian culture in their children, many of whom start dancing at powwows as soon as they can walk.

To the residents of the Wind River Reservation, life hums with work, family

and cultural activities. To the visitor, however, Wind River can seem like a step backward to a culturally rich, slower-paced time when the old chiefs and Indian guides still told their stories and when the cut-throat trout and bighorn sheep thrived.

Visitors who want to hike, fish, boat or camp on the reservation must purchase a permit from the Wind River Fish and Game Department. Permits and maps of closed areas can be obtained from the department at Fort Washakie and from various stores in the towns of Lander, Ethete, Riverton, Crowheart, Dubois, Pinedale, Shoshoni and Thermopolis. Fire permits are required but are free. Only tribal members may hunt on reservation land.

Although much of the high country is open to anyone who buys the tribal permit, most first-time visitors prefer to hire an Indian outfitter since the trails are not very well marked and non-members cannot bring their own horses. The tribe licenses outfitters, who offer a full range of services for the campers,

carrying them into the backcountry on horseback, hauling gear while the campers hike, or staying with them, moving their camp periodically, and providing meals. Meals can include prime rib, steaks and traditional delicacies such as fry bread and pemmican (dried meat) stew.

The Fish and Game Department assigns each outfitter to a different geographic area. Visitors should pick their outfitter carefully based upon fees and professionalism. Ask the Fish and Game staff or the US Fish and Wildlife Service staff in Lander for advice. The tribes regulate outfitters, but they do not attempt to fix prices.

Although small stores and snack shops can be found on the reservation, visitors will want to return to Lander or Riverton for full meals and lodging. Singing Horse Tours provides a listing of accommodations and restaurants. Contact the Visitors' Bureau, North American Indian Heritage Center, Box 275, St Stephens, Wyoming 82524, or call 307-856-6688.

Left, moccasins decorated with Shoshone-style beadwork. **Right**, enduring the ordeal of the sun dance.

SUN DANCE

An old Assiniboine medicine man calls his singers from the doorway of the sun dance lodge. His mellifluous voice weaves Anglicized names into an Assiniboine refrain. English-speakers recognize only names and several Indian words, including "Osheetogapa," the Assiniboine word for God. The chief's bearing translates the rest: "The Creator waits."

The chief and the singers sit around an ancient buffalo skin near the center pole. Three of them beat drums of rawhide stretched over wooden frames. The chief and the others thump the tattered hide with chokecherry switches.

The sun dance lodge is a circular structure 40 ft across, with a roof supported by a forked cottonwood trunk, walled and thatched with fresh boughs. A low wall hides dancers squatting on their haunches between songs. The men wear blankets wrapped around their waists. Their faces and torsos are painted. The women wear ribbon dresses or beaded buckskin. Earlier in the year, they made a vow to participate in this ceremony of personal sacrifice. They promised to live in the "Indian Way," to fast and to dance, for the good of their families, their people, themselves. Later, the men will make an offering of flesh. Their chests will

be pierced; a wooden peg will be driven through the skin and tied to the center pole.

The chief stares skyward, trembles, then begins to sing: "*Mak ay o, na gae o, Wakan Tonka...*" Dancers arise from behind the cottonwood screen wearing crowns of sweet sage. Some shake eagle-wing fans in one or both hands. Wing-bone whistles adorned with feathers scream as the dancers echo the beat.

The chief's song trails out of the lodge and across the prairie with drums in pursuit: "*Mak ay o... boom, boom, boom.*" Singers' voices join the chase, calling dancers to their feet. The whistles sound a throbbing, airy shrill. While the chief leads the singers, an assistant stokes the fire, keeps the pipes and braids of sweetgrass lit, and stretches drumheads over the coals.

An elder, the medicine man who gave the chief the right to run this Sun Dance, watches from a spot to the left of the door. The old man's presence fills the lodge. He nods to the chief. It is time to pierce. The sun dance chief nods to his second assistant, a handsome Assiniboine man with a single braid. The assistant approaches the old man, who places a small blade in his hand. "I want you to hold that knife a while," the elder says. "I don't want you to be nervous."

The elder points to a spot on the dancer's chest. The younger man pinches muscle and skin between his thumb and forefinger and pulls. The knife cuts through the tissue rising from the chest and a wooden peg is placed through the hole. The knife man fashions a slip knot in a thong hanging from the center pole, and then pulls the loop tight around the ends of the peg in the dancer's chest.

The elder smiles his approval. Not a drop of blood has spilled. The sun dance chief leads the singers in non-stop chants to provide the dancer a focus outside himself.

Soon, 12 men are dancing at the end of leather tethers attached to pegs in their breasts. Before noon, a 13-year-old boy and a woman respected for her spiritual power will sacrifice tiny pieces of flesh cut from their arms. A big Sioux will pull a train of seven buffalo skulls across the prairie by thongs tied to pegs driven through his back muscles.

One of the most important and dramatic ceremonies of the Plains tribes, the sun dance is enjoying a revival in recent years. Once outlawed by the federal government, the sun dance now attracts both young and old, men and women.

Sun dance ceremonies vary from tribe to tribe. One of the greatest differences is in the piercing of the breast. Among some tribes, dancers are not pierced. Others follow the Assiniboine style, piercing but carefully releasing the dancers from their tethers after a period of time. Still other tribes perform the sun dance in the old way, ripping free of the tethers, tearing chest muscles and bleeding profusely.

Outsiders are seldom welcome at sun dances, but the lodges remain standing and can be visited after the ceremony. Locals will usually give directions to the lodge.

CROW COUNTRY

French fur-traders wandering into Crow Country in 1742 found a race of "*beaux hommes*" living in a land of "shining mountains." The handsome men discovered by the traders in their westward quest were warriors of the Apsaloka. The mountains were the Bighorns, those craggy highlands where the Little Bighorn River begins its ramble toward the spot where another white man – Lieutenant Colonel George Armstrong Custer – would lead his Seventh Cavalry into the maw of death more than a century later.

Lords of a land as big as England and Wales combined, they called themselves Apsaloka (Children of the Big-beaked Bird). Other tribes described them in sign language with a flapping of arms which whites mistakenly translated as "Crow."

In speech, the Crow are Siouan, but the relationship with their arch-enemies, the Sioux, is lost in the mists of antiquity. More than 500 years ago, the Crow split from a group of sedentary farmers on the upper Missouri River to follow the buffalo and conquer a land of green valleys, lush grasslands and breathtaking mountains, a land that would become "Crow Country."

The introduction of the horse revolutionized life on the Great Plains. Freed from dependence on agriculture, Plains tribes blossomed, claiming great tracts of buffalo range and coming increasingly into conflict with one another. Having acquired horses and a taste for nomadic life on the plains, the Crow would plant only small patches of sacred tobacco and never farm again until the coming of the whites.

They saw themselves as "the mighty few." Though small in number (fewer than 1,500 warriors), they held their land against formidable foes. To the north ranged the Blackfeet, a fierce and powerful people who would come to be known as the "cossacks of the Plains." To the east the Crow were pressed by the great Sioux nation. The Cheyenne and Arapaho held the land to the south. All coveted Crow Country. Crow history is filled with tales of desperate stands against overwhelming numbers. Crow warriors repelled all challengers until the coming of those people too numerous to count: the White Man.

Passion for the land: Crow Country was a great triangle with its apex in Wyoming's Wind River Mountains and its base along a line between and parallel to the Missouri and Yellowstone rivers – more than 60,000 sq. miles.

Crow passion for their land is reflected in the words of the great chief Arapooish: "Crow country is good country. The Great Spirit put it in exactly the right place. Whenever you are in it you fare well. Whenever you go out of it, whichever way you may travel, you fare worse... It has snowy mountains and sunny plains, all kinds of climates and good things for every season. When the summer heat scorches the prairie, you can draw up under the mountains where the air is sweet and cool, the grass fresh and the bright

Preceding pages: fires illuminate tepees during nightlong peyote meetings. **Left**, shaking the earth and (**right**) setting up tepees at Crow Fair.

streams come tumbling out of the snow banks. There you can hunt the elk, the deer and the antelope when their skins are fit for dressing. There you will find plenty of white (grizzly) bears and mountain sheep.

"In autumn, when your horses are fat and strong from the mountain pastures, you can go down onto the plains and hunt buffalo or even trap beaver on the streams. When winter comes on, you can take shelter in the woody bottoms along the rivers. There you will find buffalo meat for yourselves and cottonwood bark for your horses. Or, you may winter in the Wind River Valley where there is salt weed in abundance.

"Crow Country is exactly in the right place. Everything good is to be found there. There is no country like Crow Country."

In 1806, members of the Lewis and Clark expedition learned what other tribes already knew about the Crow. When Captain William Clark reached the present site of Billings, Montana, on his return to St Louis, he ordered canoes hewed from huge cottonwoods. Clark and most of his men cast off to finish the trip by river. Sergeant Pryor and several men were to take the expedition's horses and return via an overland route.

Pryor camped the first night near an extension of the Bighorn Mountains. At dawn, not an animal remained in camp. Crow raiders, renowned on the Plains for their daring in taking enemy horses, had stolen every hoof. Pryor and his men sorefooted it back to the Yellowstone River to pursue the main body of the expedition in an awkward bull boat made of buffalo hide stretched over a willow frame.

The next year, fur-trader Manuel Lisa led a party of trappers to Montana, intending to build a fur fort near the headwaters of the Missouri. Lisa met John Colter, a member of the Lewis and Clark party that had stayed behind to trap beaver. Colter warned Lisa to stay out of Blackfeet country and led the trader instead to the confluence of the Bighorn and Yellowstone rivers where

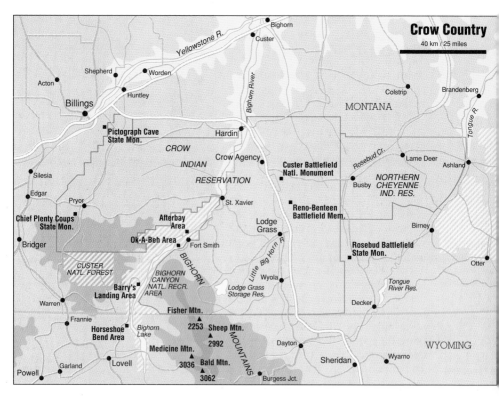

Lisa's fort, the first white man's building in Montana, was built to trade with the Crow. Colter was on a trade mission for Lisa when he discovered "Colter's Hell," better known today as Yellowstone National Park.

Chief of chiefs: Though quick to steal their horses, the Crow never waged war on whites. They were among the first of the Plains Indians to sense what the coming of white settlers meant. They aligned with the US Army in the wars against their enemies, the Sioux, Cheyenne and Arapaho.

The Battle of the Rosebud on June 17, 1876, might have been Brigadier-General George Crook's last stand had it not been for the 135 Crow scouts whose courage saved him from the fate waiting for Custer 10 days later. Six Crow scouts – Yellow Face, White Man Runs Him, Curley, Goes Ahead, Hairy Moccasin and White Swan – led Custer to the Valley of the Little Bighorn, told him he was riding to his death, and left his command.

The Crow signed a friendship treaty in 1825 that recognized the supremacy and claimed the protection of the US. But Crow friendship with whites did not save Crow Country from white encroachment. In 1851, the first Treaty of Laramie recognized Crow claims to 38 million acres. Still, the westward tide of settlers did not slacken. In 1867, the Crow were told that their treaty provisions had expired and their lands were reduced to 8 million acres. Completion of the Northern Pacific Railroad escalated the flow of outsiders, and the Crow were pressured to sell large blocks of their remaining land. Today, trust lands within the reservation total 1.5 million acres.

The Crow did succeed in saving the heart of their country – the valleys of Pryor Creek, Lodgegrass Creek and the Bighorn and Little Horn Rivers – thanks largely to the "Chief of chiefs, Plenty Coups." Among the last of the great warriors, Plenty Coups became the Crow's first modern leader.

Only nine years old when his brother was killed in a raid on the Sioux, he stole

Crow scouts in US Army uniforms.

away from camp to fast naked in the mountains. On his second attempt, he received a great vision. The "little people," a mysterious race of supernatural beings, told him he would never have children of his own but that he would become a great chief and all Crow people would be his children.

These were tumultuous times. The westward advance of white settlers intensified tribal warfare in the ever-shrinking domain of the Plains Indians.

In the 1870s, buffalo hides became suddenly valuable. The great beasts were slaughtered by the hundreds of thousands, skinned and left to rot. In 1880, one fur trader shipped 30,000 buffalo robes from the riverboat town of Coulson. Down the Yellowstone at Junction City, hides were stacked so high along the strand that the town could not be seen from across the river.

By 1884, the buffalo had disappeared, plunging the Crow from plenty to poverty. Influenza killed 600 Crow in 1849. Smallpox epidemics in 1833, 1837 and 1851 decimated the tribe. The Crow population dropped from 8,000 in 1800 to 2,000 in 1870.

Plenty Coups was only 14 when he foresaw in a vision the end of the buffalo and the coming of the strange spotted beasts that whites called "cattle." He would distinguish himself first as a warrior, counting coups many times in fearless combat against the Sioux, Cheyenne and Arapaho.

Still in his twenties, Plenty Coups understood the import of the discovery of gold in the Black Hills in 1874. Calling a council of sub-chiefs and headmen, he told them trouble was imminent because whites would drive the Sioux and Cheyenne out of the Black Hills, spilling these ancient foes into Crow Country. He decided to cast his lot with the US Army in a war against Crow enemies. Plenty Coups provided General Crook with the 135 scouts who fought at his side at the Battle of the Rosebud, prior to Custer's Last Stand. Later he would urge young Crow men to enlist with the army to "prove themselves in battle" during World War I.

After the Indian Wars, Chief Plenty Coups represented the Crow Indians in Washington, DC. He was also chosen to represent all American Indians in a moving ceremony at the tomb of the Unknown Soldier. His brief but stirring speech brought tears to the eyes of a hard-bitten, gray-haired cavalry colonel at his side: "For the Indians of America, I call upon the Great Spirit with gesture, chant and tribal tongue that the dead should not have died in vain, the war might end in peace purchased by the blood of men red and white."

None were more dignified than the old chief as he placed his war bonnet and coup stick in the grave. Marshall Foch, commander of the allied forces, would later have his train detoured in his triumphal tour of the country to visit Plenty Coups at Crow Agency.

He led his people into the 20th century by example, building a two-story log home and a store on Pryor Creek, where he ranched and traded. The chief, who had traded his bow for a gun as a

Chief Plenty Coups, 1905.

young man but fought tirelessly to keep whiskey off the reservation, told his people, "If a thing is good, pick it up. If it is bad, let it alone." Today, Plenty Coups' admonition to his "children" adorns the walls of Crow schools: "Education is your most powerful weapon. With education, you are the white man's equal. Without education, you are his victim."

Too rugged to fly over: Plenty Coups willed his home and land on Pryor Creek to "the people of all races" to use as a park. Only a half-hour's drive south of Billings, **Plenty Coups State Park** is an excellent first stop on a tour of Crow Country. A small museum on the grounds contains Indian and natural-history exhibits. The park contains picnic sites and a refreshing spring within view of dramatic limestone formations known as the **Castles.**

A gravel road, rough in spots but passable in a passenger vehicle, leads out of Pryor through a break in the mountains called "Pryor Gap." An ancient trail marked with cairns, the trail has been used by Indians since the first paleolithic hunters arrived from the north after crossing the Bering Land Bridge more than 15,000 years ago.

The road follows an old railroad grade. A number of men who died of yellow fever during construction of a tunnel through the mountain are buried near the mouth of the Gap. Crow elders say the railroad was doomed when workers began blasting through one of the Castles, a site sacred to the Crow and home of the "Little People."

At Sage Creek, the road forks. Well-marked routes branch off to Bridger in the Clarks Fork Valley and to Warren, a town of only a few souls on Highway 310. The fork that breaks to the east carries you to the lush alpine heights of the Pryor Mountains. The **Big Ice Cave,** a cavern with its own small glacier inside, is within easy reach from here, and majestic wild stallions and their harems roam the **National Horse Range** just a few miles away.

From the Pryors you can continue south to Lovell, Wyoming, via a breath-

Devil's Canyon, Crow Reservation.

taking road that winds along the lip of Crooked Creek Canyon. Locals say this country is "too rough to fly over." Though dangerous in rainy weather and too rugged for most low-slung cars, this scenic road is one of Montana's best-kept secrets.

From Pryor to Lovell, a distance of about 50 miles (80 km), the road passes through five distinct ecosystems, including cottonwood forest, sagebrush prairie, fir forest, subalpine grasslands, and desert in the rain shadow of the mountains. The route is a favorite for local ornithologists who find scores of species in its diversity. Rock hounds, fossil and arrowhead hunters find the Pryors a bonanza. A paved road leads from Pryor to **Saint Xavier**, home of a century-old mission.

South of Saint Xavier is the Bighorn Canyon and 60 miles of the Bighorn Reservoir. The lake attracts both boaters and fishermen, but the hottest action is on the Bighorn River flowing out of the canyon at Fort Smith toward the Yellowstone. The Bighorn is one of the finest "big trout" streams in North America. Fishermen with or without boats can be hired locally.

Modern Fort Smith is the site of old Fort Smith, one of several forts built to protect gold-seekers traveling the old Bozeman Trail. Just downstream from the fort, a body of soldiers was attacked in the Hayfield Fight. Constantly besieged by Sioux warriors, the forts were abandoned after the US government was pressured into making major concessions to Sioux chief Red Cloud.

Crow Agency, capital of the Crow Nation, is 25 miles northeast of Saint Xavier on Highway 90. A village on the Little Bighorn River, Crow Agency is in the heart of that land the Indians called the "Greasy Grass," grass that made ponies and buffalo fat.

During the third week in August, Crow Agency becomes the "Tepee Capital of the World" during **Crow Fair**. The fairgrounds become a huge village as Crow families erect their tepees for a week of camping, visiting, and traditional activities. Nightly pow-wow dances, hand games (Indian gambling), arts and crafts, and rodeo draw Indian participants from Canada to the Mexican border. Outsiders are welcome. A small admission is charged for the rodeo, but the dancing and other powwow events are free.

The **Rosebud Battlefield** is almost a two-hour drive northeast of Crow Agency. Take Highway 212 to Lame Deer, Route 39 north to Rosebud Creek and Route 447 (a gravel road) to the battlefield. The road is dusty but fairly smooth in fair weather. A single sign marks the battlefield, a lush meadow in spring and early summer. General Crook's defeat here put him and his command out of action. He retired to the present site of Sheridan, Wyoming, to recover. The Sioux victory may have contributed to Custer's defeat.

The mysterious Medicine Wheel: The Wyoming border, 53 miles south of Crow Agency on Highway 90, coincides with the present reservation boundary. Just south of the line, Route 14 swings westward into the uplands which fur-traders used to call "The

Getting ready for Crow Fair.

Shining Mountains," the Bighorns.

The road winding up the face of the Bighorn Mountains provides a view of hundreds of square miles of lush green valleys, rolling hills and broad prairies. This road is a favorite of hang gliders who use its pull-outs to launch colorful flights over the lowlands.

The mysterious **Medicine Wheel** waits on the alpine plateau above. A circle of stones 70 ft in diameter with a 12-ft hub and 28 spokes, it resembles the "houses of dawn" built by Aztec sun worshippers.

The object of intense curiosity, numerous articles, documentaries and endless speculation, the Medicine Wheel is seen as a New World Stonehenge by some who attribute its origin to Aztecs in exile, a vanished people, even aliens from outer space. One amateur archaeologist suggests that it was left by one of the "lost tribes of Israel." Another insists that it was built to predict the Spring Equinox.

In the saddle at sunset.

The Crow have a simpler explanation: in the 18th century, a Crow child fell face first into a cooking fire. Hideously burned, he survived but was teased and shunned by his contemporaries. Leaving the tribe to live the life of a recluse, the man called "Scarface" built the Medicine Wheel atop Medicine Mountain and two more wheels in other locations. He probably used them in his worship. They may have included a superstructure resembling a sun dance lodge built over the wheel.

From the Medicine Wheel, you can continue over the mountain on Highway 14, which crosses the 8,900-ft Granite Pass and descends via Shell Canyon to Greybull in the Bighorn Basin, or follow Highway 90 south along the flanks of the mountains to three historic sites near Story.

Fort Phil Kearney was the first garrison south of Fort Smith on the Bozeman trail. Red Cloud's Sioux warriors attacked and routed a wood-cutting team and its escort east of the fort in the Wagon Box Fight.

In December 1866, Captain William J. Fetterman led a body of men to the

rescue of a work crew attacked on a nearby ridge. Fetterman, a veteran of the Hayfield Fight, had boasted that with just 80 men he could ride through the entire Sioux nation. Eighty men followed him, but none returned. A mystical warrior, Crazy Horse, rose to prominence leading a decoy party that lured Fetterman and his command into ambush and annihilation.

Scenic Route 16 winds 95 miles through the Bighorns and the red sandstone of Ten Sleep Canyon all the way to **Thermopolis**, which sits at the mouth of the beautiful Wind River Canyon where Crow Chief Arapooish found salt weed to winter his horses. Here, the famous Crow healer, The Fringe, had his medicine dream. Both commercial and public spas are found in **Hot Springs State Park**.

Highway 120 leads north from Thermopolis to Cody, the town named for "Buffalo Bill." The **Buffalo Bill Historical Center** houses a fine collection of Western art, the large Plains Indians Museum, and a collection of Winchester arms.

Cody is also one of the gateways to that most famous corner of Crow Country, **Yellowstone National Park**. The largest US wilderness preserve, Yellowstone sprawls over 3,468 sq. miles of northwestern Wyoming, eastern Idaho and southern Montana. Most of the park rests on a high plateau in the Rocky Mountains, built up by volcanic action. The park is best known for its geothermal features, including about 200 geysers, 10,000 hot springs, and numerous smoking fumaroles. Most famous of these are Old Faithful and Mammoth Hot Springs. The park also abounds in wildlife, including elk, buffalo, moose, deer, bighorn sheep, antelope, coyote and bear.

The first national park, Yellowstone was established in 1872, four years before Custer met his end at the Battle of the Little Bighorn.

Custer's last stand: Crow Country is also home to one of the most famous battle sites in the United States, the Battle of the Little Bighorn. It was here that Custer met Sioux, Cheyenne and Arapaho warriors for the last time. Now called the **Custer-Sitting Bull National Monument**, the battlefield sprawls over gently rolling hills bordering the river.

For generations, whites called the battle Custer's Last Stand. In truth, it was a last spectacular victory in the Indians' long – and futile – struggle to hold back the Europeans. The battle is wrapped within a legend that has become etched in history's pages by the mystery of what happened on Custer's Hill, the spectacle of painted warriors clashing with saber-wielding soldiers, men larger than life: Custer, Crazy Horse, Sitting Bull, Gall, Two Moons.

The road to the Little Bighorn started in 1865 at the end of the American Civil War, when a massive wave of settlers struck out for the western frontier. To the Indians, it seemed there was an endless supply of white people with an insatiable hunger for land. War seemed inevitable, its outcome predictable.

Newspaper editors in frontier towns clamored for removal of the Indians. It was time, they said, that the redmen should give up their vast territory and become self-sufficient. No one seemed to see the contradiction in that demand.

There would be no compromise. Sitting Bull, chief of the Hunkpapa Sioux, who once declared himself "the last Indian," considered reservation Indians pitiful creatures, living off handouts like animals in a corral.

In the Treaty of Laramie of 1868, the government set aside an enormous territory west of the Missouri River as the Great Sioux Reservation and agreed to an "unceded territory" free of whites stretching from the reservation to the Bighorn Mountains. But General William Tecumseh Sherman, the commander of the US Army who helped negotiate the Treaty of Laramie, saw Indian control of unceded lands as temporary. In his view, extermination of the buffalo or a major confrontation with hostile tribes would bring a "final solution to the Indian problem."

Sherman pressed for this clash in 1874 when he granted a request to explore the Black Hills, in the very heart of the Great Sioux Reservation. Sherman wanted a fort in the area to keep an eye on the Indians. Speculators wanted confirmation of rumors of gold.

Tapped to lead this expedition was the dashing young Lieutenant Colonel George Armstrong Custer. Already a national celebrity, Custer had earned his lieutenant's bars early in the American Civil War and was promoted to brigadier-general at the age of 23. From Gettysburg to Appomattox, the golden-haired "boy general" led his troops from victory to victory.

At war's end, Custer was a national hero and a major-general at 25. A postwar cutback of generals reduced him to a line rank of captain, but a reorganization of the army in 1866 landed him in the post of lieutenant-colonel and commander of the newly formed Seventh Cavalry, the most elite unit of Indian fighters in the entire US Army.

Reporters, prospectors and territorial boomers followed Custer and his Seventh Calvary into the hills. In the pristine creeks, they found what they sought. "Gold in the Black Hills!" screamed newspaper headlines. Miners poured into the hills. Custer City, Deadwood and other mining camps sprang up like weeds. The government tried, ineffectively, to stop the miners, then attempted to buy the hills from the Sioux. Although reservation chiefs considered signing a treaty, there were still "hostile" bands roaming the Bighorn country west of the Black Hills, Chief Sitting Bull's band the most prominent among them.

Frustrated and angered, government officials decided to push the issue to its conclusion. Under the direction of General Philip Sheridan, an invasion was organized calling for a three-pronged attack on the Indian stronghold. Custer led his column on a sweep south from the Yellowstone River. On June 23 he crossed a large Indian trail heading toward the Little Bighorn River. Fearing that the Indians would break camp and scatter before he could arrange an attack, he hurried after them. By noon the next day, the trail had

"Big sky" over Custer Battlefield National Monument.

grown broader and fresher. Unaware that hundreds of warriors had broken away from the reservation to join Sitting Bull, Custer pressed on.

Both troops and horses were near exhaustion when they neared the valley of the Little Bighorn, where more than 1,000 lodges held more Indians than the army had ever encountered. Splitting his forces into three battalions, Custer rushed to the fight.

He dispatched one battalion – led by Captain Marcus Reno – in hot pursuit of a party of Sioux warriors flushed from a nearby valley. The other battalion – commanded by Captain Frederick Benteen – was ordered to swing to the left. Custer himself took 225 men and headed north to strike a large Indian village upstream.

Reaching a ridge overlooking the Indian camp, Custer sent an urgent message to Benteen: "Come quick. Big village. Bring Packs." Giovanni Martini, the Italian-born trumpeter who carried the message to Benteen, was the last survivor to see Custer alive. Benteen

received the summons but never came. Instead, both he and Reno were beaten back by the Indians to a hill about 5 miles away.

Custer's force split again at Medicine Tail Coulee. Captain George Yates charged the river with two companies and was turned back. He retreated up Deep Coulee, pursued by Chief Gall's Sioux warriors. Meeting Captain Miles Keogh and his three companies, the combined force reeled backward under Gall's assault toward what would become known as Custer Hill.

Meanwhile, Crazy Horse led a large body of Sioux and Cheyenne warriors down the valley, across the river and in a sweeping arc to attack from the north. Caught in the pincers of the Gall and Crazy Horse attacks, the Seventh Calvary made its last stand.

To relive the historic clash, stop first at the museum and interpretive center. Watch the video presentation in the museum theater, then familiarize yourself with the terrain. A topographical map in the museum stands before windows overlooking the battlefield and the Little Bighorn Valley.

Next, with the routes of Custer and his subordinates in mind, drive to the **Reno-Benteen Battlefield** and look down on the bottomland where Reno was staggered and driven back by the warriors. Follow the road that parallels Custer's route to Medicine Tail Coulee, where Gall first struck. And then drive to **Monument Hill** where Gall's Sioux warriors crushed the Seventh Calvary against the relentless attack of Crazy Horse and Chief Two Moon.

It is said that a Cheyenne woman watched this final attack from a nearby hill as the blue-clad soldiers were swallowed up by warriors and lost in the dust of battle. The woman's eyes widened in recognition. She had dreamed that the soldier known as "Yellow Hair" would be killed in a snow storm at sea. As cotton from a stand of cottonwood trees along the Little Bighorn River blew over the hills, she realized her mistake in the dream's interpretation. Yellow Hair would never again make her people cry.

Left, Crow girl wearing traditional elk-tooth dress. Right, Fire heats sacred stones.

SWEAT LODGE

A tall Gros Ventre Indian uses a pitchfork to carry stones from a bed of coals into a squat, dome-shaped sweat lodge. One by one, he drops the stones into a pit inside the lodge, pausing to pray as he lifts each of the first four from the fire of cottonwood limbs. Earlier, he lit the fire and asked the Thunder Spirit's blessing.

Inside the lodge, three men and two women sit cross-legged in silence around the pit that receives the hot stones. Ash white in daylight, the stones glow a deep red in the darkness of the lodge. A man at the back of the lodge sprinkles cedar from a buckskin pouch on the rocks. The cedar crackles and gives off an aromatic smoke. The others thrust cupped hands into the sacred smoke, pulling it toward themselves to purify their bodies.

The man with the buckskin bag speaks to the grandfather spirits in the stones and wafts smoke over a bucket of water at his knee with an eagle-wing fan. He gives a command in Gros Ventre, and the man outside drops the door flap, shutting out daylight and fresh air.

In his mother tongue, the man with the eagle wing prays: "God, O Great One, look on us, a pitiful people. Accept our pitiful pain. It is all we have to offer. All else belongs to you." He sprinkles more cedar on the stones. "O sacred cedar, carry our prayer to the Great Spirit."

Around the circle men and women begin to sweat in the dry heat radiating from the pit. The man with the fan prays several more minutes, naming each person around the circle and asking that prayers spoken in this lodge be joined with those of others who have "built sweat" this day. Dipping into the bucket with a long-handled dipper, he ladles a cupful of water onto the stones.

Steam hisses fiercely as it rises to the ceiling, then mushrooms over the men and women inside the lodge. Hot vapor washes over the worshippers, stinging shoulders and curling hair. They breathe the hot air deeply. Sweat begins to pour, purifying their bodies. Thrashing themselves with switches of dried grass, they pray aloud. Again and again, water kisses the stones and steam boils out of the pit. At last, after many prayers, the man with the eagle fan signals to the doorman. The flap opens and cool air swirls around the worshippers, their bodies gleaming with sweat.

Waiting for the next round to begin, two of the women leave the lodge and splash themselves with icy water from a creek a few yards away. One of the men immerses himself in the creek while the others smoke.

The doorman adds more hot stones to the pile in the pit. When the man with the eagle fan gives the word, it is time to go back in. They enter one by one, circling from east to west, in a sun-wise direction. They sit around the stones, and the ceremony begins again.

Practiced throughout the Great Plains, the sweat lodge is a ritual of both spiritual and physical purification. Combining the elements of water, fire and stone, it cleanses the body and revitalizes the soul. In the old days, such lodges were built of a birch or willow framework and covered with buffalo hides. Today, they are usually covered with commercial blankets or carpet. Among some tribes, like the Gros Ventre, men and women use the sweat lodge together. Other tribes are appalled by the idea of men and women entering the sweat lodge at the same time.

While traveling in Indian Country, you sometimes see a few sweat lodges near creeks or behind houses, or perhaps just the willow skeletons of lodges that are no longer being used. Although there are a few organizations that will conduct sweat lodges for tourists, most "sweats" are held in private, within the heart of the community. Men who own sweat lodges must first receive the right to conduct the ceremony from a medicine man or elder. Plumes of cottonwood smoke on Sunday afternoon summon friends and relatives to join the fire-builder in a sweat, and the ritual is often followed by a feast.

Sweat lodges can be held alone or in conjunction with other ceremonies such as the sun dance, *yuwipi* and vision quest. They are also often used in traditional healing practices and for the general well-being of the participants. As always, visitors should not attend unless they are explicitly invited by one of the participants.

THE NORTHERN CHEYENNE

In the dim mists of Cheyenne memory, there is a golden time when there were no wars and no troubles. Dislodged from that early homeland, which may have been near Lake Superior, the Cheyennes knew little peace until the establishment of their Montana reservation in 1884.

"Cheyenne" is a corruption of the Sioux term *Sha-hie-na*, meaning "people speaking a language not understood." The Cheyennes, an Algonquin-speaking people, called themselves *Tsis-tsis-tas*, which means "the people."

Driven south from the Red River by the Assiniboine, the Cheyennes lived for a time in earthen lodges and raised corn among the village tribes of the Missouri River.

In the "dog days" before the "horse days," the Cheyennes collided with the Assiniboines, a tribe armed with guns, and were driven south. Before being overcome by whites, the Cheyennes waged war against the Kiowas, Comanches, Crows, Utes, Pawnees, Apaches and Shoshones.

To be killed in battle was a likely end for a Cheyenne in pre-contact days. The tribe often found replacements and an infusion of foreign blood in raids. One historian lists 28 tribes from which captives were taken by the Cheyennes. Most captives were children who were adopted, reared as Cheyenne, and married to Cheyenne mates.

The prophet Sweet Medicine foretold centuries of tribulation for his people, the end of the buffalo, and the coming of white people. Sweet Medicine gave the Cheyennes four sacred arrows received from God at Bear Butte in the Black Hills. Many Cheyennes blame their defeat by the whites and their subsequent poverty on the loss of the arrows in a raid against the Pawnees.

Somewhere on the Great Plains between the Black Hills and Oklahoma, the Cheyennes split into two tribes as buffalo hunters ranged north and south. Groups of people constantly traveled between the Southern Cheyenne and Northern Cheyenne tribes, a practice that continues today.

Sneak attack: Westward expansion, particularly the flow of gold-seekers into Colorado, crowded Cheyenne country and increased the number of white-Indian conflicts. A growing US, impatient to settle the West and move its cattle onto Cheyenne land, found it convenient to provoke attacks on villages filled with women and children.

The Cheyennes received their first taste of the whites' determination to dispossess them in 1864. It came to a group of Cheyennes camped on Sand Creek in eastern Colorado, waiting to sign a peace treaty. The leader of the camp, Chief Black Kettle, was led to believe he could forge a lasting peace with the whites if he came into the forts. But all the while the local commander, Col. J. M. Chivington, was stalling the Indians until he could attack. "Peace without conquest would be barbarous," he said. Chivington led a sneak attack on the village at dawn in the winter of 1864. He reported killing 600 Indians. The dead were of all ages and included women and children.

In 1868 Lieutenant Colonel George Armstrong Custer led his Seventh Calvary in a winter attack on a group of Cheyennes camped along the Washita River in Oklahoma. Again, women and children were shot down in an attempt to escape. The Cheyennes say Custer later smoked a pipe in Stone Forehead's lodge and vowed never to use his guns against the Cheyennes again. Ashes from the pipe were dumped onto the floor and ground into dust. Stone Forehead warned: "If you break this promise, you and your men will be scattered like this."

In June 1876, noted Cheyenne warrior Little Hawk discovered General George Crook's soldiers marching along Rosebud Creek in eastern Montana. Little Hawk raced back to his village and led a party of warriors back to attack. Crook was leading one of three columns of soldiers converging on the Little Big Horn Valley. With this unexpected clash with the Indians, Crook withdrew to the south to regroup and mend on Little Goose Creek. Knocking Crook out of the campaign may have contributed to Custer's demise eight days later.

The Cheyennes were camped at the lower end of the great village of 1,000 lodges on the Little Big Horn River when Custer attacked. Two Moon's Cheyenne warriors joined Crazy Horse's Sioux, riding north from the river, then west to crush Custer against Gall's warriors who pressed from the east.

The Indians won a great battle, but the war's outcome was a foregone conclusion. After the fight the Indians scattered. The army struck Chief Dull Knife's Cheyenne village on the Powder River, forcing his people to abandon everything they owned in flight. General Nelson Miles sent messengers from Fort Keogh to a large Northern Cheyenne village on the Tongue River asking the villagers to surrender. Two Moon said he would go to the fort alone. Anyone who wanted to follow him could do so.

Not long after, chiefs Dull Knife and Little Wolf surrendered and were moved to a reservation occupied by the Southern Cheyennes in Oklahoma. Unaccustomed to the climate and water of the area, many sickened and died.

Defying the army, Dull Knife and Little Wolf led their people north, back to the land they loved. The small band of 300 Cheyennes held fewer than 80 fighting men. The rest were women and children. In repeated clashes with the army they made their way to the Platte River, where Dull Knife split from the main body with about 150 Cheyennes. Both bands eventually surrendered. When Dull Knife refused to return to the south, the commander at Fort Robinson decided to starve his band into submission. More than half of Dull Knife's people were slaughtered when they attempted to escape.

The Cheyenne tour: In 1884 the Northern Cheyenne Reservation was established, 46,000 acres sandwiched between the Crow Reservation and the Tongue River. **Lame Deer**, the tribal capital, is nestled in a wooded valley that greens with spring rains and is splashed with bold autumn colors in late September.

Tourist facilities are few here. The **Cheyenne Arts and Crafts Shop** features locally-made authentic articles. Love flutes made of cedar are a find. Legend holds that such flutes in the hands of expert players turn into serpents and sing songs no woman can resist. Beaded buckskin, elk ivory and porcupine quill articles vary in quality.

Each June the four-day **Northern Cheyenne Powwow** at Lame Deer features giveaways, traditional and fancy dancing. Hand games, an ancient form of gambling, are held indoors. Accompanied by drums and chanting, the players on one side try to guess the location of a piece of bone that a rival player passes from hand to hand.

Ashland, 21 miles west of Lame Deer on Highway 212 just across the reservation line, is the home of **St Labre Mission** and site of an interesting modern church built in the shape of a tepee and covered with slate. Inside, a statue portrays Christ as a dog soldier, his ankle tied to a peg on the ground and

Final resting place of Custer's Seventh Cavalry.

obviously prepared to fight to the death.

Busby, 16 miles west of Lame Deer, is a rather bleak reservation town when compared with the bustle and activity of Lame Deer. Custer passed through here on his way to the Little Big Horn, where he met the ancestors of today's Northern Cheyennes.

Custer Battlefield National Monument is 26 miles east of Busby. Though in the heart of the Crow Indian Reservation, the battlefield is frequently the site of Cheyenne ceremonies, particularly the peace ceremonies of Austin Two Moon, a modern religious leader and descendant of Chief Two Moon.

Young Cheyenne men, some of them members of the militant American Indian Movement (AIM), joined one of its leaders, Russell Means, in demonstrations at the battlefield to pressure the federal government to recognize the sacrifice of Indians who fought there in defense of their women and children. The hill where Custer fell is the designated site for a monument the Park Service hopes to erect in the early 1990s.

The **Rosebud Battlefield** sprawls across a gulch about 20 miles south of Busby on Highway 314. Here, Cheyenne warriors joined Sioux allies in the decisive defeat of General Crook. Crook retreated to the present site of Sheridan, Wyoming, to recover.

The site, just off the reservation, is beautiful, especially in spring when chokecherry, wild plum and wild roses are in bloom. There is, however, very little interpretation. The road is passable in most weather but dusty when dry.

Cheyenne reverence for warriors is reflected today in the military enlistment rate of young Cheyenne men, highest of any ethnic group in every conflict since World War I. In peacetime, Cheyennes win recognition on the basketball court. Basketball is big in Indian Country, as big as football in the South or hockey in Canada. If the sun is shining, Cheyenne youth will be shooting baskets. On Friday and Saturday nights in winter, you will find young Cheyenne men running and gunning for glory on the basketball courts of Colstrip, Ashland and Busby.

Canyon snakes through the Pryor Mountains.

THE BLACKFEET

It was January 23, 1870, and the first gore of dawn was minutes away. The Blackfeet chief was already awake, listening to his heart. Something was wrong. A pony whinnied. A chorus of dogs tore the air across the river.

The chief heard the shouts of mixed-blood scout Joe Kipp. Something was wrong. Chief Heavy Runner bolted from his bed and fumbled through a pouch for the paper he received from Lieutenant Colonel Alfred H. Sully, superintendent of Indian Affairs for Montana Territory. The paper said the chief was a "good Indian," attested to his peaceful conduct, and promised his safety.

Outside, two hundred .50-caliber carbines of the Second Cavalry were trained on the village. Lieutenant Colonel Eugene M. Baker had marched his men through the chill of 40 below zero to strike at this village on the Marias River in northern Montana, where several renegades were harbored. He found instead a village of invalids. Kipp realized the mistake, but too late. Baker ordered him to shut up and told another soldier to shoot him if he yelled again.

A gun barked. A slug the size of a pullet's egg caught Heavy Runner in the chest. He pitched face down into the snow, still clutching his paper shield. The chief would not hear the first volley sluice through the bottoms of lodges to kill women and children, many suffering from smallpox in their beds. The guns would speak again and again. Some villagers scattered into the brush along the river. A few reached the horse herd and galloped downstream, but the rest were cut down.

The Baker Massacre was finished. More than 150 Indians were killed but only 15 men of fighting age. The Blackfeet tasted the bluecoats' might. Their life was never the same again.

One hundred years later, on the 1.5-million-acre Blackfeet Indian Reservation in northern Montana, old ways echo in the powwow songs and pulsing drum beat of Blackfeet singers. Dancing men and women in colorful powwow regalia – a blur of buckskin, feathers, beadwork and bells – recall earlier days, before Lieutenant Colonel Baker came with his guns, before white ranchers came with their cattle, before Blackfeet life was changed forever.

But some things remain the same. The Blackfeet still honor the four directions with the sacred pipe, and go to the sweat lodge to purify their bodies and spirits. They still seek visions alone in the wilderness, and offer their flesh at the sun dance.

The sun still sets as it did back then, gloriously saturated with red and orange. To the west, in Glacier National Park – traditional Blackfeet land – bighorn sheep, moose and elk still roam highland trails; the sun still dazzles the surface of placid, icy lakes; the mist still shrouds remote mountain peaks. Much has changed in Blackfeet Country – but much has stayed the same.

Cossacks of the Northern Plains: Siska, Piegan and Bloods – three branches of the Blackfeet, the Cossacks of the

Northern Plains in the early 19th century. The Blackfeet pushed the Gros Ventres to the Sascatchewan River, and checked the western advance of the Sioux. The Nez Perces stole across the mountains to hunt buffalo on the plains only after the Blackfeet had settled into their winter camp. Jesuit priest Father DeSmet marveled at the neighboring Kootenais' eagerness to embrace Christianity. But the Kootenais' conversion was no miracle. The Blackfeet had already filled them with the fear of God. When Manuel Lisa established the first fur fort in the beaver-rich wilderness explored by the Lewis and Clark expedition, John Colter persuaded him to build his post on the Yellowstone River. Beaver swarmed on the headwaters of the Missouri, but so did the Blackfeet. Colter reckoned it better to take fur in Crow territory than to leave his hair in Blackfeet Country.

Then came three blows to break the back and spirit of the Blackfeet Nation. A steamboat belching black smoke pulled into Mandan Indian villages on the Missouri River with a deadly cargo. Several men aboard were dying of smallpox. Some Indian accounts say whites handed out blankets infected with the big measles. White traders said the Mandans wouldn't listen when they were warned to stay away from the boat, that they swarmed aboard and stole cloth and other trade goods.

It did not matter. Blackfeet would die for others' sins. The whites' little warriors struck the Mandans with a fury that extinguished the tribe. A few stragglers moved in with Ree and Arikara cousins and the Mandans were no more. The pox hit Assiniboines at Fort Union, where they died by the hundreds.

A keelboat carried the disease to Fort McKenzie. Trader Alexander Culbertson tried to warn the Blackfeet away, but his warnings only aroused their suspicions. Blackfeet were not easily frightened. They came and left. When they failed to return, Culbertson set out to find them. At the Three Forks of the Missouri he found a major camp where only two people remained alive. "Hun-

Traditional dancer at North American Indian Days.

168

dreds of decaying forms of human beings, horses and dogs lay scattered about," he reported.

With the close of the Civil War, "free grass" was discovered in the Missouri-Yellowstone country and Texans trailed longhorn cattle onto that grassy sea to graze the Blackfeet buffalo pasture. Bad Gun's poor people would grow poorer. In 1871, Blackfeet destiny became enmeshed in the cogs and gears of the Industrial Revolution. A tanning process invented that year could convert buffalo hides into tough, durable leather suitable for machine belts. A limited demand for buffalo pelts became an insatiable industrial market. In 1871, the northern herd, the Blackfeet's wealth, numbered a million animals. By 1883, the buffalo were gone.

Young warriors begged to carry the pipe against the white hunters and cattlemen, but chiefs who had traveled to Washington, DC, to treat with the president had seen the "great villages" of the whites and knew the futility of waging war against such numbers.

Then came the winter of 1883–84, the grim season recalled as the "Starvation Winter of the Blackfeet." Six hundred Piegans would die of starvation. The spring of 1884 would begin a sad new era for the Blackfeet. They were now dependent on the invading whites. The Cossacks of the Plains had become wards of the government.

They were driven to accept the government's handouts, the white people's largess. At Fort Benton, the government gave them hogs' heads and dried beans. They buried the pigs' heads and threw away the beans. "We didn't know how to cook these things," a survivor recalled. In the winter of starvation the Blackfeet would die at a rate of two to six a day. Tuberculosis, scrofula and other diseases, aggravated by malnutrition, filled coffins as fast as the agency carpenter could build them.

Traveling Blackfeet Country: Any tour of Blackfeet Country must begin in Browning, seat of tribal government and home of the **Northern Plains Indian Museum**. The museum is oper-

Sunset blaze over Blackfeet Reservation.

ated by the US Department of the Interior and admission is free. Just outside the museum is a medicine rock where tribal members leave offerings of tobacco and cloth. Inside, the traveler will find murals portraying Blackfeet life 200 years ago, mannequins in authentic dress, and the war history of Mountain Chief on a painted buffalo robe.

The **Historic Gallery** features displays of children's games, the Native American Church and articles of war and daily life among the buffalo hunters. Contemporary Indian artists are featured in another gallery, and a five-minute slide presentation narrated by Vincent Price traces the history of the Plains Indians.

The **Northern Plains Crafts Association** has a reputation for high quality. One-of-a-kind beaded purses and jewelry contrast sharply with tourist-trap gimcracks sold elsewhere.

Less than a block away, the **Montana Wildlife Museum** features stuffed buffalo, elk, and other animals. This museum is also a showcase for the sculp-

ture of Bob Scribner. **Scribner's Hall of Bronze** traces the history of the Blackfeet from pre-contact times to 1900 in a series of bronze statues.

While in Browning, try the cuisine. Fry bread, beef stew and Indian tacos are "soul food" here. Fry bread is bread dough that is deep fat fried and usually served with honey. Indian tacos are the Plains Indian adaptation of the Mexican fast-food favorite, using fry bread in place of tortillas.

Travelers fortunate enough to arrive during the second weekend in July will find the Blackfeet capital invaded by tribes from Canada to the Mexican border. **North American Indian Days** feature powwow dancing, singing, Indian rodeo and parades.

Glacier National Park holds the most spectacular and pristine alpine scenery of all the nation's parks, studded with 10,000-ft peaks and laced with glacier-fed lakes. The park is Blackfeet homeland, ceded to the US in 1896. The present reservation and Glacier National Park share a 60-mile boundary along

Blackfeet warriors, 1915.

the Rocky Mountain Front. Nowhere along the Continental Divide is the rise from buffalo grass to glacier-capped peaks so abrupt.

Highway 89 follows the route of the old **North Trail**, an ancient Indian road, well worn by travois that ran along the eastern slopes of the mountains from Edmonton, Alberta, to Helena, Montana. Plains Indians used the trail for war parties and horse-stealing raids. Nearly 10,000 years ago, the first paleolithic hunters followed extensions of this trail from Alaska to Mexico.

Glacier National Park's four eastern entrances are within an hour's drive of Browning. First class accommodations and fine dining are available at rustic and stately lodges at East Glacier at the southern end of the park on Highway 2 or at St Mary's Lodge or Many Glacier just off Highway 89.

Glacier is a hiker's paradise. Rugged high-country trails challenge the adventuresome. Nature walks guided by park rangers await those who would enjoy leisure amid Glacier's majesty. Hour-long cruises aboard SceniCruise Line boats plying St Mary's, Two Medicine and Swift Current lakes are a bargain at $5 for adults, $2.50 for children.

Travelers driving the Rocky Mountain Front along Highway 89 might circle north across the international border to Cardston, Alberta, to shop for Hudson Bay blankets or Canadian woolens. Alberta Routes 5 and 6 bring the visitor back to the US via Canada's **Waterton Lakes National Park**.

Chief Mountain, a distinctive peak, looms to the west of Highway 89. Northbound travelers will see it just before crossing into Canada. Sacred to the Blackfeet, this mountain is still used as a fasting and vision quest site.

Only one road crosses Glacier Park, the **Going to the Sun Highway**. This spectacular route weaves through peaks where grizzly bears roam over the Continental Divide. The highway is safe but slow and intimidating to some motorists. Accidents are rare and seldom serious, but dizzying heights can make the trip uncomfortable.

Glacier National Park.

THE NORTHWEST

From the lush rain forests of the Olympic Peninsula to the snow-capped peaks of the Cascade Range, from the frigid, raging waters of the Columbia River to the placid, rippling surface of Flathead Lake, the native Northwest is a remarkable region of vast environmental and cultural diversity.

Before the coming of white people, the Northwest coast was one of the most densely populated and culturally rich areas in the American West. The fantastic bounty of natural resources supported a great blossoming of cultures, languages and material wealth among the tribes of the Puget Sound (Duwamish, Quinault, Suquamish, Makah and others) and northward, along the Canadian coast.

To the south, the tribes of the Columbia Plateau supported their longstanding villages on the frenzied salmon runs of the Columbia River and its tributaries as well as on an abundance of game and wild foods.

To the west, the Yakimas, Shoshones, Bannocks, Salish, Kootenais, Paiutes and Nez Perces ranged across the sheltered valleys, wooded mountains and rugged canyon lands of inland Washington, Oregon, Idaho and western Montana. Among the first native people in the West to learn the arts of horsemanship, they occasionally rode onto the plains to hunt buffalo, adopting many of the customs and accoutrements of Plains Indian life.

Today, the cultures of the native Northwest live on in the beat of the powwow drum, the smoldering fires of the salmon feast, the hands of artists and craftsmen, and the beliefs and visions of the people. The Northwest is still a land of luxuriant natural beauty, rich with the traditions of its native people, and touched by the rhythms of Native American life.

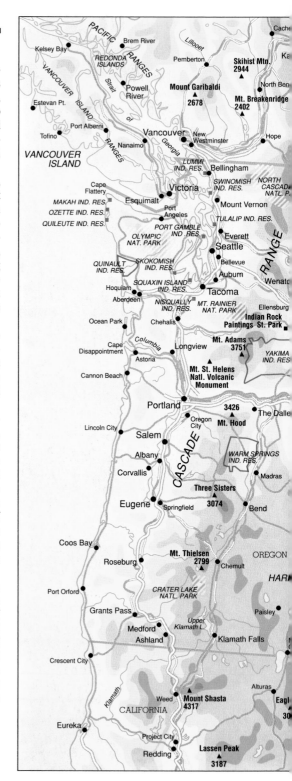

Preceding pages: traditional dancer.

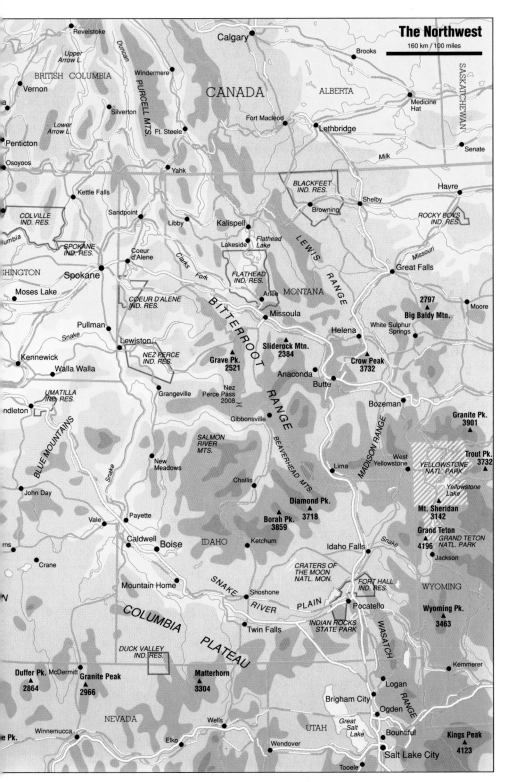

The Northwest

160 km / 100 miles

Revelstoke
Calgary
Brooks

Upper Arrow L.
Duncan
Windermere
CANADA
ALBERTA
Medicine Hat

BRITISH COLUMBIA
SASKATCHEWAN

Vernon
Silverton
Ft. Steele
Fort Macleod
Lethbridge

Lower Arrow L.
PURCELL MTS.
Senate

Penticton
Milk

Osoyoos
Yahk
Havre

Kettle Falls
BLACKFEET IND. RES.
Shelby

COLVILLE IND. RES.
Sandpoint
Libby
Kalispell
Browning
ROCKY BOYS IND. RES.

Columbia
SPOKANE IND. RES.
Coeur d'Alene
Lakeside
Flathead Lake
LEWIS
Missouri
Great Falls

WASHINGTON
Spokane
Clarks Fork
FLATHEAD IND. RES.
Arlee
MONTANA
RANGE
2797
Moore

Moses Lake
COEUR D'ALENE IND. RES.
Missoula
Helena
White Sulphur Springs
Big Baldy Mtn.

Pullman
Snake
Lewiston
NEZ PERCE IND. RES.
BITTERROOT
Sliderock Mtn. 2384
Crow Peak 3732

Kennewick
Grave Pk. 2521
Anaconda
Butte

Walla Walla
Grangeville
Nez Perce Pass 2008
RANGE
Bozeman

UMATILLA IND. RES.
Gibbonsville
BEAVERHEAD MTS.
MADISON RANGE
Granite Pk. 3901

Pendleton
BLUE MOUNTAINS
SALMON RIVER MTS.
West Yellowstone
Trout Pk. 3732

New Meadows
Lima
YELLOWSTONE NATL. PARK

John Day
Snake
Challis
Yellowstone Lake

Vale
Payette
Diamond Pk. 3718
Mt. Sheridan 3142

Crane
Caldwell
Boise
IDAHO
Ketchum
Borah Pk. 3859
Idaho Falls
Snake
Grand Teton 4196
GRAND TETON NATL. PARK

Jackson

Mountain Home
SNAKE
CRATERS OF THE MOON NATL. MON.
FORT HALL IND. RES.
WYOMING

Shoshone
RIVER
PLAIN
Pocatello
Wyoming Pk. 3463

Twin Falls
INDIAN ROCKS STATE PARK

COLUMBIA
DUCK VALLEY IND. RES.
WASATCH
Kemmerer

Duffer Pk. 2864
McDermitt
Granite Peak 2966
Matterhorn 3304
Logan
RANGE

PLATEAU
Brigham City
Ogden

NEVADA
Wells
Great Salt Lake
Bountiful
Kings Peak 4123

Winnemucca
UTAH
Salt Lake City

Pk.
Elko
Wendover
Tooele

175

THE TRIBES OF PUGET SOUND

In 1854, on the watery frontier of Puget Sound, a group of Indian tribes from Washington Territory gathered with US military officers to sign the Treaty of Medicine Creek. Whites were settling the region and wanted more land. The tide of change was flowing, and one great leader, recognized by all as a peacekeeper, uttered these words in the Duwamish tongue: "Every part of this earth is sacred to my people. Every shining pine needle, every sandy shore, every mist in the dark woods, every clearing and humming insect is holy in the memory of my people. The sap which courses through the trees carries the memories of the red man."

Chief Sealth, for whom the city of Seattle is named, watched as the Indian world succumbed to white settlement. The way of life of his tribe and many others was forever altered, but not extinguished. Over the past 150 years, many tribes in the Puget Sound area have survived the changes, evolving and yet preserving their heritage.

Like the environment in which they developed, the cultures of the Northwest coast were rich and diverse. Like the frenzy of a salmon run, they were given to explosive expressions of material wealth. Like the lush growth of Pacific forests, they spawned a blossoming of language, belief and artistic vision. Before white people came, Indians lived on a bounty of roots, berries, seeds, game, and most importantly, salmon. They wove their clothes and baskets from grasses and made houses, tools and canoes from cedar trees.

They shared their fortune at celebrations called potlatches where members of different tribes gathered to celebrate a marriage, a good hunt, a reburial, a naming, or the first salmon run of the season. The guests feasted, exchanged gifts and played stick games. The hosts were wealthy families who competed with each other in gift-giving; the more gifts given, the greater the honor.

The spiritual life of the Northwest natives was rich in its connection with the surrounding world of nature. Every living thing was believed to have a spirit, and each person had a song to summon the spirit's help. There were ceremonies throughout the year, many to honor the spirits of the animals and fish that provided their subsistence. These ceremonies were conducted before hunting, fishing or whaling to ask the animal spirits to be generous, and then again afterwards, to give thanks.

But as powerful as those days were, the Northwest has become a different place. Today, Indian people live in the modern world. Although they have preserved much of their heritage, they no longer live in longhouses, paddle canoes to their nets or wear clothes of woven reeds. What travelers see in this day and age is a mixture of old and new.

On the dark waters of Hood Canal, in a small powerboat, a Skokomish family fishes for salmon. Inland, in a tumbledown house with an abandoned car out front, a man with a graying braid weaves a basket in the old way and tells the story

eft, **Makah** *anoes*, **Neah** *ay.* **Right**, **Muckleshoot** *sherman.*

of the family argument that left the car to rust in front of his house. Down the road, tribal bureaucrats arrive at the administration building to take care of the day's business. And farther down the road, their children pile off a school bus and into the brick school where they learn not how to weave or fish, but how to multiply and divide.

Northwest natives lived undisturbed until relatively recently. Though early European explorers reached the Puget Sound, they didn't stay, and left behind only glass beads and metal tools.

It wasn't until the mid-19th century, when white settlers began streaming into the Northwest, that native people started suffering the epidemic disease and loss of land that eastern tribes had already experienced. Hundreds of thousands of acres were lost in the 1850s as a result of hastily executed treaties. Once signed, some treaties weren't ratified by the US Congress for years, and many tribes were cheated out of reservations and other benefits for which they had exchanged their homelands. In 1882, Congress passed the General Allotment Act, which broke reservations into individually owned tracts and opened the surplus (and usually most valuable) land to settlers. Some tribes are still struggling to regain control of their "checkerboard" land and to make sense of their confusing legal status.

Recently, some tribes have fought to retain their fishing rights – the very core of their economic viability. A long legal battle culminated in the 1970s with the Boldt Decision, which stated that treaties must be honored. The tribes are now entitled to half of the harvestable fish and can fish off-reservation in their "usual and accustomed places."

Starting With Seattle: Seattle, named for the great Duwamish chief, Sealth, is the aboriginal home of that tribe and a good place to begin a reservation tour. Like many regional tribes, the Duwamish are not recognized by the federal government. Thus, although they have an organized government, they have no reservation or fishing rights. A group of such tribes has joined together to form

Totem pole and longhouse, trademarks of Pacific Northwest art

STOWW, Small Tribes of Western Washington, to help provide better services to their members and strengthen their efforts for recognition.

In Seattle, travelers can get an overview of traditional and contemporary Northwest culture at the **Burke Museum** and the **Daybreak Star Art Gallery**. The Burke, on the University of Washington campus, has a recently renovated Northwest native exhibit which includes descriptions of all Washington tribes, examples of native material culture and accounts of native life before and after contact with whites. Daybreak Star, in Discovery Park, displays both contemporary and traditional art that will familiarize visitors with native motifs, little changed over time.

If time allows, you can also catch the boat (Pier 56) to **Tillicum Village** across the harbor on Blake Island, where visitors are treated to traditional Northwest dancing, storytelling, carving demonstrations and a salmon feast.

Eastern Peninsula: From downtown Seattle, the ferry sets out across the Puget Sound for Bainbridge Island. Across the island and just beyond Agate Passage Bridge lies the 7,800-acre **Port Madison Reservation**, established by the Treaty of Point Elliott in 1855 and home to the Suquamish tribe. The Suquamish are marine fishermen like their ancestors, who traveled the Sound in cedar canoes to harvest salmon and shellfish.

For the Suquamish, as for many of the region's tribes, the art of canoe-making was well developed by the time whites arrived. There were canoes designed for many different purposes: fishing, traveling, whaling and hunting. Today, tribes still make canoes, although predominantly for display or racing.

Hand-hewn canoes are on display at the **Suquamish Museum and Cultural Center** at its tribal headquarters on the shores of Agate Passage. There are also exhibits about traditional life and a slide show narrated by tribal elders.

On the Passage beach are the remains of **Old Man House**, a longhouse built by Chief Sealth to bring the region's

Lummi
Festival.

tribes together – a sort of United Nations. It was later destroyed at the direction of an Indian agent when the official federal policy was to eradicate Indian culture. Inland, near the town of Suquamish, stands the **tomb of Chief Sealth**, whose speech at the treaty-signing survives in translation as a reminder of the profoundly tragic passing of a way of life. Each August, the tribe honors him with **Chief Sealth Day**, a celebration of goodwill with games, food and music to which all visitors are welcome. The tribe also hosts an annual **Native American Art Fair** in early spring.

Farther north along the peninsula are the small Klallam tribes. Many people think the Klallam, or Strong People, once dominated the northern coast and were the first to encounter white explorers who sailed into the Straits of San Juan de Fuca. There are three Klallam tribes: the Port Gamble Klallam, Jamestown Klallam and Elwha Klallam. There are no tourist facilities, but patient travelers can learn a lot by visiting or calling the tribes to see collections of old photographs and artifacts or to get dates for an upcoming powwow.

Western Peninsula: At the northwesternmost tip of the continental US lies the **Makah Reservation**, wild and lush. The first stop on this 44-sq. mile sanctuary is the **Makah Cultural and Research Center** with displays on regional native history. Many of the artifacts, thousands of years old, were found at the nearby excavations of the Hoko and Ozette coastal fishing villages. There are also full-scale replicas of a longhouse, whaling canoes and equipment, and baskets used for everything from clam collecting to cooking. Everything was made with what nature provided: cedar, seal skins, tule, hemp, roots and grasses. There are even a few people who still practice these arts.

Makah is a hiker's paradise with trails leading through lush forest down to the beach. One moderate trail (about 6 miles round-trip) descends the wooded cliff to **Shi-Shi Beach**, one of the few remaining wild beaches in the country. A less

Makah salmon bake.

demanding trail leads to **Cape Flattery**, the northwesternmost point in the continental US, where the view is sweeping and dramatic, especially during the spring whale-watching season.

The Makah, or People of the Cape, a tribe of about 1,500, want to preserve their environment, so they ask visitors not to harvest seafood or comb the beaches without official permission. The tribe licenses freshwater anglers for fishing on the Waatch and Sooes rivers and provides guides for beach touring.

In late August, the tribe sponsors **Makah Days**, where all are welcome to enjoy salmon bakes, canoe races and other events. Motel and resort facilities are available in Neah Bay.

South of Makah, along the Pacific coast, are three tiny reservations: Ozette, Quileute and Hoh. They lack facilities, but the rare beauty of pristine beaches and rivers is reason enough to visit. Ozette is accessible by a stunning 3-mile hike from the Lake Ozette Ranger Station, and is the site of an excavation of a 2,500-year-old fishing village. The Quileute, who live near the coastal resort town of LaPush, celebrate **Elders Week** and **Quileute Days** during the summer.

Covering 196,600 acres, the **Quinault Reservation** is the largest on the western peninsula. Quinault is home to seven tribes. Some of them, like the small Waukiakum band of the Chinook tribe, signed treaties but never received land of their own. Others, like the Cowlitz, never signed treaties but maintain tribal identity through meetings and newsletters.

Like the Makah, the Quinault like to keep a close eye on their resources, including miles of untouched beaches. Travelers are asked to check in at tribal headquarters before walking on the beach or fishing the Quinault River. One of the many summer celebrations, **Chief Taholah Days**, in early July, gives visitors the best opportunity to meet people and learn about the tribes, their history and contemporary life.

At the southern tip of the Quinault Reservation, near Tokeland, is the

TOTEM POLES

Northwest natives are carvers by tradition, but it was the natives of the far north, in what is now British Columbia and Alaska, who first carved totem poles. The history of these fascinating works is surprisingly brief, for it wasn't until the mid-18th century, when European explorers first encountered these remote tribes, that the unique sculptures began to appear. Although the natives were already expert carvers of canoes, tools, longhouses and furniture, they lacked the iron tools necessary to fell a massive tree in one piece and carve its entire length.

With the iron axes they got in trade for their baskets, boxes and pelts, the coastal tribes of the far north could take advantage of the trees that grew so tall and straight in their wet climate. Initially, the poles were made to stand against the front of a house, with figures facing out and a door cut through the base, so all would enter the house through the pole. In this case, the totem pole functioned as a family crest, recounting genealogies, stories or legends that in some way identified the owner. Towards the end of the 19th century, the poles stood free on the beach or in the village outside the carvers' homes. Some villages were virtual forests of dozens, sometimes hundreds, of poles.

The family that carved the pole gave a potlatch with feasting, games and much gift-giving. The guests, in return, raised the pole. These gatherings were costly and required a great deal of preparation and participation. The custom frustrated whites trying to "civilize" the Indians, especially missionaries who solved the problem by knocking the poles down. Employers, too, complained that their Indian workers were unreliable when a pole was being carved or a potlatch planned. Eventually, both the Canadian and United States governments banned potlatches, and pole carving nearly died out. The ban was lifted in the 1950s.

The Tlingit, on the southeastern coast of Alaska, and the Haidas and Tsimshian of western Canada are known for their pole carving. On a tour in 1899, a group of Seattle businessmen visited the Tlingit village of Tongas and, finding no one there, took one of the poles. They erected it in Seattle where, at a towering 50 ft, it became one of the city's most distinctive monuments. In 1938, Tlingit carvers copied the pole after the original was destroyed by fire, and it remains in Pioneer Square today.

Poles serve the important purpose of recording the lore of a clan, much as a book would. The top figure on the pole identifies the owner's clan, and succeeding characters (read from top to bottom) tell their stories. Raven, the trickster, might tell the story of how he fooled the Creator into giving him the sun, or Frog might tell how he wooed a human woman. With slight variations between villages, everyone knew these stories, and potlatch guests dramatized them at the pole-raising with masks, drumming and songs. And so the legends were preserved from one generation to the next.

There is a story behind almost every image on the pole. For example, if an animal had the power to transform itself into other beings, the carver would portray it in all its forms. If Raven was sometimes bird, sometimes human, he would be carved with both wings and limbs, or have a human face with a raven's beak. Other images are used to describe the spirits' special abilities. Eyes are frequently used to suggest acuteness or skill. So, for example, if an eye appears in an animal's ear, it might indicate that that animal has a sharp sense of hearing. And human figures in unexpected places, like an ear or nose, might mean that the animal has great powers.

Learning to read totem poles is like learning to read a language. They speak of history, mythology, social structure and spirituality. They serve many purposes and continue to be carved by the descendants of the original carvers.

Today, Haida, Tlingit, Tsimshian, Kwakiutl and other native craftsmen carve, predominantly for the tourist trade, small "souvenir" totem poles in wood and black slate (or argillite). They also carve extraordinarily beautiful masks, effigies, boxes, house posts and figures. Totem poles can be viewed at the Museum of Anthropology (University of British Columbia) in Vancouver, and the Royal British Columbia Museum in Victoria.

Shoalwater Bay Reservation. Home to a small tribe with a proud history, this reservation is a unique environment of ocean, bay, tideland and river.

Southern Puget Sound: There are several small tribes at the base of the Puget Sound, where its narrow fingers cut into the peninsula. These include the Chehalis, Skokomish, Nisqually and Squaxin Island tribes. These reservations can be difficult to find, so it is best to begin with a trip to tribal headquarters where there are people to talk to and, on occasion, small exhibits. A few tribes host summer feasts, including the **First Salmon Celebration** at Nisqually and **Chehalis Tribal Day**.

After rounding the tip of the sound and passing through rural Nisqually, there are two more reservations before reaching Seattle. The first belongs to the Puyallup, whose original name in Salish means "Welcoming and Generous." The tribe was hit hard by white settlers who displaced them from the deepwater port now occupied by Tacoma. The tribe held onto its valuable property until 1990 when it gave up its rights to much of the port in exchange for a large settlement that included services and cash. The Puyallup still have a reservation, however, and visitors are welcome to attend the annual **Labor Day Powwow**.

Just north of Tacoma, near Auburn, is the **Muckleshoot Reservation**. Its 800 residents are descendants of the Skopmish, Stkamish and Smulkamish tribes. Aside from a smokeshop, liquor store and bingo hall, there is little of interest for most travelers, although this is as good a place as any to get a glimpse of reservation life.

Northern Puget Sound: Roughly 30 miles north of Seattle, **Tulalip** is one of the larger Puget Sound reservations, occupying some 22,000 acres. Tulalip Tribes Incorporated includes a number of tribes, all signers of the Treaty of Point Elliott. With more than 2,000 members, it operates several enterprises, including a large hatchery that welcomes visitors. During Labor Day weekend the tribes sponsor **Kla-How-Ya Days**, and there are occasional smokehouse

Cutting through the waters of the Quinault Reservation.

ceremonies and canoe races. Snoqual-mie, in Redmond, also welcomes visitors and can provide group salmon bakes.

Inland from Tulalip, toward the Cascade Mountains, are several small reservations, each with a unique history but none with facilities for travelers. The Stillaguamish, or Canoe People, recently won federal recognition. Although many were driven onto Tulalip Reservation because of white encroachment, they have now acquired their own tract of land by the Stillaguamish River. Deeper in the mountains, the Sauk-Suiattle also won recognition and a reservation recently. The tribe is working to preserve the fish and trees that are part of its heritage.

Under the Treaty of Point Elliott, the Swinomish, Lower Skagit, Kikiallus and Samish people, originally from the San Juan Islands, retained a 10-sq. mile reservation. The **Swinomish Reservation** is particularly amenable to tourism because of its proximity to the tourist town of **La Conner**. Directly across the Swinomish Channel from La Conner,

the tribe operates the Longhouse Restaurant. The tribe also plans to develop a marina and reconstruct Twiwok, an archaeological village site. Farther east, near Sedro Wooley, the **Upper Skagit Reservation** is home to the tribe known for its participation in the Indian Shaker religion, which combines native and Christian beliefs. The Upper Skagit are also known for their beautiful bentwood boxes, still made by hand, named for their bent, not cut, edges.

The **Lummi** are the farthest north of the Puget Sound tribes. Their 13,500-acre reservation is on the shores of Lummi Bay and the Puget Sound where they have fished for centuries. Traditionally, they used weirs, reef nets and stakes, sophisticated tools that have been adopted by non-Indian fishermen. The best opportunity to meet the Lummi is at the **Stommish Festival** in early summer at Gooseberry Point. Travelers can watch traditional canoe races, sample smoked salmon and buy coastal Indian art.

Up the Canadian Coast: The road continues northward into Canada ,where it soon becomes clear that the line now drawn between nations is artificial. Indian cultures north and south of the border are closely related, the thread running all the way up to Alaska and, some think, beyond. The continuity is well-documented in Canada's fine provincial and tribal museums. In the city of Vancouver, at the University of British Columbia, there are excellent exhibits on native culture at the **Museum of Anthropology**. And in Victoria, the **Royal British Columbia Museum** has native culture displays and an exceptional display of masks.

At the far end of Vancouver Island, small tribal museums in Campbell River and Alert Bay reveal something of the more northerly cultures. The thread of Pacific Northwest cultures continues unbroken all the way to the Nootka, Kwakiutl, Haida and Tlingit tribal groups along the Alaskan coast and across the Bering Strait. Many tribes and their ways of life are gone, but many others remain to teach the cultural explorer the lessons of beauty, balance and survival.

Left, canoes are still made for feasts and races. **Right**, Skokomish box carver.

COLVILLE AND YAKIMA

One of the largest reservations in the Pacific Northwest, the Colville Indian Reservation is located in north-central Washington, bounded on the east and south by the Columbia River and on the west by the Okanogan River. Within the boundaries of this 1.4-million-acre reservation, lush grasslands sweep to the edge of dense coniferous forests; lakes and rushing rivers sparkle against the backdrop of jagged gorges and mountainsides. This is inland Washington's Indian Country, marked by petroglyphs, native myths, and a rich and colorful history.

Eleven bands make up the Confederated Tribes of the Colville Indian Reservation. These include the Wenatchee, Moses/Columbia, Okanogan, Entiat/Chelan, Methow, Palouse, Nez Perce, Nespelem, Colville, Sanpoil and Lake bands. All were autonomous ethnic and political units during aboriginal times and, except for the Nez Perce and Palouse, occupied the central area of the Columbia Plateau. The original Colville Indian Reservation extended north to the Canadian border, as did the adjoining reservation of Chief Moses. The present reservation was established by executive order in 1872.

Chief Moses and his followers were removed to Colville when their own reservation was canceled in 1883 owing to the incursion of gold-hungry settlers. Moses later invited the Palouse to move to Colville after they were pushed out of the Snake River Canyon area. As a result of the move, Colville was honored by the presence of leaders like the ranking Palouse chief, Tespalus, and the sons of the highly respected Yakima chief, Kamiakin.

In 1885, a branch of the Nez Perce tribe was relocated to the Colville Reservation by the federal government. The Nez Perces were among the first Indians in the Northwest to make friendly contact with whites. The Lewis and Clark expedition spent several weeks with the Nez Perces and its men and horses were

treated well. The Nez Perces often boasted that in 70 years they had never killed a white man. But friendship was a thin shield against the onslaught of white prospectors. When gold was discovered in Chief Joseph's Wallowa Mountains in the 1870s, the cry went out for the removal of the tribe.

Rather than fight, Joseph's people fled, hoping to find refuge in Canada with Sitting Bull and his band of Hunkpapa Sioux. Led by chiefs Ollokot (Joseph's brother), Looking Glass, Toohoolhoolzote and White Bird, the Nez Perces outmaneuvered and outfought the troops over 1,500 miles with less than 100 warriors. During the retreat, Joseph supervised the rescue of the 500 women, children, elderly and wounded as well as the horse and cattle herds. Finally, on October 4, 1877, his people cold and starving, Joseph surrendered. The refugees were exiled for almost eight years in Indian Territory.

During his years of exile, Joseph never ceased trying to persuade the government to return his people to their home-

land. "You might as well expect the rivers to run backward as that any man who was born free should be contented penned up and denied liberty," he said. On May 22, 1885, Joseph and his remaining followers were released from Indian Territory and returned to the Northwest, but not to their traditional territory in the Wallowa Valley. Joseph and 140 others were sent to Colville, while 118 continued to Lapwai, Idaho, the Nez Perce Reservation.

Joseph died in Nespelem, Washington, on September 21, 1904, while sitting before his tepeefire. The agency doctor reported that he died of a broken heart. He is buried at Nespelem, his grave marked by a towering stone.

A lesser-known but nonetheless noteworthy Colville figure is Humishuma, or Cristal Quintasket, the author of the first novel by a Native American, *Cogowea, the Half-Blood* (1927). Humishuma began writing because she wanted to preserve the stories of her Okanogan people. Her efforts resulted in *Coyote Stories* (1933), a collection of Okanogan myths that feature the familiar trickster and culture hero, Coyote, who paves the way for the Indians by slaying monsters.

Woods and water: There is plenty to do and see on the Colville Reservation, but don't expect a hubbub. The area offers a wide variety of recreation with its crystal-blue lakes, rivers, unbroken wilderness, mountains and sunny climate. Wherever you are, woods and water are only a short ride away.

As progressive business people, the Confederated Tribes of Colville have invested in several tribally owned tourist ventures. The most impressive is Roosevelt Recreational Enterprises, which operates luxury houseboat rentals year-round on Lake Roosevelt in the heart of **Coulee Dam National Recreation Area**. The tribe also rents smaller fishing boats and speed boats fully equipped for waterskiing.

The Confederated Tribes also own the **Colville Cultural Museum** in the town of Coulee Dam. Exhibits include native crafts and artwork, coyote stories

Fancy dancer shows his colors.

CHIEF JOSEPH AND THE NEZ PERCES

Before he died in 1871, Chief Joseph's father, Tuekakas, counseled his son: "When I am gone, think of your country. You are the chief of these people. They look to you to guide them. A few more years and the whites will be all around you. They have eyes on this land."

The old man knew well white people's appetite for land. Twice government men had come with treaties pushing the Nez Perces out of their country, and twice Tuekakas refused. "This country holds your father's body," he told his son. "Never sell the bones of your father and mother."

Before the Americans came, the Nez Perces ranged over the grasslands, canyons and high-country forests west of the Bitterroot Mountains. They welcomed Lewis and Clark's ragged expedition in 1805 and befriended the whites that followed. Some Nez Perces, including Tuekakas and Joseph, even accepted the white people's faith and called themselves by Christian names.

But Nez Perce friendship was not enough for the Americans; they wanted Nez Perce land, too. In 1873, after Tuekakas' death, the government men came back to Joseph's band with an old treaty and demanded that they move to a reservation. But Tuekakas had never signed that treaty; he had never agreed to give up his country. "If ever we owned the land," Joseph explained, "we own it still, for we have never sold it."

The young chief's logic fell on deaf ears. The government gave Joseph's people an ultimatum: leave their homes in 30 days or be driven out by force. There were warriors among the band that cried out for blood, but Joseph knew that the odds were hopeless. "Better to live at peace," he said, "than to begin a war and lie dead."

Within 30 days, Joseph's people began their journey, losing much of their livestock to raging rivers and predatory whites. But before the band could finish its march, a group of young braves fired with anger slipped out of camp and murdered 11 whites. "I would have given my own life if I could have undone the killing of white men," Joseph said

later, but before any reparations could be made, the soldiers were upon them.

What followed over the next four months was one of the most daring, heroic and strategic retreats ever fought by Indian warriors. Together with chiefs Toohoolhoolzote, Looking Glass and Ollokot, Joseph led the band of 650 over 1,300 rugged miles, evading and engaging troops far superior in numbers and firepower.

They had hoped to take refuge in Canada, possibly joining Sitting Bull's band. But only 30 miles from the border, they were halted in their tracks. With his camp bogged down by snow and surrounded by soldiers, Joseph gave up his rifle.

His message to the soldiers is one of the best known passages in Native American history: "I am tired of fighting. Our chiefs are killed. Looking Glass is dead. Toohoolhoolzote is dead. The old men are all dead. It is the young men who say yes and no. He who led the young men (Ollokot) is dead. It is cold and we have no blankets. The little children are freezing to death. My people, some of them, have run away to the hills, and have no blankets; no food; no one knows where they are, perhaps freezing to death. I want to have time to look for my children and see how many I can find. Maybe I shall find them among the dead. Hear me, my chiefs. I am tired. My heart is sick and sad. From where the sun now stands, I will fight no more forever."

Despite the promises made that day, Joseph and his people were not sent to a reservation but to an internment camp in Kansas, where nearly 100 died. After a subsequent period in Indian Territory, and a deadly bout with malaria, a few of the survivors were allowed to return to the Nez Perce Indian Reservation at Lapwai, Idaho. But not Joseph. Despite pleas to join his people, Joseph was exiled to the Colville Reservation in Washington State, where he died in 1904.

Recalling the Nez Perce war, a military man expressed the opinion of many: "I think that, in his long career, Joseph cannot accuse the Government of the US of one single act of justice."

Today, the Nez Perce Tribe is headquartered at the Nez Perce Indian Reservation in northwest Idaho. They sponsor several powwows during the spring and summer; visitors are welcome.

told in the native tongue as well as exhibits on native foods, traditional clothing and housing. The Museum Gift Shop also offers a large inventory of locally crafted moccasins, beaded items and cedar baskets.

The **Trading Post**, near tribal headquarters in Nespelem, is also tribally owned and operated. In addition to the usual small-town groceries, the Trading Post carries a good selection of beadwork, Pendelton blankets, T-shirts designed by Indian artists, and a Colville delicacy, huckleberries. Beadwork, books and a good selection of Indian music can also be found at Video Quest, north of the Trading Post on Highway 155. It is worth the trip.

Elsewhere on the reservation, a little investigation goes a long way. At the **History and Archaeology Program** building near the Trading Post, for example, the staff keeps a showcase of artifacts dating from 200 to 8,000 years ago. Visitors can also inquire about several pictograph and petroglyph sites. One little-known site is located within walking distance of downtown Coulee Dam, but because many sites have been destroyed by thoughtless visitors, locals may be reluctant to give directions.

Colville holds its major **powwow** at Nespelem during the Fourth of July holiday. The week-long celebration attracts drum groups from as far away as the Dakotas and Montana.

Small community rodeos are held in the area all summer long, including the **Omak Stampede** rodeo and Indian encampment. The Omak Stampede is world-famous for its Suicide Race in which young riders guide their mounts down an impossibly steep hill, rush headlong into the treacherous currents of the Okanogan River, swim across, and then dash into the rodeo arena.

Once a year people come from all over the country to the increasingly popular **Sobriety Camp Out**. The Camp Out was begun by Pierre Louie, who wanted to find a way of "gathering the people" in order to provide an alternative to the destructive force of alcohol and to encourage spiritual enrichment **Mount St Helens.**

and traditional well-being. Concern for his mountain community of Inchelium inspired Louie to provide a place for families to come together and enjoy themselves in a wholesome, supportive environment. It is now so popular that he has need of many helpers. The Sobriety Camp Out is open to the public and is advertised as a family gathering with a fun run, boating, hiking, beautiful vistas and peace of mind. It is located at Twin Lakes, near Inchelium, for a solid week in July. Bring your own tents, tepees, campers and sleeping bags.

One other event you may want to keep in mind is the **Spokane Labor Day Celebration**, which is held on the small **Spokane Indian Reservation** adjacent to Colville. The event features dancing, crafts, food and traditional games.

About 30 miles away, in the city of Spokane, the **Museum of Native American Cultures** maintains one of the most extensive collections of American Indian artifacts in the West.

Yakima Nation: About 200 miles southeast of Colville, nestled against the snow-capped peaks of the Cascade Range, the **Yakima Indian Reservation** spreads over 1.4 million acres of plateau and mountain slopes. Like Colville, the modern Yakima Tribe is a confederation of several smaller bands including the Palouse, Pisquose, Yakima, Wenatchapam, Klickitat, Klinquit and others.

The Yakima Nation was created by the Walla Walla Treaty of 1855 in which 14 bands agreed to a large cession of land in return for peace. The Indians were promised that they could remain in their traditional homelands for two years after the ratification of the treaty, but whites began moving into the territory immediately after the signing and hostilities quickly broke out. Led by Yakima chief Kamiakan and others, warriors from several bands and tribes attacked troops who were sent to hunt down the Indians. A number of volunteer "exterminators" were also involved in the effort to rid the region of Indian tribes.

Scattered hostilities persisted for three years and spread to the Coeur d'Alenes, Palouses, Cayuses, Northern Paiutes and Spokanes. Despite a few early victories, the Indians suffered heavy losses and the confederacy broke up. Fifteen Indian leaders were eventually captured and hanged by the whites; many others were imprisoned. Wounded in 1858, Chief Kamiakan escaped to Canada. He returned several years later and settled on the Spokane Indian Reservation.

The best place to start a visit to the Yakima Indian Reservation is at the **Cultural Heritage Center**, near tribal headquarters in Toppenish. In addition to a library, theater and restaurant (try its traditional fish chowder), the complex houses the **Yakima Nation Museum**, which features exhibits on the region's ecology and native cultures. There are full-size models of a willow earth lodge, tule (reed) tepee and sweat house, and special exhibits that feature the work of native artists. There is also a gift shop with a good selection of beadwork, baskets and silver jewelry, all by Yakima or other native artists.

The Cultural Center is the place to inquire about the **Toppenish Powwow** and **Yakima Nation Summer Encampment**, the biggest social gatherings of the year. Both are held over the Fourth of July weekend and feature intertribal dancing, crafts, and hand games. The **Yakima Powwow**, in September, is also an important event on the national powwow scene.

To the west of Toppenish, **Fort Simcoe State Park** preserves one of the many garrisons that were involved in the Yakima War and other Indian–white hostilities. In some cases, the soldiers were called out to protect the local tribes from white vigilantes who were bent on Indian extermination.

In the distance, the 12,000-ft peak of **Mount Adams** looms over the western half of the reservation. This is Pahto, the sacred mountain of the Yakima bands, giver of water, plants and animals. The only geological mass that rises higher is **Mount Rainier**, immediately to the north, which reaches more than 14,000 ft. To the west of Pahto, the deadly volcanic cone of **Mount St Helen's** continues to belch out an ominous gray cloud.

WARM SPRINGS

"You are now entering the Warm Springs Indian Reservation." More than 11,000 cars pass the sign every day, but only a fraction of the drivers stop to savor the magnificent roadside vistas or the clouds tumbling over the nearby Cascade Mountains.

Even fewer take time to get to know the people who live here. They are members of three distinct tribes – the Warm Springs, Wasco and Paiute – living together on the largest Indian reservation in Oregon and developing one of the country's most progressive approaches to sustaining tribal culture in the late 20th century.

The Warm Springs Reservation is nestled in a geographic basin bordered on the west by the blue evergreen ridge of the Cascade Mountains and on the east by the cold, swift waters of the Deschutes River. Most people imagine the Pacific Northwest as a land of emerald forests and ceaseless rain, but this isn't a country cut from a single stamp. Central Oregon – and the Warm Springs Reservation in particular – is a land of dramatic rimrock cliffs, volcanic formations, and ancient geological upheavals. It is also a land of vast, almost unimaginable spaces. Enormous expanses of high desert stretch out to a meeting of sky and land, holding the earth in two great hands, palm to palm, cupping a thriving ecosystem in warm and pungent air.

Needless to say, driving across this terrain is a lesson in geologic variation, from sharp mountain curves to wide-open highways; from the bottom of deep canyons to the panoramic circle of grasses, juniper and sagebrush. And as you travel through the reservation, the visual constants of Mount Jefferson, Black Butte, Bald Peter, Ollallie Butte and Mount Hood rise in the distance.

Three tribes, one people: Like many Indian people, the three tribes of the Warm Springs Reservation no longer occupy their traditional homelands. In fact, the 640,000-acre reservation is only a pinch of the 10 million acres that was ceded by tribal leaders in 1855.

Originally, the Wasco and Warm Springs tribes – the first two groups to be settled on the reservation – lived on the Columbia River in ancient villages that served for more than 10,000 years as centers of a lively continental trade. They took their sustenance from the salmon-rich waters, wild roots and berries and occasionally deer and other game that ranged over the plateau and the slopes of the Cascade Mountains.

In the beginning, relations between the Warm Springs (also known as Walla Wallas), Wascos and Americans were good. Following the Columbia River to the Pacific Ocean, the Lewis and Clark expedition encountered the tribes in 1805, describing them as people of "great kindness." But by the mid-1800s, with settlers pouring into the rich country around the Columbia River Gorge, pressure mounted for the forceful relocation of the region's native people. Believing it wiser to accept the protection of a reservation than to be

Preceding pages: Shoshone-Bannock moccasins. **Left**, Warm Springs logger. **Right**, Ske-metze, or Chopped Up, with bow and arrow in quiver, *circa* 1877.

overrun by white settlers, tribal leaders signed the Treaty of 1855 exchanging all but a small portion of their ancestral territory in return for an assurance of peace and tribal sovereignty.

The third member of the Confederated Tribes – the Northern Paiutes (or Snakes) – weren't relocated to the Warm Springs Reservation until 1879, about 25 years after the Wascos and Warm Springs. The Paiutes were largely a foraging people centered in the Great Basin region of present-day Nevada, although far-ranging bands occasionally ventured into the Southwest, the western slopes of the Rocky Mountains, and the plateau country of southern Idaho and Oregon.

An independent and rugged people, the Northern Paiutes were quick to respond to the incursion of white people, a good number of them prospectors drawn by the gold rush of the 1850s. With the US Army occupied by the American Civil War, they raided mining camps, ranches and stagecoaches with little fear of retribution. But after the close of the war in 1865, troops began arriving at local forts, and under the command of General George Crook, they forced the Northern Paiutes to relent, killing or capturing some 550 Indians in less than two years.

The survivors of the so-called Snake War of 1866–68 were shipped off to various forts and reservations for internment. One group, which eventually became the third member of the Confederated Tribes, was held as prisoners of war at Fort Vancouver for more than 10 years before being allowed to resettle on the Warm Springs Reservation. Twenty-five years after the ratification of the Treaty of 1855, the Confederated Tribes became one people.

Bask in the warmth: Despite their hardships since the arrival of the Lewis and Clark expedition, kindness and generosity are still a basic quality in the makeup of the Warm Springs people. The tribes maintain an open-door policy, encouraging Indians and non-Indians to come and visit. More than 100 years removed from their ancestral **Drummers set the cadence.**

homelands, they are still dedicated to cultural preservation and to innovation for the benefit of individual tribal members within the whole circle of the community. They are also serious about economic development and meeting the challenges of environmental protection. The tribal timber industry, for example – one of the tribes' most lucrative and reliable ventures – is regulated by a strict code of conservation.

But as one council member put it, lumber is not the only resource that needs to be protected: "The roots, berries and moss that grow in the forest have value for us, too. Grass is a resource, not just for cattle and horses, but for deer, elk and other grazing animals. Clean water is a resource for the salmon and trout. We must protect all habitats that have special significance for us."

Make no mistake, the culture of the Confederated Tribes is alive and looking to the future. The Warm Springs people are self-sufficient, well-intentioned and clearly in touch with the modern world, and as such, they can serve as a bridge of understanding for travelers with a serious interest in Native American life and culture.

The main visitors' facility on the Warm Springs Indian Reservation is the **Kah-Nee-Tah Vacation Resort**, a 144-room luxury lodge named after the Indian woman, Kah-Nee-Tah, who once owned the site. The resort is a perfect example of progressive business development informed and directed by traditional tribal values. "Bask in the warmth… of an ancient tradition," the brochure urges, and considering that every visitor is a valued guest in the most traditional sense, it's not difficult to see the attraction.

Whether you are looking for a comfortable getaway or a rugged outdoor adventure, Kah-Nee-Tah has what you want. In addition to luxury suites with Jacuzzis and fireplaces, the lodge offers a number of cabins, a campground with a cluster of tepees, horseback riding, fishing and golfing. Nearby, hot springs have been enjoyed for centuries for their soothing and healthful mineral

Mount Jefferson.

waters, and are now used by the resort to heat several pools. The resort also offers regular salmon bakes, the traditional food of the Columbia River tribes, and a chance to experience ceremonial dancing and music.

It makes a great base from which to explore the surrounding wilderness, too. The **Pacific Crest National Scenic Trail** winds its way around the peaks of the Cascade Range at the very edge of the reservation, heading north into the wilds of **Mount Hood National Forest** all the way to Canada and south into the Three Sisters Wilderness Area and, some 200 miles later, California. The reservation is convenient to one of the state's best ski areas, too, only about 15 miles to the north.

The Kah-Nee-Tah lodge also features an interesting collection of artwork, much of which illustrates the myths and legends of the Confederated Tribes. One work in particular represents Coyote, the magical hero-trickster who appears in the myths of tribal people throughout the Northwest.

Coyote typically has one foot in the mythological realm and the other in the human world. Unfortunately, he doesn't acknowledge the limits of either, which makes him likeable but often impulsive and brash. Over the years, stories of his adventures have given Indian people much to think about.

Elsewhere on the reservation, visitors can stop at the Warm Springs **National Fish Hatchery**, where a variety of interpretive materials tell of the importance of salmon to the tribal community and the entire region. Some Warm Springs fishermen still catch salmon in the traditional way at Shears Bridge with dip nets lowered from platforms that are balanced precariously on the edge of the riverbank, white water rushing below. At one time, the immense runs of these silvery, darting fish enabled the tribes to survive through the lean months, attract traders, and restore their spiritual needs in the shortened days of winter with medicine dances and storytelling.

Winter was also the time for making tools and other objects, many of them exquisite works of art. Unfortunately, many of these artifacts are now housed in off-reservation museums where the community is unable to reach them or use them to educate their young people about the traditional way of life.

In order to address this problem, the Confederated Tribes plan on opening their own museum. The $4.5 million project was launched in 1990 and promises to be a "living cultural laboratory" with computerized archives, facilities to preserve and restore artifacts, an aggressive acquisitions program, and interpretive exhibits detailing the culture and history of the Confederated Tribes for both tribal members and visitors.

Celebrating life: During the course of the year, the people of Warm Springs also welcome guests to a number of special events that celebrate the existence of tribal cultures and the cyclical renewal of life. Indian people from all over the country travel to Warm Springs for the **Pi-Ume-Sha Treaty Days Powwow**, usually held in the third

Fishing with dip nets at Shears Bridge.

weekend in June, and the **Lincoln's Birthday Powwow** in February.

Ceremonial events, including the **Root Feast** and **Huckleberry Feast**, are also open to the public, although it is best to get information from the tribes' Public Relations or Culture and Heritage departments before attending. The Root Feast is held in spring, usually the first Sunday in April. The Huckleberry Feast is celebrated in early August. The exact date of these first fruit celebrations are determined by the maturity of roots and berries. The feasts are declared by the tribes' Elder Woman as the proper time to give thanks and begin the year's harvest.

Drawn from ancient ceremonies, these celebrations of life – like so much at Warm Springs – represents a layering of old and new, age and youth, cultural preservation and innovation. Perhaps it's the mountains that symbolize it best – their permanence and peacefulness, their raw beauty, the signs of upheaval and change. "Faith and patience have held our people together since the first contact with Europeans," a contemporary Wasco chief has noted. "They have been our strength. I see a resurgence of traditional life. Faith and patience, together with technology, are bringing much of what we lost back to life."

The Warm Springs Indian Reservation is a place to be understood with a delicate and discerning gaze. The diversity of the landscape, like the Warm Springs, Wasco and Paiute people, has an age-old beauty matched only by its powers of regeneration.

This is a unique place, unlike any other reservation in the American West. It is here that three tribes took a treaty and considerable hardship and turned themselves into a major economic and cultural force. The tribes have achieved success, a difficult endeavor during a tumultuous period. But perhaps the powers of tribal commitment were learned from the legendary Coyote – one foot in the old world and the other in the new – who taught that a people in transition are not irrevocably bound to the limitations of a distressed humanity.

Looking on at a Warm Springs powwow.

FLATHEAD RESERVATION

In the beginning, the Salish elders say, the Creator sent Coyote to that part of the planet that was land, to prepare it for habitation by the animal people and humans. The wise old Coyote gave shape to the world and taught humans how to live. He gave people many good and useful things, but he also left them with hunger, greed, anger and other imperfections as spurs to growth, learning and human understanding.

Salish legend says Coyote and his brother, Fox, wait at the edge of this island called "land." When they return it will be the end of time, the end of this stage of the universe's existence.

Elders say the Creator made one people. Over the ages, they scattered into the many tribes of the Northwest, including the Salish of the Bitterroot Mountains and their neighbors to the northwest, the Kootenai. Today, the Salish and Kootenai tribes live together in northwestern Montana on the Flathead Indian Reservation, more than a million acres of forested mountains and sheltered valleys nestled against the icy blue waters of Flathead Lake. The name "Flathead," which originally applied to only one of the Salish bands, has long been used by whites to refer to all members of the Salish-Kootenai Confederacy.

Powerful medicine: The great river valleys and timber-clad mountains were good to the Flathead people. Buffalo, elk and deer provided food, clothing and utensils. Bottomlands grew rich in bitterroot, wild parsnips and other foods. Mountains offered a cool retreat in summer. Timber-ringed meadows provided shelter in winter.

But the lives of the Flathead people were changed profoundly with the coming of Europeans, and white contact came earlier to the Flatheads than to other Montana tribes. In the early 19th century, pelts of American beaver, mink and other fur-bearing animals were in great demand in Europe, where felt hats and fur coats adorned the rich. Fortunes

to be made in fur sparked intense competition between the British and French, and later between Britain and the fledgling US.

In the early 1800s, John Jacob Astor's American Fur Company was racing the British Hudson Bay Company to the Pacific, building a string of fur forts and trading posts and making trading alliances with tribes along the way. Flathead people met a succession of French, British and American trappers and traders. The whites sought furs, of course, but they had something the Flatheads wanted.

When a fur company brought Iroquois trappers to this land to teach the local Indians how to use steel traps and dress furs in the manner preferred by traders, it was no accident that Christian converts were selected for the mission. The Iroquois told of powerful white medicine men in the East, the "black robes" with their medicine book, the Bible. The power described was exactly the kind the Flatheads sought.

Threatened by their neighbors, the

fierce and numerous Blackfeet, the Salish sent a succession of four delegations to St Louis, Missouri, to bring back priests and the white man's powerful medicine. The first delegation found a receptive Protestant denomination but produced no results. Two of the Salish died in St Louis and two perished on the return trip. The Protestants sent missionaries to the Pacific coast, but not to the shores of Flathead Lake. A second delegation was massacred by the Sioux Indians. A third secured promises but no results. At last, a delegation in 1839 reached the remarkable Jesuit priest, Father Pierre Jean DeSmet.

Whites marveled at the alacrity and intensity with which the Salish immersed themselves in Christianity. The new religion fitted not only their needs but their prophecy as well. Shining Shirt had seen the future in a vision as a youth. Spirits had told him, "When you grow up there will come men wearing long black dresses. They will teach you about Amotgen, the good spirit who sits on top, and about Emtep, the evil one who sits at the bottom. From them you will learn to live your life on earth."

But acceptance of the white man's medicine was no protection against the white man's greed. In the late 1890s, white settlers were beginning to crowd the tribes of western Montana. Gold strikes, first at Alder Gulch, then at Helena's Last Chance Gulch, drew whites to the territory they considered theirs by manifest destiny.

Whites felt that the Indians occupied far more land than they would ever use. "Use," in the minds of frontier whites, meant to farm, mine or graze. Living off the land in the traditional Salish or Kootenai manner did not fit the invaders' definition. In 1897 a commission was appointed to negotiate with the Indians to buy part of the reservation. But both the Salish and Kootenai were resolutely against the proposition. Chief Charlo of the Salish said he would not sell a foot of land. Isaac Big Knife, chief of the Kootenai, said the whites would do better finding someone wanting money more than his people.

Railroads snaked across Montana. Cities blossomed. Mines thrived. And at the turn of the century, Montana's whites complained that Indians were impeding "progress." US Senator Joe Dixon became the state's champion in the drive to separate Indian tribes from their lands. A bill he introduced in 1903 allotted tribal lands to individual Indians and opened the rest of the reservation to white homesteaders.

Exclusive ownership of small tracts of land was foreign to the Indian way of life. In a short time, Indian allotments, like most small holdings, passed into the hands of men with money. In most cases this meant whites. Most of the white-owned homesteads suffered the same fate. As a result, the best farmlands and town sites on the reservation became alienated from tribal ownership. Today, more than 40 percent of the reservation is no longer tribally owned.

God's country: The Flathead Reservation is set in some of the most beautiful land in Indian Country. "This is where God would vacation if he had the time,"

Flathead Delegation to Washington DC, 1884.

local people say. In spring the air is heady with the aroma of cherry orchards. In early summer the bitterroot blooms. This flower was the Creator's gift to tribes of the Northwest. Other tribes ground bitterroot as medicine, mixing it with tea or sprinkling it on the hot rocks inside a sweat lodge and inhaling the smoke. Here, the bitterroot was a staple of the Salish and Kootenai diets.

Visitors will find easy access to the majestic mountain country to the east of Flathead Valley. The Confederated Salish-Kootenai Tribe's Wild Land Recreation Department manages a 93,000-acre **Tribal Wilderness Area** along the fringes of the **Mission Mountains**. Backpackers, hikers, rock climbers and campers find the tribal wilderness a paradise. Campgrounds are primitive (with outhouses and no concessions or laundry facilities), and hiking trails are uncrowded. There are also more than 100 lakes and ponds an acre or more in size. Many are "kettle lakes," potholes left in the wake of retreating glaciers at the end of the last Ice Age.

West slope cutthroat and dolly varden (bull trout) are the natives here. Rainbow and brook trout have been planted and are plentiful. Check local regulations when you purchase your fishing license. Limits vary from year to year, and bull trout caught in the lower streams must be released.

Huckleberries are a prized resource in this mountain country. Huckleberry lovers gloat when they find good picking, and lie to protect their favorite patch from discovery. Some swap recipes for jam, pancake syrup and wine. Others wonder how anyone can pick fast enough to fill a pail with the berries that make it past the picker's mouth.

Campers in the wilderness must be aware that this is grizzly country. Precautions are advisable. Store food in a tree away from camp, and bury garbage. Bear bells are worn by some hikers to avoid surprising big bruins. In midsummer, the great bears flock to **McDonald Peak**, where they feed on clusters of lady bugs. Wild Land Recreation managers close a 10,000-acre

Horse logging on the Flathead Reservation.

section of the wilderness area during this time to protect both bears and humans.

Before striking out into the Tribal Wilderness Area, be sure to pick up a copy of the tribe's land-use map, which gives the location of campgrounds, picnic areas, hiking and cross-country skiing trails. They are available at sporting-goods shops in Polson, Kalispell and other nearby towns, or at tribal headquarters. Since private, non-tribal lands checkerboard the reservation, the map is also a key to fishing jurisdiction. Tribal game wardens police tribal lands where a $5 tribal conservation permit and a $10 fish stamp is good for the season. A three-day permit can be purchased for $13. On state lands or private lands not owned by Indians, a state fishing license is required in addition to the tribal permit.

In addition to the Tribal Wilderness Area, the tribes have also designated two Primitive Areas. These pristine lands are off-limits to all but tribal members. The primitive areas, where the Salish

and Kootenai may practice ancient arts and skills in surroundings isolated from the modern world, serve to preserve Indian identity and keep it vital.

Tribal members pack off to the mountains to hunt, fish and camp, listen to a grandfather tell Coyote stories, watch a grandmother prepare berry pudding, and recall the feeling of membership in the tribes whose holdings spread beyond these mountains and valleys.

Sports, saints and powwows: The center of attention in this corner of Montana, however, is **Flathead Lake**, the largest freshwater lake west of the Mississippi River. Flathead Lake offers a variety of watersports. Sailboats, cruisers, houseboats and even rowboats can be rented in Polson. The lake contains trout, whitefish, perch, bass and huge sturgeon.

In Polson you may also hire a fishing guide, rent a jet boat or windsurfing outfit, or take a parasail ride. Polson outfitters also offer white-water raft trips on the Flathead River. At present, there are no scuba equipment rental shops, but air is available in Kalispell. Divers find the submarine canyons near the outlet intriguing.

Off the western shore of the lake, 2,700-acre **Wild Horse Island State Park** is accessible only by boat. Wild bighorn sheep live on the island. Several smaller islands contain blue heron rookeries, and osprey nests are common in dead trees along the shore. Two smaller bodies of water, **Ninepipe** and **Kicking Horse reservoirs**, are excellent fisheries and the source of record largemouth bass. Birders will find both reservoirs to be birding hot spots.

Wildlife also abounds at the **National Bison Range**, located in the middle of the reservation about 25 miles south of Polson. A herd of 400–500 bison roam freely across 19,000 acres of grassland and timber. The shaggy, slow-moving beasts are truly awesome. You will pass within 100 ft of some. Do not leave your car. Bison prefer to ignore you, but are dangerous if crowded. The Bison Range also contains mule deer, white tail deer, pronghorn antelope, bighorn sheep and elk.

Nearby, outside the little town of St

Flathead Lake.

Ignatius, travelers will find one of the most beautiful churches in the American West. Certainly none has a more striking background than the Mission Mountains. **St Ignatius Mission** was built under the supervision of Father DeSmet and his Jesuit "soldiers of Christ," who learned the local native languages and began teaching Indian children decades before white gold-seekers poured into Flathead land. The original chapel, built in 1854, still stands. The chapel houses a collection of Indian artifacts and photos of the early mission days. The building is listed on the National Register of Historic Places and remains a religious center of the Flathead people.

Among the special attractions of the mission are the paintings of an Italian monk, Brother Cariganano. The mission fields of the 19th-century American West could not afford a man with only one talent, a man wearing only one hat. Cariganano spent his evenings and early mornings painting the walls of the chapel. During the day, he was the mis-

sion cook. The paintings are a series of Old Testament scenes and portraits of saints. Cariganano's masterpiece is a triptych, behind the altar, of St Ignatius of Loyola's three visions.

If you visit the Flathead Reservation in July, you will have your choice of two powwows. The **Arlee Fourth of July Powwow** runs three days and includes parades, stick games, bronc riding, races, calf roping and dance competitions. Concessionaires come from all over the West with arts and crafts. Dancers compete for $15,000 in prizes. If you own a tepee, the Arlee Powwow committee will furnish poles. There are also campsites for tents and recreational vehicles. A poster advertising the Arlee celebration warns: "The Powwow committee will not be responsible for theft, vandalism or lost spouses."

The **Elmo Powwow**, though smaller, is much like the Arlee celebration. It is held the second weekend after the Fourth of July weekend. Beaded buckskin articles and other crafts sold during this event are exquisite.

Harvest time in Flathead Valley.

Alcohol is banned at both powwows, but beer flows freely at the **Fourth of July Mule Celebration** at Joe's Smoke Ring in Evro. This is essentially a country western concert featuring big-name performers.

Best of both worlds: For a good look at 20th-century Indian life, visit **Salish-Kootenai College** (SKC) at Pablo. About 800 students pursue associate degrees on this beautiful junior-college campus. But SKC is more than a college; it is a concept exciting to tribal members who follow both modern and traditional ways of life. It is a fertile environment for the languages and world view that were nearly exterminated by an encroaching dominant society.

The European assault on Salish and Kootenai cultures was even greater than that experienced by most tribes. Being squeezed into one governmental unit by the US Department of the Interior extinguished most subtle cultural and social differences among the several Salish-speaking tribes.

Intermarriage between Salish and

Kootenai people tended to make English the common language of both. Long contact with whites and the early opening of the reservation to white homesteading diluted both blood lines. Today, very few full-blooded Salish or Kootenai remain. Sadly, a 1980s survey found not a single Indian first-grader fluent in either tongue.

The college embodies not only the hope for the future but is an active guardian of the past. At SKC, a student may learn computer sciences or the ancient art of beading buckskin, take up nursing or learn the Salish and Kootenai languages. Whatever students choose to study, they leave SKC ready to claim the best of two cultures.

And in many respects, that sums up the Flathead experience. The Flathead Indian Reservation is not typical of Western America's reservations or Canada's reserves. In fact, much of it is more resort than reservation. A visitor may spend a day in Polson, dining in stylish restaurants, browsing in trendy boutiques, playing golf or sailing, and then spend the night at a powwow, entranced by the pulsing rhythm and stirring melody of an age-old Indian song.

That doesn't mean there aren't any problems. The troubled history of Indian-white relations in this area has left a legacy of questions about tribal membership and treaty rights. There is still more than a little confusion, for example, about the tribal enrollment process. There are cases of brothers in which one is enrolled and one is not. One is "Indian," the other is not.

There is also a good deal of controversy surrounding the extent of Indian treaty rights, especially fishing rights at Flathead Lake. Here, as elsewhere, protestors argue forcefully that the exercise of tribal authority over fishing, hunting and other activities is clearly "treaty abuse."

But despite these difficulties, the Flathead Indian Reservation is still one of the most exciting travel experiences in Indian Country. Rich in tradition and surrounded by natural beauty, the Flathead Reservation is one of the gems of Native America.

Arlee Indian Encampment.

THE PEYOTE ROAD

Peyote is a hallucinogenic cactus that grows in northern Mexico and is used as a sacrament by the Native American Church, a loose intertribal organization that was first chartered in Oklahoma in 1918 and now claims members among Indian people throughout the American West.

The religious use of peyote goes at least as far back as the Aztecs, who called the cactus *peyotl*, from which the English word is derived. Although the Yaqui and Apache tribes continued to use peyote after European contact, it wasn't widely known among other North American tribes until the late 1800s, probably via the Comanches and Kiowas living in Oklahoma. The influential Comanche chief, Quanah Parker, who learned about peyote from a Mexican *curandera*, may have been the first to conduct regular peyote ceremonies and to teach its ritual use to other tribes.

Peyote buttons are cut from the top of the cactus and usually eaten dried, or soaked in water and taken as tea. Experienced peyotists may eat as many as 20 or 30 buttons during the nightlong ceremonies, and the effects may include colorful visions, a sense of well-being, focused energy and increased concentration.

To members of the Native American Church, peyote represents spiritual power. According to the late J.S. Slotkin, an anthropologist and member of the Native American Church, ceremonial peyote-use is a way of gaining spiritual insight and communing with God: "Long ago God took pity on the Indian… So God created Peyote and put some of his power into it for the use of Indians. Therefore the Peyotist takes the sacramental Peyote to absorb God's power contained in it, in the same way that the white Christian takes the sacramental bread and wine."

Peyote meetings are conducted by informal leaders called "road men" or "road chiefs," and are usually held in a tepee. The road man is responsible for initiating and guiding the ceremony and supplying the necessary ritual paraphernalia, such as an eagle-wing fan, eagle-bone whistle, rattle, fire stick,

water drum and sometimes a Bible. The participants sit cross-legged around the edge of the tepee, and a fire, which is tended by an appointed fire man, burns in the center. A crescent-shaped altar is made on the ground in front of the road man, who sits on the west side of the tepee. A particularly large peyote button known as "father peyote" or "peyote chief" is usually placed on the altar.

Although ceremonies vary from one road man to another, they are generally divided into four segments, each with its own songs, prayers and periods of meditation. Peyote is passed around the circle at various times throughout the night, and the participants take turns singing a series of four songs while the person sitting on the right beats the water drum (usually a skin-covered kettle filled with water). Sacred water is brought into the tepee and drunk at midnight after the singing of the midnight water song, and again at dawn after the singing of the morning water song. The ceremony ends in the morning with the singing of four quitting songs, and a feast or gathering usually follows.

The legal status of sacramental peyote-use has been questioned from the very beginning. Over the years, missionaries, government officials and others have argued that peyote is a drug and that its use and distribution ought to be criminalized. Some crusaders have fabricated stories about wild, licentious "peyote parties," although clearly the recreational use of the cactus is alien to the tenets of the Native American Church.

Peyotists generally respond to these charges by pointing out that peyote is not addictive, that peyote meetings are serious religious events, and that peyote-use is only one part of a sober and generally conservative way of life. It was thought that the issue was put to rest in 1978, when Congress passed the American Indian Religious Freedom Act protecting the sacramental use of peyote by members of the Native American Church. In 1990, however, the US Supreme Court challenged the law. The legality of peyote-use may now to be decided on a state-by-state basis.

Peyote ceremonies are not open to visitors. Unless you are invited by a participant and accepted by the road man, do not attempt to find or attend peyote meetings.

209

THE SHOSHONE-BANNOCK OF IDAHO

Entry into the world of the Shoshone-Bannock people begins at the Fort Hall exit of Interstate 15. Eight miles north of Pocatello, Idaho, the tribe's Trading Post is an instant relief from freeway hypnosis. Inside the **Clothes Horse**, a large building on the northern edge of the complex, you can see walls packed with hundreds of moccasins, gloves, beaded belt-buckles, purses and other jewelry made by Shoshone and Bannock artisans.

Shoshones and Bannocks have a national reputation as designers of cut-bead jewelry. And of course, there is nothing quite like handmade beaded moccasins. The smell of tanned deer hide is beautiful and alluring. Better yet, moccasins get better with age, reaching their peak comfort after you've worn them a few years.

Some of the beaded craft is art that is meant to be worn every day. Belt buckles are made with both traditional patterns and modern designs. You can even get one with your name or initials on it. The same is true for fancy beaded earrings, handbags, wallets and purses.

You will also find strands of beads (if you want to try it yourself), buckskin to sew it on, and even instruction books. Or you can opt for the ready-made, museum-quality material for sale by the tribe. If you want to see older beadwork, the **tribal museum** is across the road in the same complex. There you can see exhibits on Shoshone and Bannock history as well as older regalia once worn by local people.

Having seen pictures of the buffalo hunt, you may want to taste some – buffalo, that is. Once again, it's here, at the **Oregon Trail Restaurant**. Order up a bowl of buffalo stew and fry bread.

The beauty of the Trading Post complex is that in just a few hours you can sample the culture of the Shoshone and Bannock people. There is also a bit of modern life here: a grocery store, gas station, and even an ice cream parlor. During the summer months, powwow dancers and singers entertain visitors.

Trail of immigrants: It's appropriate that the freeway brings people from the outside world to Fort Hall. It's now a time-worn tradition. Most of the reservation is near the Snake River bottoms, rolling hills that flow into rich swampland along the Snake River. This land has been a freeway for generations of Indians who came to meet, trade, talk and make war. Two generations ago it became a different kind of freeway, a trail of immigrants.

Because of the rich lands near the river, the area has always been the winter home for Shoshone and Bannock bands. Several mountains can be seen from the Snake River, landmarks for travelers who did not carry maps. Mount Putnam sits on the eastern edge of the reservation, and at nearly 7,000 ft it can be seen from almost anywhere in the region.

Most of the land is high desert, populated by jackrabbits, rock chucks, antelope, deer and elk. The rivers and streams are full of trout and other fish.

Preceding pages: Skokomish blanket. **Left**, the T-shirt says it all. **Right**, drummer sets the pace of traditional hand games.

And the bottoms also draw tens of thousands of Canada geese and nearly a half-million ducks each year.

It was, and still is, a rich country. No wonder that the Shoshone and Bannock bands who made this region their home two centuries ago were the wealthiest lot of the Shoshone bands that roamed throughout the western states. There were Eastern Shoshone in Idaho and Wyoming, Lemhi Shoshone (Sheep-eaters) in central Idaho, Bruneau Shoshone in western Idaho and Oregon, Western Shoshone in central Nevada, and Southern Shoshone in the Mohave Desert of California. Most of the people at the Fort Hall Reservation today are Eastern Shoshone and Bannock. The Bannock were a Paiute band that roamed with Shoshones but spoke their own tongue. A few people at Fort Hall are trilingual, speaking Shoshone, Bannock and English. Other bands of Shoshone were moved onto the reservation in the late 1800s.

Tribal elders tell stories from their parents and grandparents about the days

before the Europeans came: "Everything used to be Indian. The *Neme* – the human beings – talked Indian. The trees among us also talked Indian. And all living things talked Indian. They talked Shoshone. That very one, the Indian father, put the living things down to grow. All creatures talked Shoshone, even the eagles, coyotes and deer."

But then the world changed. New four-legged beings and new two-legged beings came to live in the land of the *Neme*. The four-leggeds were useful. The *punku*, or horse, allowed Shoshone bands freedom to seek better hunting and fishing grounds in summer and the safety of warmer climates in winter.

In the 19th century, the four-legged creatures changed Shoshone and Bannock society forever. The horse made the Shoshone and Bannock bands powerful, giving them wealth and prestige. But the two-leggeds were not useful, the elders say.

A century later, two-leggeds began arriving in force. Most were Mormon pioneers pushing the kingdom of Zion north from Utah. The Mormons wanted to farm the rich lands of southeast Idaho. Other two-leggeds preferred to march through the bottom country on their way to California or Oregon, destroying important habitat areas that fed Indian people. The opening of the Oregon Trail in 1843 brought 19th-century traffic jams directly onto Shoshone and Bannock lands. The Indians mockingly called the trail, "the Holy Road." Fort Hall was built along the trail as a way-station for travelers and an army supply station.

During the winter of 1862, the Shoshone and Bannock bands began to run out of food in the once fertile land. On the banks of Bear River, in what is now Franklin, Idaho, a large number of Indians insisted that the Mormons give food to the Indians as payment for destroying their hunting grounds.

"But as their demands became more insistent, the Mormons became frightened," wrote Mont Faulkner, a tribal secretary in the 1930s. Troops were sent to protect the Saints. William Hull, one of the Mormons sent to the battlefield

Couple in powwow dress.

the next day, commented upon the scene in a different light: "Never will I forget the scene – dead bodies everywhere. I counted eight deep in one place... all in all we counted nearly four hundred; two-thirds of this number being women and children."

The slaughter at Bear River convinced the chiefs of the Shoshone and Bannock to submit to the US. But most whites in the area did not want peace. They wanted extermination. An editorial in the *Idaho Statesman* in 1867 called for a council of all Idaho Indians followed by a feast. "Then just before the big feast, put strychnine in their meat and poison to death the last mother's son of them."

A year later, a peace treaty was signed at Fort Bridger, Utah Territory, now Wyoming, between the eastern band of Shoshones and Bannocks and the US government establishing the Fort Hall Indian Reservation. Chief Washakie and Chief Tagee, among others, were the signers for the Shoshones and Bannocks respectively. The treaty did not guarantee a permanent homeland for the two tribal groups. The reservation was to have been 1.8 million acres, but was cut in third because the treaty misspelled the name Camas Prairie as Kansas Prairie, creating more new land for settlers.

Hard times to good times: In the decades following the treaty, Fort Hall remained one of the poorest reservations in the country. Its rate of poverty, suicide and other social problems regularly ranked it among the most troubled locations in Indian Country. In recent years, the tribal government began to control more and more of the reservation's resources. Farming on the reservation, for example, had been leased out to non-Indian farmers at bargain rates. Thus, tribal members neither received the profits nor learned how to farm. In the late 1970s, the tribe began to operate its own farm, which still operates at a profit today.

The tribe's government center is an interesting set of buildings. The first, which houses the library and education

Spearfishing.

programs, is a modern tepee. The second, which houses the tribal administration, is a modern version of a tribal lodge. Both are at the **Fort Hall Indian Agency**, the official government site. The rest of Fort Hall's town site is along Highway 191. It includes a few small stores and businesses.

In the late 1970s, the Trading Post complex was built by the tribe. It started with a small log cabin selling tax-free cigarettes called the "Big Smoke Shop," which is both a general food store and a successful retailer of cigarettes (still a truckers' favorite).

The tribe's buffalo herd has become a boom in recent years. Non-Indian sportsmen are allowed to buy permits to shoot one of the herd which roams in the bottoms. Fishing permits are also sold by the tribal government for certain rivers, lakes and creeks on the reservation. You can also visit the site of the original Fort Hall in the bottoms, although, aside from a marker and the beautiful setting, there really isn't a great deal to see. A replica of the old fort

is at Ross Creek Park in Pocatello.

The highlight of summer on the reservation is the annual **Shoshone-Bannock Indian Festival**, held the first week of August. The four-day tribal fair features singers and dancers from across North America, competing for top prize money. The tepees form a large circle around the grounds in the center of town west of the Trading Post. A small grandstand on the festival grounds affords an excellent view of fancy dancers, traditional dancers, gourd dancers and shawl dancers who compete each day. Arts and crafts booths from tribes across North America surround the festivities.

An all-Indian rodeo is also held during the festival, with wicked bulls and bucking horses challenging cowboys from Canada and several western states. Rodeo is a year-round sport at Fort Hall. In the winter months, cowboys hone their skills in the Roping Arena, a metal structure north of Fort Hall on Highway 191. And in the summer, jackpot rodeos are held nearly every weekend at the **Young couple...**

Rodeo Grounds. Several larger rodeos are held each year for regional all-Indian rodeo associations.

Shoshone-Bannock rodeo has an additional twist: Indian relays. These are teams of horses with one rider who switches mounts every lap of the arena. Few riders are adept at making the switch. Some riders end up chasing their horse around before they can get back into the saddle.

Traditionally, Shoshones and Bannocks have been fond of gambling. At the festival grounds, a central hub is an open tent where Indians from around the US and Canada play hand games. The hand games, sometimes also called stick games, are played by two teams who bet each other equal amounts on victory. Spectators can add to the pot, placing their money on their favorite team. Before the game is played, one side may have trouble getting an equal share, and you will hear its leader sing out, "Short, short, winning side," in an attempt to interest investors in the next round of play.

Once the two pots are equal, the teams play a guessing game using bones that can be hid inside a player's fist. Teams take turns guessing which hand the bone is hidden in. Sticks are used to keep score; when one side collects all the sticks, the game is over and the winnings are two-to-one for all players and investors. The games take hours and are accompanied by fervent gaming songs that draw crowds to watch and listen. In the summer, hand games are also played at one of the tribe's traditional lodges. On weekends, **Buffalo Lodge,** a few miles from Fort Hall, is jokingly called Buff-Vegas.

The Shoshone-Bannock Tribe also operates modern high-stakes gaming, running bingo on weekends in **Timbee Hall** in the center of town. Most of the 200 or so people who play are on their way north to Yellowstone National Park or are "regulars" from Boise, Salt Lake City, Idaho Falls and other nearby towns. Pots are a guaranteed payoff of $1,000 but run as high as $10,000 on weekend nights.

...and singers at Shoshone-Bannock Indian Festival.

THE SOUTHWEST

Geologically, the American Southwest is one of the most spectacular regions in North America – a land of stunning canyons, scorched deserts, towering mesas and rolling plateaus. This is the very heart of America's Indian Country, a cornucopia of native arts, dances, ceremonies, ruins and ancient villages.

Native people developed great civilizations in the Southwest as much as 1,500 years ago. The ancient Anasazi built apartment-like pueblos on the mesas and canyons of the Four Corners area, where their cultural descendants, the Pueblo people of New Mexico and the Hopis of Arizona, still gather in kivas and perform their sacred dances.

In the desert country of southern Arizona, the ancient Hohokam built villages and irrigated crops on the same parched landscape occupied today by the Tohono O'odhams, Pimas, Yaquis and Maricopas.

Before whites came, these village-dwelling people were invaded by Athabascans from the north. These invaders were the ancestors of the Navajos and Apaches, fierce warriors and raiders who later came into bloody conflict with Spanish and American soldiers. The Apaches maintained their hunting-and-gathering way of life well into the colonial period, breaking up into small bands scattered throughout the Southwest.

The Navajos borrowed heavily from the Pueblos and Spanish, took up sheepherding, horsemanship, weaving, silversmithing and various elements of Pueblo religion. Today, they are one of the largest Indian tribes in the US; the Navajo Nation occupies the better part of northeastern Arizona.

And there are other tribes, too: Havasupai, Hualapai, Paiute, Ute, Cocopah, Mojave. All share in the heritage of the native Southwest. All are part of the cultural vitality that places the Southwest at the core of Native America.

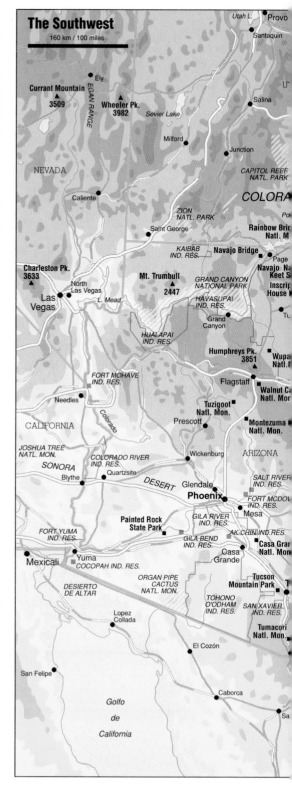

Kremmling
Boulder
Lakewood
Denver
Burlington
Winona
Limon

Mount Elbert
▲ 4399

Grand Junction
Thompson
reen ver
ND OURAY RES.
ROCKY

COLORADO

Buena Vista
Colorado Springs
Kit Carson
KANSAS

Montrose

MOUNTAINS

Uncompahgre Pk.
▲ 4361

Pueblo
Deerfield
Lamar
Arkansas
La Junta

Wolf Creek Pass
3309

SANGRE
GREAT SAND DUNES NATL. MON.
Blanca Pk.
▲ 4378
Walsenburg
Springfield

MESA VERDE NATL. PARK
Durango
Alamosa

UTE MOUNTAIN IND. RES.
SOUTHERN UTE IND. RES.

NT VALLEY
San Juan

Trinidad

DE

MONUMENT VALLEY NAVAJO TRIBAL PARK
AztecRuins Natl. Mon.
Tierra Amarilla
Wheeler Pk.
▲ 4011
Cimarron
OKLAHOMA

Farmington

CRISTO

Taos Pueblo
Taos
Springer
Clayton

NAVAJO IND. RES.

JICARILLA APACHE IND. RES.

Sta. Clara Pueblo
San Juan Pueblo

Dalhart

CANYON DE CHELLY NATL. MON.

CHACO CULTURE NATL. HIS. PARK

Los Alamos
S. Ildefonso Pueblo
Bandelier Natl. Mon.

MTS.

Canadian
Borger

Hubbell g Post t. Site

NEW MEXICO

Jemez Pueblo
Santa Fe

Window Rock
Gallup
Zia Pueblo
Santo Domingo Pueblo
San Felipe Pueblo
Las Vegas
Tucumcari
Amarillo

TEAU

ZUNI IND. RES.
Grants
LAGUNA IND. RES.
Sandia Pueblo
Albuquerque
Hereford

EL MORRO NATL. MON.

PETRIFIED FOREST NATL. PARK

Mal Pais Lava Beds
ACOMA IND. RES.
Acoma Pueblo (Sky City)
ISLETA IND. RES.
Vaughn
Fort Sumner
Farwell
Plainview

Saint Johns

ALAMO NAVAJO IND. RES.

Clovis
Levelland
Lubbock

Springerville IN

Quemado

Socorro
San Antonio

Carrizozo
LINCOLN NATL. FOREST
Pecos
LLANO

ESTACADO

RLOS ES.

Gila Cliff Dwellings Natl. Mon.

Roswell
Plains

MESCALERO IND. RES.

PECOS PLAINS

Brownfield

Truth or Consequences

WHITE SANDS NATL. MON.
Alamogordo
LINCOLN NATL. FOREST

Artesia
Hobbs
Lamesa

ford Solomon

Lordsburg

Rio Grande

Las Cruces

Carlsbad

Midland

Odessa

Chiricahua Natl. Mon.
oronado atl. Forest

El Paso
Salt Basin
Kermit

Douglas

Ciudad Juarez
TEXAS
Pecos
McCamey

La Candelaria

Rio Grande
Bravo del Norte

Van Horn

Fort Stockton

MEXICO

Marfa

221

NAVAJO NATION

Entering the Navajo Reservation from any direction, on any road, you quickly sense its most striking quality: space, openness, unbounded landscape. Everywhere you look there are dramatic views of distant, angular mesas, expansive plateaus and wide, pale-green valleys. No other land in the Southwest quite compares in scale or beauty to the 17-million-acre Navajo Reservation, the largest in the country. After seeing it, being within it, you may wonder why it remains so unknown and empty.

Today's Navajoland *(Dine' bikeyah)* dominates the northeast corner of Arizona and spills over into New Mexico and Utah. In every direction, the treeless Navajo horizon stretches out before you in a landscape of tawny dunes, orange-and-pink canyons, and faraway blue mountains rising more than 10,000 ft.

On most days, the land is flooded in brilliant sunlight and domed by a nearly cloudless blue sky. But in the summer, when moist air arriving from the Gulf of Mexico collides with hot air rising from the desert floor, ominous thunderheads gather overhead. Then entire weather systems are created before your eyes. Huge anvil-shaped clouds rise to a center point in the sky and then spread, darkening like blue-black mountains in the air. Desert rainclouds can open at any time and pour out their burden in a 15- or 20-minute thunderstorm, pelting the ground with the hard "male" rains that send torrents rushing across slickrock and into arroyos.

Geologically, Navajoland is absolutely awe-inspiring. Buttes and cliffs dwarf human figures. Huge slabs of sandstone and limestone appear freshly broken from rocky abutments, making them look as if they have emerged through heaps of geological debris. From a distance, these huge chunks of rock take on a different aspect, like sleeping giants occupying the earth.

In fact, Navajo mythology teaches that the huge expanses of mesa and plateau are the petrified bodies of mon-

sters who inhabited the earth before it was fit for humans. The Navajos' Hero Twins – Monster Slayer and Child Born of Water – slew the monsters of the third or Yellow World to make the land safe for the emergence of the "five-fingered people" into the fourth or Glittering World.

The land was an obstacle to the earliest white visitors – the Spanish in the 1500s followed by the Mexicans and Americans. But the indigenous people – the Navajos, Hopis and Paiutes – held it in reverence and adapted to the vagaries of climate, precipitation and resources.

The Navajos, relatives of the Athabascan people who migrated to the Southwest from the frozen arctic north, made the land their religion. It is home to their deities, the Holy People, an immense pantheon of supernatural personalities still remembered today in the chants of Navajo medicine men, singers, hand tremblers and crystal gazers, all known simply as *hatahli.*

Over the past 600 years, the Navajos have embraced this land with as much

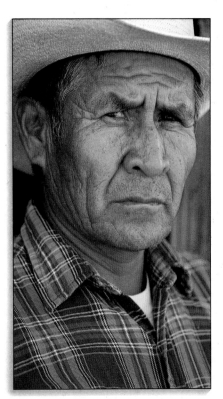

reverence as tenacity, adapting to it with a light touch. Today, the most common symbol of their relationship with the land is the hogan, the traditional domed dwelling once made exclusively of stacked or standing logs and covered with mud. Although dwindling in number, these ancient homes can still be seen across the reservation, especially in areas where modern facilities have arrived late.

Since the 1970s, though, the old mud hogan has been used by Navajos more for ceremonial and religious purposes and less for housing. Today, federally-subsidized housing and mobile homes are proliferating as the Navajo population mushrooms. But this change is more indicative of Navajo adaptability than of an abandonment of culture. In fact, modern eight-sided hogans, usually built of plywood and lumber, are still quite common. Traditional or modern, with its entrance always facing the rising sun, the hogan symbolizes the security of the Navajo mother, *shimah* – Mother Earth as much as the woman who serves

as the anchor of the Navajo family.

Holy people: In Navajo cosmology, the land lies between two protective parents. Below, supporting and nurturing the people, is Mother Earth, provider of sustenance – corn, water, grazing land. Above is Father Sky, providing life-giving rain to make the plants grow and the water run. In the morning, before sunrise, traditional Navajos still offer a few sprinkles of corn pollen and, in their prayers to the rising sun, ask for the blessings of the Holy People.

Navajos believe they emerged from an underworld known as the first or Black World. This was a timeless place known only to spirit-beings and the Holy People. Here lived First Man and First Woman, but separately, in the east and west. They were united when First Man burned a crystal (symbolizing the awakening of the mind) and First Woman burned a piece of turquoise. Seeing each other's fire, they were united after four attempts.

But soon, the insect-beings of the First World began to quarrel and create

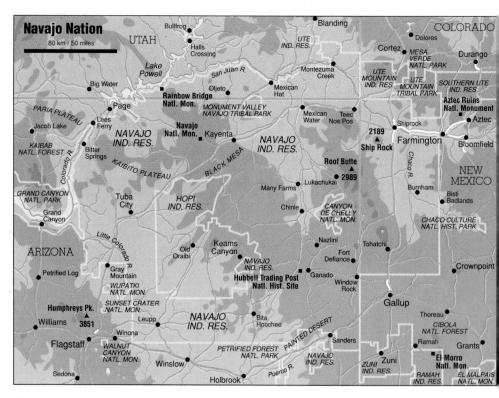

chaos, forcing First Man and First Woman to leave through the east. Their migrations, brought on by disunity, led them to the Blue World, and then to the Yellow World, where they found the six sacred mountains still revered by the Navajos. These are Blanco Peak in Colorado to the east, Mount Taylor in New Mexico to the south, the San Francisco Peaks of Arizona to the west, and the La Plata Range of Colorado to the north. Within this area is Huerfano Mesa in New Mexico at the center, and Gobernador Knob, also in New Mexico, as the inner mountain.

It was Coyote who began the turmoil of the Yellow World by stealing the child of Water Monster. Furious, Water Monster flooded the world. First Man planted a female reed that grew to the sky, permitting the living things to escape the rising waters. As the flood receded, the First People found themselves in the Glittering World, where the Navajos live today.

First Man and First Woman are also the parents of Changing Woman, who they found as a baby atop Gobernador Knob and who is the mother of the four principal Navajo clans. Together with her sister, White Shell Woman, these are the most important figures in the Navajo pantheon.

Despite the influx of various Christian denominations, most Navajos continue to practice their own religion, remain superstitious, respect taboos, and try to adhere to the teachings handed down from previous generations. Most families still have medicine men they rely on to perform any number of ceremonies that help restore a sense of harmony, balance, beauty and prosperity – the highest ideals of Navajo life, expressed by the concept of *hozjo*.

Among the most common ceremonies still practiced by the Navajos are the *kinaalda*, a girl's puberty rite; the *nidaa*, or squaw dance, a three-day ceremony performed in the summer; and the *yei-be-chei*, a winter healing ceremony that lasts up to nine days and features masked dancers that are somewhat similar to Hopi kachina dancers.

La Plata Range, sacred mountains of the north.

Although sacred to the Navajos, some ceremonies also serve as social gatherings. The *nidaa*, for instance, is often advertised on hand-painted signs posted along the highway. Visitors may attend, but it is highly recommended that they come with someone who is already familiar with the ceremony. (Bear in mind that in the past some Squaw Dances have been the site of alcohol-related disturbances.) The *yei-be-chei* is also open to outsiders, but tends to be less common these days because of its nine-day length and expense. It may cost a Navajo family as much as $5,000 to pay for preparations, food, helpers and the services of a medicine-man fees.

The long walk: Navajos have long been known for their ability to adapt to the changing circumstances of their lives. They borrowed from all the people with whom they have been in contact – the Spanish, Hopis, Americans – adopting and transforming various aspects of their cultures. From the Spanish they acquired sheep and horses and became some of the best herdsmen and riders in the

Southwest. It's uncertain from whom they learned silversmithing, possibly the Spanish, Mexicans or eastern tribes, but it continues to be one of the most popular and distinctive Navajo art forms. From the Hopis and other Pueblo people, they learned desert agriculture and weaving. For more than a century now, the Navajos have been renowned for their exquisite, hand-woven rugs. Certain aspects of Navajo religion also seem influenced by Pueblo belief.

But like other native people, the Navajos did not always enjoy peaceful relations with their neighbors. In the 1770s, the Spanish were able to subdue them brutally, beginning a long and bitter period of slave-raiding and territorial encroachment. In 1804, the Navajos made war on them, but suffered a bloody defeat at Canyon de Chelly, where the Spanish shot people retreating into caves and then destroyed hogans, burned crops, seized sheep and horse herds, and captured dozens of women and children. In 1821, at a truce conference with a Spanish commander, 24

Young woman tests her endurance during the *kinaalda* ceremony.

Navajos were treacherously murdered, each stabbed in the heart as he smoked in peace and hope.

When Americans started moving toward Navajo territory in the 1840s, there was hope that they would dispatch the Mexicans and free their relatives from slavery. In less than 10 years of their coming, however, relations between the white people, or *bilagaana*, and the Navajos were already dismal. The Americans had failed not only to free Navajo slaves as promised in treaties, but were instrumental in allowing slave-raiding to continue. They had also invaded Navajo land and destroyed crops, and, in 1849, shot and killed the aged Narbona, the most prominent Navajo leader of his time.

The first American military post built in Navajo territory, Fort Defiance, was established in 1851. Several treaties followed, but none of them held the peace for more than a few years. Then, in 1862, General James H. Carleton took command and immediately set about clearing the Indians off the land. It was Carleton who devised the ill-fated plan to march 8,000 Navajos 300 miles to the flat, featureless no-man's-land called Bosque Redondo, east of Santa Fe. This was the infamous Long Walk, remembered bitterly to this day. Carleton wrote that the only peace the Indians would find was imprisonment at the Bosque, where they would supposedly learn to farm. "Entire subjugation, or destruction of all the men, are the alternatives," he said.

In 1863, Colonel Christopher "Kit" Carson was assigned to carry out Carleton's orders by slashing, burning and shooting his way across Navajo territory. As winter came, Carson's patrols hunted the Navajos like animals, forcing them to surrender a few at a time after weeks of cold and hunger. The campaign's most bitter episode came in January 1864, when Carson and 300 soldiers swept through Canyon de Chelly, repeating the destruction of the Spanish years earlier. Those who tried to escape were shot down. Many of the elderly, too weak to make the Long Walk, were left behind to die. Only a few Navajos are known to have made it into the rugged canyon country around Monument Valley, led by the well-known headman Manuelito.

Within four years, Carleton's plan ended in disaster. A quarter of the Navajos imprisoned at Bosque Redondo (renamed Fort Sumner) starved or died of illness. Their crops failed from drought. The little water available was too brackish to drink. There was no wood. A grief-stricken Ganado Mucho told the government superintendent that the Navajos would live on a reservation if it could be in their own country.

Outcry over the Navajos' fate finally reached Washington, and on June 1, 1868, Navajo headmen agreed to peace by signing the Treaty of 1868, a document still held sacred by the tribe. The US government granted the Navajos a reservation in their old country and allowed the survivors to return.

The early decades of the 1900s saw more lands added to the reservation and improvement of the Navajos' condition, although confrontations with whites

Navajo weaver.

continued. In the 1930s, for example, the federal government implemented a livestock-reduction program designed to reverse the effects of over-grazing. Thousands of sheep were bought by the government for a dollar a head, and then slaughtered in canyons and left to rot. The Navajos were horrified as the source of their wealth and sustenance was destroyed before their eyes.

The Navajos also became involved in a long-term land dispute with the Hopis, whose mesa-top homes are completely surrounded by the larger Navajo Reservation. For years the Hopis had charged that Navajos were robbing their fields and stealing their cattle. Tensions escalated to a high point in 1974 when the US Congress passed the Navajo-Hopi Relocation Act. The law, which divided nearly 2 million acres between the tribes, will eventually force 11,000 Navajos and about 100 Hopis to leave homes they have known for generations. About half the Navajos have already received new government housing, but many who moved, called "refugees" by the tribe, are still waiting. Others have vowed never to leave and continue to resist from strongholds at Big Mountain and Teesto.

Finally, in the late 1980s, the Navajos seemed to turn on each other. At the height of a fractious corruption scandal involving former chairman Peter MacDonald, two MacDonald supporters were shot and killed by police at a demonstration that turned violent. MacDonald's downfall was sealed in 1990, when he was convicted on 41 charges of corruption in the Navajos' own court. The following month, his arch-rival, former chairman Peterson Zah, was chosen to lead the tribe as its first elected president.

Canyon de Chelly and East: Today, calm has returned to tribal politics, although great challenges lie ahead for Navajos. **Window Rock**, next to the New Mexico state line, is the seat of Navajo government and the most impressive of all tribal capitals. Navajo government offices and federal Bureau of Indian Affairs offices are housed in historic sandstone buildings of classic Southwestern design tucked into a small canyon where the famed "window rock" arch rises above. The Navajo Tribal Council is a one-of-a-kind, hogan-shaped building with a high log ceiling. Around the eight interior walls is a mural depicting the history of the tribe.

Window Rock is the home of the tribally-owned **Navajo Arts and Crafts Enterprise**, an excellent place to purchase all kinds of Navajo rugs, jewelry, sand paintings, pottery and beadwork. The building also houses the **Navajo Tribal Museum** and art museum, well worth a stop.

Over the Fourth of July, Window Rock is the site of one of the biggest **all-Indian rodeos** in the country. Rodeo, it goes without saying, is the most popular sport on the reservation, and travelers can find one any summer weekend. For nine days in September, Window Rock also hosts the **Navajo Nation Fair**, the largest in the country. It is like a county fair with an Indian flavor, bringing together as many as 50,000 Navajos and members of neighboring tribes, a cor-

Navajo code talkers baffled the enemy during World War II.

nucopia of produce, rugs, jewelry, continuous powwows, traditional dancing and one booth after another selling mutton stew and fry bread, Navajo favorites.

Twenty-eight miles west of Window Rock on Highway 264 is Ganado, site of the **Hubbell Trading Post**. The post was opened by the legendary John Lorenzo Hubbell in 1876 and has been open for business ever since. The most important trader of his day, Hubbell was much-loved by the Navajos, whom he tended during the devastating smallpox epidemic of 1886. His biggest influence on the tribe was popularizing Navajo rugs and blankets, encouraging weavers to use color, and essentially creating the distinctive Ganado Red design that became so popular with the outside world. Hubbell's place retains the look and feel of an old-time trading post, and Navajos still travel for miles to do business here. The post is now administered by the National Park Service.

Perhaps the most important destination on the reservation is **Canyon de Chelly**, the very heart of Navajoland. The main entrance is about 2 miles from the large town of Chinle, and about 30 miles north of Highway 264. This extraordinary three-branched canyon, enclosed within 800-ft sandstone walls, has been home to desert people for more than 1,000 years. The prehistoric Anasazi left behind hundreds of cliff-dwellings and thousands of artifacts. Like the Navajos, who moved in centuries later, the Anasazi farmed the canyon's bottomland (for additional information see *Ancestral Ground*).

Travel within the canyon is restricted to guided tours by the National Park Service, because Canyon de Chelly remains home to many Navajo families who still herd sheep and raise crops within its confines. Good paved roads along the rim offer excellent views of the canyon's depths. There is one hiking trail to the bottom of the canyon at White House Ruin.

It takes about two hours to make the trip down and across the wide, shaded stream to the ancient Anasazi pueblo

Herding sheep in Canyon de Chelly.

tucked into a ledge in the cliff face.

The Canyon de Chelly visitors' center is an excellent place to learn about the Anasazi people who occupied the entire Four Corners region. The Thunderbird Lodge, just inside the park, sells hundreds of Navajo rugs at reasonable prices, often better than those at local trading posts. Many talented Navajo weavers live in the Chinle area and earn their entire incomes with their looms.

Canyon de Chelly's north-rim drive takes you 10 miles east to Tsaile, home of **Navajo Community College**. Founded 20 years ago, this is the country's first Indian community college, offering two-year associate degrees. Although humble, the campus features a gleaming glass hogan-shaped building surrounded by several traditional hogans. This is another good place to learn more about Navajos and the reservation. The college runs an excellent book store packed with titles on Native American cultures. It also is host to two annual powwows; for exact dates consult the college.

East of Tsaile, across the heavily wooded Chuska Mountains, you can pick up Highway 666. To the south is **Gallup**, New Mexico, the so-called "Indian Capital of the World," where Navajos, Zunis and other Pueblo people do a good deal of trading. Gallup pawn shops and trading posts usually carry an extensive stock of Navajo jewelry and rugs, Hopi kachina dolls and Pueblo pottery, although prices are never as good as buying directly from the artists. For excellent buys on Navajo rugs, try the town of **Crownpoint**, about 50 miles northwest of Gallup, where six times a year a rug auction attracts buyers from all over the US. Crownpoint is also a convenient stepping-off point for the magnificent Anasazi ruins at **Chaco Culture National Historical Park**, located at the end of a rutted 20-mile dirt road.

About 80 miles north of Crownpoint, past the bizarre, twisted rock formations of the **Bisti Badlands**, is Farmington, a major agricultural center though not very interesting. Another Anasazi site, **Aztec**

Bizarre shapes of Bisti Badlands.

Ruins National Monument, is about 15 miles to the east. The little town of **Shiprock**, named after the jagged cinder cone that soars to an elevation of some 7,000 ft, is located about 25 miles west.

Monument Valley and West: Starting back at Canyon de Chelly, you can head north to Many Farms and catch Highway 59 to **Kayenta**. This is a 66-mile trip through some of the area's most spectacular landscape. The road skirts the northeast flank of huge **Black Mesa**, perhaps the most significant and isolated land mass on the reservation. When you get to the intersection of Highways 59 and 160, take a few minutes to look around. Across a wide expanse to the north is Monument Valley; to the west, beyond Kayenta, is the remote canyonland of Skeleton Mesa. Before you is Church Rock, one of several volcanic plugs jutting out of the area's bright orange sandstone.

Kayenta is not only one of the reservation's prettiest towns, it's a remarkable blend of traditional and modern ways of life. Kayenta's economy is fueled by the Peabody Coal Company, which operates the two largest mines in the country atop Black Mesa. Many of the company's 800 miners live here, giving the town an air of prosperity. With a number of motels, restaurants and service stations, Kayenta also does a brisk business with travelers.

From Kayenta, Highway 163 takes you through wide sandy valleys enclosed by giant plateaus and buttes to **Monument Valley**, the crown jewel of the Navajos' spectacular red-rock country and familiar from countless John Ford westerns. Today it's a tribal park, requiring a $1 fee to travel along the dusty loop road. While the unpaved road may seem inconvenient, especially in the heat of summer, it adds to the ambience and helps retain some of the park's natural quality. Like Canyon de Chelly, Monument Valley is the home of several Navajo families. Children may flag you down to offer a cedar-bead necklace for a few dollars. The money this and other items brings may be a significant addition to their family's income. If you would rather not drive yourself, a number of companies offer van tours with Navajo guides. For many tourists, this is the best way to get off the main trail and see some of the less-traveled areas.

To the west of Kayenta, there is another, perhaps less well-known site, every bit as beautiful and culturally rich as Monument Valley. This is **Navajo National Monument**, site of the Southwest's largest and prettiest prehistoric Indian ruins. From the visitors' center high on the rim of Tsegi Canyon, you can see **Betatakin** ("Ledge House" in Navajo), a ruin of 135 rooms built into a 500-ft-high, scallop-shaped cave hollowed into the canyon wall. Built around AD 1300, Betatakin is thought to be one of three major centers of Anasazi culture, the other two being Chaco Canyon, New Mexico, and Mesa Verde, Colorado (see *Ancestral Ground*). For a closer look at the ruins, the Park Service offers at least one guided trip daily during the summer months.

For those seeking more adventure, the 160-room **Keet Seel** ruin is down an

Shonto Dunes, near Monument Valley.

8-mile trail into Dowozhiebito Canyon. Horses and local guides can be hired to make the trip in a single day. Backpackers usually camp the night. Check with park rangers to make the necessary arrangements.

West of Kayenta, in the low-lying Klethla valley, Highway 98 turns toward the town of **Page**, just over the reservation's northwestern border. Page is the site of **Glen Canyon Dam** and gateway to **Lake Powell**, perhaps the most beautiful body of water in the entire Southwest. The dam is a 710-ft-high concrete plug jammed into a narrow section of Glen Canyon. It was designed to deliver a regular supply of water to downstream users, produce a clean source of electricity, and provide recreation for millions.

But since the dam's completion in 1963, environmentalists have decried the loss of the enchanted Glen Canyon, now sunk in a watery grave beneath Lake Powell. They have also criticized the dam's impact on the Colorado River. More than 40 federally-sponsored environmental impact studies are currently under way.

The most convenient way to explore Lake Powell is by boat. Both houseboats and motorboats may be rented at Wahweap Marina, 5 miles from Page. It is possible to spend weeks exploring the winding sandstone canyons, isolated beaches, remote trails and hidden ruins. Of particular interest is the famed **Rainbow Bridge National Monument**, tucked deep into the recesses of Forbidding Canyon. At 309 feet, Rainbow Bridge is the world's largest natural stone arch. If time is limited, you can catch a one-day tour boat to Rainbow Bridge at Wahweap Marina. Hardy backpackers can also reach it by land on two of the prettiest trails in Arizona. One is 13 miles long, the other 16 miles. Guides can be obtained by inquiring a few days in advance at the Tuba Trading Post (Tuba City) or Navajo Mountain Trading Post (Navajo Mountain).

Leaving Page on Highway 89 south takes you across more miles of beautiful open desert rising into the Navajo sand-

Evening sky over Black Mesa.

stone formations high above House Rock Valley and the Colorado River. About 24 miles south of Page the road passes through the giant "cut" blasted into the cliff face. Pullouts here offer stunning views of the valley below, the high Kaibab and Paria plateaus 10 miles across, and the tips of the San Francisco Peaks more than 100 miles south.

A quick detour on Highway 89A leads you north again across the dangerously narrow Navajo Bridge, spanning **Marble Canyon Gorge** and the Colorado River 467 ft below. Historic **Lee's Ferry**, where all raft trips into the Grand Canyon begin, is another 6 miles north.

Returning to Highway 89 and continuing south, the road quickly descends to the desert floor and is bounded by the rocky face of Echo Cliffs. Aside from a couple of old trading posts, Navajo hogans and cornfields, there is nothing but lovely scenery all the way to the bright-red badlands around the little settlement of **Moenave**. Dinosaur tracks at the Moenave turnoff have been a popular attraction since the turn of the century. The 12-inch, three-toed tracks were left by a dilophosaurus about 60 million years ago.

Nearby, **Tuba City** is the major town in the western portion of the reservation. It was settled in 1870 by Mormon pioneers and named after a Hopi chief. In addition to government offices and medical facilities, Tuba City has one motel, several restaurants, a theater and large supermarket. If you happen to be passing through on a Friday, be sure to stop at the local flea market behind the big white community center. Dozens of vendors and hundreds of shoppers gather here to buy and sell everything from herbal medicines and Indian art to hot mutton sandwiches. It's a cultural treat to drift through the booths, enjoy the smell of cooking fires, and hear the old people talking in their native languages.

Across the road from Tuba City is the Hopi village of **Moenkopi**, the Hopi Indians' westernmost settlement. Hopis say they have used the lovely canyon as a farming satellite for some 300 years before the Navajos arrived in this re-

Stringing beads at a roadside stand near Tuba City.

gion. A ruin high on a promontory across from the village shows evidence of prehistoric habitation.

This small Hopi town was permanently settled about the time the Mormons arrived in 1870. In fact, the old Mormon church still stands in the village next to the cemetery where Tuba's first pioneers now rest. Just past the entrance, you can see that the village is divided into upper and lower sections. The old stone pueblos of Lower Moenkopi are considered to be the most traditional part of the village, similar in appearance to the original settlement. This is a good place to buy kachina carvings, paintings and other Hopi art directly from the makers, and for very reasonable prices. Ask for the information at the Clifford Honahnie Building as you enter the village.

South of Tuba City, the highway heads across the ice-cream-colored rocks of the **Painted Desert**. This is where 200-million-year-old shale, mudstone and sandstone streak the landscape with bands of brilliant red, green and tawny rock. Although bare and alkaline, the desert is scattered with bits of petrified wood, a survival of the ancient forest that once flourished here. To the east, **Petrified Forest National Park** offers trails, information and some of the most dramatic vistas in the Painted Desert.

Travelers have convenient access to Grand Canyon National Park, adjacent to the reservation's western border; the ancient ruins at Wupatki and Walnut Canyon national monuments; and the cities of Flagstaff and Sedona.

If you want to find out more about the Navajos, two excellent museums are within reasonable driving distance of the reservation: the **Museum of Northern Arizona** in Flagstaff and the **Heard Museum** in Phoenix. The Museum of Northern Arizona sponsors an annual Navajo art show and exhibition, usually in July. Farther afield, the Museum of Indian Arts and Culture and the Wheelwright Museum in Santa Fe, and the great Southwest Museum in Los Angeles all maintain first-class collections of Navajo art and artifacts. **Navajo elder.**

NAVAJO SAND PAINTING

Over the past 40 years, Navajo sand painting has moved out of the relative obscurity of the hogan floor into trading posts, gift shops, museums and galleries throughout the Southwest and beyond.

The exact origin of sand painting – once also known as dry painting – is lost in the mists of Navajo mythology, although it seems possible that the practice was borrowed from the Pueblo people after the Navajos' ancestors migrated into the Southwest some 700 years ago.

Traditionally, sand paintings are made during nightlong Navajo healing rituals, known as "sings." They are created on the floor of a ceremonial hogan by specially trained medicine men, who often spend years learning the elaborate prayers, chants and sand painting designs.

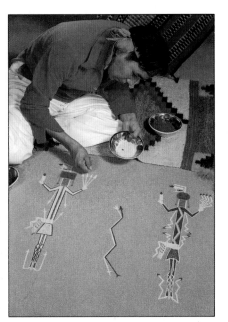

Softly singing the various chants of the rite, and depending on the cure required by the patient, the medicine man sifts the colorful crushed stone, corn pollen and other sacred materials through his thumb and index finger, slowly creating the appropriate design. Most sand paintings tend to be about 2 or 3 feet across, but others reach as much as 20 ft and require helpers to complete.

The most common designs feature the Navajo gods, or yeis, who are invoked during the ceremony to help cure the patient. The stick-figure yeis may be encircled by the Navajo rainbow, with crossed lines holding the four sacred directions, feathers or representations of animals. At the end of the ceremony, just before dawn, the sacred images are destroyed. The sand is collected and buried north of the hogan; a little may be given to the patient. If the ceremony continues for several nights, different sand paintings are created for each part of the cure.

Little was known of sand painting until the 1880s when Washington Matthews, a military doctor stationed on the Navajo Reservation, became the first white man to observe and study a Mountainway Chant.

While Matthews is credited with being the first to translate Navajo ceremonies, it was some 30 years before a scholar delved into the sand paint-ing rituals. In the 1920s, Gladys A. Reichard committed herself to learning the ceremonies. First she spent five years mastering the compli-cated Navajo language and then learned the chants themselves from a singer named Miguelito.

Today, permanent sand paintings are made spe-cifically for the non-Indian market. In addition to traditional paintings of yeis, rainbows, shooting stars and whirling logs, contemporary paintings incorporate landscapes, Indian portraits, pottery and rug designs, and abstract images. The tech-nique is also being applied to badges, name plates, wall hangings, even lamps and figurines.

Like other forms of native religious art, the market for Navajo sand painting was virtually created by traders and collectors, and it has stead-ily grown in popularity ever since. Prices range from a simple $8 piece up to $2,000 or more for large, framed collectibles by a well-known artist.

The tools of the sand painter are quite simple. The piece begins with a board upon which glue is applied in the shape of the design. Sand is then care-fully sprinkled from above. There is little room for error, so patience is essential, especially as the work becomes more de-tailed.

Although commercial sand paintings are made by hundreds of Navajos throughout the reserva-tion, the best-known art-ists are centered around the Shiprock area of New Mexico. According to trader Jed Foutz of the Shiprock Trading Post, the most talented of these artists come from Sheep Springs, 45 miles south.

For traditional sand paintings, says Foutz, the Myerson family – father Cecil, mother Jean and son Sammy – and any of the dozen relatives and in-laws of the Ben family are highly regarded. For the contemporary style, no one comes close to Eugene Joe. But Foutz advises visitors to ask about the many up-and-coming sand painters from the Shiprock area and elsewhere.

Like other Indian arts and crafts, sand paintings can be purchased at galleries, gift shops, even Southwestern department stores. But to get a good buy, the best places to go are the trading posts on or near the Navajo Reservation. Traders often know the artists personally and can steer travelers to quality pieces at the best price.

HOPI HOMELAND

Hopi tradition says that before the earth was created, the spirits lived in a world called Tokpela, which means boundless space. It was a beautiful world and the spirit people lived happily with one another. Then came the time for the earth to be created and for the spirit people to take human form. There was a great gathering and the Creator chose the spirits who were to begin life on earth in physical form. But before long, the people strayed from the instructions of the Creator Spirit and became wicked. And so, this First World was destroyed by fire, and only those who still remembered the Creator Spirit's instructions were saved.

When the fires cooled, the Second World rose up and flourished. But once again, the people grew evil, desiring material goods and forgetting the Creator's way. As before, the Creator Spirit caused the Second World to be destroyed, this time with ice.

Another civilization, the Third World, rose up. It was less beautiful than the first two worlds, but the people were content, until again, many became corrupt and made war with each other. Immorality was rife, and the people did not heed the Creator or their own leaders. The people who still remembered the Creator's instructions began to look for sanctuary in another world. They heard sounds of movement above. They searched for a path and finally emerged into the Fourth World, the present world, where Masaw, caretaker of the Earth, resided. The people asked Masaw's permission to live with him in the Fourth World. He agreed but told them that life in this world was difficult.

And then the Hopi clans migrated for countless generations, traveling in all four directions in search of the Center of the Earth. They were given divine instructions to build communities of stone, because these stone houses would endure long after they departed and mark the boundaries of their domain for others to see in the future. They finally settled on an arid plateau between the Rio Grande and Colorado River, a place so barren that they would have to depend on prayer for rain and food; where they would never again forget to be thankful to the Creator Spirit.

And this is where the Hopis now live, their old stone villages perched atop three finger-like mesas protruding from the Colorado Plateau, modern villages below. The most ancient, Old Oraibi, was settled as much as 1,000 years ago and is reputed to be the oldest continuously inhabited village in the US.

It is a stark and rugged country dominated by tones of red and brown, by jagged sandstone outcroppings, and by the striking enormity of earth and sky. Made of stone blocks, the old pueblos are almost indistinguishable from the mesas themselves. They are low and flat-roofed, and built to the very edge of the cliffs. Dust clouds spin through the alleys and are hurled to the desert floor, more than 200 ft below. In June and July, eagles sit impassively on the roofs of one or two homes, waiting to fulfill

their sacred purpose. Their feathers will be used for *pahos*, or prayer sticks – offerings to the spirits that are left in shrines all over the mesas. Later, the eagles will be sacrificed, sent back to the ancestors with prayers for rain.

White People Come: When Francisco de Coronado made his *entrada* into the Southwest in 1540, the Hopis had already been settled in their mesa homes for hundreds of years, practicing dry farming, miraculously coaxing corn, beans and melons from the desert in much the same way as the ancestral Hisatsinom – People of the Ancient Times – more commonly known as the Anasazi (a Navajo word meaning "Enemy Ancestor"). Many Hopi farmers use the same techniques today.

In their quest for gold and "pagan" souls, the Spanish brought the Hopis to their knees. They closed kivas (underground ceremonial chambers), forbade Hopi ceremonies, and forced the Indians into virtual slavery. Spanish oppression among the Hopis and other Pueblo people erupted in the Pueblo Revolt of 1680. The normally pacifist Hopis participated in the uprising and executed all the friars on the Hopi mesas and destroyed the missions. The Catholic Church never re-established itself in Hopi country, although other denominations have set up churches. None, however, has a large following.

Following the Pueblo Revolt, the Hopi enjoyed a brief period of independence. The Spanish and Mexican governments never had the vitality to exert much influence over the remote Hopi villages, and they were left in relative peace until the westward settlement of Americans once again disrupted the tranquility of Hopi life. American expansionism in the mid-1800s also forced Navajo Indians into Hopi territory, instigating a land dispute between the two tribes that is still being fought today, although the battlefields are now in Congress and the courts.

Traditionally, the Hopi villages were autonomous, self-governing bodies. Village government consisted of a spiritual leader known as a *kikmongwi*, a **Bird's-eye view of Hopi village.**

group of officials called "decision makers," and a *qaleetaqa* (or war captain). In effect, it resembled a theocracy.

More recently, the majority of the Hopi villages have organized themselves along modern lines in accordance with the Indian Reorganization Act of 1934. In so doing, the Hopi people became – at least officially – a "tribe," a foreign concept to a people who had organized themselves by clans and villages for millennia. But the Hopis were no longer alone on their ancestral land. Americans proved more powerful than the Mexicans, and the elders saw that it was necessary to "provide a way to deal with modern problems… and with the outside world generally." A constitution was adopted authorizing a democratic form of government at the tribal level.

Spiritual life: The Hopis are noted above all for being a deeply religious people. Religion is so completely intertwined with the rest of life that isolating it is like unraveling the entire Hopi universe. And for the Hopis, spirituality is truly a universal concern. Hopi elders believe that they have inherited stewardship over Mother Earth. They are obliged to protect her and maintain the religion on behalf of all humankind. This stewardship is carried out through priesthood societies called *wuutsim*. These societies conduct religious ceremonies to ensure the temporal and spiritual well-being of all people, and to achieve a balanced and peaceful relationship with the spirit world and the natural environment.

There are also priestess societies and other religious groups such as the Snake and Kachina societies, each assigned a specific time of year to conduct their ceremonies. Together, they form the spiritual infrastructure of Hopi society. Their ceremonies, like the insistent beating of a Hopi drum, mark the cadence of traditional Hopi life.

In the Hopi view, kinship is not limited to the mortal world. Men and women who have been initiated into the Kachina Society are also fathers and mothers of the kachina spirits. When they manifest themselves as rain clouds, the kachinas

Left, traditional desert farming. Right, Hopi dancer.

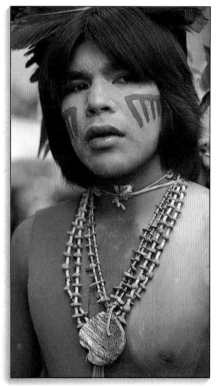

in turn become fathers of the people.

Kachinas are spiritual beings – intermediaries between people and the Great Spirit. As ancestral spirits, they connect the Hopis with the past. As spirits of plants, animals and other natural forces, they link the Hopis with the natural world. Kachinas also act as messengers between the Hopis and the domain of the Rain People. They manifest themselves as clouds and bring life-giving rain to the Hopis' arid fields.

From late July to December, the kachinas live in San Franciso Peaks, about 90 miles south of the pueblos. In midwinter they come to the villages, where they dance in the kivas and plazas. Dances are held in one of the villages almost every weekend during the spring and early summer, and many are open to visitors, so long as they abide by a few rules. In particular, photography, sketching, audio and video taping are strictly forbidden.

Before the kachinas arrive, the people gather on the rooftops and along the edges of the dusty plaza. Ritual clowns – sometimes striped with black and white paint – wander about the plaza playing jokes on the spectators, turning everything sacred upside-down. Later, when the kachinas dance, they act as attendants, blessing the dancers with cornmeal and fixing their elaborate outfits.

And then the kachinas arrive. They are magnificent beings, their heads covered with beautiful masks, their painted bodies resplendent with turquoise jewelry, eagle feathers, pine boughs, sashes and kilts. They move in unison, chanting a melodic prayer in deep muffled voices, their tortoise-shell rattles sending up a hollow, rhythmic clatter as their feet pound the earth in time with the drum. At the end of the dance, the kachinas may give the people gifts – baskets filled with traditional food, bread, fruit and store goods. At some dances they give little girls kachina carvings, so the young ones will come to know them. Although some Hopis frown on the practice, many Hopi artists carve kachina dolls for sale. The best carvings can be extraordinary works of art and bring in much-needed income.

The kachinas return to their mountain home in July after the Niman or Home Dance. During this phase of the ritual cycle, other ceremonies are held, including the famous Snake Dance in which members of the Snake Society dance with snakes in their mouths – many of them poisonous rattlesnakes – while other snakes writhe on the plaza floor. At the end of the ceremony the snakes are allowed to return to the desert carrying prayers for rain on the Hopis' behalf. This is also the time for summer social dances – the Butterfly Dance, among others – in which young men and unmarried young women dance together.

With only 10 inches of precipitation per year, the main concern of much Hopi religion is rain and the growth of corn, their most important crop. Traditionally, corn is the lifeblood of Hopi society, the very cornerstone of survival, and as such, it figures prominently in ceremonial life. The four colors of Indian corn represent the four directions of the Hopi universe, and sacred corn meal is used in many rituals to purify and bless and as a sacramental offering to give thanks for the good things gathered from Mother Earth.

The connection between corn and life is made at the time of birth when a perfectly formed ear of native white corn is placed next to the newborn child and another next to the mother for a period of 20 days. The ear of corn represents their spiritual mother, Mother Earth, from whence the corn was formed and to which the bodies of the baby and mother will return upon death. On the twentieth day, the perfect ear of corn is used to bless the baby at a naming ritual, completing the child's passage from the spirit world to earthly existence. This ritual is repeated at the kachina initiation rite at about 11 years of age and at the tribal initiation rites into the priesthood societies upon reaching adulthood. At the final rite of passage back into the spirit world, cornmeal is applied to the face of the deceased.

Blue corn meal is also used in the Hopis' paper-thin piki bread. Hopi women make piki by spreading a thin batter across a hot polished stone, then peeling off and folding the bread. Piki is served on most ceremonial occasions and other special events, and is often available at the Hopi Cultural Center on Second Mesa.

Artistic tradition: The Hopis have a long and distinguished history as artists. In fact, some of the finest pottery, jewelry, baskets and carvings to come out of the Southwest are crafted by Hopi hands. The artists of First Mesa are especially noted for their pottery, which is built by hand (without a potter's wheel), smoothed with a polishing stone and fired outdoors, usually with dung. The pots are then hand-painted with intricate designs using fine yucca-fiber brushes and natural paints.

Second and Third mesas are renowned for basketry, one variety made of woven wicker, the other of coiled yucca. Kachina dolls are made on all the mesas and are carved from cottonwood roots.

Hopi silversmiths specialize in the distinctive overlay style, although a number of talented jewelers are now branching off into inlay and channel work with turquoise, jet, corral, shell and other semiprecious stones, and a few jewelers work with gold settings.

The best place to start looking for Hopi art is at the **Hopi Cultural Center** on Second Mesa, which contains both a museum and a gift shop as well as a motel and restaurant. Many craftspeople also work out of their homes, where visitors can buy direct and see them at work. Ordinarily you can stop by at any reasonable hour, but it's always best to make prior arrangements. Call the Hopi Cultural Center for details. Tours usually include stops at workshops, craft stores, the old picturesque villages, and other places of interest. They may also include piki-making demonstrations, video tapes about Hopi life, and other special exhibitions. Although guided tours do not include kachina dances in the village plazas, dances are open to the public during the "kachina season" and visitors may see them on their own. There are also about a dozen gift shops on the reservation, most of them close to the main highway. Watch for signs.

Corn, the lifeblood of Hopi society.

Being a good guest: While attending dances, visitors are expected to be respectful, quiet and unobtrusive. It is particularly important not to ask questions about the identity of the participants, about the masks, or to ask children about relatives who might be involved in the dance in any way. Children are not told until they go through the proper initiation that kachinas are only impersonators and not the real spirit people. Later, in private, visitors can try asking a guide or a Hopi friend about the ceremonies, although when the question is of an esoteric nature, answers are often not forthcoming.

Again, photography, sketching and recording is not permitted at the dances or in many villages. Doing so will result in confiscation of film, and perhaps even the camera, by Indian police.

It is also strongly recommended that conservative clothing be worn by visitors attending the dances – especially women. This is a way of making life easier for the participants, mostly men, who are called upon to undergo a devotional period of abstinence before the ceremony.

There are shrines of various kinds within the confines of the villages as well as on the outskirts, including the edge of the mesas. Offerings – especially prayer sticks – are deposited regularly at these shrines and hold a great deal of spiritual significance for Hopi people. If you accidentally encounter an offering, do not disturb it. Taking objects or artifacts of any type is highly offensive to the Hopis and is an infraction of tribal law. At the very least you will be escorted off the reservation, if not charged with a criminal act. Similarly, it is unwise to buy ritual objects such as prayer sticks, masks or fetishes, or ancient artifacts such as pottery shards, from any questionable source.

Finally, remember that the old pueblos are still the private homes of the Hopi people and should not be entered without an invitation. If invited into a home while the family is sitting at the meal table, you may be invited to eat. It is only polite to join them and partake of at least a little bit.

Accommodation at the Hopi Cultural Center is frequently difficult to obtain during the kachina season – early spring through late summer – so make reservations well in advance, a few months if possible. Limited accommodation on the reservation is also available at the Keams Canyon Motel, located 20 miles east of the Hopi Cultural Center and 10 miles from the closest Hopi villages at First Mesa. Otherwise, the nearest available rooms are in the peripheral towns of Flagstaff, Holbrook, Winslow and Tuba City.

According to tradition, the Hopi homeland is the spiritual center of the earth. It is a chosen place where the Hopis' spiritual fathers have inherited the duty to preserve the spiritual well-being of all humankind on behalf of the Great Spirit. Indeed, people from all over the world come to the Center of the Earth for spiritual rejuvenation. The Hopis hope that all people will share these thoughts and an aspiration for a good life when they come to visit Hopiland.

Hopi basket maker.

THE ART OF HOPI KACHINA CARVING

Since time immemorial, Hopi men have carved wooden replicas of the Hopi spirit-beings, *katsinam*, known as kachinas among non-Hopis. Called *tihu* in Hopi and "kachina dolls" in English, these effigies are given to Hopi children to teach them about religion. Today, kachina dolls are one of the Hopis' most developed and highly valued art forms and a Hopi trademark recognized around the world.

Unlike pottery and silversmithing, which tend to be done by specialists on First and Second mesas, kachina carving is practiced in all of Hopis' 12 villages. And much of the craftsmanship is truly exquisite.

Kachina carving is deeply rooted in Hopi religion, still a vital and pervasive part of the culture, binding one aspect of Hopi life to another. In earliest times, the Hopi say, religion inspired the ancestors' migration to their remote mesa homeland. More recently, it has enabled the Hopi to withstand the encroachment of the modern world into their simpler, humbler way of life.

Among the most important aspects of Hopi religion are the kachina societies into which all Hopis are initiated at about the age of nine or ten. The kachina spirits are as innumerable as the laws of nature, for that is what they are. Some are the spirits of ancestors hidden by the clouds. Others make the rain fall and the corn grow, or bestow blessings upon the people.

For half the year, from about the winter solstice in December until the Niman Kachina ceremony, or Home Dance, in July, these spirits live among the Hopis in their mesa villages. During these months they are represented by ornately costumed men – kachina dancers – who perform various dances in the kivas and village plazas. The rest of the year, the kachinas reside in the high mountains of the San Francisco Peaks, in clear view about 90 miles south of the reservation, just north of Flagstaff, Arizona.

It is believed that there are some 350 kinds of kachinas depicted by the carvings, but like all works of art, no two are exactly alike. Like all things Hopi, the carvings are considered sacred. Although dolls, they are not toys. And although religious in origin, they are now a major source of income for many Hopi families.

Some carvers, like Dennis Tewa of Moenkopi, Ronald Honyouti of Hotevilla and Neil David of Kykotsmovi, bring prices in the thousands of dollars for their work, much of which is immediately snatched up by museums and private collectors. The talents of these and other artists have elevated kachina carving into the realm of fine, rare and high-priced art.

There are two basic styles of kachina carving, traditional and sculptural. Traditional pieces are crafted from the soft root of the native cottonwood tree and come closest in appearance to the kachina dancers who take part in the plaza ceremonies. At one time, these figures were fashioned in rigid poses with legs together and arms to the side. Today, they are more often depicted in a dancing pose, in the middle of a ritualistic act.

Traditional carvings are usually painted in minute detail, adorned with leather, shell, turquoise, fur and feathers. The carver's name can be found beneath the cottonwood stand, ensuring that it is Hopi-made and not an imitation.

Sculptural carvings feature the virtuosity of the artist as much as traditional religious symbolism, making them even more valuable to collectors. Pieces carved from a single piece of wood, either following the curve of the grain or taking its own shape, may, for instance, have all the intricate lines of a feather etched in impeccable minuscule detail. These works are frequently stained rather than painted, with the exception of adornments applied with natural dyes.

Travelers can find kachina dolls for sale at trading posts, gift shops and galleries throughout Hopi and Navajo country. But the best way to save money and learn what the dolls represent is to buy directly from the carvers who make them. Hopi-owned galleries on the reservation, as well as the Hopi Arts and Crafts Guild on Second Mesa, are also highly recommended. To learn more about Hopi kachinas, visit the Heard Museum in Phoenix or the Museum of Northern Arizona in Flagstaff.

NEW MEXICO'S PUEBLO COUNTRY

In the quiet hours before dusk, long finger-like shadows creep along the cut-stone houses of Zuni Pueblo. At the main plaza, people gather on the rooftops. Children play along the edges, jumping from one roof to another, while old women in colorful shawls sit in the gallery below. Smoke rises from the chimneys into the sky, sending the sweet sting of cedar over the crowd. To the east, thunderheads darken the sky over Corn Mountain, Zuni's sacred mesa.

Huddled on a ridge near a trickling stream, the village seems a defense against the vast spaces of the high New Mexican desert. Before the Spanish arrived, the Zuni called this place *Halona Itwana* – the Middle Anthill of the World – and at the end of the day, when the village is backlit by the sun, it's easy to see how the old terraced pueblo must have resembled mounds of ant-sifted dirt. The Zuni say their ancestors emerged from beneath the earth and, after years of wandering, settled on this dry plateau. Today, the ancestors return to the village in the form of clouds, bearing the scarce blessing of rain.

A muffled cry carries over the dusty labyrinth of alleyways, and a hush falls over the crowd. A rhythmic jingle grows louder and louder. And then, as if from thin air, the kachinas stride into the plaza. They are colorful, commanding figures – part beast, part human, part spirit. Their masks are a riot of colors – red, black and brilliant turquoise. Their bodies are adorned with exquisite jewelry, feathered ruffs, pine boughs, rattles and ankle bells. Even the children know their names – Shulawitsi, the little fire god; Sayatasha, the rain god of the north; Yamukato, the frightful warrior.

As usual, the *koyemshi*, or mudheads, are also in attendance. They are ritual clowns, representing the deranged children of incest. Their masks are like knobby helmets with protruding eyes and puckered lips. They are at once the funniest and most sacred of the Zuni kachinas, and the men who impersonate

them must often give up work for an entire year to fulfill their many ceremonial obligations.

The kachinas file into the plaza and form a circle. A drum sounds, and a group of masked singers takes up the rhythm. The kachinas hesitate for a moment, and then, bowing at the knee, begin the trotting, back-and-forth dance that one sees in countless variations throughout Pueblo Country. It is a dance to wake the earth, to stir the clouds. It brings rain to the parched landscape and life to the people.

The ancient ones: Zuni is one of 19 Indian pueblos in New Mexico, most clustered along the Rio Grande between Albuquerque and Taos. Although they share a common history and culture, Pueblo Indians don't consider themselves a single people so much as a collection of autonomous units. Each pueblo is governed independently by civic and religious leaders, and stubbornly maintains a distinct identity.

Nor do they all speak the same language. Including the Hopi villages in

Arizona, Pueblo people represent four language families – Zunian, Tanoan, Keresan and Shoshonean – and six distinct languages. Although nobody knows for sure where the Pueblo people migrated from, it is clear that they are the cultural descendants of the Anasazi – a Navajo word meaning "ancient ones" – whose dramatic cliff-dwellings, rock art and pottery are scattered throughout the Four Corners area.

The Anasazi ruins at Mesa Verde, Chaco Canyon, Aztec ruins, Canyon de Chelly, Bandelier National Monument and hundreds of other sites, speak volumes to archaeologists about the complexity of Anasazi life, but exactly why this great civilization collapsed in the 14th century is still something of a mystery. Some archaeologists point to severe climatic change, others to overpopulation, Athabaskan raiders and depletion of resources.

According to traditional Zuni beliefs, however, the deeper truth about the past is to be found in the ancient stories of emergence. Although details vary from pueblo to pueblo, the basic outline of the creation story is the same, tracing the journey of the ancestors through four successive underworlds and their eventual emergence into this, the middle world, through an opening commonly referred to as the *sipapu.*

The historical trail picks up again with the arrival of the Spanish in 1539. The first Spanish explorer to make contact with the Pueblo people was a Franciscan priest, Fray Marcos de Niza, whose desire for treasure and heathen souls led him in search of the mythical Seven Cities of Cibola. Together with a black guide named Estevan and a retinue of Indian servants, Fray Marcos approached within sight of the Zuni village of Hawikuh, now in ruins. Estevan had been sent ahead of the party in order to make contact with the Indians, but, according to Zuni legend, the "Black Kachina" showed so little respect for his hosts that the Zuni killed him and cut up his body. Terrified by the murder, Fray Marcos fled to Mexico with exaggerated accounts of the great treasure-laden cities that lay to the north.

The following year, a second and larger expedition was launched under the leadership of Francisco Vásquez de Coronado. With several hundred horsemen under his command, Coronado easily overran the Zuni villages, and after a brief stay pushed on to the Rio Grande, where he commandeered an entire pueblo, demanded to be fed, and then burned several villages and executed hundreds of Indians after they resisted. It was the beginning of a long and abusive relationship.

Coronado returned to Mexico in 1542, and for nearly 40 years the Pueblo people enjoyed relative peace. By 1581, the Spanish took a new interest in the New Mexican territories, and several small expeditions set out to make contact with the pueblos – all of whom shed more Indian blood. In 1598, a formal effort to colonize the area was launched by the Spanish. It was led by Don Juan de Oñate, who, with a large force of soldiers, priests and servants quickly established a program of "civilizing" and converting the Indians.

San Ildefonso Pueblo corn dance.

Although the Pueblo Indians offered little in the way of gold and treasure, they possessed a bounty of land, labor and souls, and Oñate wasted no time in exploiting them all. The Pueblo people were not only required to pay burdensome tributes to the Spanish, they were forced to work on mission compounds and private ranches.

Worse yet, they were forbidden to practice their native religion. Determined to exterminate the Indians' "pagan" beliefs, the Franciscan fathers raided kivas and destroyed masks, prayer plumes and other sacred objects. Men who were caught performing kachina dances were whipped or killed. The Pueblos were forced to conduct their ceremonies in secret. To this day, they are extremely protective about their native beliefs. Access to kivas and most ceremonial events is strictly prohibited to outsiders.

By 1680, the Pueblo Indians had had enough of Spanish domination. Under the clandestine leadership of a San Juan medicine man named Po Pay, they plotted a general insurrection. On August 10, 1680, Pueblo warriors rose as a single body against the Spanish, slaughtering priests and administrators, destroying missions and laying siege to the capital at Santa Fe. Badly outnumbered, the Spanish beat a quick retreat south to El Paso.

The Revolt of 1680 freed the villages of Spanish influence, but the period of liberation – 12 precious years – was all too brief. In 1692, Diego de Vargas marched into Santa Fe and spent the next four years re-establishing colonial rule. The Spanish retained power over the Pueblo people until 1821, when Mexico took command of the territory, only to lose it to the US in 1846. At the time of Coronado's arrival, there were approximately 85 pueblos in New Mexico. Today, only 19 survive. But despite the destructive power of the government and church, of war and disease, Pueblo people have managed to make it into the 20th century with their native cultures intact.

The western fringe: Zuni is the

Anasazi ruins at Chaco Canyon.

westernmost and largest pueblo in New Mexico. Culturally, Zuni is more akin to Hopi than to the Rio Grande villages; the similarity is most apparent in its elaborate kachina dances. Although Zuni was the first pueblo to be contacted by the Spanish, it didn't suffer quite the same depredation that the Rio Grande pueblos did, partly because the villages were located so far off the beaten path. As a result, Zunis seem fairly secure about the presence of outsiders, even on ceremonial occasions.

Most travelers come to Zuni for one of two reasons: dances and jewelry. Zuni kachina dances are truly spectacular; but because they are rarely announced in advance, and only then within the small circle of the pueblo community, they are often difficult to catch. You can try calling the tribal council, but your best bet is to visit in late winter and early spring, when a good deal of dancing takes place at the main plaza (near the mission church) for a couple of hours before sunset. The one exception to this rule is the magnificent Shalako

ceremony, a year-long ritual that culminates in the winter when the 12-ft bird-like figures known as Shalakos visit the pueblo and dance all night long. It is one of the most magnificent ceremonies in Indian Country and open to visitors. There are strict regulations, and some talk about restricting non-Indians in the future, so contact the tribal council beforehand for details.

The Zunis are also well known for their exquisite jewelry, which tends to be highly refined and delicate. They specialize in mosaic-like inlay and channel work as well as a bead-like style called needlepoint. There are a number of trading posts clustered outside the village on Highway 58, including the tribally owned arts and crafts co-op and privately owned **Turquoise Village**, **Shiwi Village** and **Pueblo Trading Post**. Visitors may also visit a number of unexcavated archaeological sites, including **Hawikuh**, one of the seven villages occupied by the Zuni at the time of Spanish contact, and the **Village of the Great Kivas**, which has

Zuni jewelry.

a number of well-preserved petroglyphs. It is absolutely essential to get permission from the Zuni tribal government before visiting the sites.

Standing 90 miles to the east of the Zuni Reservation, **Acoma** is the most dramatic of the New Mexican pueblos. One of the oldest continuously inhabited villages in the country, the village of Acoma, now called **Sky City**, is perched atop a 365-ft sandstone mesa. Although most Acomas now live in outlying towns, the old pueblo is still inhabited by about 12 families year-round and is kept in excellent repair for a variety of ceremonial events. The two- and three-story buildings, many entered only via ladder, have no electricity or plumbing. Rainwater is still collected from "water pots" carved into the rock as much as 800 years ago.

Contact with the Spanish was particularly devastating at Acoma. After Acoma warriors killed a party of tribute-collectors, Juan de Oñate's army stormed the pueblo and slaughtered 800 villagers. As punishment for their impudence,

all Acoma men over 25 years old were sentenced to the amputation of one foot and 20 years of slavery. Women over 25 were also sentenced to 20 years of labor, while the children were handed over to the priests to be raised.

Today, access to Sky City is tightly monitored. Outsiders must stop at the visitors' center at the base of the mesa and then ride to the village with a tour guide. There is an admission charge, plus an optional fee for photography and sketching. The tour includes a stop at **San Esteban Rey Mission**, a monumental adobe church originally built in the 17th century. All the materials used in construction were carried to the mesa-top by Acoma laborers, including the massive ceiling beams, which came from Mount Taylor, nearly 50 miles away. Legend has it that the giant logs never touched the ground.

During the tour of the village, there are plenty of opportunities to buy Acoma pottery, considered some of the finest in New Mexico. Prices and quality vary, but the best pieces are hand-built, thin-

walled and painstakingly painted with natural dyes. Among the many fine potters at Acoma, Lucy Lewis, and the Lewis sisters, are perhaps the most famous. Their work is exquisite, and predictably high-priced.

Laguna Pueblo, located adjacent to Acoma on the opposite side of Highway 40, consists of several small villages, with the original, Old Laguna, in the center. Laguna was founded in 1699 by Keresan refugees who had been chased out of their old villages by the Spanish. It also attracted settlers from Zuni, Jemez and Hopi. Old Laguna has none of the drama of Acoma, although the **Church of St Stephen**, built nearly 300 years ago, is one of the prettiest pueblo missions in New Mexico.

Rio Grande Pueblos: Adjacent to Laguna, the large **Isleta Reservation** stretches across the fertile bottomland of the Rio Grande just south of Albuquerque. For reasons that are not entirely clear, Isleta was the only pueblo that did not join the Revolt of 1680. Routed by the northern pueblos, the Spanish re-

treated to the garrison at Isleta, and together with about 300 Indians, continued south to El Paso. After 20 years in exile, the Isletas returned and rebuilt the village, including the massive **Church of St Augustine**, reputedly the oldest continuously used church in the US still standing on its original foundation. The church still dominates Isleta's broad dusty plaza, and visitors are welcome to enter. There are a number of small arts and crafts shops in the squat, lopsided adobes that surround the plaza, although none are especially distinctive. Isleta is famous for its homemade bread, however, baked each morning in the beehive ovens, or *hornos,* found outside most homes.

From Isleta, Highway 25 passes through Albuquerque and then, about 15 miles farther north, cuts through the **Sandia Reservation**. The dusty village offers little of interest for most travelers, but the pueblo runs the exceptional **Bien Mur** arts and crafts market just off the highway at the base of Sandia Peak. The selection of jewelry, pottery, weavings

San Juan Pueblo deer dance.

and other arts and crafts is quite good and prices are reasonable, certainly better than at most shops in Albuquerque or Santa Fe.

Sandia is the first in a cluster of seven pueblos nestled at the foot of the San Pedro Mountains just north of Albuquerque. Generally speaking, they are quite conservative when it comes to tourism, so an extra measure of circumspection is in order. One pueblo, **Santa Ana**, is closed to outsiders on all but its feast day. The others are all well worth visiting during public dances, and most have lively trading posts and beautiful Spanish missions.

Starting from the south, both **San Felipe** and **Santo Domingo** are highly traditional pueblos well known for their large and inspiring Corn Dances, a dignified ceremony of chanting and dancing performed by as many as 500 men, women and children. Black-and-white striped clowns known as *koshare* often accompany the dance, playing tricks on the audience and tending to the dancers' needs. In addition to the dances,

there are a number of trading posts near the entrance to Santo Domingo Pueblo, and at least one – Martin Rosetta Trading Co. – carries a fine selection of local work. Pay particular attention to the strands of shell known as heishi, a Santo Domingo specialty.

Just north of Santo Domingo is the pueblo of **Cochiti**. Aside from the 300-year-old **San Buenaventura Mission**, there isn't much at Cochiti to attract visitors. The old village has largely been abandoned for modern housing, and there are no trading posts or shops to speak of, although for the past 30 years or so Cochiti has made a name for itself with clay "storyteller" figurines, usually an Indian woman with a passel of tiny children crawling on her lap. Cochiti Lake is also located on the reservation, with a small marina, golf course and campground nearby.

The other pueblos in this cluster – **Zia** and **Jemez** – are of varying interest to the casual visitor. Zia Pueblo is located atop a mound of volcanic rock and makes quite a dramatic impression but offers

little in the way of shops or trading posts. About 10 miles away, Jemez Pueblo is located at the entrance to **Jemez Canyon**, a stunning gorge scatter-shot with natural hot springs. The passage through the canyon takes you past the ruins of the old village of Giusewa at **Jemez State Monument**, occupied by the ancestors of the Jemez Indians before the arrival of the Spanish. Looping through the canyon toward Los Alamos also brings you past the fascinating Anasazi ruins at **Bandelier National Monument**, occupied between AD 1100 and 1500.

Pushing north, a second cluster of pueblos is located between Santa Fe and Taos. The southernmost of these – **Tesuque**, **Nambe** and **Pojoaque** – are rather modest communities, although both Tesuque and Nambe are well-maintained villages with a traditional core. Nambe also offers camping, fishing and sightseeing at the **Nambe Falls Recreation Area**, located against the stunning snow-capped peaks of the Sangre de Cristo Mountains.

The story is quite different a few miles away at **Santa Clara** and **San Ildefonso**. Both of these Tewa-speaking pueblos are trim, neatly kept villages that have carved a lucrative niche for themselves in the pottery market. The black-on-black pottery style created by Maria and Julian Martinez in the 1920s and refined by the Tafoya, Naranjo and other families has spawned a lively trade in Indian pottery of all types. Tourists and collectors are often surprised at how much even the tiny ornamental pots can fetch these days.

San Ildefonso is a bit more restrictive than Santa Clara when it comes to tourism. Visitors must pay an entrance fee and are not allowed to wander freely around the village. There is a modest pottery exhibition next to pueblo headquarters and several small pottery shops, including one owned by Maria Martinez's daughter-in-law, Anita Da. Santa Clara also has several good shops, including **Singing Water Pottery**, near the pueblo entrance. Just outside the village, the dramatic Anasazi ruins at

Left, Matachina dancer. Right, Taos Pueblo, traditional adobe dwelling.

Puye Cliffs are also administered by Santa Clara. Puye is said to be the ancestral home of Santa Clara as well as other Tewa pueblos. Like the ruins at Bandelier, the cliff-dwellings are cut directly into the soft volcanic tuff and require some fairly precarious ladder-climbing to visit.

About 5 miles north of Santa Clara is **San Juan Pueblo**, a political leader among the pueblos, with a strong traditional backbone. In addition to a year-round offering of public ceremonies, the pueblo offers a number of shops dealing in locally produced arts and crafts, including the large **O'ke Oweenge Crafts Cooperative**. San Juan is also the headquarters of the Eight Northern Indian Pueblos Council, a great place to get information about upcoming events.

Nestled in the wooded foothills of the Sangre de Cristo Mountains, the little pueblo of **Picuris** makes an interesting stop on the way to Taos. Like Taos, Picuris was heavily influenced by the Plains Indian culture of the Jicarilla Apaches, Kiowas and Comanches. The best time to visit is in August, during the annual **Feast of San Lorenzo**.

The terraced adobe homes at **Taos Pueblo** are probably the most picturesque and visited Indian site in New Mexico. Only 5 miles from the famous artists' colony, Taos has nonetheless managed to detach itself from the off-reservation world. Typical of many of the northern pueblos, Taos is divided into two social groups, the North House and South House, on either side of the Taos River. The two halves of the village alternate civic and religious responsibilities, and compete in footraces during the pueblo's well-known **Feast of San Geronimo**.

In 1847, Mexican rebels instigated a revolt of Taos Indians against the new American government. After murdering Governor Charles Bent, Taos warriors fled to the pueblo church, which American soldiers then blew apart with cannons, killing 150 Indians. The remains of the church are still standing outside the village and can be visited on the self-guided tour.

Rules and regulations: Wherever you travel in Pueblo Country, the best time to visit is undoubtedly during ceremonial dances and feast days. Among the dances you are likely to see are the imitative Buffalo, Deer, Elk and Eagle dances, the dignified Corn and Basket dances, and the dramatic, Spanish-derived Matachina Dance. All dances are ceremonial events – prayers for rain, crops, game or thanksgiving – and should be approached with appropriate respect.

Not all dances are open to the public, however, so be sure to do your homework. The best place to get information about dances and other special events is at the Indian Pueblo Cultural Center in Albuquerque, which runs a terrific museum, gift shop and restaurant, as well as a packed schedule of special events. Other museums in the area with extensive Pueblo Indian collections are the Maxwell Museum of Anthropology in Albuquerque; the Museum of Indian Arts and Culture and the Museum of New Mexico in Santa Fe; and the Millicent Rogers Museum in Taos. Far-

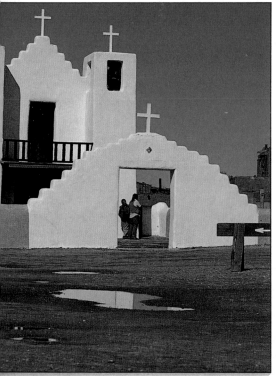

San Geronimo Mission, Taos Pueblo.

ther afield, the Heard Museum in Phoenix and the Museum of Northern Arizona in Flagstaff both have excellent collections of Pueblo art and artifacts.

Visiting the pueblos can be tremendously rewarding – especially during dances – but there are a few things to keep in mind. Generally speaking, Pueblo people share a deep sense of ambivalence when it comes to tourism. While tourist dollars have proved a boon to local economies, there are very powerful factions within each pueblo that consider tourism a threat to traditional culture. Privacy is highly valued, and although gregarious by nature, Pueblo people may not always be very warm to outsiders.

In some pueblos, photography, audio recording and sketching is prohibited. In others, a permit must be purchased from the tribal council. In either case, do not take a picture of a person unless you request permission. A gratuity of $2 or $3 may be in order. In almost all cases, it is absolutely forbidden to photograph, record or sketch dances or any other religious events. Offenders may have their film confiscated or may be asked to leave the reservation. If you are attending a dance, be quiet and respectful, don't stand in front of anyone or sit in a seat that doesn't belong to you, and be sure to dress appropriately (no shorts, halter tops or brief clothing). Remember that dancers – especially kachinas – are very sacred. Don't talk to them or walk across the dance plaza. If they approach you, stand back, avert your eyes, and let them pass.

It is also forbidden to enter a kiva or any other area that is marked off-limits. If you're not sure, stay away. Keep in mind that the old adobe buildings are usually private homes. Do not climb on them, and do not enter without an explicit invitation.

Finally, collecting artifacts, prayer plumes or any other objects on Indian land is prohibited. If you would like to visit an archaeological site on a reservation, it is essential to ask the tribal council for permission and, if necessary, to pay for a guide.

Below, antlers adorn a Santa Clara adobe. Right, Julian and Maria Martinez in 1931.

MARIA MARTINEZ

If there is a single person associated with the revival of Pueblo pottery, it is the late Maria Martinez. A native of San Ildefonso Pueblo, Maria remains the most famous Indian artist of the 20th century and a potter of international repute. Inspired by ancient Anasazi pottery, she and her husband, Julian, developed San Ildefonso's trademark black-on-black ware and sparked a new interest in Pueblo pottery of every style.

Maria's career was shaped by a curious combination of skill, vision and circumstance. Like other Pueblo women, she learned to fashion hand-built pottery as a child, making pieces as they were needed at home or for trade with other Indians. At the time, manufactured goods had virtually replaced handmade pottery, and the art form was quickly dying out.

Then, in 1907, Maria's husband, Julian, took a job with a group of archaeologists who were excavating an ancient pueblo site on the nearby Pajarito Plateau. Among the artifacts recovered at the site was a potsherd of extraordinarily high quality. The man in charge of the project, Dr Edgar Hewett, director of the School of American Research in Santa Fe, New Mexico, asked Maria and Julian if they could reproduce pottery of a similar style. In the following months, Maria made several pots, and Julian painted and fired them.

Although their early pots were polychromes – a cream-colored slip with red and black designs – a few were accidentally discolored during the open-air firing. Rather than red, black and cream, these "rejects" turned a lustrous black, not unlike the style of pottery that was being made at neighboring Santa Clara Pueblo.

Several months later, Julian was asked to supply pots to a Santa Fe storekeeper and, having nearly run out of the polychromes, he brought the black pots. To his and Maria's surprise, the storekeeper bought them. And it wasn't too long before he came back for more.

While experimenting with the new firing process, Julian made a second discovery, again quite by accident. Among the pots he tested were a few that had already been painted. Rather than a solid black finish, the pots had a black matte design against a polished black background. Julian had stumbled on the secret of the black-on-black technique that would eventually bring them international attention.

As Maria's skill and repertoire expanded over the next several years, demand for her work grew beyond all expectation. Julian, perhaps the more innovative of the two, continued to experiment with new firing processes and attained a new level of excellence in his use of traditional motifs, including the well-known water-snake, feather and kiva-step designs.

In 1943 Julian died, and Maria's son, Popovi Da, took up the painting chores several years later. Popovi Da was an innovator in his own right; he introduced new firing techniques and a broader range of colors. His son, Tony Da, also an artist, became well-known for integrating turquoise, heishi, incising techniques, and unconventional shapes into his pottery designs.

Throughout her career, Maria remained at San Ildefonso. Her commitment to Pueblo life never seemed to waver. As Alice Marriott notes in her excellent biography: "Her life has been, as nearly as she could make it, the normal life of a woman of her culture. She herself is the first to say that San Ildefonso has other potters who are more skilled than she."

Maria Martinez died in 1980 at the age of 94. Vessels that Maria and Julian sold for $5 or $10 in the 1920s and 1930s are now considered priceless. But perhaps even more valuable than her work is the tradition of personal integrity that she left behind. Maria and Julian had always felt it was important to share their good fortune. Maria devoted a good deal of time to teaching, and today, thanks largely to her groundbreaking work, pottery remains a major source of income for many Pueblo communities. "I was never selfish with my work, for what God gave me," Maria said. "I just thank God because it's not only for me; it's for all the people."

Collections of Maria's work may be found at the Popovi Da Studio in San Ildefonso Pueblo; the Millicent Rogers Museum in Taos; and the Heard Museum in Phoenix, Arizona.

PEOPLE OF THE BLUE-GREEN WATER

Deep within the sun-drenched, rocky environs of the Grand Canyon is the most isolated Indian reservation in the country. It's at the bottom of a remote side-canyon, far to the west of where most travelers go to view the desert's dramatic landscape. But unlike the 2,000 sq. miles of parched, open land that surround it, this is a lush paradise of cascading waterfalls, sky-blue travertine pools, shady trees filled with songbirds, fenced cornfields and melon patches, all tucked into a stunning red gorge split by a turquoise creek.

This is the home of the Havasupai Indians, the "people of the blue-green water." They are a small tribe of some 700 people who have called this canyon and surrounding plateau home since the 14th century. But even today, the Havasupais seem to have been forgotten by the 20th century.

The only way to reach Havasupai, besides helicopter, is to hike a rugged 8-mile trail into Havasu Canyon. Their one village, Supai, remains a quiet place where the sounds of children's laughter still carries down the canyon before breakfast, and where, most of the time, the only other noises are the swishing of horse tails brushing away flies, the purr of the village's one tractor making its way along a powdery trail, or the gurgle of Havasu Creek, the stream from which the people take their name.

For the most part, Supai village is cut off from the outside world. There are no roads, no cars, no street signs. It's far beyond the reach of daily newspapers, television, and most radio signals. The only telephones, which work sporadically, are connected to the tribal office, the tribal store and one pay phone at Havasupai Lodge. This is a world apart, still connected to the rhythms of the people, the animals and the canyon itself.

A well-kept secret: Tourism is Havasupai's only industry. Although some 15,000 people venture here each year, the place remains a secret to most of the world. Considering that 4 million tourists annually view the Grand Canyon's world-renowned vistas just 35 air-miles to the east, many people apparently don't realize that Indians still occupy one of its branches, as they have for at least 4,000 years.

This is a place most people hear about by word of mouth, often in glowing terms. Some equate Havasupai's beauty with a landlocked Polynesia. Whatever the comparison, it does seem to be an anomaly in the high Arizona desert. There's no place quite like it. And getting there is part of the adventure.

The trip to Havasupai begins at the trailhead in Hualapai Hilltop, some 63 miles over well-paved Route 18, off the old Route 66, northwest of Flagstaff, Arizona. Before setting out, it's best to buy gas and any other supplies either at Kingman or Seligman. These can also be purchased at Grand Canyon Caverns or Peach Springs during regular business hours, but you'll be out of luck any time afterward. Once you turn onto Route 18, it's an hour's drive over the high plateau country where the Havasupais

used to spend winters before being confined to their narrow canyon by the federal government in 1882.

Once at the trailhead, the only land-route into the canyon is the single pack trail. (Helicopters may also be arranged; contact Havasupai Tourist Enterprise for details and reservations, tel: 602-448-2121.) The Havasupais long ago decided against bringing the modern mechanized world into their village by refusing to have a road built into the canyon. This maintained trail is still used by these people today to bring in everything they need: mail, groceries, household items, fuel and various equipment.

The Havasupais rely on their horses not only for transportation but for a good part of their family income. Each family takes turns hiring out their horses to pack the mail in and out, bring down all the supplies sold in the tribal store, and guide tourists. Many Havasupai men work as packers. With advance booking, visitors can ride the trail to the easy gait of a canyon-bred horse. Most visitors

still choose to make the three-hour hike down, saving the ride for the more strenuous return trip.

All three modes of getting into Havasupai – flying, hiking or riding – offer distinct advantages. The choice should depend on your physical condition. As Grand Canyon hikes go, this one is moderate but can be taxing on the way out. Like most of the surrounding country, it's a dry trail with no services, no water, little shade and scorching summer temperatures. Carrying and drinking a gallon of water per person is highly recommended. A horse ride is more relaxed but still exposes you to the glare of the sun. Experienced canyoneers always use a hat, sunglasses and sun-screen. By making arrangements 24 hours in advance at the campground, you can have your heavy backpack carried out for $15 on the day of your departure. For those who can afford the $55 fee, the 10-minute helicopter ride provides a view of the canyon not seen in any other way.

The trail to the canyon floor drops

Navajo cowboy waiting at the gate.

steeply for almost 2 miles as it cuts through the rimrock to the wash below in Hualapi Canyon. Here the canyon is wide, offering the trail's broadest views of the surrounding landscape. Along the way you'll see the small signs placed by the Havasupais warning of the impending uranium development, which the people fear may someday contaminate their canyon and water. After an hour's walk the trail drops into a dry, rocky stream bed that finds its way into the shady, narrowing gorge, offering the first relief from the relentless sun. Shortly past the junction of Havasu Canyon, you cross clear little Havasu Creek, which snakes through the village, widens, and eventually falls over cliffs more than 100 ft high.

From the first crossing of the sparkling creek, it's a 1½ mile walk into the heart of the village. The dusty trail leads under high cottonwood trees, offering wonderful views of Supai and giving you a first glimpse of the place's grandeur. The trail passes the rodeo grounds. On either side are Havasupai homes and

Havasu Canyon, with Supai village in distance.

fields, all sandwiched between the towering walls of the canyon. Arriving in Supai village, you pass the gift shop and museum and the red-frame Havasupai Tourist Enterprise building, where all visitors must register and pay an entry fee of $9 (for non-Indians) and a camping fee of $21. While this may seem a bit steep, bear in mind that tourism is the Havasupais' only independent source of tribal revenue.

After your long walk in, the Havasupai Café is a good place to slake a thirst with a tall, if pricey, lemonade. It's the village's only gathering place, so relax under the shade of a cottonwood tree and join the elderly Havasupais who gather outside the post office to watch tourists straggle in. You may want to look around the village for a while before setting off on the 2-mile trail to the campground and the first of Havasupai's visitors' most spectacular sights, its beautiful waterfalls.

Havasu Canyon is known for its high red walls, towering 300 ft or more above the village floor, with huge carved-out

waterfall spouts, called "hanging canyons," waiting to be filled by a thunderstorm. Majestic shade-giving trees line the lovely creek and trail. One word of caution about the water: Although it is safe to swim in, do not drink it. The terraced travertine pools along the creek were created by calcium carbonate, a natural laxative, in the water. Drink water only from the spring at the campground.

Heading down the canyon, the first three waterfalls are within 2 miles of each other. The first is **Navajo Falls**, smallest of them all, but lovely with its frame of dense trees, vines and moss. Next is the 100-foot **Havasu Falls**, pouring clean and clear through spouts of ragged travertine into a pool of turquoise green. The travertine has the appearance of torrents of mud frozen in mid-fall.

Below this waterfall is the most popular swimming hole in the canyon, created by the high cascade of 190-foot **Mooney Falls**. This waterfall was named after a miner who lost his life in 1882 after dangling from a rope for nearly three days when it became ensnared by the sharp rocks. It finally broke, sending him plummeting into the gorge. To get to the pool below Mooney, the trail goes through two tunnels cut into the travertine by miners back in the 1880s.

Equally stunning, **Beaver Falls** is 4 miles farther down the trail. The canyon becomes wilder and the trail more challenging from here to the Colorado River, about 8 miles, but it makes a good day hike.

At several spots along the trail, you have to make your way along dangerously exposed cliffs, so think twice before taking children along. As the canyon narrows, you may notice what appear at first to be caves high above in the sheer walls. These are, in fact, mines left by prospectors who dug for silver, zinc, lead and vanadium. Some old steel ladders are still hammered into the rock. They may be unsafe, so don't attempt to climb them.

Reclaiming the land: It would be a mistake – one made by the federal

Havasupai basket weaver in front of a willow wickiup, 1901.

266

government a century ago – to think that Havasupais have always been exclusively canyon-dwellers. Before the coming of white people, they spent winters hunting and gathering on the forested plateau and then retreated to the canyon to plant corn and beans in summer. They are believed to be related to the Cerbat and Cohonina people, prehistoric groups who occupied the Grand Canyon area at least 1,500 years ago.

Traditionally, the Havasupais lived in thatched dome-shaped wickiups, and men and women shared labor in the fields. They are still well-known for their skillful basketry, utilizing the reeds and willows that grow in abundance throughout the canyon. Visitors can purchase Havasupai baskets at the museum, lodge, or, even better, directly from the makers.

In the 1860s and '70s, the Havasupais watched as their land outside the tiny canyon was taken over by cattlemen, railroads and settlers, but they never took up arms against white people. A government survey in 1882 reduced their huge aboriginal territory to a 518-acre reservation within the confines of the canyon walls. In 1883, their relatives and closest neighbors, the Hualapais, or "Pine Tree People," had a reservation established on the plateau above. By 1900, almost all of their traditional hunting and gathering land was gone, eliminating the basis of their subsistence and livelihood.

The Havasupais' transformation from hunters and farmers to wage-earners was sudden by any measure. They began by working as packers for miners, and then as laborers, mail carriers and construction workers. By the 1940s, the tribe had changed from a nomadic group of hunter-gatherers to a small, short-term labor pool for the federal government and private interests. The government was beginning to recognize the problem it had created at Havasupai and tried to remedy it by forming tribally-run enterprises. Most of these programs failed until tourism began to catch on in the 1960s.

In more recent years, the Havasupais **Havasu Falls.** have fought a series of legal battles to regain the land taken away from them by the federal government. In 1974, after eight attempts, the tribe finally won from Congress and the administration the return of 185,000 acres and use-rights to an additional 93,500 acres in Grand Canyon National Park.

Today, the Havasupais still survive with a fragile economy based on tourism. Most families continue to spend winter in the canyon, although many have jobs off the reservation.

The best time to visit Havasupai is between late spring and early fall, before the weather turns cold and snow blankets the plateau. The tribe continues to hold its annual **Peach Festival** on Labor Day weekend, which usually brings in hundreds of visitors and members of other tribes. Dozens of horses and cattle are driven down the trail for a rodeo. It's a wonderful opportunity to enjoy the hospitality of these gentle people, learn about Havasupai culture, buy the women's exquisite baskets, and take in the exceptional beauty of their isolated canyon home.

ARIZONA'S APACHE COUNTRY

On a recent trip to Disneyland, Apache elders were treated to a parade, rides and amusements. When a little girl was introduced to a tribal elder, the girl burst into tears. "You don't have to be afraid of me," the old woman smiled. "We're tame now."

In the history of the American West, "A" stands for "Apache." Whenever the word is spoken, it provokes an immediate emotional response. Flickering images of old John Wayne movies, silent warriors waiting in ambush, fast and fearless Indian ponies climbing to an isolated mountain hideout inflame the emotions like burning arrows.

The historic Apaches long ago merged with myth. In play, American, German and French boys become Apache warriors. Remains of the real past lie in museum cases, in sudden and inexplicable reactions, and in the group consciousness of a nation that defeated an "enemy" it also admired.

The last Apache scout: January 30, 1988, mourners gathered at the old military cemetery at Fort Apache in Arizona. They came for the passing of a man named Julius Colelay – the last Apache Scout. Bright sun drew the chill from winter skies as they gathered among the cemetery's yucca and prickly pear. A drill team from Fort Huachuca offered slow salutes, then bore the coffin slowly onto a slab over an open grave. As volleys of rifle fire cracked the silence, the death wails of Apache women for a dead warrior rose to the sacred mountains. Tenderly, female relatives placed mortuary offerings in the open casket. Food, a ceremonial blanket, a black felt hat. Things he would need in his journey to the spirit world where he would meet his old comrades in arms again – the legendary Apache Scouts.

As early as 1866, Congress authorized the Army to enlist Indians as scouts. But the first Apache Scouts, from Cibecue to Carrizo, did not enlist until 1871, followed by volunteers from the White Mountain and San Carlos tribes. They served as guides, gathered information on enemy movements, engaged in combat and helped keep order on the reservations. The last Apache Scouts were discharged in 1947.

"The Apache Scout could look at the mountains, look at the trees, and see signs no one else could see," said Apache veteran Broadus Bones. "He was sent forward on horseback to listen and look and report back to his commander. He knew the enemy's dialects, his ways of movement, campsites, hunting grounds, watering places. He went into the enemy's camp and offered peace. We should not forget that he was a peacemaker as well as a warrior."

History will take note of Julius Colelay, the last Apache Scout, but his tribe will remember the husband, father, friend and medicine man who walked down the streets of Whiteriver, leaning on his cane, singing the old songs. Vietnam veteran Alvino Hawkins said, "This man would get up early in the morning, before the sun rose, to ask the Great Spirit to give us another beautiful

Preceding pages: Colorado River courses through the Grand Canyon. **Left,** Cienega Falls, Salt River Canyon, San Carlos Indian Reservation. **Right, Apache man, Nethla,** *circa* 1904.

day, to bless and protect us… When I was leaving late one autumn for a place I'd never been, a place called Vietnam, this man put eagle feathers on me and prayed for me."

Apaches were great warriors not because they loved battle, but because they loved their families and their homeland and were determined to protect them. The White Mountain Apaches are the only Apache group who have never been displaced from their homeland. The mountains of east central Arizona have been their ancestral home for perhaps 500 years.

A warm welcome: In ancient times, these southern Athabascans traveled in small bands, hunting and gathering wild foods. With the arrival of the Spanish, the Apaches became horsemen, extending their territory from the prairies of Nebraska to the mountains of Durango, Mexico; from the Staked Plains of Texas to the Colorado River. Apachean people mingled freely with one another and with their linguistic cousins, the Navajos. By that time, the western Apaches

had gathered into five distinct groups. The White Mountain and Cibecue Apaches lived in their present domain, trading with their former enemies, the Zuni people. The northern and southern Tonto and San Carlos groups had more contact with the Yavapai people to the west and south.

Contact with the US government came late to this region, after many tribes had learned bitter lessons. In 1859, the Indian Agent Michael Steck wrote in his annual report: "In all their intercourse with the government, their deportment toward travelers and traders [the White Mountain and Cibecue Apaches], have shown themselves to be the most reliable of all the bands of Apaches."

In 1869, Major John Green was sent by the US Army to determine whether the White Mountain Apaches were indeed friendly. As his expedition proceeded north from Camp Grant toward the White Mountains, smoke signals of welcome appeared on the cliffs. Green had orders to destroy Apache crops, villages and people, "if necessary." But instead of defiance, the major found a welcome so warm he was dumbfounded. When his troops burned 100 acres of ripe corn belonging to Chief Pedro, the chief reportedly apologized and said, "The corn should not have been there."

So impressed was Green with the White Mountain and Cibecue Apache bands and their leaders Miguel, Pedro, Diablo and Capitan Chiquito, he recommended the establishment of a regional military post at the confluence of the east and north forks of the White Mountain River. He wrote: "I have selected a site for a military post on the White Mountain River which is the finest I ever saw. The climate is delicious, and said by the Indians to be perfectly healthy, free from all malaria. Excellently well wooded and watered, it seems as though this one corner of Arizona were almost its garden spot, the beauty of its scenery, the fertility of soil and facilities of irrigation are not surpassed by any place that ever came under my observation."

While under the spell of the White Mountains, Green wrote his command-

White Mountain elder.

ing officer that establishing a post would create a good scouting base against hostile tribes, and compel the White Mountain Indians to live on their reservation or be driven from their "beautiful country which they almost worship." Surprisingly, Green's plea was heeded and Washington approved a reservation for the White Mountain Apache Tribe, more to protect them from greedy mineral, ranching and timber interests on the outside than to protect settlers from Apache depredations.

From the time the first Apache Scouts enlisted, in 1871, to the time the military left in 1922, relations between the military and the Indians were unique in the history of the American West. Soldiers often attended Apache ceremonies, and some married and had children with Apache women. Scouts drew regular military pay and were issued arms and ammunition, but they functioned as individuals, never compelled to follow orders. General George Crook, who stayed at Fort Apache in 1871 and 1872, had to buck his superiors to get the

Scouts into the Army, but he never lost faith in their ability and intelligence, calling the Apache Scout "the perfect, the ideal, scout of the whole world."

Celebrate the land: Today, the descendants of the Apache Scouts are still avid outdoorsmen. Apaches are sports lovers and basketball fanatics. Any day of the week, men and women are out running at daybreak. Boys and girls grow up swimming in the rivers, riding horses in the mountains, and fishing in the lakes. Apaches take great pleasure in family outings, such as excursions into the forest to cut firewood, pick berries or picnic. Apache elders are treated to field trips to gather wild foods such as piñon nuts, acorns and berries. Elders hold an esteemed place in traditional Apache culture, respected as repositories of tribal culture and wisdom. Still deeply influenced by traditional values, Apache society is stitched together by the clan system. Ancestry is traced through four major clans – Roadrunner, Bear, Eagle and Butterfly – and is a determining factor in marriage

Chief Alchesay and Apache scouts, *circa* 1886.

rules, family obligations and a personal sense of identity.

Perhaps no Americans are more aware of the value of their land, their resources and their traditions, or more determined to preserve them for future generations. The challenge of young Apaches is to hold fast to traditional values while adapting to a high-tech, fast-paced outside society. With the same tenacity, shrewd judgment and resourcefulness that won the respect of a nation a century ago, the tribe is moving forward into the 21st century.

Few tribes are as blessed with natural resources as the Apaches of Arizona. But gradually, an economy based on the consumption of natural resources such as timber, rangeland and minerals is being superseded. Tourism, especially outdoor recreation, is seen as the key to their financial future.

Outdoor events open to outsiders begin in April with the **Spring Roundup All-Indian Rodeo** in San Carlos and team roping in Whiteriver. In May, White Mountain goes all out for the **Head Start Parade and Rodeo**. In June, tribal elders from all over Arizona convene in Whiteriver for *Shiwoye*, or **Elderfest**. Elders are honored with a barbecue, daylong entertainment, dances and displays of arts and crafts. The **Fourth of July** is celebrated in cowboy style with a rodeo, fireworks and western dance and music.

Also in July is one of the Southwest's prime events – the **Native American Art Festival** in the off-reservation community of Pinetop-Lakeside. This two-day event features artists, dancers, singers and storytellers from many tribes, as well as Native American food.

The **White Mountain Tribal Fair and Rodeo** is held in Whiteriver on Labor Day weekend, and all tribal offices are closed. The fair includes a parade, rodeo, night dances, and a queen and princess pageant. In November, San Carlos and Cibecue both sponsor a **Veteran's Day Rodeo**.

Traditional Apache crafts are definitely not mass-produced, and not easily obtained. They include buckskin and

Saddling up at an all-Indian rodeo.

beadwork, basketry, carving, doll-making and cradleboards. A few artisans still make the unique musical instrument known as the Apache violin. Contemporary artists who have attained national acclaim are Philip Titla of San Carlos and Michael Lacapa of White Mountain. Apache beadwork and some crafts are available at Forestdale Trading Post (west of Show Low), the Whiteriver Restaurant and Apache Culture Center at Fort Apache.

Sportsmen's paradise: For sportsmen, the reservations offer 26 lakes, 300 miles of trout streams and more than 1,000 campsites. Outdoor recreation, including fishing, camping, hiking, whitewater rafting and skiing, is by far the biggest attraction on the reservation, drawing thousands of tourists every year. But there are miles of wilderness for the lone birdwatcher or wildlife photographer to explore, prehistoric ruins to ponder, and history to relive. Fees are required for all activities on the reservation, but they are nominal and well worth the money. Some areas require

special use permits and some are off-limits to non-Apaches. Tourists should check with the White Mountain Apache Game and Fish Department before embarking on any adventures.

One of the biggest attractions on the Whiteriver reservation is the tribal trophy elk hunt, which draws big-game hunters from all over the world, producing revenue of $500,000 a year for the tribe. For a fee of $10,000, hunters live in a rustic camp for a week with their Apache guides, and are guaranteed good camp cooking, privacy and a 99 percent chance to bag trophy rack. The trophy hunt has been used as a tool for game management, serving to cull from the elk herd the older males who would soon die naturally if they were not taken. Largely because of this policy, Arizona's elk population is at an all-time high, and the Apaches have been recognized by Harvard University researchers as having one of the most successful resource management programs in the world.

Efforts to restore the once-endangered native Apache trout have met with equal

success. "Salmo Apache" is a small, shy, flickering fish with iridescent gold on its sides, blending to olive green on top, speckled with black spots. Along with rainbow, German brown, brook and cutthroat trout, the Apache trouts are among the million fish raised at local hatcheries in order to stock the many pure, cold streams in this high country paradise.

For nearly a century, the White Mountains have been a retreat for Arizona's desert dwellers. Today, the reservation is even better known for winter sports. Snowplows keep Highway 260 open, even in the worst storms, as that is the route to **Sunrise Ski Area**. One of the major winter playgrounds in the Southwest, Sunrise has more than 1,000 acres of ski terrain on three mountains. Three triple chair lifts and five double lifts have a capacity of 13,000 skiers a day. In addition to a base lodge and mountaintop day lodge, Sunrise has a convention center and resort hotel used year-round. Miles of cross-country trails are being developed every year. Sunrise

Ski Area is usually open from late November to early April.

Before each new run is dedicated, it is blessed by Apache medicine men. All the mountains of the Southwest are held sacred by the Apaches, but none is as sacred as 11,590-ft high **Mount Baldy**. Called Dzil Ligaye, White Mountain, by the Apaches, the bald peak is the source of water and of life, home of the wind and of the Ga'an, Mountain Spirits, who bring blessings to the Apache people. Silent and serene, Dzil Ligaye is a symbol of the eternal bond between the Creator and the White Mountain people. Tribal members, young and old, still make pilgrimages to the wind-beaten top of White Mountain to give thanks for the immense beauty of their land and for all the blessings bestowed on them.

San Carlos Apache Reservation: Ask a San Carlos Apache what the difference is between him and a White Mountain Apache, and he will probably say "location." The tribes are governed independently by their respective tribal councils, but they share the same lan-

Cradleboards and burden basket, rare Apache treasures.

guage, culture, ceremonies and clans.

The San Carlos Reservation is larger (1.8 million acres) and less trammeled than the adjacent White Mountain Reservation. Visitors will find developed campsites at San Carlos Lake, Talkalai Lake, Seneca Lake and Point of Pines. The remainder of the reservation is pristine territory. Although much of San Carlos is lower-elevation desert scrubland inhabited by chaparral and mesquite, there are trout streams in the high country and hundreds of cattle impoundments stocked with catfish, bluegills and bass.

The San Carlos Reservation is easily reached from Phoenix by taking Highway 60 to Globe, then turning east on Highway 70 to Peridot. Getting there from the north is another story. For a real adventure, try the trail Coronado is believed to have taken in his quest for the legendary Seven Cities of Cibola. It is better to start from Fort Apache Junction in the north, because it is a downhill run the whole way. Tribal Road 9 is best in dry weather, and is most easily traveled in a four-wheel drive vehicle.

History looks down from every rock and cliff. Imagine, if you like, Coronado's motley troops on tired horses, moving slowly through this pass with their herd of cattle and remuda of horses. Imagine Major Green's feelings of wonder and suspicion as he saw smoke signals welcoming him into the territory held by the White Mountain Apache bands. Or imagine the pioneers who braved a rutted and gutted road in a rickety Model T when Black River Crossing was the only way of getting to Phoenix from northeastern Arizona.

Black River runs clear and dark, alive with the quick shadows of fish. On the other side, purebred Hereford cattle belonging to the San Carlos Livestock Association graze among the juniper, piñon, gambel oak and manzanita. An ascent through one more mountain range brings the scent of pine, spruce and fir fresh and clean. On the other side of a park-like forest is Hilltop, with a natural spring coming out of the mountain. A charming old government house has

Silver Butte.

just been renovated for game rangers. At Hilltop, one road turns west toward Seneca Lake; the other heads south toward San Carlos. The crest below Hilltop offers a dusty panorama of the Gila River Valley and Mount Graham. Pine-pungent air from the highlands recedes into the soapy smell of chaparral brush. A steep grade cuts down through thickets of mesquite to true desert of ocotillo, prickly pear and cholla. The temperature climbs higher as the road drops in elevation.

The return trip from San Carlos through Globe to Show Low descends Arizona's *other* canyon, **Salt River Canyon**. Roadside vistas and rest stops allow drivers time to meditate on the 2,000-ft vertical drop to the salty waters of the river that begins pure and cold on Mount Baldy, and has become the River of Dispute for Apaches eager to protect their water rights against the intrigues of "water-rustlers" who want to divert the flow to Phoenix and other urban centers. If time is not essential, and at this point it shouldn't be, try a side trip

to Cibecue, 12 miles north of Highway 260 on Tribal Road 12. Groceries and gasoline may be purchased at a modern shopping center in this small sawmill community. Those equipped for backcountry travel may want to explore the primitive country north of Cibecue, stopping at **Grasshopper Prehistoric Site**, or fishing for legendary German brown trout in Cibecue Creek. A special use permit is required for this area.

From the claypot striations of Salt River Canyon to the blue mirage of San Carlos Lake; from pale aspens and thin air to the bold buckskin cliffs of Whiteriver, the land itself remains the main attraction of Apache Country. The open-door policy of the Whiteriver and San Carlos Apaches assures a warm welcome for visitors as long as they mind their manners. As Captain James M. Williams, US Eighth Cavalry, wrote in 1869 after meeting chiefs Miguel and Pedro: "The appearance and manners of these two chiefs and their people was calculated to make me have confidence in their protestations of friendship." **Salt River Canyon.**

278

THE APACHE SUNRISE CEREMONY

Sparks from the campfire join the stars. Men's voices, low and even above the heartbeat of the drum, call the Mountain Spirits out of the deep well of time. Cries not animal, not human, emerge from the darkness as the Ga'an step into the circle of light. Black-hooded, painted, ghostly figures in buckskin skirts, moccasins and fantastic headdresses dance with jerky, unearthly movements. Harness bells mark the rhythm of their steps. The clown's bullroarer whirrs like a nighthawk overhead.

It is the second night in the four-day Sunrise Ceremony. The Ga'an are blessing the young woman on the occasion of her first menstruation. She is celebrating her womanhood in the embrace of her family, clan and tribe. For four days, she will be the embodiment of White Painted Woman, the Holy Woman of the Apaches. In this holy state, the girl has special powers to heal and bless her people.

Women, as the source of human life, are held in high esteem in traditional Apache culture. A girl's puberty rite is the oldest and most sacred of Apache ceremonies. An Apache woman is expected to be strong, patient, hardworking and wise. From her godmother and her female relatives she learns the skills she must know to become a good homemaker and mother. A decade ago, only a handful of Sunrise Ceremonies were performed every year. Today, the intricate and expensive ceremonies occur almost every weekend from April through October somewhere on the reservations.

The Sunrise Ceremony involves a commitment of time and money from the girl's parents and godparents. Godparents must be willing to sacrifice their own needs for those of the girl for years to come, but being chosen as a godparent is a great honor for the traditional Apache.

At least six months before the ceremony, preparations begin. Early one morning, the godparents are visited by the girl's parents. Her father presents an eagle feather and turquoise bead to the godmother. The eagle feather is a symbol of purity and power. If the godparents accept, the girl's father sponsors a large feast in their honor.

Because most people work during the week, the first day of the ceremony is usually a Friday. On Friday evening, the girl is dressed publicly in her ceremonial buckskin cape and beaded necklace. A shell pendant is placed on her forehead and a yellow feather fastened to her hair. The medicine man sings the first four songs of the 32-song ceremony. From that time until the ceremony is over, the girl may touch herself only with a "scratching stick" and drink only with a reed attached to her ceremonial cane.

As the first rays of the sun strike the shell pendant the next morning, the girl is purified and acquires supernatural healing powers. During Saturday's ceremony, she kneels on a stack of blankets and "dances" on her knees. Her godmother massages her body to make her strong. In the last part of the strenuous ceremony, the girl must run in each of the four directions, in ever widening circles. She is then blessed with yellow cattail pollen. That night, as people gather, food is served and the Ga'an come out to dance.

At daylight, the girl must run about 5 miles, then goes to the ceremonial wickiup or *gowah*, a structure made of poles and bear grass once used as homes by Apache people. The girl's head is painted with yellow pollen, signifying a cleansing of the mind, body and spirit. Following the painting, she dances with her godfather, then returns to the wickiup where she is visited by all who wish to receive her blessing and paint themselves with yellow pollen.

On the fourth day, the medicine man "undresses" the ceremonial cane, removing the reed and scratching stick. The girl must wear the shell pendant and feather for another four days.

Finally, she will bathe and wash her hair. Outwardly she will resume the life of an American teenager, a life of Cokes, dances, school sports, rock music and videotapes. Inwardly she will remember the lessons taught by her relatives and godparents in the Apache Way. She will know her purpose in life and remember the ceremony in which, for four days, she became the embodiment of the Holy Woman of the Apaches.

NEW MEXICO'S APACHES

There are two Apache reservations in New Mexico: the Jicarilla Apache Reservation in the San Juan Mountains of northern New Mexico and the Mescalero Apache Reservation in the Sacramento Mountains of southern New Mexico. Both reservations are located in areas of extraordinary natural beauty, and both tribes work hard to attract and accommodate travelers.

Like their cousins in Arizona, the Jicarillas and Mescaleros are an Athabascan people who migrated into the Southwest about 600 years ago. They were primarily a hunting and gathering people, although by the time the Spanish arrived a few were also practicing some small-scale farming. Living on the edge of the Great Plains, they were deeply influenced by the horse-and-buffalo culture of the Southern Plains tribes and were routinely harassed by their long-time enemy, the Comanches. They also had regular contact with the Pueblo Indians, especially Taos and Picuris, and were regular participants at the yearly trading fair at Taos Pueblo.

The arrival of Americans went hard on the eastern Apaches. The Santa Fe Trail cut directly through their territory, channeling thousands of miners and ranchers into northern New Mexico. By 1870, the southern buffalo herd was virtually exterminated and the area's best foraging and farmland was occupied by settlers. Weakened by disease and hunger, and pressured by the US Army, there was little choice for the Apaches but to accept reservations.

It took years for the Jicarillas and Mescaleros to recover their strength, but after a difficult start on their reservations they managed to bootstrap themselves into two of the most progressive tribes in the country. With interests in timber, ranching, oil and tourism, the tribes have proved themselves resourceful and tenacious businessmen. As one Apache official put it, comparing his people to the other native groups in the area, "The Navajos make rugs, the Pueblos make pottery, and the Apaches make money!"

Mescalero: Traditionally, the Mescalero Apaches ranged between the Rio Grande and the Staked Plains of Texas and as far south as the Mexican provinces of Chihuahua and Coahuila. It is an enormously diverse territory, with the peaks of the Sacramento and San Andres Mountains rising as high as 12,000 ft, surrounded by arid, desert-like plains.

When the Spanish moved north into New Mexico in the late 17th century, settlers were encouraged to occupy Indian land however – and wherever – they wished. Slave raids against the Mescaleros and other Apache bands were tolerated by the Spanish, as was the wholesale slaughter of Apache "hostiles." But the Apaches were skilled guerilla fighters. By sweeping down into settlements and then swiftly retreating into mountain hideouts, the Mescaleros held back the Spanish frontier for more than 100 years.

When New Mexico was annexed by the US in 1848, however, the Mescaleros didn't fare so well. The tide of Anglo pioneers – some crossing Apache territory in order to reach the goldfields of California, others establishing ranches in the area – encroached on Mescalero land and depleted game and wild foods. Mescalero raids intensified along the Santa Fe Trails as well as on frontier ranches, and before long the US Army was called out to "pacify" them.

The man in charge was General James H. Carleton, the same General Carleton who was harassing the Chiricahua Apaches in southern Arizona and who in later years would drive the Navajos from their ancestral homeland. As his field officer, Carleton chose Christopher "Kit" Carson, a former Indian trader and army scout. In 1863, Carson launched a punishing campaign against the Mescaleros, and within about nine months the exhausted and hungry warriors were prepared to surrender.

Carleton ordered the Mescaleros to an internment camp at Bosque Redondo (Fort Sumner), a dry and dusty plain on the Pecos River. For the free-ranging Apaches, confinement was an ordeal.

Hooded Ga'an, the Apache spirit.

But when Carleton also forced some 9,000 Navajos to the Bosque – compared to only 500 Apaches – the Mescaleros were overwhelmed.

Smallpox, crop failure and hostilities with the Navajos cut deeply into Mescalero numbers. After two years of misery, they could take it no more; they escaped to their old country. There they remained for about five years while negotiating with the government for a new reservation. In 1873, a new home was established in the Sacramento Mountains. It was by all accounts inadequate, but with the bitter memory of the Bosque still fresh in their minds, the Mescaleros had little choice but to take what was offered.

In the early years, the new reservation wasn't much better than the Bosque. Smallpox ravaged the tribe, white ranchers crowded their borders, and rations were chronically low. To add insult to injury, the Mescaleros were rounded up and imprisoned a second time after a band of Chiricahua Apache fugitives came to them for help.

The Chiricahua connection: While the Mescaleros were in confinement, their closest Apache relatives, the Chiricahuas, were being ruthlessly pursued by the US military. Since the hostilities with Cochise had started nearly 10 years earlier, the Chiricahuas were almost constantly on the run. After Cochise's death in 1874, a younger generation of leaders, including Geronimo, Naiche (Cochise's son) and Victorio, took up the struggle. Their repeated escapes from the San Carlos Reservation, and the bloody cycle of raids and skirmishes that followed, dragged on until 1882, when the last of the Apache guerilla leaders, Geronimo, finally surrendered.

After 27 years of imprisonment in Florida and Oklahoma, the banished Chiricahuas were given the option of joining their cousins on the Mescalero Reservation or staying in Oklahoma. In 1913, 187 Chiricahuas relocated to Mescalero. The remaining 84 chose to stay in Oklahoma. In 1903, the Mescaleros were also joined by a small band of Lipan Apaches who had taken refuge in Mexico. Although uneasy with

Ski Apache, Sacramento Mountains.

GERONIMO

In 1905, while a prisoner of war at Fort Sill, Indian Territory, Geronimo recounted the Apache creation story: "In the beginning the world was covered with darkness," he said. "There was no sun, no day. The perpetual night had no moon or stars. There were, however, all manner of beasts and birds. Among the beasts were many hideous, nameless monsters... Mankind could not prosper under such conditions, for the beasts and serpents destroyed all human offspring."

But there was one boy who was not eaten by the monsters, Geronimo said. His mother, White Painted Woman, hid him from a dragon who ate human children. When the boy grew up, he went hunting and met the dragon in the mountains. He shot three arrows into the dragon's scales, and then, with the fourth arrow, he pierced the dragon's heart. "This boy's name was Apache."

It must have seemed odd to the men who heard this tale that the old story-teller was once the most feared warrior in the American Southwest. Goyathlay (The One Who Yawns), known to whites as Geronimo, was a war leader of the Chiricahua Apaches, the most truculent and fiercesome of the Apache bands. Between 1876 and 1886, Geronimo and his warriors terrorized settlers and frustrated soldiers with lightning raids, elusive retreats, and repeated escapes.

Like many of his Chiricahua compatriots, Geronimo's early life was surrounded by raids and warfare. As a young man he married and had children, but his entire family was wiped out by Mexican troopers. He launched bloody raids against the Mexicans in revenge for the massacre, and emerged as a leading warrior. He later fought alongside Cochise and Mangas Colorado in engagements against American and Mexican soldiers, and continued to plunder ranches, wagon trains and villages on both sides of the border.

Geronimo joined Cochise in 1874 on his newly created Chiricahua reservation, but when the reservation was dissolved two years later, he escaped and returned to raiding. He was captured in New Mexico in 1877 and brought to San Carlos, where many Arizona Apaches were being confined and encouraged to take up farming. It had no appeal for Geronimo. He broke out of San Carlos in 1881 and the raiding started again.

Twice more Geronimo agreed to return to San Carlos, and twice he bolted. Finally, in 1886, with some 5,000 soldiers and 500 Indian scouts chasing his band of 24 warriors, Geronimo surrendered for the last time.

Back home in Arizona, whites wanted him tried for murder and executed. Newspapers across the country painted him as a savage killer. Even President Grover Cleveland suggested that he be hanged. But Geronimo's punishment may have been worse. He and the Chiricahuas – even many who had served as army scouts – were shipped in chains to a prison camp in Florida, and then, one year later, to another in Alabama. They were ravaged by tuberculosis, homesickness, despair. Within a few years, more than 100 died.

In 1894, after much lobbying by friends, Geronimo and his people were relocated to Fort Sill, Indian Territory. Here he reflected grimly on his people's fate: "We are vanishing from the earth, yet I cannot think we are useless or Usen (God) would not have created us... For each tribe of men Usen created He also made a home... When Usen created the Apaches He also created their homes in the West... Thus it was in the beginning: the Apaches and their homes each created for the other by Usen himself. When they are taken from these homes they sicken and die. How long will it be until it is said, there are no Apaches?"

Throughout his imprisonment, Geronimo begged to go home. "Other Indians have homes where they can live and be happy," he told President Theodore Roosevelt. "I and my people have no home... Let me die in my own country." But Geronimo's request was not granted. He died of pneumonia in 1909. He was still a prisoner of war at Fort Sill.

Finally, in 1913, after 27 years of internment, the Chiricahuas were released. Some resettled with the Mescalero Apaches in New Mexico; others remained in Oklahoma. But none were allowed to return to their Arizona homeland as Geronimo so often requested.

each other at first, the three tribes were soon bound by ties of marriage and friendship. In 1964, all Apaches on the Mescalero Reservation were officially recognized as members of the Mescalero Tribe regardless of their original band.

Today, the Mescaleros are one of the most progressive and economically secure tribes in the US. In addition to their investments in timber and ranching, the tribe is a forerunner in the field of tourism. **Ski Apache**, the tribe's skiing facility, provides world-class conditions atop 12,000-foot **Sierra Blanca Peak**. The facility boasts 40 trails, eight lifts, open bowl skiing, more than 15 ft of snow each year, and a spine-tingling 1,800 ft of vertical drop. The tribe also operates the **Inn of the Mountain Gods**, a luxury lodge nestled next to a high valley lake. In addition to its excellent restaurant and convention center, the resort offers golfing, tennis, swimming, boating, horseback riding, skeet-shooting and fishing. Horse racing takes place at **Ruidoso Downs** about 15 miles away.

The Inn also makes an excellent base from which to explore the **White Mountain Wilderness Area**, which covers hundreds of acres of spectacular mountain country crisscrossed with hiking and cross-country skiing trails. The mountains quickly slope down to a vast desert plateau known as **Jornada del Muerto**. Laced with the jagged black rubble of ancient lava flows and studded with razor-edged yucca plants, this is some of the most forbidding – and awesome – terrain in the Southwest.

About 35 miles southwest of the reservation, the brilliant dunes of **White Sands National Monument** slowly migrate across the desert floor. The dunes – which are made of gypsum sand eroded from the nearby Sacramento and San Andres mountains – can reach a height of 30 feet. The place is an enormous sandbox, some 230 sq. miles of rippling dunes set in constant motion by the wind.

The Mescaleros' biggest festival is held over the **Fourth of July** weekend. The central event of the celebration is the Sunrise Ceremony, a girl's coming-

White Sands National Monument.

of-age ritual at which masked Mountain Spirits (or Ga'an) with fantastic crested headdresses come to dance. The dancers represent spirits who came to the Apaches at creation and taught them how to live in balance with each other and the earth. The weekend also features a powwow, rodeo, and crafts sale.

Jicarilla Apache: Like the Mescaleros, the Jicarillas underwent severe hardships during the colonial period, not only because of the Spanish, but because of the Comanches, who were being armed by French traders to the north. Originally Jicarilla territory stretched from the mountains of northeastern New Mexico into the plains of Colorado and Oklahoma, where they regularly hunted buffalo. But with the Comanches threatening war, they turned to the Spanish and the Pueblo Indians of Taos and Picuris for protection.

When New Mexico became an American territory in 1848, the Jicarillas quickly found themselves displaced by white settlers. Like other Apaches, they took to the warpath, raiding ranches, farms and wagon trains on the Santa Fe Trail. Between 1851 and 1880, a number of treaties were signed by the Jicarillas, only to be ignored by land-hungry whites or smothered in the government's cumbersome ratification process. The Jicarillas were even packed off to the Mescalero Reservation for several years, but were so desperately unhappy they eventually escaped.

Finally, in 1887, a suitable reservation was created for them in the San Juan Mountains of northern New Mexico. Poverty, neglect and disease (especially tuberculosis) drove the Jicarillas to the brink of extinction, but with the institution of tribal self-government in the 1930s, the tribe's situation started to turn around. The Jicarillas now derive much of their income from gas, oil, minerals, timber and ranching.

Today, the reservation is a haven for sportsmen and naturalists looking for an out-of-the-way place to enjoy the rugged beauty of New Mexico's high country. The terrain is dominated by wooded mesas and sagebrush valleys. There are several lakes nestled between the mesas where the trout-fishing is excellent. The tribe's Game and Fish Department can arrange Apache guides for big-game hunting.

The newly developed **Horse Lake Mesa Game Park** specializes in bull elk, mule deer, black bear and wild turkeys. Guides are required for all hunting expeditions and vary in price depending on the type of hunt and the services provided. Primitive campsites are located throughout the reservation, and two motels are located at **Dulce**, the tribe's headquarters and the reservation's main town. Otherwise, the reservation is a wonderful place for hikers and campers, with nearly three-quarters of a million acres of wilderness to explore and two ancient Indian ruins.

There are also a number of special events that are well worth catching. The **Little Beaver Roundup**, usually held on the third weekend of July, includes a three-day rodeo, traditional dances and an arts and crafts fair. The **Stone Lake Fiesta**, in September, is a massive Apache campout with feasting, arts and crafts, dances and the traditional relay race between the Llaneros (plains people) and Olleros (mountain people), representing the major social division among the Jicarillas. The two teams also represent the mythical sun and moon, and their legendary race to escape the underworld.

Like the Mescaleros, the Jicarillas also perform their version of the Sunrise Ceremony. Without an explicit invitation, however, it is not advisable to attend.

Renowned for their basket-making (*jicarilla* means "little basket"), the Jicarillas have established a permanent crafts outlet at the **Tribal Arts and Crafts Shop and Museum** in Dulce, where visitors will also find beadwork, jewelry and paintings.

The Jicarillas and Mescaleros have suffered many hardships over the years, but with determination, strength and business savvy, they are blazing a trail into the 21st century. Visiting the land and people, and glimpsing Apache culture, is an experience that most travelers will never forget.

PEOPLE OF THE DESERT

They hear her last name, but it touches nothing in their memory. It brings no place names to mind. So they ask her, "Where are you from?"

"I'm from Casa Grande."

It is an off-reservation town, a cotton-growing area. Most Tohono O'odhams, or Papagos, who live there come from somewhere else. And so they ask, "Where were your parents really from?"

"They are from the other side. They are from Quitovac."

"Ah, yes. The place where they do that rain ceremony. Yes, that is an old place. The people on this side used to do that ceremony, but they quit. I don't know why they quit. Yes, I know who you are. My mother is from that side, too. She used to go to the ceremony every year. She probably knows your family. She is probably related to you. All the people from down there are related to each other. Yes, I know exactly who you are."

They now have a place associated with her name. A place that is an old Tohono O'odham settlement, one that is rich in history and culture. She is now put in a perspective that has meaning for all Tohono O'odham people.

Desert People – Tohono O'odham: The village may be any number of small communities dotting the 2½ million acres (1 million hectares) of the Tohono O'odham Reservation or the nearby Ak Chin and San Xavier Indian reservations, also occupied by the O'odham people, all located south of Phoenix, Arizona. The village may be one of any number that have such unassuming names as Si:l Naggia (Saddle Hanging), Hawan Naggia (Crow Hanging), Hodai Son Wo'o (Rock Basin Tank) or even Gogs Mek (Dog Burnt).

The villages are scattered across the northern reaches of the Sonoran Desert, a hot and arid plain broken by isolated mountain ranges and studded with creosote brush, mesquite and cacti. The austere beauty and fantastic plant life of the region are preserved at **Organ Pipe National Monument**, on the Tohono O'odham Reservation's western border, and **Saguaro National Monument**, a short drive to the east.

The biggest town on the Tohono O'odham Reservation is Sells, which in the past decade has become a melting-pot village. Tohono O'odhams who live in Sells have settled from somewhere else. Most come for job opportunities with the Bureau of Indian Affairs; others come for government housing, which in past years has become prevalent at most reservation communities. It is also the location of the **Arts and Crafts Center**, where local art work, including highly valued Tohono O'odham basketry, may be seen and purchased.

Sells is a quasi-ubanized sprawl nestled below the sacred mountain, Waw Giwulk, or Baboquivari, the home of the Protector of the Tohono O'odham people. Despite the non-traditional housing, many Tohono O'odhams call this place home. But the entire reservation is home as well, since all of it is the aboriginal land of the O'odhams. To-

Left, Yaqui deer dancer. Right, prickly inhabitants of Saguaro National Monument.

day, the oral history of the Tohono O'odhams tell of their emergence from this ground. This sacred event is held in the memory of the people, a memory reinforced by the telling of the creation story. There are places on the reservation where a Tohono O'odham can point and say, "This is where we came from." One emergence point is only a few feet from a paved road. Some people joke, "When we came out, a tribal van pulled up and we drove off."

Today, people still use the Tohono O'odham names of those areas that are not within the reservation's boundaries and, by doing so, maintain their special connection to them. To the east lies Tucson, whose name is a bastardization of Cuk Son (Black Base Mountain). To the west, there is a mining town called Ajo; the Tohono O'odhams call this area Moik Wahia (Soft Well). To the south, there is Sonoita, called Son Oidag (Spring Field). And in Mexico, there is Poso Verde, called Ce:dagi Wahia (Green Well).

The Pima – River People: About 50 miles (80 km) north of Tohono O'odham land, lies the **Gila River Indian Reservation**, home of the Pima tribe. Here another dialogue of memory begins.

An old man is talking: "People used to like to work together. When the wheat was ready, all the people would come together to harvest. They would cut the wheat down by hand. They would wait for a windy day or night and they would all get together and throw the wheat up in the air so that the grass and things would blow out. A night that had a full moon and the wind blowing was the best time. The people would work all night. That is how they used to do things."

About 10,000 Pima Indians reside on this 3,000-acre reservation as well as a few hundred Maricopa Indians. The Maricopa belong to the Yuman linguistic family and are not related to the Pimas in any way. The tribes own the **Gila River Arts and Crafts Center**, which specializes in their own outstanding pottery and basketry. Nearby, the **Gila Heritage Village and Museum** features

O'odham schoolboys strolling through Sells

288

a reconstructed village of traditional Pima, Maricopa, Tohono O'odham and Apache houses. The **Mul-Cha-Ta** (Gathering of the People) celebration is usually held in March at Sacaton and features a rodeo, art exhibit, and basket and rain dances.

Anthropological evidence suggests that the Pimas and Tohono O'odhams were, at one time, a single people. They are said to be descendants of the Hohokam – or as they are called by the people, *Huhukam*, "the ones that have gone now." Linguistically the two groups are very closely related. Their languages are mutually intelligible, and socially the two tribes resemble one another. Many of their rituals, stories and songs are similar, too.

Among the ancient Hohokam sites that may be visited by travelers are **Casa Grande Ruins**, immediately south of the Gila River Reservation, and **Pueblo Grande Museum** in Phoenix. Both sites feature the ruins of a Hohokam village, including their elaborate irrigation system. Ancient Hohokam rock art may be viewed at **Painted Rocks State Park**, west of the Gila River Reservation about 20 miles outside the town of Gila Bend.

Tohono O'odhams and Pimas distinguish each other by location. The name "Tohono O'odham" means Desert People; they have traditionally lived in the torrid flatlands of the Sonoran Desert. The Pimas call themselves Akimel O'odham, or River People; they traditionally lived along riverbanks in the valleys of south central Arizona.

The "River People," the Pimas, are well-documented by the Spanish and later by Anglos as having had a truly rich agrarian society. Hundreds of Pimas throwing wheat into the wind on a moonlit night was once a common sight, but this practice, as the old Pima recalls, is no more. With the coming of Anglos, the fight for domination over the water of the Gila River became a major struggle for the Pima people.

The Pimas are still called River People even though the river that winds through their reservation no longer carries water. The riverbed is now cracked and dusty, a home only to lizards, horned toads and rattlesnakes. There is no traditional farming, only that which uses water brought from other places in concrete canals or pumped from wells deep below the ground. But this place along the dry river is home. Other Pima lands, such as the Salt River Indian Reservation, which is on Phoenix's eastern boundary, are only a small part of the aboriginal holdings of the Pima. Another tiny segment, which is shared by the Tohono O'odhams, is called, ironically, Ak Chin, "River's Mouth."

The O'odham people – both the Pimas and the Tohono O'odhams – were more open to the religious and cultural influences of Spanish missionaries than any other Southwestern tribes. Though they were probably more interested in Spanish cattle than religion, there was in fact more demand for missionaries than the Jesuits could provide. This early acculturation was hastened by a common enemy – the Apaches – and continued when US troops arrived. American forts were a welcome refuge from Apache

Stone chapel, Tohono O'odham Reservation.

raiders, and the O'odhams formed a standing army to help US troops.

The written history of the O'odham people was probably first recorded when they met the Spanish and were introduced to Catholicism. Their history was not only collected in the flowery script of the mission historians, it was recorded in the structures they built to house the new religion. These are the missions, structures ranging from the quaint little churches dotting the reservations to the grand **San Xavier del Bac Mission**, an 18th-century Byzantine masterpiece that shines like a gem in the desert sun. San Xavier Mission is located on the O'odhams' small San Xavier Reservation immediately south of Tucson.

In accepting Christianity, the O'odhams also transformed it. Even during holiday celebrations, Catholicism and traditional O'odham beliefs are intertwined. On Christmas Eve, for example, it's not uncommon for people to speak of sighting the Holy Family. They talk about seeing them as ordinary people, doing ordinary things like washing their hands at an outdoor faucet or sitting on a stump to rest.

The same is true of Easter. On Good Friday, people say the devil runs rampant among ordinary folks. He is human; he is real. He can be your uncle or father. He plays mischief and spends the evening playing cards, the devil's game. Or the fiddle, the devil's music. Children are warned not to play on precarious edges or the devil might push them down. Don't climb on trees! Don't walk too close to the irrigation ditch!

It is a solemn day. The saints on the saints' table are covered in black. The children play quiet games – staying as safe as possible during this most unholy time. It is said there was even a tradition that allowed mean people, truly mean people, to run about the village all day doing dreadful things to their neighbors. People locked up their possessions and stayed indoors as the mean ones wandered about kicking any dogs or cats they came upon, stealing any personal belongings that were in sight, and harassing women.

San Xavier del Bac Mission.

Pascua Yaqui: Indian beliefs and Catholicism are also brought together by the Pascua Yaqui tribe, neighbors of the O'odhams who live in small towns throughout the Tucson and Phoenix area. Towns with large Yaqui communities include Guadalupe, Coolidge, Florence and Chandler, all south of Phoenix; Marana, outside of Tucson; and Barrio Libre, which is a settlement in South Tucson. The Yaquis also have a small reservation adjacent to the Tohono O'odham Reservation near Tucson. Although the Yaquis are not related to the O'odhams linguistically, the two tribes interact socially and attend each other's ceremonies and festivals.

Yaquis have lived in Arizona for more than 100 years, but their songs and stories don't speak of sacred places in this area. Their sacred mountains and other sites are all in Sonora, Mexico, where they lived before migrating north and where the majority of Yaquis still reside today. Currently, there are some 6,000 Yaquis residing in Arizona and some 30,000 in villages in Sonora.

Like the O'odhams, the Yaquis were introduced to Catholicism early. After nearly a century of repelling Spanish domination, the Yaquis requested Jesuit missions in the early 1600s and began practicing Catholicism. The Spanish presence grew heavy-handed, however, and in 1740 the Yaquis revolted. In later years, they also came into conflict with the Mexican government, which drove several villages north. The first Yaqui refugees started trickling into present-day Arizona in the 1880s.

Yaqui religion is a distinct blend of Catholic and native beliefs. Central to much of their traditional ceremonies are the mystical realms – the "wilderness world" and "flower world" – where things are said to be enchanted. Deer songs and deer dances are also a critical part of the ceremony, representing a hunter's request for permission to take the animal's life. The pascola dancer is also a central figure. He is the master of ceremonies and ritual clown all in one. He dances for happy occasions as well as sad. Sometimes O'odham people hire Yaqui pascolas to dance for them. The O'odhams have their own *pako'ola* dancers, but they often say the Yaqui pascola is the best.

The best-known and most dramatic Yaqui ceremony is a passion play celebrated on Holy Saturday (the day before Easter). The O'odhams call it *mat o wo:p g jijiawul*, "the chasing of the devils." The ceremony is a battle played out between the symbolic forces of good and evil. Flowers – representing the blood of Jesus – are thrown at the black-cloaked devils to drive them off. All in attendance watch as the two spirits fight. In the end, the forces of good win for another year. Everyone is blessed with holy water or the confetti from *kaskalones*, decorated eggshells. Ceremonial dancers perform through the night, including deer dancers, matachines, and the clownish pascolas.

To find out more about the Yaquis, O'odhams and other Southwestern tribes, visit the **Heard Museum** in Phoenix or the **Arizona State Museum** in Tucson on the campus of the University of Arizona.

Yaqui flute player.

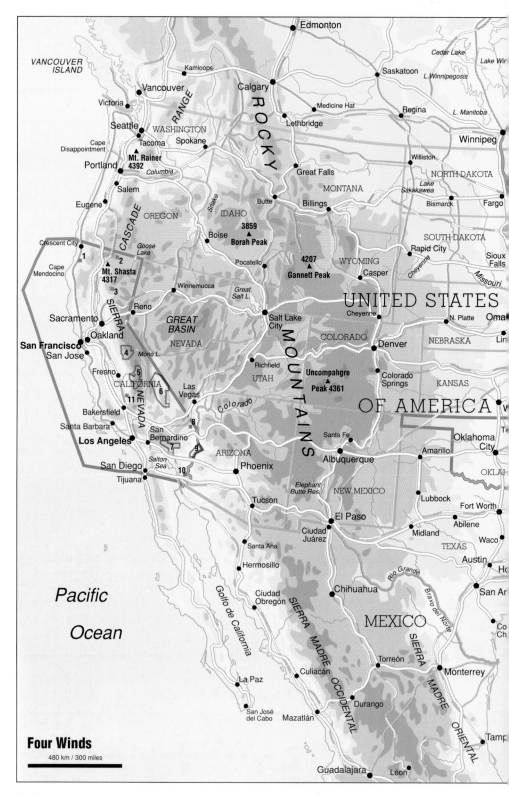

Pacific

Ocean

Four Winds
480 km / 300 miles

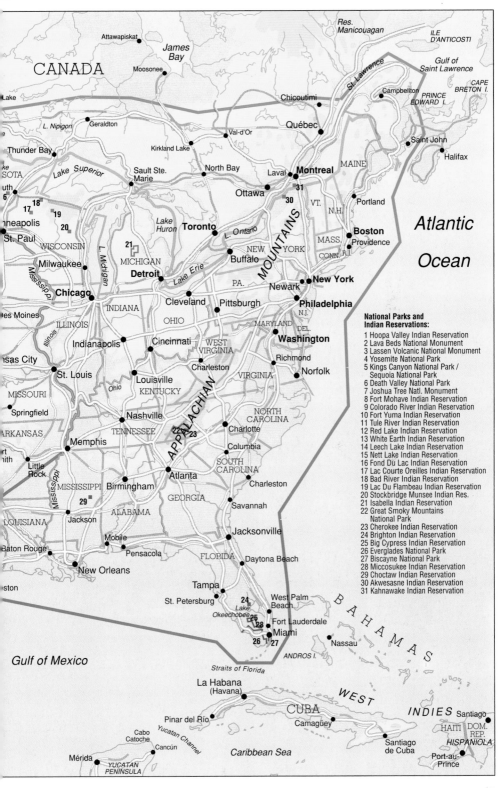

CANADA

Attawapiskat
James Bay
Moosonee
Res. Manicouagan
ILE D'ANTICOSTI
Gulf of Saint Lawrence
CAPE BRETON I.
Lake
L. Nipigon
Geraldton
Chicoutimi
Campbellton
PRINCE EDWARD I.
Saint John
Halifax
Thunder Bay
SOTA
uth
6
18
17
19
20
St. Paul
Val-d'Or
Québec
Kirkland Lake
North Bay
Laval
Montreal
MAINE
Portland
Sault Ste. Marie
Ottawa
31
30
VT.
N.H.
MASS.
Boston
Providence
R.I.
CONN.
neapolis
WISCONSIN
Milwaukee
21
MICHIGAN
Lake Huron
Toronto
L. Ontario
NEW YORK
Buffalo
Atlantic Ocean
Chicago
Detroit
Lake Erie
PA.
Newark
New York
INDIANA
Cleveland
Pittsburgh
Philadelphia
N.J.
es Moines
ILLINOIS
OHIO
MARYLAND
DEL.
Washington
Indianapolis
Cincinnati
WEST VIRGINIA
Richmond
sas City
St. Louis
Charleston
Norfolk
MISSOURI
Louisville
KENTUCKY
VIRGINIA
Springfield
Ohio
Nashville
NORTH CAROLINA
ARKANSAS
TENNESSEE
22
23
Charlotte
rt
ith
Memphis
Columbia
Little Rock
SOUTH CAROLINA
MISSISSIPPI
Atlanta
Charleston
Birmingham
29
GEORGIA
Savannah
LOUISIANA
ALABAMA
Jackson
Jacksonville
Baton Rouge
Mobile
Pensacola
FLORIDA
Daytona Beach
ston
New Orleans
Tampa
St. Petersburg
24
West Palm Beach
Lake Okeechobee
25
Fort Lauderdale
28
Miami
26
27
Nassau
ANDROS I.
Gulf of Mexico
Straits of Florida
B A H A M A S
La Habana (Havana)
W E S T
I N D I E S
Santiago
Pinar del Río
CUBA
Camagüey
HAITI
DOM. REP.
Cabo Catoche
Yucatan Channel
Cancún
HISPANIOLA
Mérida
YUCATAN PENINSULA
Caribbean Sea
Santiago de Cuba
Port-au-Prince

MINNESOTA
APPALACHIAN
MOUNTAINS
Mississippi
Lake Superior
L. Michigan

National Parks and Indian Reservations:

1 Hoopa Valley Indian Reservation
2 Lava Beds National Monument
3 Lassen Volcanic National Monument
4 Yosemite National Park
5 Kings Canyon National Park / Sequoia National Park
6 Death Valley National Park
7 Joshua Tree Natl. Monument
8 Fort Mohave Indian Reservation
9 Colorado River Indian Reservation
10 Fort Yuma Indian Reservation
11 Tule River Indian Reservation
12 Red Lake Indian Reservation
13 White Earth Indian Reservation
14 Leech Lake Indian Reservation
15 Nett Lake Indian Reservation
16 Fond Du Lac Indian Reservation
17 Lac Courte Oreilles Indian Reservation
18 Bad River Indian Reservation
19 Lac Du Flambeau Indian Reservation
20 Stockbridge Munsee Indian Res.
21 Isabella Indian Reservation
22 Great Smoky Mountains National Park
23 Cherokee Indian Reservation
24 Brighton Indian Reservation
25 Big Cypress Indian Reservation
26 Everglades National Park
27 Biscayne National Park
28 Miccosukee Indian Reservation
29 Choctaw Indian Reservation
30 Akwesasne Indian Reservation
31 Kahnawake Indian Reservation

THE FOUR WINDS

The Four Winds are the four directions: east, west, north and south. With Father Sky above and Mother Earth below, this is the Indian universe.

In the "Four Winds," we travel to every corner of Native America. We start in the Northeastern Woodlands, where the Chippewa Nation shares the lake country of Minnesota, Wisconsin, Michigan and Ontario with the Menominees, Winnebagos, Potawatomis, Oneidas and other tribes, and where the descendants of the mighty Five Nation Iroquois League still reside in the dense woodlands of Ontario, Quebec and northern New York.

In the Southeast, descendants of the Five Civilized Tribes – those that escaped the Trail of Tears – still occupy lands where ancient Mississippian people built earthen pyramids and temple mounds. In North Carolina, the Eastern Band of Cherokees is headquartered at the foot of the Great Smoky Mountains. In southern Florida, the Seminoles and Miccosukees remain in the watery jungles of the Everglades. And in Mississippi, the Choctaw Nation stands fast after years of adversity.

In Oklahoma (once known as Indian Territory) some 30 indigenous and exile tribes, including the Cherokees, Creeks, Choctaws, Pawnees, Miamis, Shawnees, Comanches, Kiowas and others, now live shoulder to shoulder at the nation's Indian crossroads.

And in California, still the most densely populated and culturally diverse native region in the US, native Californians – including Pomos, Miwoks, Shoshones, Hupas and Cahuillas – as well as immigrants from other tribes are nurturing a rebirth of Native American life and cultures.

Preceding pages: San Xavier Mission. **Left, praying with a sacred pipe, Grand Portage, Minnesota.**

THE NORTHEASTERN WOODLANDS

In the late 1600s, the great Northeastern Woodlands was a region in turmoil. Propelled by the arrival of Europeans and the rich rewards of the fur trade, Indian people traveled, traded and vied for power.

Small European villages – so tiny and helpless only 20 years before – had multiplied and grown in size. Giant ships crossed the ocean with a seemingly endless supply of settlers. And all of them, it seemed, wanted a piece of Indian Country to call their own.

Indian people learned quickly that not all whites were the same. French voyaguers worked out a complex fur-trading network with the Micmac, Abnaki, Cree, Huron, Ottawa and Chippewa tribes around the Great Lakes and along the St Lawrence River. English planters settled in the heart of the mighty Powhattan Confederacy near the Chesapeake Bay and in the rocky soil of New England where the Wampanoags, Massachusets, Pequots and Narragansets lived. The Dutch established a lucrative partnership with the powerful Iroquois League in the northern reaches of the Hudson River and with Algonquin tribes surrounding Manhattan Island. About 100 miles (160 km) away, in the territory of the Delaware Indians, a small colony of Swedes broke ground on the banks of the Delaware River.

Even before the whites built their towns, there were signs that they would come. Entire villages on the New England coast were wiped out by a strange new illness – smallpox – carried by early traders and fishermen. One group of whites, the famous Pilgrims, built their houses on the bones of a Wampanoag village. And as more whites arrived, the epidemics only grew worse.

By the time most tribes realized what was happening, it was already too late to resist. First the Powhattans rose up, then the Wampanoags, Narragansets, Nipmucs and Delawares – all trying to push the invaders back into the ocean. Many whites died, but many fought back. They hunted the Indians like animals, or sold them into slavery.

By the early 1700s, whites were also fighting each other, spoiling for the biggest chunk of Indian land. The tribes joined them in war, hoping to regain some of their former strength or to strike against longstanding Indian.

But even in victory, Indians seemed to lose. They were pushed farther west, beyond the Appalachian Mountains into the Ohio Valley and around the Great Lakes. One after another, charismatic leaders organized the refugee tribes into confederacies capable of striking back against the whites: first Pontiac, the great Ottawa chief, in 1763; then Little Turtle, a Miami, in 1790; the brilliant Shawnee, Tecumseh, in 1811; and Sauk Chief Black Hawk in 1832. All led their warriors in a few initial victories, but none could break the back of the invaders' military might.

In the late 1800s, many Northeastern tribes were relocated by the government to Indian Territory, now Oklahoma. Many Indian people remain on or near

Left, Winnebago singer slings a drum across his back. Right, Sauk Chief Black Hawk.

their traditional homes, however, and much of their culture is still intact. Among these groups, the Chippewas and Iroquois are perhaps the most rewarding to visit.

Chippewa Nation: Canoeing through the remote lake country of northeastern Minnesota, it's not difficult to imagine what the life of 17th-century voyaguers must have been like. They were French fur-traders who paddled the labyrinth of waterways that connected one tribe with another and who often adopted Indian ways and learned Indian languages.

Today, much of this country is contained within **Superior National Forest**, and looks much as it did 300 years ago. There are still miles of unbroken wilderness here: thick stands of birch and spruce, enormous outcroppings of jagged gray rock. Walleye flicker in the shallows of the lakes, and waterfowl rustle in wild-rice marshes near the banks. This is the traditional territory of the Chippewa Nation, now divided among several reservations in the Great Lakes region of the US and Canada.

Not too far away, within the Chippewas' **Grand Portage Reservation**, a 260-year-old fort still stands at **Grand Portage National Monument**. It was once an important link in the French fur-trading network, and visitors can still walk the 8-mile trail that winds around the waterfalls and rapids.

Although the French were eventually pushed north by the English, they left their mark on the names of Chippewa bands. There are the Fond du Lac, Lac du Flambeau, and Lac Courte Oreilles, among others – more than 10 in all, most with their own small reservations. In fact, "Chippewa" is also a French-derived word. In their own language, the Chippewas call themselves "Anishinabe," the Original People. They make up the largest Indian nation in the area.

The best time to visit these reservations is during the powwow season, when local communities open their doors to visitors from all over North America. In Minnesota, powwows are held at the Leech Lake, Fond du Lac, Nett Lake and White Earth reservations; in Wis-

Chippewa's lake country.

consin at the Lac du Flambeau, Lac Courte Oreilles and Red Cliff reservations (see *Travel Tips* for a complete listing). The most affecting location, however, is probably the Grand Portage Reservation. It is set along the shore of Lake Superior on the easternmost finger of Minnesota, cut off from the rest of the world by the trackless forests of Superior National Forest and **Quetico Provincial Park**. The **Grand Portage Inn**, a luxury lodge owned by the Grand Portage Chippewa Band, makes the perfect base from which to explore the wilderness on foot, by canoe, or, in winter, on 70 miles of cross-country skiing trails. The band also runs a marina and boat rental operation. A 20-mile cruise takes visitors to **Isle Royale National Park**, home to wolves, moose, beaver and other wildlife.

Wild rice – one of the area's great Indian delicacies – is usually harvested in September. At least one band, the Bad River Chippewas in northern Wisconsin, holds a wild rice celebration around Labor Day with feasts, dancing, crafts and traditional games. In August, the Fond du Lac Band holds its annual **Ni-mi-Win Celebration** at the Spirit Mountain Ski Complex near Duluth, which brings together Chippewa bands and visitors for an entertaining and informative series of historians, anthropologists, spiritual leaders, drum groups, dancers and artists.

The **Lake of the Woods Ojibwa Center** in Kenora, Ontario, coordinates exhibitions, powwows and other cultural events. There is a powwow in the Kenora area almost every weekend during the summer and early fall. Contact the Center for up-to-date information.

Spearfishing wars: Recently, Chippewa communities in northern Wisconsin have become embroiled in a bitter dispute over treaty rights. The controversy stems from the traditional Chippewa practice of spearfishing, usually done at night with torches, or, more commonly now, with high-intensity flashlights. Angry locals claim that the Chippewas are depleting stocks of prized walleye pike and muskellunge, one of the main

Grand Portage Powwow.

attractions of the area's tourist industry.

According to treaties dating back to the mid-1800s, however, Chippewas retained the right to harvest fish and game in their traditional manner both on and off their reservations. Although a federal court decision reaffirmed that right in 1983, anti-spearfishing protestors continue to voice their opinion, some resorting to intimidation and racist slurs in order to make their point. In 1989 and 1990, angry mobs gathered to jeer at Chippewa fishermen, pelt them with stones, buzz their canoes, and heckle them with slogans like "Spear an Indian, save a walleye!"

Although there is little hard evidence that the game-fish population is suffering because of spearfishing, several bands have suspended the practice for the time being in order to mollify the protestors and work out a compromise. In the meantime, tribal leaders, state officials and anti-spearfishing organizations are faced with the difficult task of reaching an agreement that will satisfy everyone concerned.

Immigrants and natives: There are a number of non-Chippewa communities in the Great Lakes region as well. Some are indigenous to the area; others are immigrants that were pushed west by the crush of European occupation.

Among the immigrant groups is the Oneida Tribe, a member of the once mighty Iroquois League originally located between the Hudson River and Lake Ontario. The Oneidas were forced out of their homeland after the American Revolution despite their alliance with the American rebels. Their 5,000-acre (2,000-hectare) reservation is located 10 miles (16 km) from Green Bay, Wisconsin. In addition to a bingo enterprise and an annual powwow, the tribe runs the **Oneida Nation Museum**, which houses an impressive collection of Oneida artifacts, crafts, historic exhibits and a reconstructed village with an authentic birch longhouse.

Nearby, the **Stockbridge-Munsee Reservation** is home to two Algonquin-speaking tribes also from the east: the Munsee, a Delaware tribe, and the

Chippewas harvesting wild rice.

302

Stockbridge, or Mohican, originally from New England. The tribes have developed the **Stockbridge-Munsee Historical Museum** and hold an annual powwow in August.

Among the tribes native to the region are the Potawatomis, Winnebagos (a non-reservation tribe), a branch of the eastern Sioux, and, the one with most to offer travelers, the Menominees. Nearly destroyed by the federal government's termination policy in the 1950s, the Menominees have managed to regain their tribal status and some of their land. In addition to other enterprises, the tribe now runs a white-water rafting outfit, a fascinating **Logging Camp Museum** and the **Menominee Nation Casino** – a little piece of Las Vegas in northern Wisconsin. The other tribes are less tourism-oriented, although some run bingo halls and hold yearly powwows.

Elsewhere in the region, **Pipestone National Monument**, located in Minnesota's southwestern corner, preserves the quarries where generations of Indians have come for catlinite, the soft red rock used in the making of sacred pipes. Pipe-makers and other craftspeople are usually on hand in the summer months to demonstrate their work.

Farther afield, several ancient mound-builder sites are also well worth investigating. The most dramatic include **Effigy Mounds National Monument** in Marquette, Iowa; **Serpent Mound State Memorial and Museum** in Locust Grove, Ohio; **Mound City Group National Monument** in Chillicothe, Ohio; and **Cahokia Mounds State Historic Site** in Collinsville, Illinois. All are Adena or Hopewell sites dating from 1,000 to 2,000 years ago. Some feature enormous bear, bird and snake-shaped effigy mounds. Others, like Monks Mound at Cahokia, reach a height of 100 ft. These mounds are all the more amazing when you consider that the Adena and Hopewell people had neither wheels nor beasts of burden to transport the thousands of tons of earth necessary to build them.

Modern warriors: Moving eastward, Indian communities thin out, testimony to the devastation wrought by white

encroachment and the many colonial battles fought between the French, English and Americans near the present Canadian–US border. This was formerly the homeland of the powerful six-nation Iroquois League comprised of the Mohawk, Seneca, Oneida, Onondaga, Cayuga and Tuscarora tribes. There is still a vital – and militant – Iroquois presence here, and in recent years they have managed to focus international attention on the issues of Indian rights, land claims and tribal sovereignty.

The struggle between tribal members and the Canadian government – as well as between Indian militants and traditional tribal leaders – came to a head in July 1990 after a shootout between Mohawk activists and Quebec provincial police left one policeman dead.

Nominally, at least, the conflict started when a developer announced plans to build a golf course on land that was claimed by the Mohawks. Considering the intensity of the Mohawks' reaction, however, it was clear that there were larger issues involved. Protests quickly

Waterfall at Pipestone National Monument.

spun off into violent demonstrations, road blockades and, in the end, a two-month siege at Oka, Quebec, near Montreal, where 20 heavily armed members of the Mohawk Warrior Society were holed up against 400 Canadian soldiers. At issue were not only questions of Indian land claims, but the growing reliance on illegal on-reservation gambling, the involvement of organized crime in gambling operations, and, in much broader terms, the direction of Indian activism.

The standoff came to an end with promises of negotiation but few concrete solutions for the Mohawks. It was clear, however, that the incident at Oka struck a chord in Native American communities throughout the US and Canada and may foreshadow similar acts of militancy elsewhere in Indian Country.

Needless to say, visiting Iroquois communities in this area may be somewhat dicey for non-Indians. There are a number of sites that are strictly for tourists, however, and they should present little if any trouble.

At Brantford, Ontario – named after famous Iroquois leader Joseph Brant (Thayendanegea) – the **Woodland Indian Cultural Education Center** offers an informative exhibit on Iroquois culture and history, research facilities, and contemporary arts and crafts. Nearby, the **Six Nations Grand River Indian Reserve** is home to thousands of Iroquois, mostly Mohawks and Cayugas, and offers several fine crafts stores.

About 40 miles (65 km) east, at Niagara Falls, New York, the **Turtle: Native American Center for the Living Arts** is an Iroquois-operated museum, art gallery and craft shop which also has occasional lectures, classes, and, in the summer, traditional Iroquois dancing.

Farther east, on the Kahnawake Indian Reserve about 15 miles (24 km) downriver from Montreal, the **St-Francois Xavier Mission** maintains the Shrine of Kateri Tekakwitha, a young Mohawk woman converted by French Jesuits in the late 1600s and subsequently persecuted by the Iroquois. She was beatified by the Catholic Church, a major step toward sainthood.

Living heritage: Other Indian communities are scattered throughout the Northeast, although none are as large as the Chippewa or Iroquois. The Passamaquoddy and Penobscot tribes occupy state reservations in Maine and hold occasional public dances. Hundreds of Micmac Indians live on Nova Scotia and Prince Edward Island, and a small group of Wampanoags still live on Martha's Vineyard.

The Nipmuc Tribe has a small state reservation in Massachusetts, as do the Mattaponi and Pamunkey in Virginia, both formerly members of the Powhattan Confederacy. The Shinnecock Tribe has a reservation near the tip of Long Island and sponsors an annual powwow. The Delaware Indians of Pennsylvania, New Jersey and Delaware gather each year for a powwow, usually in Philadelphia.

There are other tribes, too, some represented only by a handful of people of mixed blood. Their heritage lives on, however, if only in the memory of their scattered descendants.

Left, Witch Tree on shore of Lake Superior, Grand Portage. **Right**, Indian ball player, by George Catlin.

THE GREAT SOUTHEAST

In 1539, when Hernando de Soto landed on the west coast of Florida with 550 conquistadores, he found a land of wild and luxuriant beauty. There were expansive saltwater marshes, blinding white beaches, dense forests of cypress and yellow pine, and gentle hills shrouded with mist.

For the most part, the people he encountered in the interior were farmers who lived in small villages often affiliated by blood, culture and language. There were the Timucuas and Apalachees on the coast, the fierce Caddos near the Mississippi River, the powerful Creeks and Choctaws in the woods of Georgia and Alabama, and the Cherokees in the mountains and river valleys of the Carolinas.

By the time de Soto arrived, the ancient Temple Mound-builders – or Mississippian Culture – had all but disappeared. With the exception of the Natchez, whose highly stratified, theocratic society survived well into the 1700s, the only remnants of the Mississippian Culture were embedded in overgrown temple mounds and in the cultures of their scattered descendants.

Like so many Spanish explorers, de Soto came with conquest in his heart. He and his small army roamed from village to village for two years, killing or kidnapping hundreds of Indians and stealing whatever treasures they could find. For many tribes, it was a bloody and tragic introduction to the ways of the white invaders.

Nearly 300 years later, the terrible work started by de Soto was finished by the US government. In 1830, President Andrew Jackson signed the Indian Removal Act calling for the relocation of eastern tribes to Indian Territory west of the Mississippi River. The Five Civilized Tribes – Cherokee, Choctaw, Chickasaw, Creek and Seminole – were the main target of Jackson's new law. Their desperate march – and the exodus of all eastern tribes to Indian Territory – came to be known as the Trail of Tears.

But the Indian people of the Southeast have by no means disappeared. Reservation communities in Florida, North Carolina and Mississippi, as well as thousands of people of Indian descent, still identify with their tribal heritage. And the temple mounds of the ancient Mississippian Culture give mute testimony to the complexity and splendor of the people who built them.

The Eastern Cherokees: In the western corner of North Carolina, nestled against the densely wooded, blue-green swells of **Great Smoky Mountains National Park**, is the **Qualla Reservation** of the Cherokee Indian Tribe. This is the home of the eastern band of Cherokees. They are descendants of refugees who escaped the Trail of Tears and hid themselves for years in the lush backwoods of the Carolina highlands.

Little wonder why the Cherokees were so reluctant to give up their homeland. This is a stunningly beautiful country, blanketed with forests of oak and pine, and painted with the pinks, purples and whites of blossoming mountain laurels

SE-QUO-YAH

and wild rhododendron. The Smoky Mountains have been called the Land of Moving Water, and everywhere you look cold, clear streams tumble down rocky slopes. Deer, black bear and wild boar roam the woods. Falcons and owls command the sky. And of course, there is the Smoky Mountains' famous milky-blue mist – a combination of moisture and pine oil that drifts in the folds of slopes and valleys.

This spectacular scenery has helped make Great Smoky Mountains the most visited national park in the country. About 10 million people pass through the area each year, and as a result, the tourism industry is booming. And like most people who live and work around the park, the Cherokees depend on their share of tourist dollars.

What this means for many travelers is that the Qualla Reservation isn't the remote mountain sanctuary you might expect, or that the "reverence and respect" for nature that is commonly associated with the "Indian Way" prevents some Cherokees from exploiting the endless demand for trinkets and entertainment. Chances are you'll pass more than one roadside Indian decked out in war bonnet and buckskin (traditionally, a Plains Indian outfit) posing for pictures with passing tourists. In the gift shops, toy tomahawks and peace pipes bear the unsettling label "Made In Taiwan." The Cherokees have obviously learned the lesson of the marketplace: give consumers what they want.

But appearances aside, there is still a good deal worth visiting for those with a sincere interest in Cherokee culture and history. At **Ocanaluftee Indian Village**, a reconstructed 18th-century settlement built by tribal members, guides give informative talks about the traditional way of life. Basket makers weave beautiful vessels from white oak and river cane; canoe makers demonstrate the construction of traditional dugouts; potters and weavers give detailed demonstrations. Much of their work, and the work of other Cherokee artists, is available at the **Qualla Arts and Crafts Store**. During the summer,

North Carolina's Great Smoky Mountains.

Unto These Hills, a dramatic retelling of Cherokee history, is presented at an outdoor theater. A more detailed account of Cherokee history, life and culture is presented at the nearby **Museum of the Cherokee**.

About 60 miles (95 km) south of Cherokee, just outside Calhoun, Georgia, travelers can also visit **New Echota State Historic Site**, the original capital of the Cherokee Nation. This is where John Ross, the elected chief of the Cherokee Tribe at the time of removal, presided over the Cherokee Council.

While the notorious Georgia Guard ransacked Cherokee plantations, Ross was petitioning lawmakers in Washington. Finally, in 1832, after many months of legal wrangling, the US Supreme Court handed down its landmark Worcester vs. Georgia decision, ruling that "the Cherokee Nation… is a distinct community, occupying its own territory, with boundaries accurately described, and which the citizens of Georgia have no right to enter, but with the assent of the Cherokee themselves…" Although

this decision upheld the principle of tribal sovereignty, it was no help to the Cherokees. President Jackson ignored the court and encouraged Georgia and other states to continue the policy of Indian removal.

New Echota is also where Sequoyah, a former Cherokee warrior, began working on the Cherokee system of writing, the first written Indian language north of Mexico. "I thought that would be like catching a wild animal and taming it," Sequoyah later said. Within months, the tribe learned to read and write their own language and began publishing a newspaper, the *Cherokee Phoenix*. Among the restored buildings at the site is the original *Phoenix* office.

Nearby, several ancient mound-builder sites make a fascinating detour. The best-known include **Etowah Indian Mounds Historic Site** in Cartersville, Georgia; **Ocmulgee National Monument** in Macon, Georgia; and **Kolomoki Indian Mounds State Park** in Blakely, Georgia. **Mound State Monument** in Moundville, Alabama;

Miccosukee alligator wrestling.

Chucalissa Indian Museum and Moundbuilder Site in Memphis, Tennessee, and the **Eva Archaelogical site near Knoxville, Tennessee**, are also within reasonable driving distance. These sites feature reconstructed temples, excavations and excellent exhibits on the life, culture and art of the ancient Mississippian people.

Seminoles and Miccosukees: Although the Cherokee Trail of Tears came to symbolize the tragic fate of the Five Civilized Tribes, it was the Seminole Tribe and its offshoot, the Miccosukee Tribe, that suffered most at the hands of Andrew Jackson and his brutal policy of Indian relocation.

By the time Jackson became president, he and the Seminoles already had a long history of bad blood. In 1818, when Jackson was still a military officer, he led troops against the Seminoles in an attempt to drive them out of northern Florida and claim the land for the US government. The First Seminole War, as the campaign came to be known, dealt the Indians a painful and damaging blow. Although Seminole warriors managed to evade Jackson's army, they were driven deep into the jungles south of Tampa Bay and forced into a major cession of tribal territory.

In 1835, a full five years after Jackson signed the Indian Removal Act, the Seminoles were still hiding out in their Florida stronghold. Although a few Seminole spokesmen accepted relocation, the majority of the tribe – under the leadership of warriors like Osceola, Alligator and Billy Bowlegs – steadfastly refused to go. Jackson dispatched troops to dislodge the recalcitrant Indians, but the Seminoles put up a punishing hit-and-run defense.

The Second Seminole War lasted seven years and cost the US government $20 million. But slowly, as the Seminoles were pushed deeper and deeper into the Florida Everglades, small groups of Indians surrendered or, like Osceola, were captured under a flag of truce.

By 1842, the government decided that the Seminole War was more trouble than it was worth and called its army

Miccosukee elder.

home. In the end, 3,000 Seminoles had been shipped to Indian Territory, two for every soldier killed in the fighting. A few hundred Seminoles remained in the swamps. Their descendants proudly claim to be the only undefeated Indian tribe in the US.

Today, the Seminole and Miccosukee tribes occupy four federal reservations in south Florida: the Miccosukee Indian Reservation and Big Cypress Seminole Reservation in the Everglades, Brighton Seminole Reservation near Lake Okeechobee, and the tiny Hollywood Reservation just north of Miami.

The **Miccosukee Indian Reservation** (reached via the Tamiami Trail) is the most visited of these, and like Qualla, it relies heavily on tourism. Again, some travelers may be disappointed by the stagy entertainment – alligator-wrestling, for example – but it's important to remember that tourism has been a mainstay of the local economy for many years and affords a level of self-sufficiency that other tribes are still unable to attain. The **Miccosukee Culture Center**

and **Museum** are informative, and a small village of traditional, open-sided "chickee" huts is a pleasure to stroll through. Brightly colored patchwork garments and other crafts are also available at the Culture Center.

Although somewhat forbidding, the **Everglades** do have a certain seductive quality, especially at dusk, when the horizon is streaked with pink and orange light, illuminating wandering patches of mist. It's worth getting a closer look at the swamp and its tree-crested "hammocks" by taking one of the airboat tours offered by the tribe.

The Miccosukee also sponsor an annual **Indian Arts Festival**, usually held the week after Christmas. The festival features native dancers, singers, artists and craftspeople from the US, Canada and Mexico.

Elsewhere in the area, the **Seminole Arts and Crafts Center** in Dania (near Fort Lauderdale) offers a good selection of local handicrafts, including the Seminoles' trademark patchwork clothing. And at the **Big Cypress**

Miccosukee airboat streaks across the Everglades.

Seminole Reservation, about 60 miles from Fort Lauderdale, the Seminole Tribe runs what is possibly the biggest bingo operation in the world.

Florida also has its share of prehistoric mound sites, including the **Madira Bickel Mound State Archaeological Site** at Bradenton (south of Tampa), **Turtle Mound Site** and **Green Mound State Archaeological Site** south of Daytona Beach, **Crystal River State Archaeological Site** at Crystal River, and the **Indian Temple Mound Museum** at Fort Walton Beach. Exhibits at each site explain the excavations and describe their significance in Native American prehistory.

The Mississippi Choctaws: Another member of the Five Civilized Tribes to remain in the Southeast is the Choctaw Tribe. Although most Choctaws were moved out of their Mississippi homeland during the Trail of Tears, a small band remained behind, and today, after several generations of severe hardship, they are one of the region's most successful business communities.

The Choctaws were among the first tribes to be relocated under Jackson's Indian removal plan. Their profound love of the land was observed by whites who watched as they touched trees, rocks and streams before turning away from their homes.

Many of the Choctaws who remained in Mississippi were quickly run off their farms by whites and driven into poverty. Their numbers started to dwindle, and, as early as the 1920s, it very much looked as if they might not survive through the 20th century.

Today, their situation is entirely different. With the help of the federal government and private investors, the tribe has staged one of the most impressive turn-arounds in recent memory. Thanks largely to Chief Philip Martin, who spearheaded a campaign to attract outside businesses, the Choctaws now run one of the country's largest greeting-card production companies, and they are branching off into the manufacture of automobile parts.

The best time to visit the Choctaws is during the **Choctaw Annual Fair**, held on their reservation outside Philadelphia, Mississippi, usually in July. As many as 20,000 visitors come to the fair to watch traditional Choctaw dancing, buy Choctaw arts and crafts, and see the fast-paced stickball game the tribe has played for centuries. The Choctaws are well-known for their ribbon applique work and fine basket making. Both items may be purchased at the **Choctaw Museum of the Southern Indian**, which also features exhibits on traditional Indian art, culture and important figures in Choctaw history.

The Choctaws trace their ancestry to **Mother Mound**, about 20 miles (30 km) north of the reservation. A second important mound site, **Emerald Mound**, is located near Natchez. Both sites were abandoned about AD 1500.

Like the Cherokees and Seminoles, the Choctaws are a divided people. Part of the tribe remains in the Southeast; the others were forced to resettle in Indian Territory, now Oklahoma, where they created a new life at the end of the Trail of Tears.

Left, selling colorful Miccosukee clothing. **Right**, floating through the Everglades in a dugout canoe.

OKLAHOMA

Oklahoma is an American Indian melting pot, a patchwork of native people from every corner of the US. This is Indian Territory, a remnant of the supposedly inviolable country created by President Andrew Jackson "to be guaranteed to the Indian tribes, as long as they shall occupy it." It was a land of Indian exiles. For some, like Geronimo and the Chiricahua Apaches, it was a prison. For others, like the Five Civilized Tribes, it was a last-chance refuge.

More than 25 tribes are now represented in Oklahoma, the vast majority descendants of refugees who were forced out of their original homelands. Although the American Indian population is larger than in almost any other state, there are no Indian reservations. Indian communities are spread throughout Oklahoma, often indistinguishable from their non-Indian neighbors.

Oklahoma's story started in 1830 when President Jackson, bent on removing eastern Indian tribes, signed the Indian Removal Act, creating a "permanent Indian frontier" west of the Mississippi River where Indian people were forced to relocate. The Five Civilized Tribes (Cherokee, Creek, Choctaw, Chickasaw and Seminole) were the first to go, losing as much as one-quarter of their people to the unspeakable hardships of the Trail of Tears.

But, painful as it was, Indian Territory was theirs. Jackson signed the papers. Congress made a promise. This was to be a land of sovereign Indian nations. "No Territory or State shall ever have a right to pass laws for the government of the Choctaw Nation," a typical treaty said. "No part of the land granted them shall ever be embraced in any Territory or State..." But the Choctaws' treaty, like so many made with Indian tribes, was quickly forgotten.

While the Five Civilized Tribes were busy with the work of nation-building, Northeastern and Plains tribes were also being relocated to Indian Territory. The Potawatomis, Shawnees, Kickapoos, Ottawas and others were removed from the Great Lakes region. The Pawnees, Iowas, Poncas and Osages were pushed out of the nearby eastern prairie. Immediately to the west, Plains tribes like the Cheyenne, Arapaho, Comanche and Kiowa still ranged freely in what is now the western half of Oklahoma and the Staked Plains of Texas.

By the 1850s, hardly more than 20 years after the signing of the Removal Act, the reduction of Indian Territory was already in the works with large tracts of land ceded to Kansas and Nebraska territories. More ground was lost during the Civil War, partly due to the alliance between many tribes and the rebellious Confederacy.

Then, in the late 1880s, Congress delivered a crushing blow. Railroads, commercial developers and hundreds of squatters (called Boomers) had long coveted Indian Territory, and with the passage of the General Allotment Act of 1887 the government virtually gave it to them. The Allotment Act broke up tribal holdings and deeded them directly to

Preceding pages: Quapaw Powwow. Left, singing at the Cherokee Nation Powwow. Right, Satanta, Kiowa chief.

individual Indians, who, with the help of liquor, coercion and fraud, were encouraged to sell. All land that remained unclaimed or unallotted was thrown open to homesteaders. Two million acres of tribal land were lost in a single year. And in 1890, much of Indian Territory became Oklahoma Territory.

Later, when the Cherokees and Choctaws resisted allotment, Congress passed the Curtis Act of 1898, which dismantled tribal governments and dissolved all hopes of maintaining tribal sovereignty. White homesteaders swarmed in once again, taking legal possession of land that had been promised to the tribes "as long as the grass grows and the rivers run."

In 1907, the State of Oklahoma was admitted to the Union. Indian Territory no longer existed.

End of the trail: Because Indian communities are scattered throughout the state, tracking down tribal sites and events involves a good deal of traveling. Generally speaking, there are two centers of Indian activity in Oklahoma, one in the eastern half of the state and the other in the western half. In the east, Muskogee, Okmulgee and Tahlequah form a three-pronged anchor around which the Five Civilized Tribes and other immigrant tribes settled. In western Oklahoma, Anadarko is the center of activity. The headquarters of several western tribes, including the Southern Cheyenne, Kiowa and Comanche, are located here as well as a number of important tourist attractions.

After the ordeal of the Trail of Tears, the Five Civilized Tribes gathered their strength and set about the business of establishing governments and rebuilding farms and communities. The leaders in this movement were undoubtedly the Cherokees, who, under the leadership of John Ross, headquartered their new council at **Tahlequa** and started publishing a tribal newspaper, *The Cherokee Advocate*. Today, Tahlequah is still the headquarters of the western band of Cherokees, and a must-see for anyone with a serious interest in Native American life in Oklahoma.

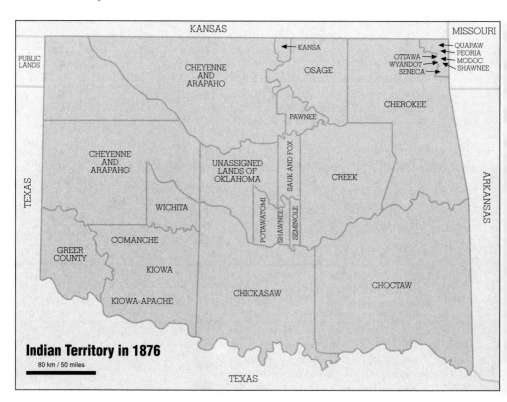

Indian Territory in 1876
80 km / 50 miles

The tribe owns and operates the **Cherokee Heritage Center**, which encompasses a museum featuring historic exhibits and contemporary Indian art; the **Tsa-La-Gi Ancient Village**, which is a detailed recreation of a traditional Cherokee village; and **Adams Corner Rural Village**, a historic enclave modeled after a 19th-century Cherokee settlement. The Heritage Center also sponsors the *Trail of Tears*, a dramatic reenactment of the Cherokee removal performed in an open-air theater. The graves of John Ross and his family as well as the original capitol building and Cherokee Supreme Court may also be visited.

About 30 miles (50 km) from Tahlequah, the history and culture of the southern tribes is presented at the **Five Civilized Tribes Museum** in Muskogee. In addition to a regular series of special exhibits, the museum hosts the annual **Five Civilized Tribes Art Show**, one of the area's major Indian art events.

At nearby Okmulgee, about another 30 miles west, the leaders of the Creek Nation meet at their new tribal complex. The old **Creek Capitol Building**, one of the most historic and charming buildings in Oklahoma, is also in town. It now houses the **Creek Council House Museum**, which traces Creek history from the pre-contact period to the present day. It offers a first-rate gift shop where Creek arts and crafts are sold. Okmulgee is also the site of the annual **Muskogee Creek Festival**, which features arts and crafts shows, a rodeo, stomp dancing and Creek music.

The original capitals of the other three Civilized Tribes are located in the southwest quarter of the state. The Seminoles, most of whom now live in Oklahoma rather than Florida, maintain the **Seminole Nation Museum** in the little town of Wewoka, where their historic capitol building still stands. Farther south, at Tuskahoma, the old **Choctaw Council** now houses a museum and gift shop. Tuskahoma is also the site of the **Choctaw Nation Labor Day Festivities**. At Tishomingo, about

Cherokee
Powwow,
Tahlequa.

30 miles from Durant, the Chickasaws have installed a museum in their historic **Council House** as well.

Elsewhere in the eastern half of Oklahoma, museums, cultural centers and powwows are sponsored by a number of immigrant tribes, most from the Great Lakes region or the eastern prairie. In Miami, in the northeasternmost corner of the state, the **Inter-Tribal Council Building** and gift shop represent members of eight tribes: the Ottawa, Miami, Wyandot, Peoria and Seneca-Cayuga from the northeast; the Eastern Shawnee and Quapaw from the eastern plains; and the Modoc from the Pacific Northwest. The Inter-Tribal Council holds its annual **Oklahoma Indian Heritage Days**, and the Quapaw and Ottawa hold their powwows, during the summer.

About 60 miles (95 km) west of Miami, the Osage Tribe – which originally ranged in this general area – operates the **Osage Museum** at Pawhuska, where it also holds its yearly powwow. The Pawnee Tribe, which also hails from the eastern prairie, holds a highly regarded powwow at the town of Pawnee near its tribal offices. Just outside of town, the **Pawnee Bill Museum** presents an interesting collection of art and artifacts. The Poncas hold their annual powwow at nearby Ponca City, also home to the **Indian Museum of the Ponca City Cultural Center**, a fine collection of artifacts representing several Oklahoma-based tribes, including the Ponca, Tonkawa, Otoe and Osage.

Heading south, the **Sac and Fox Library** and gallery is located at Stroud, about 50 miles (80 km) from Tulsa on Highway 44. The exhibits feature memorials to a number of famous tribal members, including Black Hawk, leader of the failed 1832 uprising; Keokuk, chief of the Sauks; and Jim Thorpe, world-famous Olympic gold-medal winner. Outside Oklahoma City, Shawnee is the headquarters of the Citizen Band of the Potawatomi Tribe, originally from the Great Lakes region where much of the tribe still resides. The band sponsors a summer powwow with both Plains and traditional Potawatomi dancing, and has developed a fine museum and archives chronicling the tribe's history and culture. Powwows and other cultural events are also held at Potawatomi communities in Kansas, Michigan and Wisconsin.

Finally, eastern Oklahoma has an exceptional mound-builder site. **Spiro Mounds Archaeological State Park** is found outside Poteau near the Arkansas border. Artifacts recovered from the mounds are exhibited at the **Kerr Museum**, outside Poteau.

The western connection: Anadarko is the center of Indian activity in western Oklahoma and an essential destination for anyone with an interest in historic and contemporary Native American cultures. Each year thousands of Indian and non-Indian visitors come to Anadarko for the **American Indian Exposition**, one of the largest Indian gatherings in the country. The exposition is a weeklong celebration of Native American cultures featuring drums and dancers, craftspeople, artists and spectators from the US and Canada. Of course, many participants are from lo-

Patriotic beadwork at the Cherokee Powwow.

cal Oklahoma tribes, including the Southern Cheyenne, Arapaho, Comanche, Apache, Kiowa, Delaware, Wichita and Ponca, just to name a few. In addition to the opening and closing parades, the exposition features the "pageant," an unforgettable procession of traditional dancers and singers.

There are a number of important attractions that operate year-round, too, and if possible, they shouldn't be missed. **Indian City**, **USA**, is a walk-through recreation of several Indian villages, including Apache wickiups, Navajo hogans, Kiowa tepees and Wichita grass lodges, all explained by knowledgeable Indian guides. There is a museum and gift shop here too, and a series of dance and music exhibitions, art shows and lectures. Contact Indian City directly for an up-to-date calendar of events.

Across the highway, the **National Hall of Fame for Famous American Indians** pays tribute to exceptional figures in Native American history – some well known, others fairly obscure. The **Southern Plains Indian Museum**

is in Anadarko, too, and, in addition to its fine collection of artifacts, provides an excellent outlet for contemporary Plains arts and crafts. Just outside of town, the Wichita and Kiowa tribes also run tribal museums. The Wichita usually hold their powwow in August. The Kiowas host an annual **Gourd Dance** over the Fourth of July weekend.

Fort Sill Military Reservation is about 35 miles (55 km) south of Anadarko. The historic frontier post and Indian internment camp is now a modern military facility, but a few of the original buildings are still intact, including the guardhouse that once held Geronimo and other Chiricahua Apache prisoners. Although many of the Chiricahuas were eventually shipped to the Mescalero Apache Reservation in New Mexico, some chose to stay in western Oklahoma. Their descendants still live in the area. Geronimo was never released from exile, however. He died and was buried at Fort Sill in 1909, already enshrined in Wild West mythology. His gravesite, and the grave of Comanche

Iowa Indian dancer.

chief Quanah Parker, are located on the base. Ask the staff at the **Fort Sill Museum** for directions.

While you are in the area, it's worthwhile to make a side trip to the **Wichita Mountains National Wildlife Refuge**, where a herd of buffalo once again roam the grasslands of the Southern Plains. These burly, seemingly placid, animals were the very lifeblood of the Plains Indian tribes, and figured prominently in their spiritual life. Seeing the prairie littered with carcasses left to rot by professional hide-hunters, Satanta, the war chief of the Kiowas, asked a delegation of military men, "Has the white man become a child that he should recklessly kill and not eat? When the red men slay game, they do so that they may live and not starve."

The tragedy of the Southern Plains is recalled again at the **Washita Battleground Historic Site**, about 120 miles west of Oklahoma City within the **Black Kettle National Grassland**. It was here that, in 1868, a young glory-seeking officer named George Armstrong Custer

rode down upon a Cheyenne village headed by Chief Black Kettle. Only three years earlier, Black Kettle had survived the Sand Creek Massacre, and he had worked hard since then to maintain peace between his people and the whites. His efforts came to nothing on that cold winter dawn as Custer's troops swept into camp cutting down Indians indiscriminately.

More than 100 Cheyennes were killed that day, including Black Kettle and his wife. Only 11 of the dead were warriors. Upon his return, Custer was publicly congratulated by his commanding officer for "efficient and gallant services."

The memory of the Washita Massacre, the Trail of Tears, the Allotment Act and other tragedies haunt Oklahoma, but Indian people have not given up their cultures or lost a sense of who they are. Originally a land of exile, Oklahoma is now home to more than 25 tribes, and a cradle of intertribal culture and activities. The name has changed, the land has been taken away, but Oklahoma is still Indian Territory.

George Catlin's *Comanche Feats of Horsemanship.*

QUANAH PARKER AND THE COMANCHES

They were known as the Lords of the Southern Plains, and they ruled over the boundless grasslands and buffalo herds of northern Texas, western Oklahoma and eastern New Mexico. Skilled horsemen and fiercesome warriors, they held the Spanish frontier in check for more than a century. Later, when Americans began to trickle into their territory across the Santa Fe and Butterfield trails, they swept down on travelers, plundered ranches, and fought a 20-year running battle with the Texas Rangers.

Together with their long-time allies, the Kiowas, the Comanches fought what was to be the last great war of the Southern Plains, the Red River War. At the Medicine Lodge council of 1867, several Comanche and Kiowa leaders agreed to move their bands onto a reservation in Indian Territory. There were a few bands that were unwilling to give up the old ways, however, and they continued to range freely over the remaining buffalo plains of western Texas.

The most powerful of these "wild" bands was the Kwahadi Comanches. Their leader was a young man of extraordinary strength and intelligence known to Comanches as Quanah, the Eagle, and to whites as Quanah Parker. The surname was his mother's, a white woman who had been captured as a child, adopted by the tribe, and later married to a Comanche chief.

In the 1870s, after decades of battling Americans over land, the Comanches faced a new threat to their traditional way of life. Buffalo-hunters were invading Comanche territory and slaughtering the great beasts by the hundreds, leaving their unused carcasses to rot on the prairie. Enraged, Quanah helped organize a party of Comanche, Kiowa and Cheyenne warriors to attack a group of hunters at Adobe Walls, an abandoned trading post on the Texas Panhandle. A Comanche prophet named Isatai assured the warriors of success. He claimed that he had visited the spirit world and that his "medicine" would protect them from the hunters' guns.

But neither Quanah's rage nor the prophet's magic could match the hunter's high-powered rifles. After several unsuccessful charges, the Indians pulled back. Within weeks, American troops were converging on the Indians, most of whom had gathered on the Texas plains. After a few small skirmishes, the soldiers finally stumbled on a large Comanche and Kiowa camp at Palo Duro Canyon. Although few warriors were killed in the attack, the Indians' horses were captured and their village was torched.

Destitute, scattered, their buffalo nearly destroyed, the beleaguered Indians began to surrender. In February 1875, the Kiowa leader, Lone Wolf, brought his ragged band into Fort Sill in what is now Oklahoma. Reluctantly, Quanah and the Kwahadi Comanches surrendered a few months later. They were the last American Indians to roam freely over the Southern Plains.

Quanah adjusted to reservation existence extraordinarily well. He was as determined to succeed in his new way of life as he was to hang on to the old. While visiting his white relatives, in Texas, Quanah learned about cattle-raising, and upon returning home, he started his own ranch. Before long, he was one of the most prosperous cattlemen in the region. And at the center of his expansive landholdings, he built his family an enormous white house.

Not that Quanah gave up all his Indian ways. Despite the urgings of government and church people, he remained a firm believer in polygamy, a Comanche custom. At one time he had eight wives, each with her own room in "the big white house." Quanah himself never got the knack of sleeping under a roof, though. He stayed in a tepee out in the backyard.

Quanah learned something else while visiting his white relatives. Shortly after arriving, he became deathly ill. Quanah begged for a traditional healer, but the best the family could do was a Mexican Indian *curandera*. The old woman gave Quanah tea made of peyote cactus, a natural hallucinogen. While Quanah recovered, he learned the *curandera's* peyote ceremonies. When he returned to Indian Territory, he taught the ceremonies to his friends and family. The new peyote religion passed from tribe to tribe, and eventually became the basis of the Native American Church.

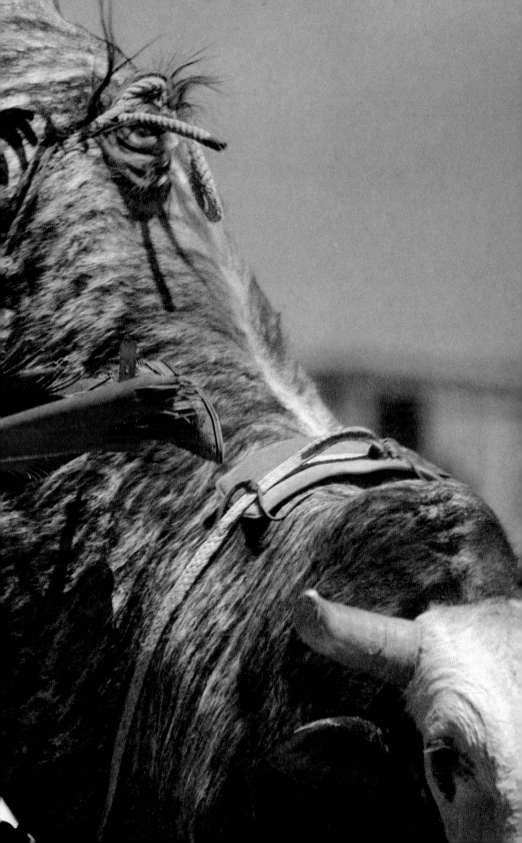

CALIFORNIA

Twice a year, at the old San Juan Bautista Mission near San Jose, California, an Indian market attracts native artists from as far away as Oklahoma, Washington, New Mexico, even Guatemala and Peru, and, of course, all parts of California. This gathering of native peoples is not unusual in California. The region's rich and varied environment has attracted Indians for thousands of years. When the first white explorers reached the region in the 1700s, they found a bewildering array of native peoples speaking perhaps 65 different languages. And the situation is much the same today. California has a larger and more diverse Native American population than any other state.

Stone tools unearthed at the **Calico Early Man Site** (visitors welcome), about 15 miles east of Barstow, date Indian occupation to about 15,000 years ago. Athabascans migrated into California about 3000 BC, pushing aside the earliest Hokan inhabitants. Penutians and Shoshoneans moved into the region some time later, settling on either side of the Sierra Nevada.

Although contact with Europeans occured fairly late in California, the displacement of Indians was swift and devastating. The first sizable incursion didn't begin until 1769, when Padre Fray Junípero Serra and Capitán Gaspar de Portola established the first of about 20 missions along the El Camino Real, stretching over 500 miles from San Diego to San Francisco.

Most of these missions were made to prosper by teaching the natives Spanish agriculture, ranching, weaving and other trades, while new "converts" were procured by the troops. Disease ran wild, carrying away hundreds of Indians with every outbreak. The imposition of Spanish law was so severe that rebellion broke out at nearly every mission. Today, few visitors realize that these lovely old churches were built by Indian hands or that there are thousands of unnamed Indians buried in their cemeteries.

Preceding pages: Indian bull rider. Left, Maidu dancer.

But as bad as the mission days were, they paled in comparison to the wholesale slaughter perpetrated by Americans. In 1849, gold was discovered at Sutter's Mill and the floodgates of American migration were opened. Thousands of miners and settlers poured into California and in a matter of 25 years, the native population was nearly wiped out. At worst, Indian people were hunted like animals; many were taken as slaves. At best, they were marched at gunpoint to desolate reservations.

Seven large reservations were set aside between 1853 and 1887, although only portions of four survive. Tiny rancherias were added in the early 1900s, but many were "terminated" in the 1960s. Today, the total area of Indian-occupied land is about 600,000 acres for an enrolled tribal population of some 300,000 Native Americans.

But the old ways of most tribes were not entirely forgotten. The elders remembered, taught the young ones, and the cycle was renewed. Human and political rights were slowly, painfully, regained. Health and education improved. Families began to grow. Today, native California is undergoing a cultural renewal. The old spirits are being reawakened; dances and ceremonies are being performed, not for entertainment, but because they must be.

Southern California: Starting in the desert country of California's southeasternmost corner, the Quechan Indians' **Fort Yuma Reservation** straddles the Colorado River. The first visible structure on the reservation is St Thomas Catholic Church (1922), which stands on the site of the original Misión Purísima Concepción, founded by Fray Junípero Serra, but totally destroyed by the Quechans after only one year. Part of the old US Army fort still stands on the same prominent hill and contains an excellent period museum. The tribe maintains at least two RV parks, and plenty of bingo and high-stakes card play. Fishing is good here (with a tribal license), and powwows are held in March and September.

About 80 miles north of Fort Yuma is the immense **Colorado River Indian**

Reservation. This bi-state reservation is the ancestral home of the Chemehuevi Indians, although Mohave, Navajo and Hopi Indians also reside here. A visit to the Colorado River Reservation Museum at Parker is highly recommended; it's the only Indian art museum in the region with a live art program. The Chemehuevi also live on the fairly barren **Chemehuevi Reservation**, a few miles north at Lake Havasu. To the east of the Colorado River Reservation, about 13½ miles north of Blythe on Highway 95, is one of the most impressive works of rock art in California – the **Desert Intaglios** – giant figures of animals and hunters, 95–167 ft long, scooped out of the desert floor.

Farther north on Highway 95 is the tri-state **Fort Mojave Reservation**, home of the Hamákhava (Mohave) people. Most of the Indian land is in Arizona, and occurs in one-mile checkerboard squares (one of the peculiarities of some Southern California reservations). Ask someone at the tribal office in Needles to point you to the ancient **Rock Maze**, which is still used in ceremonies to prevent evil spirits from following spirits of the dead down the river. The reservation borders the **Havasu National Wildlife Preserve**, a quiet year-round retreat.

Traveling across the state, near the Mexican border, there are a number of small, sparsely-settled Kamia reservations nestled in the rolling plateau of the Southern Coast Range west of San Diego. These include the Campo, La Posta and Manzanita reservations, largely unavailable to visitors but worth a glance from the highway just to see what a magnificent ecological preserve unspoiled Indian land can be. To the north, the Viejas and Barona reservations occupy the high, chapparal-green valleys of the Coast Range. In San Diego itself, you will find the oldest Indian mission in California, **San Diego de Alcalá** (1769); it never looked as good as it does today. In the excellent **Museum of Man** in Balboa Park, you can find a good presentation of early Kamia Indian (also called Kumeyaay, Ipai-Tipai

Shake Head Dance, north California coast.

or Diegueño) life as well as other Indian artifacts.

North of San Diego, starting near the historic and colorful **Santa Ysabel Mission Asistencia** (a branch of Misión San Diego), is another cluster of small reservations, including Santa Ysabel, Mesa Grande, Los Coyotes, Rincon, La Jolla, Pauma and Pala. Several, **Mesa Grande** and **Los Coyotes** in particular, offer remarkable high-country scenery in what is practically a natural preserve, overlooked by the distant presence of sacred Mount Palomar. **La Jolla Reservation** is notable not only for its water park (slides, swimming, etc.) and full-service campground, but for its tiny mountain village with picturesque chapel and cactus-lined adobes.

But perhaps the **Pala Reservation** leaves the most lasting impression. The **Pala Asistencia** chapel (1816) is probably the most moving of the Indian missions – with unusual grave markers in the cemetery and strange Indian-painted faces on the walls. The people of three Indian cultures reside here –

Luiseño, Cupa and Ipai. Although culturally similar, they still keep some degree of distinctiveness. Cupa Days are held in May, and a general fiesta is held in September. Corpus Christi, Easter, and Christmas services are also memorable. Staying at the newly-remodeled full-service tribal campground is a good way to experience this quiet meeting of native cultures.

Want something completely different? Half of the City of Palm Springs *is* the **Agua Caliente Reservation** of the Cahuilla people. The federal government checkerboarded this land when handing out reservations in 1896. Every other square mile is Indian land, and much of it is leased to developers, making the Agua Caliente band the wealthiest Indian people, per capita, in the US. The tribe carefully protects the area's extraordinary palm canyons. For directions, see either the tribal offices or the beautiful and informative **Desert Museum**. The Agua Caliente **Indian Market** is held in late March.

To the west of Palm Springs lies the

Basket weaving.

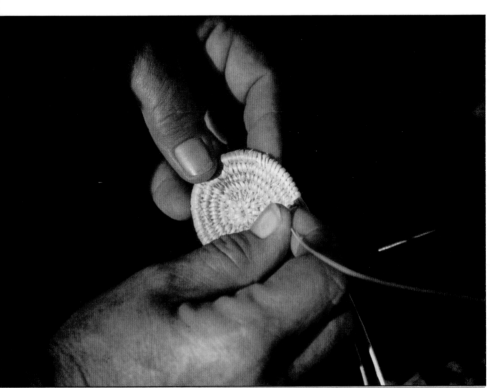

Morongo Reservation and its small but interesting **Malki Museum**. Unusual here is the 1890 Moravian Church, a relic of days when the government used Christian organizations to supervise many reservations. Rare music is performed here on Memorial Day – their big time for fiesta and powwow.

Heading west into Los Angeles County, the **San Manuel Reservation**, in San Bernardino operates the most magnificent bingo palace in the state, worthy of Vegas.

Elsewhere in the Los Angeles area, there is only one real spot of Indian-dedicated land – **Satwiwa**, site of an ancient village, located in the extensive **Santa Monica Mountains National Recreation Area.** This wild mountain spot is used by the Gabrielino (Tóngva) peoples of the Los Angeles basin and by the Chumash people to the west for ceremonies and for weekly Sunday storytelling and historical presentations open to the general public.

Tens of thousands of Native Americans live in the Los Angeles area –

people from all over the continent. It is no surprise, then, that powwows are scheduled every Saturday somewhere in the area. Check the local American Indian Center for a listing. There are also three excellent museums: the **Los Angeles Museum of Natural History**, the **Bowers Museum** in Santa Ana, and the stunning **Southwest Museum** in Pasadena, which is dedicated exclusively to the Southwestern tribes. **San Fernando** and **San Gabriel missions** also possess a number of Indian artifacts from the colonial period.

Central California: The mission trail continues north of Los Angeles at **Misión Santa Barbara**, an imposing structure built by the Chumash Indians. Nearby, the **Santa Barbara Museum of Natural History** features an excellent collection of Chumash artifacts. Ask the museum staff for directions to the **Chumash Painted Cave**, *the* most extraordinary ancient Indian painting in California. **Misión Purísima Concepción** is located in Lompoc about 50 miles farther up the coast, and **Misión San Miguel**, once home of hundreds of Salinan Indians, is about another 80 miles north on Highway 101. A few remnants of this small tribe are still members of the congregation at **Misión San Antonio de Padua**, about 20 miles to the northwest.

Continuing northward, you cross the road to the famous **Carmel Mission**, an extraordinary place, but whose Esselen and Rumsen Indian cemetery is overwhelmed by charm. Preferably, go a bit further to **Misión San Juan Bautista**, mentioned earlier.

Crossing the state into the Central Valley, the **Tule River Reservation**, occupied principally by Yokuts, offers quiet vistas of the Sierra Nevada and a fine rural atmosphere. An astounding rock painting is located beside the Tule River. To see this **Painted Rock**, you must hire a guide at the tribal office.

Farther east, the tenacious band of Timbi-Sha Shoshone Indians have held on to their heritage in a most unlikely place, the aptly named Furnace Creek of **Death Valley National Monument**. There is not much to see of their homes,

Yurok dancers, northwest California.

but their homeland is fascinating.

The Owens Valley, deep between the Sierra Nevada and the Inyo and White mountains is home to other Shoshone and Paiute peoples. The largest of some five reservations is the **Bishop Reservation**, on a 875-acre patch of land set dramatically alongside beautiful, plunging mountains. An architecturally fine museum displays dioramas, artifacts, crafts, and arts (some for sale). Horseback pack trips into the Sierra are also available.

Continuing northward, you have the first opportunity to visit a roundhouse at **Ahwahnee**, site of the **Wassama Roundhouse**. Central and Northern California Indians use roundhouses for ceremonial dances. California dancehouses are not unlike Hopi kivas, except that the fire pit is in the center, and the entrance is through a small alcove facing east. Most roundhouses are semi-subterranean, though the one at Ahwahnee is not. Roundhouses are sacred places, and most are off-limits. The dances invoke the spirits to bring well-being to the dancers and to the people taking part. Dances are occasionally open to the public. They may be seen at Wassama on the second weekend in July. Contact the park for details.

Outside the roundhouse, there are ancient grinding rocks used to process acorns, a native California staple. A sweathouse structure, used for prayer and purification, is also on the grounds.

Like Death Valley, an Indian community lives within **Yosemite National Park** – descendants of the original Miwok and Shoshone inhabitants of the valley. An Indian village is set up at the visitor center. Although the bark tepees are not inhabited, the roundhouse and sweat lodge are used by Indian people on the third weekend in June (and at other times deemed appropriate by spiritual leaders). Ask one of the resident Indian guides to show you around. Pay particular attention to the basketry demonstrations. Some of the most beautiful basketry in the world has come from native California. Intricate designs, watertight weaves, the use of feathers

Death Valley, stark homeland of the Timbi-Sha Shoshone.

and beads, and miniatures are characteristic of California basketry.

From Yosemite you can head into the gold country on Highway 49 to **Tuolumne Rancheria** and **Chaw-Se Indian Grinding Rocks State Park**. Tuolumne is quite typical of the smaller residential rancherias of Central and Northern California. Here, next to the tribal office, one finds a small roundhouse and a dance ground. An **Acorn Festival** is sponsored the weekend after Labor Day. Chaw-Se is the site of ancient acorn grinding rocks adorned with religious carvings. Here also is California's largest roundhouse, a large state museum featuring the Sierra Miwok people and a campground. Local Miwoks use the site for dances several times a year and invite other Central California peoples to present their dances.

In Sacramento, the **State Indian Museum** has modest but well-rounded exhibits devoted exclusively to "California cultures." The **California Academy of Sciences** in San Francisco has a small section covering native California, as does the **Lowie Museum of Anthropology** at the University of California, Berkeley.

Northern California: To the north of San Francisco, the **Kule Loklo Coastal Indian Village** is located at **Point Reyes National Seashore**. Although a "new" site, it has been adopted by the local Indian community. When the first dedicatory ceremonies were held an amazing thing happened: people from "extinct" local tribes (Wappo and Coastal Miwok) appeared. Since then, events at the village have drawn even more Indian people. Indian and non-Indian visitors are always invited.

Farther north, the **Clear Lake** region is peppered with dozens of small rancherias representing Pomo, Nomlaki, Wintun and Miwok bands. In recent years, the population of these groups has grown as has an awareness and pride in Indian culture. Within a 40-mile radius of the lake, there are five active roundhouses and several dance groups. Most dancing is done privately, but occasional demonstrations are given

Half Dome, Yosemite National Park.

at the beautiful **Pomo Museum** on Lake Mendocino (Ukiah), staffed by members of local Pomo bands.

If you're feeling particularly adventuresome, head north on Highway 101 to the scenic Eel River and the **Round Valley Reservation**, residence of about five different Indian groups brought here in the 1850s in one of California's tragic "trail of tears." Round Valley is one of the most remote reservations in California. With the exception of an Indian celebration and powwow in September, life is exceedingly quiet.

Even farther up the coast, some miles east of Eureka, the 12-sq.-mile **Hoopa Reservation**, largest in the state, is located in the stunning Trinity River gorge. Ten of the original 13 Hupa villages are still located on the reservation, in various states of repair. One of the religious centers, still in use, dates back over 5,000 years. In some of the ancient villages, the old-style sunken square homes have been reconstructed, and visits are encouraged. July Fourth is the big day here: a rodeo is held during the day and the deeply religious Brush Dance starts in the evening and may last all night. The tribal hall, which is built in the form of a giant roundhouse, is a marvel of environmental architecture. The tribal museum and old military fort are located nearby.

For those willing to make a real trip into the wilderness, **Lava Beds National Park**, near the Oregon border, has the largest set of ancient petroglyphs in the state – an entire cliffside carved with stories and figures (sadly, some have been disfigured by vandals). In the lava beds themselves, 60 Modoc Indians, led by Kintpuash, or "Captain Jack," held off 600 soldiers for four months in 1872. After their defeat, Kintpuash was hanged, and most of the Modocs were shipped off to Oklahoma. In 1990, a special ceremony was held in honor of the Modocs. Nearly 200 members of this "extinct" tribe showed up from the surrounding area.

Once again, the native peoples of California are regaining their strength. Their renaissance seems imminent.

Below, a restored Hupa home. **Overpage**, an elder of Taos Pueblo.

GETTING THERE

BY AIR

If driving to a reservation is impractical because of distance, the next best way to get to Indian Country is to fly to a major city and rent a car. The major hubs closest to Indian areas are:

Great Plains: Billings-Logan International; Denver-Stapleton International; Great Falls International; Rapid City Regional; Winnepeg International.

Northwest: Calgary International; Portland International; Seattle-Tacoma International; Spokane International; Vancouver International.

Southwest: Albuquerque International; Las Vegas-McCarran International; Phoenix Sky Harbor International; Tucson International.

Northeast: Chicago-Midway International; Chicago-O'Hare International; Minneapolis-St Paul International; Montreal-Dorval International; Montreal-Mirabel International; Newark International; New York-LaGuardia International; New York-Kennedy International; Toronto-Pearson International.

Southeast: Charlotte-Douglas International; Miami International; New Orleans-Moisant Field International.

Oklahoma: Oklahoma City-Will Rogers International.

California: Los Angeles International; Oakland International; San Francisco International; San Diego International; San Jose International.

NATIONAL AIRLINES

Air Canada: tel: 800-776-3000
American Airlines: tel: 800-433-7300
Continental Airlines: tel: 800-525-0280
Delta Airlines: tel: 800-221-1212
Midway Airlines: tel: 800-866-9000
Northwest Airlines: tel: 800-225-2525
Pan Am Airlines: tel: 800-221-1111
TWA: tel: 800-221-2000
United Airlines: tel: 800-241-6522
US Air: tel: 800-428-4322

BY TRAIN

Amtrak offers over 500 destinations across the US. There is something special about traveling on a train, and Amtrak tries to make the journey even more pleasant by offering lounges, restaurants and snack bars. Some trains show movies or offer live entertainment.

There are several lines that cross Indian Country in the American West. Amtrak's Southwest Chief runs from Chicago to Los Angeles with stops at Kansas City, Missouri; Topeka and Dodge City, Kansas; Albuquerque and Gallup, New Mexico; and Flagstaff, Arizona. The train runs along the old Santa Fe Trail, first followed by Indians, then by Spanish conquistadores and later, by American pioneers. Between Albuquerque and Gallup, an Indian Country guide points out scenic highlights and discusses regional history, culture and folklore.

The Sunset Limited runs from New Orleans to Los Angeles with major stops at Houston, San Antonio and El Paso, Texas; Deming and Lordsburg, New Mexico; Tucson and Phoenix, Arizona.

The California Zephyr runs from Chicago to San Francisco with major stops at Omaha, Nebraska; Denver, Colorado; Salt Lake City, Utah; Reno, Nevada; and Sacramento, California.

The Pioneer follows the old Oregon Trail from Chicago to Seattle, with stops at Omaha, Nebraska; Denver, Colorado; Salt Lake City, Utah; Pocatello and Boise, Idaho; Portland, Oregon and Tacoma, Washington.

The Empire Builder also runs from Chicago to Seattle, with stops at Minneapolis, Minnesota; Minot, North Dakota; Whitefish and Havre, Montana; and Spokane, Washington.

Be sure to ask about two or three-stopover discounts, senior citizen and children discounts. Tel: 1-800-USA-RAIL for detailed scheduling information.

BY BUS

One of the least expensive ways to travel in America is by bus. The biggest national bus company is Greyhound (tel: 800-528-0447), which acquired Trailways Lines in 1987. The company routinely offers discounts such as a $99 go-anywhere fare and a $1 ticket for moms on Mother's Day. Call the Greyhound/Trailways office nearest you for information on special rates and package tours. However, Greyhound generally does not service remote reservation areas. A car rental or other mode of transportation will be necessary from the major hubs.

BY CAR

Driving is by far the most flexible and convenient way of traveling in Indian Country. Major roads are well-maintained on nearly all reservations, although many will also have dirt and gravel roads as well. If you plan on driving into remote backcountry areas or will be encountering snow, mud or severe weather, it's a good idea to use a four-wheel-drive vehicle with high chassis clearance.

Your greatest asset as a driver in Indian Country is a good road map. Maps can be obtained from state tourism offices, filling stations and convenience stores. Keep in mind, however, that reservation areas are sometimes misrepresented. Geographical details may be lacking, and secondary, dirt or gravel roads may be overlooked. Also, not all reservation roads are open to visitors. Do not enter any area that is marked off-limits.

Although roads are maintained even in remote areas, it is advisable to listen to local radio stations and to check with highway officials for the latest information on weather conditions, especially if you plan on leaving paved roads. Driving conditions vary depending on elevation. During the fall and winter, your car should be equipped with snow tires or chains and an ice scraper for mountain driving. Also, be prepared for the longer amount of time it takes to travel winding mountain roads.

If you plan on driving in desert areas, carry extra water – at least 1 gallon (4 liters) per person. It's a good idea to take along some food, too. Flash floods can occur during the rainy season, from early summer to fall. Stay out of arroyos, washes and drainage areas.

Service stations are few and far between in Indian Country. Not every town will have one, and many close early. Check your gas tank frequently. It's always better to have more fuel than you think you need.

A word of caution: If your car breaks down on a back road do not attempt to strike out on foot, even with water. A car is easier to spot than a person, and gives shelter from the weather. Sit tight and wait to be found.

Finally, if you plan on driving any distance, it's a good idea to join the American Automobile Association. The AAA offers emergency road service, maps (ask for their *Indian Country* map, covering the Southwest), insurance and bail bond protection.

CAR RENTALS

National car rental agencies are located at all airports, cities and large towns. In most cases, you must be at least 21 years old to rent a car, and you must have at least one major credit card. Be sure that you are properly insured for both collision and liability. Insurance may not be included in the base rental fee. Additional cost varies depending on the car and the type of coverage, but usually ranges between $10 and $20 per day. It is also a good idea to inquire about an unlimited mileage package. If not, you may be charged an extra 10¢ to 25¢ per mile over a given limit. Rental fees vary depending on the time of year, how far in advance you book your rental, and if you travel on weekdays or weekends. Be sure to inquire about any discounts or benefits you may be eligible for, including corporate, credit card or frequent flyer programs.

Alamo: tel: 800-327-9633
American International: tel: 800-527-0202
Avis: tel: 800-331-1212
Budget: tel: 800-527-0700
Dollar: tel: 800-421-6868
Enterprise: tel: 800-325-8007
General: tel: 800-327-7607
Hertz: tel: 800-654-3131
National: tel: 800-227-7368
Thrifty: tel: 800-331-4200

Travel Essentials

VISAS & PASSPORTS

The Consular Affairs Division of the US Department of State recently began a pilot program which waives the visa requirements for the following countries: Britain, Japan, Germany, Italy, France, Switzerland, Sweden and the Netherlands. Travelers from these countries need only present a valid passport upon entry into the US. All other foreign nationals must obtain a visa from the US consulate in their country. Two exceptions are Canadians entering from the Western Hemisphere and Mexicans with border passes. Neither needs a visa or passport to enter the US.

Once admitted to the US, you may visit Canada or Mexico for up to 30 days and re-enter the US without a new visa. If you lose your visa or passport, arrange to get a new one at your country's nearest consulate or embassy (see Directory for a list of embassies). Visa extensions are granted by the Immigration and Naturalization Service (2401 E St, Washington, DC 20520; 202-514-4330).

CURRENCY & EXCHANGE

Foreign currency is rarely accepted in the US. You can exchange currency at selected banks in large border towns, major big-city banks and hotels, and international airports. The best rates are usually found at banks.

It's advisable to arrive with at least $100 in cash (in small bills) to pay for ground transportation and other incidentals. It's always a good idea to carry internationally recognized traveler's checks rather than cash. Major credit cards are also a big help (American Express, Visa, Mastercard, Diners Club, Discover, etc.) and will be necessary if you want to rent a car. Traveler's checks and/or credit cards are accepted at most gas stations, trading posts and motels, even in remote areas.

American money is based on the decimal system. The basic unit, a dollar ($1.00), is equal to 100 cents. There are four basic coins, each worth less than a dollar. A penny is worth 1 cent (1¢). A nickel is worth 5 cents (5¢). A dime is worth 10 cents (10¢). And a quarter is worth 25 cents (25¢).

In addition there are several denominations of paper money. They are: $1, $5, $10, $20, $50, $100 and rarely, $2. Each bill is the same color, size and shape, so be sure to check the dollar amount on the face of the bill before handing it over the counter.

CUSTOMS

All people entering the US must go through Customs. Be prepared to have your luggage inspected and keep the following guidelines in mind:

1. There is no limit to the amount of cash you can bring into the US. If the amount exceeds $10,000, however, you must file a special report.

2. Any objects brought for personal use may enter duty-free.

3. Adults may enter with a maximum of 200 cigarettes or 50 cigars or 3 pounds of tobacco and/or 1 liter of alcohol.

4. Gifts valued at less than $400 can enter duty-free; gifts of $100 or less need not be declared.

5. Agricultural products, meat and animals are subject to restrictions; to avoid delays, leave these items at home unless absolutely necessary.

For additional information, contact US Customs at 1501 Constitution Ave, Washington, DC 20229; Tel: 202-566-8195.

With **Insight Guides** you can make the whole world your home. From Bali to the Balearic Islands, from Munich to Moscow, from Thailand to Texas, from Zurich to Zaire.

With **Insight Guides** the journey begins even before you leave home. With stunning photographs that put you in the picture, journalistic stories and features that give insight, valuable practical information and maps that map out your journey for you.

Insight Guides enrich the travel experience. They can be used before, during and after a journey — as a travel planner, as an indispensable companion and as a way of reliving memorable sights and moments.

We now have over 100 titles in print in various languages. Thanks to our extensive distribution channels your bookseller will have them available. Nevertheless, should you have problems purchasing certain titles, feel free to contact us:

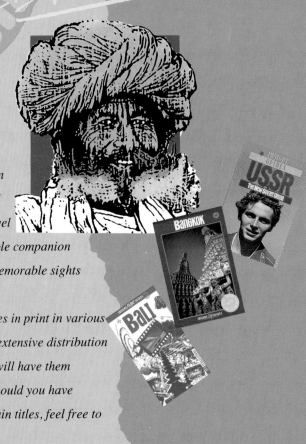

"SEE YOU SOON!"

Höfer Communications
38 Joo Koon Road
Singapore 2262
Fax: (65) 8612755

A P A
INSIGHT
GUIDES

*Experience the diversity of the United States with **Crossing America**, a guidebook that is colourful, informative and fun. Or explore the Sunshine State of Florida, check out the Californian lifestyle or the spirit of aloha in Hawaii, see the unforgettable scenery of the Rocky Mountains, visit the large metropolises of New York and Chicago. Canada is also a land of many images, mirrored vividly in the **Insight Guide**. From the beaches of the Atlantic to Ontario's stunningly beautiful parks to the cobblestone streets of romantic Montreal.*

DUNGEK CHE CUM CAN CHULLY!

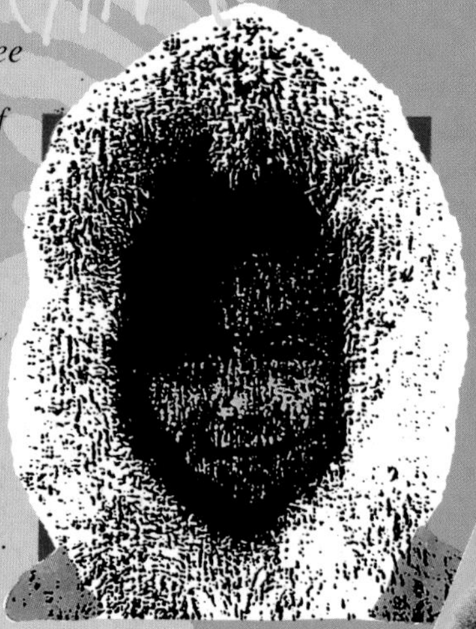

Texas

alaska

INSIGHT GUIDES
NEW YORK State

Alaska
American Southwest
Boston
California
Canada
Crossing America
Florida
Hawaii
Los Angeles
Miami

New England
New York City
New York State
Northern California
Pacific Northwest USA
Rockies
San Francisco
Southern California
Texas

APA
INSIGHT
GUIDES

GETTING ACQUAINTED

HOW TO BEHAVE IN INDIAN COUNTRY

Cultural sensitivity is absolutely vital in Indian Country. Because some Indian people may feel uncomfortable or ambivalent about the presence of outsiders, it is very important to be on your best behavior. Here are a few "dos" and "don'ts" to keep in mind:

1. Don't use racist terms. Referring to an American Indian as chief, redskin, squaw, buck, Pocahontas, Hiawatha, or other off-color terms, is highly offensive.

2. Abide by all rules and regulations while on Indian land or at Indian events. These may include prohibitions on photography, sketching, taking notes, video and audio recording. In some cases a photography fee may be required. If you wish to take an individual's picture, you must ask permission first (a gratuity of $2 or $3 may be appropriate).

3. Respect all restricted areas. These are usually posted, but it is advisable to ask permission before hiking into wilderness or archaeological areas, driving on back roads, wandering around villages, and entering churches or other ceremonial structures.

4. Try to be unobtrusive. Remember that you are a guest at Indian communities and events. Be polite and accommodating. In general, it is better to be too formal than too casual.

5. Don't ask questions or interrupt during Indian ceremonies or dances. Even if an Indian event is not explicitly religious (such as a powwow), it may have a spiritual component. Show the same respect at Indian ceremonials that you would at any other religious service. At all events, try to maintain a low profile. Do not talk loudly, push to the front of a crowd, block anyone's view, or sit in chairs that do not belong to you.

6. Dress casually but neatly when on In-dian reservations. Indian people tend to be conservative when it comes to dress. Wear clothes that are comfortable but show respect for Indian people and ceremonies. Shorts, halter tops and other brief clothing are inappropriate, even when it's hot.

7. Keep in mind that many Indian people have a looser sense of time than non-Indians. You may hear jokes about "Indian time." Don't be surprised at long delays in the start of ceremonies, powwows, etc.

TIME ZONES

The continental US is divided into four time zones. From east to west, later to earlier, they are Eastern, Central, Mountain and Pacific, each separated by one hour. Thus, when it is 3 p.m. in New York City, it is 2 p.m. in Chicago, 1 p.m. in Denver, and 12 p.m. in Los Angeles. In spring, most states move the clock ahead one hour for Daylight Savings Time. In fall, the clock is moved back one hour to return to Standard Time.

One peculiarity to keep in mind: Arizona does not observe Daylight Savings Time, but the Navajo Nation does. Thus, during the spring and summer, "Arizona time" is one hour behind "Navajo time."

PUBLIC HOLIDAYS

All government offices, banks and post offices are closed on public holidays. Additionally, mass transportation often runs less frequently on these days. In addition to the dates listed below, many states and tribes observe public holidays.

January 1: New Year's Day.
January 15: Martin Luther King, Jr's Birthday.
February 12: Lincoln's Birthday.
Third Monday in February: Washington's Birthday (observed).
March/April: Easter Sunday.
Last Monday in May: Memorial Day.
July 4: Independence Day.
First Monday in September: Labor Day.
Second Monday in October: Columbus Day (observed).
November 11: Veteran's Day.
Fourth Thursday in November: Thanksgiving Day.
December 25: Christmas Day.

COMMUNICATIONS

POSTAL SERVICES

Even the most remote reservation communities are serviced by the US Postal Service. Smaller post offices tend to be limited to business hours (9 a.m.–5 p.m. Mon–Fri), although central, big-city branches may have extended weekday and Saturday morning hours.

If you do not know where you will be staying in a given town, you can have your mail sent to General Delivery, care of the local post office. General delivery mail must be picked up in person; identification is required.

Stamps are sold at all post offices and at some convenience stores, filling stations, hotels and transportation terminals, usually from a vending machine.

For expedited deliveries, often overnight, try US Express Mail, Federal Express (tel: 800-238-5355), DHL (tel: 800-345-2727), United Parcel Service (tel: 800-272-4877) or other local services listed in the telephone directory.

TELEPHONES

Public telephones are located at many highway rest areas, service stations, convenience stores, bars, motels and restaurants. The quickest way to get assistance is to dial 0 for the operator; or if you need to find a number, call information at 555-1212 (411 in some areas). Local calls cost 25¢ and can be dialed directly. Rates vary for long distance calls, but they can also be dialed directly with the proper area and country code. If you don't know the codes, call information or dial 0 and ask for the international operator.

Make use of toll free numbers whenever possible. For information on toll free numbers, dial 800-555-1212. For personal calls, take advantage of lower long-distance rates on weekends and after 5 p.m. on weekdays.

Telephone service on nearly all reservations is good, although problems occasionally occur in the most remote areas. If you are trying to reach an Indian person who doesn't have a telephone, try calling a relative or neighbor. Word of mouth is often the most effective means of communication in isolated backcountry areas.

TELEGRAMS & FAX

Western Union (tel: 800-325-6000) and International Telephone and Telegraph will take telegram and telex messages by phone. Check the local phone directory or call information for local offices.

Fax machines are available at most large hotels. Printing shops, stationers and office supply shops might also have them. They are even cropping up in a number of big-city convenience stores.

MAGAZINES & NEWSPAPERS

Trying to find information about upcoming Indian events can be frustrating. Many tribes publish modest newsletters, bulletins and weekly newspapers, but these tend to be limited to local news and events and are rarely available beyond the immediate area. News and information about regional or national Indian events can be found in the following publications:

American Indian Art
7314 E. Osborn Dr.
Scottsdale, AZ 85251
Tel: 602-994-5445

Arizona Highways
2039 W. Lewis Ave
Phoenix, AZ 85009
Tel: 800-543-5432

Gallup Independent
500 N. Ninth St
Gallup, NM 87305
Tel: 505-863-6811

Indian Trader
PO Box 1421
Gallup, NM 87305
Tel: 800-748-1624

Native Peoples
PO Box 36820
Phoenix, AZ 85067-6820
Tel: 602-277-7852

New Mexico Magazine
1100 Saint Francis Dr.
Joseph Montoya Bldg
Santa Fe, NM 87503
Tel: 505-827-0220

News of Native California
2054 University Ave #403
Berkeley, CA 94704
Tel: 415-549-3564

A few established Indian newspapers include:
Akwesasne Notes
Mohawk Nation of Akwesasne
Via Rooseveltown, NY 13683

Apache Scout
PO Box 898
Whiteriver, AZ 85941
Tel: 602-338-4813

Hopi Tribal News
PO Box 123
Kykotsmovi, AZ 86039
Tel: 602-734-2401

The Lakota Times
1920 Lombardy Dr.
Rapid City, SD 57701
Tel: 605-341-0011

Navajo Nation Today
PO Box 2466
Window Rock, AZ 86515
Tel: 602-871-4289

News From Indian Country
Rt. 2, Box 2900-A
Hayward, WI 54843
Tel: 715-634-5226

Sho-Ban News
PO Box 306
Fort Hall, ID 83203
Tel: 208-238-3700

Yakima Nation Review
PO Box 151
Toppenish, WA 98948
Tel: 509-865-5121

EMERGENCIES

SAFETY

In general, travel on Indian reservations is safe. There are, however, a number of special safety considerations to keep in mind:

1. Although many reservations prohibit alcohol, alcohol abuse is still a major problem. Avoid any events or gatherings where alcohol is being used illegally, or where legal drinking is excessive. It is also a good idea to avoid nearby off-reservation bars; many are notoriously rowdy. In fact, there are a number of reservation border towns whose main industry is selling alcohol to Indians.

2. Needless to say, motorists need to be especially wary of intoxicated drivers. If you see someone driving recklessly or erratically – on or off reservations – pull over and let them pass. Cautious driving is also advised on winding or mountainous backcountry roads. Although main roads are usually well-paved, they may not have guardrails or adequate snow and ice removal.

3. The violent-crime rate on reservations is twice as high as the national average. The rates for robbery, burglary and other crimes are similarly elevated. It is necessary, therefore, to take precautions. Again, avoid situations in which people are drinking illegally or excessively. Lock unattended cars, and keep valuables out of sight or in the trunk. If you are harassed, robbed, or assaulted by an Indian or non-Indian while on a reservation, report the crime immediately to tribal officials and to the nearest off-reservation law-enforcement agency. If they are unable to help you, ask to be directed to the appropriate authorities. Depending on the type of crime, the people involved and the location, this will probably be the tribal police, BIA police, FBI, state police or county sheriff.

Many reservations have federally-subsidized Indian Health Service hospitals and clinics. Eligibility varies from tribe to tribe but, in general, you must be a tribal member, or a tribal member's spouse, to receive non-emergency medical care. If you need emergency medical treatment while on a reservation, you will be taken to the nearest hospital, whether or not it is on the reservation.

RESERVATIONS & THE LAW

The US Supreme Court has recently wrestled with several cases involving the issue of tribal jurisdiction on reservation lands. There is no general formula for determining whose laws (federal, state, county or tribal) apply while on reservations; it varies from state to state. Generally speaking, tribal officials have jurisdiction over misdemeanor crimes involving tribal members only. The situation becomes more complicated when the crime involves non-Indians, both Indians and non-Indians, or Indian people of different tribes. Many Indian officials complain that jurisdictional loopholes have contributed to the high crime rate on some reservations and are partially responsible for the low arrest and prosecution rates for crimes committed on Indian lands.

To be safe, the Bureau of Indian Affairs (BIA) recommends that you check with the state Indian commission before you visit reservations. BIA area offices may also be of some help. Two constants, though, are: (1) If you violate traffic laws while on reservation roads, you will be remanded to a local off-reservation court; and (2) while on reservation land you must abide by all tribal laws and regulations and obey all tribal law-enforcement officials.

LIQUOR LAWS

Many tribes do not allow possession, consumption or sale of alcohol on their reservations. Alcohol is forbidden at most Indian events as well. It is absolutely essential to obey these rules, even if you see a few Indian people who do not. If alcohol is permitted, you must be at least 21 years of age to buy or drink alcohol.

WHERE TO STAY

TRIBALLY OWNED LODGINGS

In addition to campgrounds and RV sites, a number of tribes operate their own tourist lodgings, ranging from basic motels to luxury lodges with an abundance of recreational facilities. The following are all tribally owned and operated.

APACHE

Best Western Jicarilla Inn
US 64 and Jicarilla Blvd
Dulce, NM 87528
Tel: 505-759-3663
Fine motel with restaurant and gift shop owned and operated by the Jicarilla Apache Tribe.
Rates: $45 single; $55 double.

Inn of the Mountain Gods
PO Box 269
Mescalero, NM 88340
Tel: 800-545-9011
A 250-room luxury lodge run by the Mescalero Apaches set on a lake in the beautiful Sacramento Mountains. Fine restaurant, convention center, golfing, boating, skeet shooting. Access to Ski Apache and White Sands National Monument.
Rates: $110 single/double; $120 suite.

White Mountain Apache Motel
PO Box 1149
White River, AZ 85941
Tel: 602-338-4927
Basic, comfortable lodging with 20 rooms and restaurant.
Rates: $30 single/double.

CHICKASAW

Chickasaw Motor Inn
West First and Muscogee
Sulphur, OK 73086
Tel: 405-622-2156
Basic, comfortable motel with restaurant and pool.
Rates: $34 single; $39 double.

CHIPPEWA

Grand Portage Lodge
PO Box 248
Grand Portage, MN 55605
Tel: 218-475-2401
Luxury lodge on Lake Superior owned by the Grand Portage Chippewa Tribe with 100 rooms, conference facilities, restaurant, swimming pool, cross-country hiking and skiing trails and marina. Access to Isle Royale National Park, Superior National Forest and Quetico Provincial Park.
Rates: $69 - 65 single; $59 - 55 double.

HAVASUPAI

Havasupai Lodge
General Delivery
Supai, AZ 86435
Tel: 602-448-2111
Basic lodging at the bottom of Havasupai Canyon, a remote branch of the Grand Canyon. A beautiful setting, eight miles from the nearest road.
Rates: $45 single; $50 double.

HOPI

Hopi Cultural Center Motel
PO Box 67
Second Mesa, AZ 36039
Tel: 602-734-2401
Includes a 33-unit motel located next to the tribal museum, crafts shop and restaurant. In the center of the Hopi Reservation.
Rates: $52 single; $58 double.

NAVAJO

Kayenta Holiday Inn
PO Box 307
Kayenta, AZ 86033
Tel: 602-697-3221
Comfortable, 160-room motel with restaurant. Near Monument Valley and Navajo National Monument.
Rates: $90 single; $100 double.

Navajo Nation Motor Inn
PO Box 1687
Window Rock, AZ 86515
Tel:602-871-4108
56-room motel with restaurant, in the Navajo Nation capital. Close to Canyon de Chelly.
Rates: $55 single; $60 double.

Tuba Motel
PO Box 247
Tuba City, AZ 86045
Tel: 602-283-4545
80-room motel with restaurant. Reasonable rates, basic accommodations. Within reasonable driving distance to Lake Powell, Grand Canyon and Painted Desert.
Rates: $45 single; $55 double.

UTE

Bottle Hollow Inn
PO Box 190
Fort Duchesne, UT 84026
Tel: 801-722-3941
Basic motel on the Uintah and Ouray Reservation with 18 units, restaurant, pool and tennis. Near Dinosaur National Monument.
Rates: $21 single; $25 double.

Sky Ute Lodge
PO Box 550
Ignacio, CO 81137
Tel: 303-563-4531
36-room lodge on the Southern Ute Reservation with a restaurant, indoor and outdoor pool. Near Mesa Verde National Park.
Rates: $35 single; $42 double.

WARM SPRINGS

Kah Nee Ta Vacation Resort
PO Box K
Warm Springs, OR 97761
Tel: 503-553-1112
300-room luxury lodge owned by the Warm Springs Tribe. Also offers cottages, teepees and RV sites. Recreation facilities include two pools (one heated by natural hot springs), two golf courses, tennis courts, horseback riding and bicycle rentals.
Rates: $80–90 single; $150 suite; $75 cottage.

Cliff Castle Lodge
Highway 17 & Middle Verde Rd
Camp Verde, AZ 86322
Tel: 602-567-6611
Well-maintained, comfortable motor lodge with restaurant, pool and volleyball courts. Access to Sedona, Oak Creek Canyon, Montezuma's Castle, Walnut Canyon. Rates: $61 single; $63 double.

THINGS TO DO

BUYER'S GUIDE

Indian arts and crafts can be purchased at several retail outlets, but it is always most rewarding to buy directly from the artists themselves. You will not only learn about the work first-hand (you might even see it being made), you will probably get a good deal. Haggling is expected by most Indian artists and craftspeople, so don't be afraid to negotiate about price. Indians know what their work is worth, however, so don't expect to get a steal. You can usually find artists selling their work at powwows, art shows, flea markets and festivals or at the year-round outdoor markets at the main plaza in Santa Fe and the Old Town Plaza in Albuquerque. Some artists work out of their homes and welcome visitors. Look for signs, or inquire at a cultural center or tribal office.

The second best place to buy Indian arts and crafts is at trading posts. Old-time trading posts are a dying breed, but there are still a few doing business, especially in the Southwest. Many traders have been working with Indian people for years, and they are a great source of information about local culture, history, people and news. They also tend to be very knowledgeable about arts and crafts and local artists. If you are looking for something, or someone, in particular, the local trading post is an invaluable resource.

Prices tend be much lower than other retailers. You can try haggling but, again, traders know what their merchandise is worth; don't expect them to go below their bottom line.

If you like rummaging through second-hand merchandise, you may want to try a pawnshop. Basically, pawnbrokers hold property as security against a loan. If the loan isn't repaid, the merchandise gets sold. Pawnshops can be a little seedy sometimes. It's hard to shake the feeling that you're taking advantage of another person's desperation, especially in reservation border towns where Indian alcoholism is a major problem. The merchandise at pawnshops is of varying quality, so be sure you know what you're buying.

Finally, there are regular arts and crafts shops and art galleries. There are hundreds of these in the major Indian art centers: Santa Fe, Taos and Gallup, New Mexico; Sedona, Flagstaff and Phoenix, Arizona; Jackson,Wyoming; Vancouver, British Columbia; Anadarko and Oklahoma City, Oklahoma. Prices and quality vary from store to store, but with a little browsing you should be able to find something for any taste and budget. At places like Santa Fe, Sedona and Jackson, the selection is truly staggering. A dedicated shopper can spend days jumping from shop to shop. Don't forget to ask about discounts. Although some shops are pricey, most offer across-the-board discounts anywhere from 10 to 60 percent.

In addition to making the merchandise, many Indian people are also opening their own shops and galleries. The **Indian Arts and Crafts Board** publishes a directory of Indian-owned arts and crafts shops. A free copy of this guide can be obtained by contacting the Board at the US Bureau of Indian Affairs, 1849 C St NW, Mail Stop 400, Washington, DC 20240, tel: 202-208-3773.

AUTHENTICITY

Unfortunately, the demand for Indian arts and crafts has encouraged the production of imitations. In some cases, mass-produced items are being passed off as handmade items. In others, non-Indians are selling their work as genuine Indian art.

The Indian Arts and Crafts Board recommends that you take the following precautions when making an important purchase.

1) Buy from someone with a regularly established place of business.

2) Obtain a written receipt of your purchase which includes a description of the item and, if known, the artist's name.

Be especially wary if someone approaches you about buying ancient artifacts or ceremonial paraphernalia (masks, prayer sticks, ancient pottery, etc.). Illegal pot-hunting is a problem particularly in the Southwest. Remember, excavating or removing artifacts from federal, state or tribal land is against the law. Indian people have already lost too much of their heritage to the black market.

QUALITY

The quality of Indian craftsmanship varies from artist to artist, piece to piece. Obviously, the higher the quality of workmanship, design and materials, the more a piece is worth. And while it is true that beauty is in the eye of the beholder – and that it is often the imperfections of a work that make it most endearing – there are a few things you may wish to keep in mind when judging arts and crafts. Here are a few guidelines:

Jewelry: Most Indian jewelry is made with silver and semiprecious stones. Be sure to ask what kind of silver you are buying. If it is sterling, there should be a small stamp on the back. Nickel silver, a lower grade alloy, is also sometimes used. You should also ask the seller to identify the types of stones that are used. Be especially careful about turquoise; various forms of mock turquoise (usually involving plastic) can fool an inexperienced eye. Jewelry should look clean and finished. Check the piece for file marks, sloppy soldering and other irregularities. Check the stones for cracks, pits or discoloration, and make sure the settings are adequate to hold the stones. Finally, find out if the design is original. Is the piece one-of-a-kind? One of a limited number? Or a reproduction?

Pottery: Traditional Indian pottery is made by hand without a potter's wheel, painted with natural dyes, and fired over an open flame. The first thing you should ask about pottery is whether it is handmade or manufactured. Because the price of handmade pottery is so high, manufactured, or "ce-

ramic," pots have become quite common. They are often handpainted in the traditional way and – so long as you know what you're buying – can be quite beautiful. Most Indian vendors make a point of distinguishing between handmade and manufactured pottery. Gift shops may not always be so scrupulous. Manufactured pots tend to be lighter in color and weight and uniform in size and shape. If you're shopping for handmade pottery, look for a graceful, symmetrical form, fairly thin walls, and precise, neatly applied decoration. As always, watch out for irregularities: cracks, discoloration, bumps or pits in the clay, lopsidedness, slanted or uneven decorations. Keep in mind that firing clouds, which usually appear as dark smudges, are sometimes quite desirable, even though many potters consider them a problem. You may also want to know how the vessel was produced. Was it made with local clay? Are the paints natural or commercial? Was it painted with a traditional or commercial brush? Was it fired over an open flame or in a kiln? You should also ask if the vessel was made by the same person who painted it. At some Pueblos, for example, it is traditional for women to make the pots and men to decorate them.

Basketry: Fine, handmade baskets are quite rare these days, but there are still a few Indian people who are producing exquisite traditional work. First of all, make sure you are buying an American Indian basket. Imports from Africa, Asia and Latin America have found their way into the Southwest and occasionally crop up next to genuine American Indian arts and crafts without any explanation. (Actually, Indian people sometimes buy these baskets for ceremonial or other uses.) There are basically two types of basketry: coiled and woven. In both cases, look for tight, even and sturdy construction, a pleasing shape, clear and even designs. To test the tightness of the weave, hold the basket up to a light. You should also check how the basket was started; the first coil should not stick out or be loose.

Weaving: Again, be absolutely sure you are buying Indian work. The popularity of Navajo rugs has created an entire industry of imitations, many from Mexico. Also, don't confuse Navajo weaving with the Hispanic weaving of northern New Mexico (based in

Chimayo), which is also of very high quality. A few traditional Navajo weavers still do their own washing, carding, dyeing (with vegetal pigments) and spinning, but most buy prepared wool. Some use a mixture of commercial products and traditional techniques. In any case, the finished product should be tightly woven, with a "balanced tension" of design and color. The rug or blanket should have a smooth texture and the corners should not curl. It should also have fairly even edges (all four corners should meet when folded). Ask if the rug is 100 percent wool. Some weavers will use cotton or synthetic fibers in the warp. You should also know if the dyes are vegetal, commercial or both. Commercial dyes tend to give brighter, more saturated colors. Vegetal dyes are said to be subtler and richer and are made by hand.

Kachina Carving: Although most often associated with the Hopis, kachina dolls are also made by Zunis and other Pueblo people as well as by Navajos. The most valuable kachina dolls are carved from a single piece of cottonwood root. Less expensive pieces may have separate legs or arms and possibly leather, feather or other adornments attached to the figure. Most reputable dealers will tell you if the figure is Hopi-made. Many people feel that Navajo kachinas are less authentic and therefore less valuable, but considering the high price of Hopi work (a good kachina doll will probably start at $300 or more), Navajo work may be a reasonable option. Let your eyes, conscience and wallet be your judge.

Beadwork: The mark of fine beadwork is tight, even and closely spaced stitching. Keep an eye out for the "lazy stitch" in which several beads are strung on a single stitch. The smaller the beads and more intricate the design, the more you can expect to pay. Watch out, too, for cheap machine-made imitations. Make sure there aren't any frayed edges or loose ends. Once poor beadwork starts to unravel, it is very difficult to repair.

MAJOR ART FAIRS, MARKETS & EXHIBITIONS

American Indian Intertribal Arts and Crafts Show
1713 W. Buchanan
PO Box 504
Phoenix, AZ 85007
Tel: 602-253-1594
Shows are held several times a year at the Civic Plaza in Phoenix, AZ.

Native American Arts and Crafts Market
Native American Tourism Center
4130 N. Goldwater Blvd
Scottsdale, AZ 85251
Tel: 602-945-0771
The market is held the first weekend of every month between November and April.

Navajo Rug Auctions
Crownpoint Rug Weavers Association
PO Box 1630
Crownpoint, NM 87313
Tel: 505-786-5302
Auctions are held several times a year.

MARCH

Heard Museum Indian Fair and Market
22 E. Monte Vista Rd
Phoenix, AZ 85004
Tel: 602-252-8848

Speelyi Mi Indian Arts and Crafts Fair
Yakima Nation Cultural Center
Highway 97
Toppenish, WA 98948
Tel: 509-865-2800

APRIL

Native American Art Fair
Suquamish Tribal Council
PO Box 498
Suquamish, WA 98392
Tel: 206-598-3311

MAY

Eight Northern Indian Pueblos Artist and Craftsman Show
PO Box 969
San Juan Pueblo, NM 87566
Tel: 505-852-4265

Museum of Northern Arizona Zuni Exhibition
Ft Valley Rd
Rt. 4, Box 720
Flagstaff, AZ 86001
Tel: 602-774-5211

JUNE/JULY

Museum of Northern Arizona Hopi and Navajo Shows
Ft Valley Rd
Rt. 4, Box 720
Flagstaff, AZ 86001
Tel: 602-774-5211

AUGUST

Intertribal Indian Ceremonial
Red Rock State Park
PO Box 328
Church Rock, NM 87311
Tel: 505-722-3839

Santa Fe Indian Market
Santa Fe Chamber of Commerce
PO Box 1928
Santa Fe, NM 87504
Tel: 505-983-7317

SEPTEMBER

New Mexico State Fair
State Fairgrounds
1900 San Pedro SE
Albuquerque, NM 87108
Tel: 505-265-1791

OCTOBER

Arizona State Fair
State Fairgrounds
19th & McDowell Rd
PO Box 6728
Phoenix, AZ 85005
Tel: 602-252-6771

TRIBAL MUSEUMS & CRAFTS SHOPS

GREAT PLAINS

Cheyenne Arts and Crafts Shop
Northern Cheyenne Tribe
PO Box 128
Lame Deer, MT 59043
Tel: 406-477-8283

H.V. Johnston Cultural Center
Cheyenne River Sioux Tribe
PO Box 590
Eagle Butte, SD 57625
Tel: 605-964-2542

Three Affiliated Tribes Museum
PO Box 220
New Town, ND 58763
Tel: 701-627-4781

NORTHWEST

Clothes Horse Trading Post
PO Box 848
Fort Hall, ID 83203
Tel: 208-237-8433

Colville Cultural Museum
PO Box 233
Coulee Dam, WA 99116
Tel: 509-633-0751

Kwagiulth Museum and Cultural Center
PO Box 8
Quathiaski Cove, British Columbia V0P 1N0
Tel: 604-285-3733

Makah Cultural Center and Museum
Highway 112
PO Box 95
Neah Bay, WA 98357
Tel: 206-645-2711

Suquamish Museum
PO Box 498
Suquamish, WA 98392
Tel: 206-598-3311

U'Mista Cultural Centre
PO Box 253
Alert Bay, British Columbia V0N 1A0
Tel: 604-974-5403

Yakima Nation Museum
PO Box 151
Toppenish, WA 98948
Tel: 509-865-2800

Apache Culture Center
PO Box 507
Fort Apache, AZ 85926
Tel: 602-338-4625

Bien Mur Indian Market Center
PO Box 91148
Sandia Pueblo, NM 87199
Tel: 505-821-5400

Gila River Arts and Crafts Center
PO Box 457
Sacaton, AZ 85247
Tel: 602-562-3411

Hopi Museum and Cultural Center
PO Box 67
Second Mesa, AZ 86043
Tel: 602-734-2401

Indian Pueblo Cultural Center
2401 12th St NW
Albuquerque, NM 87102
Tel: 505-843-7270

Jicarilla Arts and Crafts Shop/Museum
PO Box 507
Dulce, NM 87528
Tel: 505-759-3242

Mescalero Apache Cultural Center
PO Box 176
Mescalero, NM 88340
Tel: 505-671-4495

Navajo Tribal Museum/Arts and Crafts Enterprise
Postal Drawer A
Window Rock, AZ 86515
Tel: 602-871-4090

O'ke Oweenge Crafts Cooperative
PO Box 1095
San Juan Pueblo, NM 87566
Tel: 505-852-2372

San Ildefonso Pueblo Museum
Governor's Office
Rt. 5, Box 315-A
Santa Fe, NM 87501
Tel: 505-455-3549 or 455-2273

Southern Ute Arts and Crafts
PO Box 550
Ignacio, CO 81137
Tel: 303-563-9466

Tigua Indian Reservation Cultural Center
122 S. Old Pueblo
El Paso, TX 79917
Tel: 915-859-3916

Zuni Craftsmen Cooperative Association
PO Box 426
Zuni, NM 87327
Tel: 505-782-4425

Akwesasne Museum
Rt. 37
Hogansburg, NY 13655
Tel: 518-358-2461

American Indian Community House Gallery
708 Broadway
New York, NY 10003
Tel: 212-598-0100

Lake of the Woods Ojibwa Cultural Center
PO Box 1720
Kenora, Ontario P9N 3X7
Tel: 807-548-5744

Museum of the Woodland Indian
184 Mohawk St
PO Box 1506
Brantford, Ontario N3T 5V6
Tel: 519-759-2650

Oneida Nation Museum
PO Box 365
Oneida, WI 54155
Tel: 414-869-2768
The Turtle: Native American Center of the Living Arts
25 Rainbow Mall
Niagara Falls, NY 14801
Tel: 716-284-2427

Choctaw Museum of the Southern Indian
PO Box 6010
Philadelphia, MS 39350

Tel: 601-656-5251 (ext. 317)

Miccosukee Cultural Center and Museum
PO Box 440021
Tamiami Trail
Miami, FL 33144
Tel: 305-223-8380

Museum of the Cherokee Indian
US Highway 441 N.
PO Box 1599
Cherokee, NC 28719
Tel: 704-497-3481

Seminole Arts and Crafts Center
5847 Rt. 7
Ft. Lauderdale, FL 33314
Tel: 305-321-9655

OKLAHOMA

Cherokee Heritage Center and National Museum
PO Box 515
Tahlequah, OK 74465
Tel: 918-456-6007

Creek Council House Museum
106 W. 6th St
Okmulgee, OK 74447
Tel: 918-756-2324

Five Civilized Tribes Museum
Agency Hill, Honor Heights Dr.
Muskogee, OK 74401
Tel: 918-683-1701

Oklahoma Indian Arts and Crafts Cooperative
PO Box 966
Anadarko, OK 73005
Tel: 405-247-3486
Osage Tribal Museum
c/o Tribal Agency
Pawhuska, OK 74056
Tel: 918-287-2495

Seminole Nation Museum
PO Box 1532
Wewoka, OK 74884
Tel: 405-257-5580

CALIFORNIA

Colorado River Indian Tribes Museum
Rt. 1, Box 23-B
Second and Mojave St
Parker, AZ
Tel: 602-669-9211

Hupa Tribal Museum
PO Box 1348
Hoopa, CA 95546
Tel: 916-625-4110 or 916-625-4211

Malki Museum
11-795 Fields Rd
Banning, CA 92220
Tel: 714-849-7289

Sacramento Indian Center
Arts and Crafts Store
2612 K St
Sacramento, CA 95816
Tel: 916-442-0593

Sierra Mono Museum
PO Box 275
North Fork, CA 93643
Tel: 209-877-2115

MAJOR MUSEUM COLLECTIONS

GREAT PLAINS

Buffalo Bill Historical Center Plains Indian Museum
PO Box 1000
Cody, WY 82414
Tel: 307-587-4771

Denver Art Museum
100 W. 14th Ave Parkway
Denver, CO 80204
Tel: 303-575-2793
Denver Museum of Natural History
2001 Colorado Blvd
Denver, CO 80205
Tel: 303-322-7009

Glenbow Museum
130 9th Ave SE
Calgary, Alberta T2G 0P3
Tel: 403-264-8300

Museum of the Plains Indians
Highways 2 & 89

PO Box 400
Browning, MT 59417
Tel: 406-338-2230

Sioux Indian Museum
515 West Blvd.
PO Box 1504
Rapid City, SD 57709
Tel: 605-348-0557

W.H. Over State Museum
University of South Dakota
PO Box 414
Vermillion, SD 57069
Tel: 605-677-5228

NORTHWEST

Burke Museum
University of Washington
Mail Stop DB-10
17th Ave NE & NE 45th St
Seattle, WA 98195
Tel: 206-543-5590

Daybreak Star Arts Center
Discovery Park
PO Box 99100
Seattle, WA 98199
Tel: 206-285-4425

Museum of Anthropology
University of British Columbia
6393 NW Marine Dr.
Vancouver, British Columbia V6T 1Z2
Tel: 604-228-5087

Museum of Native American Cultures
200 Cataldo
Spokane, WA 99202
Tel: 509-326-4550

Portland Art Museum
1219 SW Park Ave
Portland, OR 97205
Tel: 503-226-2811

Royal British Columbia Museum
675 Belleville St
Victoria, BC V8V 1X4
Tel: 604-387-3701

SOUTHWEST

Arizona State Museum
University of Arizona
Park Ave and University Blvd.
Tucson, AZ 85721
Tel: 602-621-6302

Heard Museum
22 E. Monte Vista Rd
Phoenix, AZ 85004
Tel: 602-252-8848

Institute of American Indian Arts Museum
1369 Cerrillos Rd
Santa Fe, NM 87501
Tel: 505-988-6281

Maxwell Museum of Anthropology
University of New Mexico
Albuquerque, NM 87131-1201
Tel: 505-277-4404

Red Rock Museum
Red Rock State Park
PO Box 328
Church Rock, NM 87311
Tel: 505-722-3839

Museum of Indian Arts and Culture
710 Camino Lejo
Santa Fe, NM 87501
Tel: 505-827-6344

Museum of New Mexico
113 Lincoln Ave
Santa Fe, NM 87501
Tel: 505-827-6451

Museum of Northern Arizona
Ft Valley Rd
Rt. 4, Box 720
Flagstaff, AZ 86001
Tel: 602-774-5211

Wheelwright Museum
704 Camino Lejo
Santa Fe, NM 87501
Tel: 505-982-4636

NORTHEAST

American Museum of Natural History
Central Park W. at 79th St
New York, NY 10024

Tel: 212-769-5000

Brooklyn Museum
200 Eastern Parkway
Brooklyn, NY 11238
Tel: 718-638-5000

Canadian Museum of Civilization
100 Laurier St
PO Box 3100 Station B
Hull, Quebec J8X 4H2
Tel: 819-776-7000

Field Museum
1200 S. Lakeshore Dr.
Chicago, IL 60605
Tel: 312-922-9410

Iroquois Indian Museum
N. Main St
PO Box 158
Schoharie, NY 12157
Tel: 518-295-8553

McCord Museum
690 Sherbrooke
Montreal, Quebec H4C 1B1
Tel: 514-398-7100
To reopen in spring 1992.

McMichael Museum
10365 Islington Ave
Kleinburg, Ontario LOJ 1CL
Tel: 416-893-1121

National Museum of the American Indian
3753 Broadway
New York, NY 10032
Tel: 212-283-2420
This museum will be moved to a new facility
in Washington, DC, after 1992.

New Jersey State Museum
205 W. State St
Trenton, NJ 08625-0530
Tel: 609-292-6308

Newark Museum
49 Washington St
Newark, NJ 07101
Tel: 201-596-6550

Peabody Museum of Archaeology
Harvard University
11 Divinity Ave

Cambridge, MA 02138
Tel: 617-495-2248

Royal Ontario Museum
100 Queens Park
Toronto, Ontario M5S 2C6
Tel: 416-586-5549

Smithsonian Institution
National Museum of Natural History
10th St and Constitution Ave NW
Washington, DC 20560
Tel: 202-357-2700

University Museum
University of Pennsylvania
33rd & Spruce St
Philadelphia, PA 19104
Tel: 215-898-4000

SOUTHEAST

Museum of Science
3280 S. Miami Ave
Miami, FL 33129
Tel: 305-854-4247

OKLAHOMA

Bacone College Museum
Bacone College
99 Bacone Rd
Muskogee, OK 74403-1597
Tel: 918-683-4581

Fort Sill Museum
437 Kwanah Rd
Fort Sill, OK 73503
Tel: 405-351-5123

Museum of Art
University of Oklahoma
410 W. Boyd St
Norman, OK 73019
Tel: 405-325-3272

Southern Plains Indian Museum and Crafts Center
PO Box 749
Anadarko, OK 73005
Tel: 405-247-6221

CALIFORNIA

Kearn County Museum
3801 Chester Ave
Bakersfield, CA 93301
Tel: 805-861-2132

Lowie Museum of Anthropology
University of California, Berkeley
103 Kroeber Hall
Berkeley, CA 94720
Tel: 415-642-3681

Museum of Man
1350 El Prado
Balboa Park
San Diego, CA 92101
Tel: 619-239-2001

Southwest Museum
234 Museum Dr.
Highland Park
Los Angeles, CA 90041
Tel: 213-221-2163

State Indian Museum
2618 K St
Sacramento, CA 95816
916-324-0971

PARKS, MONUMENTS & ARCHAEOLOGICAL SITES

GREAT PLAINS

Alibates National Monument
Sanford, TX

Badlands National Park
PO Box 6
Interior, SD 57750
Tel: 605-433-5361

Black Hills National Forest
803 Soo San Rd
Rapid City, SD 57702
Tel: 605-343-1567

Chief Plenty Coups State Monument
Pryor, MT

Custer Battlefield National Monument
PO Box 39
Crow Agency, MT 59022
Tel: 406-638-2621

Devil's Tower National Monument
PO Box 8
Devil's Tower, WY 82714
Tel: 307-467-5370

Glacier National Park
West Glacier, MT 59936
Tel: 406-888-5441

Great Sand Dunes National Monument
11500 Highway 150
Mosca, CO 81146
Tel: 719-378-2312

Madison Buffalo Jump State Park
Logan, MT

Rosebud Battlefield State Monument
Kirby, MT

Sitting Bull State Historic Site
Fort Yates, ND

Wind Cave National Park
Rt. 1, Box 190-WCNT
Hot Springs, SD 57747
Tel: 605-745-4600

Yellowstone National Park
PO Box 168
Yellowstone National Park, WY 82190
Tel: 307-344-7381

NORTHWEST

Mount Rainier National Park
Tahoma Woods Star Rt.
Ashford, WA 98304
Tel: 206-569-2211

National Bison Range
132 Bison Range Rd
Moiese, MT 59824
Tel: 406-644-2211

Nez Perce National Historic Park
PO Box 93
Spalding, ID 83551
Tel: 208-843-2261

Olympic National Park
600 E. Park Ave
Port Angeles, WA 98362
Tel: 206-452-4501

Aztec Ruins National Monument
PO Box 640
Aztec, NM 87410
Tel: 505-334-6174

Bandelier National Monument
HCR1, Box 1
Suite 15
Los Alamos, NM 87544-9701
Tel: 505-672-3861

Canyon de Chelly National Monument
PO Box 588
Chinle, AZ 86503
Tel: 602-674-5436

Casa Grande National Monument
1100 Ruins Dr.
Coolidge, AZ 85228
Tel: 602-723-3172

Chaco Culture National Historical Park
SR 4, Box 6500
Bloomfield, NM
Tel: 505-786-5384

Chiricahua National Monument
Dos Cabezas Rt. Box 6500
Willcox, AZ 85643
Tel: 602-824-3460

Coronado State Monument
PO Box 95
Bernalillo, NM 87004
Tel: 505-867-5351
Danger Cave State Park
Wendover, UT

El Morro National Monument
Highway 53
Rt. 2, Box 43
Ramah, NM 87321
Tel: 505-783-4226

Gila Cliff Dwelling National Monument
Rt. 11, Box 100
Silver City, NM 88061
Tel: 505-536-9461

Glen Canyon National Recreation Area
PO Box 1507
Page, AZ 86040
Tel: 602-645-2511

Grand Canyon National Park
PO Box 129
Grand Canyon, AZ 86023
Tel: 602-638-7888

Gran Quivira National Monument
Rt. 1, Box 36
Mountainair, NM 87036
Tel: 505-847-2770

Hovenweep National Monument
McElmo Rt.
Cortez, CO 81321
Tel: 303-562-4248 or 529-4465

Hubbell Trading Post National Historic Site
Highway 264
PO Box 150
Ganado, AZ 86505
Tel: 602-755-3475

Jemez State Monument
PO Box 143
Jemez Springs, NM 87025
Tel: 505-829-3530

Mesa Verde National Park
PO Box 8
Mesa Verde, CO 81330
Tel: 303-529-4465

Montezuma Castle National Monument
PO Box 219
Camp Verde, AZ 86322
Tel: 602-567-3322
Monument Valley Navajo Tribal Park
PO Box 308
Kayenta, AZ 86515

Navajo National Monument
HC 71 Box 3
Tonalea, AZ 86044-9704
Tel: 602-672-2366

Organ Pipe Cactus National Monument
Rt. 1, Box 100
Ajo, AZ 85321
Tel: 602-387-6849

Pecos National Monument
PO Drawer 418
Pecos, NM 87552-0418
Tel: 505-757-6414

Petrified Forest National Park
PO Box 2217
Petrified Forest National Park, AZ 86028
Tel: 602-524-6228

Pueblo Grande Museum
4619 E. Washington St
Phoenix, AZ
Tel: 602-495-0900

Puye Cliff Dwellings
Santa Clara Pueblo
PO Box 580
Espanola, NM 87532
Tel: 505-753-7326

Saguaro National Monument
3693 S. Old Spanish Trail
Tucson, AZ 85730
Tel: 602-670-6680

Salinas National Monument
PO Box 496
Mountainair, NM 87036
Tel: 505-847-2585

Three Rivers Petroglyph Site
Alamogordo, NM

Tonto National Monument
PO Box 707
Roosevelt, AZ 85545
Tel: 602-467-2241

Tuzigoot National Monument
PO Box 68
Clarkdale, AZ 86324
Tel: 602-634-5564

Walnut Canyon National Monument
Walnut Canyon Rd
Flagstaff, AZ 86004
Tel: 602-526-3367

White Sands National Monument
PO Box 458
Alamogordo, NM 88310
Tel: 505-437-1058

Wupatki National Monument
HC 33, Box 444A
Flagstaff, AZ 86004
Tel: 602-527-7040

NORTHEAST

Aztalan State Park
Aztalan, WI

Cahokia Mounds State Historic Site
Old Highway 40
PO Box 681
Collinsville, IL 62234
Tel: 618-346-5160

Copper Culture State Park
Oconto, WI

Effigy Mounds National Monument
Highway 76
Marquette, IA

Grand Portage National Monument
PO Box 426
Grand Portage, MN 55605
Tel: 218-475-2228

Isle Royale National Park
87 N. Ripley
Houghton, MI 49931
Tel: 906-482-0986

Mound City Group National Monument
16062 Rt. 104
Chillicothe, OH 45601
Tel: 614-774-1125

Pipestone National Monument
PO Box 727
Pipestone, MN 56164
Tel: 507-825-5463

Port Au Choix National Historic Park
PO Box 70
Griquet, Newfoundland AOK 2XO
Tel: 709-623-2608

Serpent Mound State Memorial
3850 Rt. 73
Locust Grove, OH 45660
Tel: 513-587-2796

SOUTHEAST

Chucalissa Indian Village
1987 Indian Village Dr.
Memphis, TN 38109
Tel: 901-785-3160

Etowah Indian Mounds Historic Site
813 Indian Mounds Rd SW
Cartersville, GA 30120
Tel: 404-387-3747

Everglades National Park
PO Box 279
Homestead, FL 33030
Tel: 305-247-6211

Grand Village of the Nachez Indians
400 Jefferson Davis Blvd
Nachez, MS 39120
Tel: 601-446-6502

Kolomoki Indian Mounds State Park
Rt. 1, Box 114
Blakely, GA 31723
Tel: 912-723-5296

Mound State Monument and Museum
Highway 69
PO Box 66
Moundville, AL 35474
Tel: 205-371-2572

New Echota Historic Site
1211 Chatsworth Highway
Calhoun, GA 30701
Tel: 404-629-8151

Ocmulgee National Monument
1207 Emery Highway
Macon, GA 31201
Tel: 912-752-8257

Toltec Mounds State Park
1 Toltec Mounds Rd
Scott, AK 72142
Tel: 501-961-9442

Rock Eagle Indian Mound
350 Rock Eagle Rd
Eatonton, GA 31024
Tel: 404-485-2831

OKLAHOMA

Battle of the Washita Historic Site
Highway 47A
Cheyenne, OK
Tel: 405-497-3929

Spiro Mounds Archaeological State Park
Highway 59
Spiro, OK
Tel: 918-962-2062

Wichita Mountain National Wildlife Refuge
Rt. 1, Box 448
Indiahoma, OK 73552
Tel: 405-429-3222

CALIFORNIA

Calico Early Man Archaeological Site
Mineola Rd
Barstow, CA 92311
Tel: 619-256-3591

Chaw Se Indian Grinding Rock State Park
14881 Pine Grove-Volcano Rd
Pine Grove, CA 95665
Tel: 209-296-7488

Death Valley National Monument
PO Box 579
Death Valley, CA 92328
Tel: 619-786-2331

Lassen Volcanic National Park
PO Box 100
Mineral, CA 96063
Tel: 916-595-4444

Lava Beds National Monument
PO Box 867
Tulelake, CA 96134
Tel: 916-667-2282

Point Reyes National Seashore
Kule Loklo Miwok Indian Village
Point Reyes, CA 94956
Tel: 415-663-1092

Wassama Roundhouse State Park
Ahwahnee, CA

Yosemite National Park
PO Box 577
Yosemite, CA 95389
Tel: 209-372-0283

CALENDAR OF EVENTS

The following is a list of powwows, ceremonies, feast days, rodeos, festivals and other special events. It is not a comprehensive list but covers most of the major events. Dates often change, so we have listed only the month. Be sure to contact the sponsors in advance to get more detailed information.

GREAT PLAINS

JUNE
Big Wind Powwow
Shoshone Business Council
Northern Arapaho Business Council
Fort Washakie, WY 82514
Tel: 307-332-4932

Oglala Lakota College Graduation Powwow
Oglala Lakota College Activities Committee
PO Box 490
Kyle, SD 57752
Tel: 605-455-2321

Plains Indian Museum Powwow
Buffalo Bill Historical Center
PO Box 1000
Cody, WY 82414
Tel: 307-587-4771
Red Bottom Celebration
Fort Peck Executive Board
PO Box 1027
Poplar, MT 59255
Tel: 406-768-5155

Shoshone Indian Days Powwow and Rodeo
Shoshone Business Council
Fort Washakie, WY 82514
Tel: 307-332-4932

JULY
Black Hills and Northern Plains Indian Exposition
Black Hills Powwow Association
PO Box 1476
Rapid City, SD 57709

Ethete Powwow and Rodeo
Northern Arapaho Business Council
PO Box 396
Fort Washakie, WY 82514
Tel: 307-332-6120

Flandreau Santee Sioux Traditional Powwow
PO Box 283
Flandreau, SD 57028

Tel: 605-997-3891

Mandaree Powwow
Three Affiliated Tribes
PO Box 220
New Town, ND 58763
Tel: 701-627-4781

Milk River Indian Days
Fort Belknap Tribal Office
Rt. 1, Box 66
Harlem, MT 59526
Tel: 406-353-2205

North American Indian Days
Blackfeet Tribal Council
PO Box 850
Browning, MT 59417
Tel: 406-338-7522

Northern Cheyenne Fourth of July Powwow
Northern Cheyenne Tribal Council
PO Box 128
Lame Deer, MT 59043
Tel: 406-477-8283
Shoshone-Paiute Fourth of July Powwow
Shoshone-Paiute Tribal Council
PO Box 219
Owyhee, NV 89832
Tel: 702-757-3161

Sisseton-Wahpeton Powwow
Sisseton-Wahpeton Tribal Council
CPO Box 689
Sisseton, ND 57262
Tel: 701-698-3911

AUGUST
Cherry Creek Powwow
Cheyenne River Sioux Tribe
H.V. Johnston Cultural Center
PO Box 590
Eagle Butte, SD 57625
Tel: 605-964-2542

Crow Creek Powwow
PO Box 50
Fort Thompson, SD 57339
Tel: 605-245-2221

Crow Fair
Crow Tribal Council
PO Box 159
Crow Agency, MT 59022

Tel: 406-638-2601

Fort Randall Powwow
Yankton Sioux Tribal Office
PO Box 248
Marty, SD 57361
Tel: 605-384-3804

Little Shell Powwow
Three Affiliated Tribes
PO Box 220
New Town, ND 58763
Tel: 701-627-4781

Lower Brule Powwow
PO Box 187
Lower Brule, SD 57548
Tel: 605-473-5561
Oglala Nation Powwow and Rodeo
Oglala Sioux Tribe
PO Box H
Pine Ridge, SD 57770
Tel: 605-867-5821

Rocky Boys Powwow
Chippewa Cree Tribe
Rocky Boy Rt. Box 544
Box Elder, MT 59521
Tel: 406-395-4282

Rosebud Fair and Rodeo
Rosebud Tribal Office
PO Box 430
Rosebud, SD 57570
Tel: 605-747-2381

Standing Rock Powwow
Standing Rock Sioux Tribal Council
PO Box D
Fort Yates, ND 58538
Tel: 701-854-7231

Wazi Paha Oyate Festival
Oglala Lakota Community College
PO Box 490
Kyle, SD 57752
Tel: 605-455-2321

SEPTEMBER
Cheyenne River Labor Day Powwow
Cheyenne River Sioux Tribal Council
PO Box 590
Eagle Butte, SD 57625
Tel: 605-964-4155

Mah-Kato Powwow
Mdewakanton Club
PO Box 3608
Mankato, MN 56001
Tel: 507-389-6125

Turtle Mountain Labor Day Powwow
Turtle Mountain Tribal Council
PO Box 900
Belcourt, ND 58316
Tel: 701-477-6451

NORTHWEST

FEBRUARY
Lincoln's Birthday Powwow
Warm Springs Tribal Council
PO Box C
Warm Springs, OR 97761
Tel: 503-553-1161
MARCH
Epethes Powwow
Nez Perce Tribe
PO Box 305
Lapwai, ID 83540
Tel: 208-843-2253

MAY
Chehalis Tribal Day Celebration
Chehalis Community Council
Howanud Rd
Oakville, WA 98568
Tel: 206-273-5911

Satus Longhouse Powwow
Yakima Nation Cultural Center
PO Box 151
Toppenish, WA 98948
Tel: 509-865-2800

University of Washington Powwow
Seattle, WA
Tel: 206-543-9082

JUNE
Stommish Festival
Lummi Indian Tribe
2616 Kwina Rd
Bellingham, WA 98226
Tel: 206-734-8180

Tinowit International Powwow, Treaty Days Celebration and Rodeo
Yakima Nation Cultural Center
PO Box 151

Toppenish, WA 98948
Tel: 509-865-2800

Warm Springs Treaty Days
Warm Springs Tribal Council
PO Box C
Warm Springs, OR 97761
Tel: 503-553-1161

Warriors Memorial Powwow (honoring Chief Joseph)
Nez Perce Tribe
PO Box 305
Lapwai, ID 83540
Tel: 208-843-2253

JULY

Arlee Fourth of July Powwow
Confederated Salish and Kootenai Tribal Council
PO Box 278
Pablo, MT 59855
Tel: 406-675-2700

Chief Taholah Days
Quinault Tribal Council
PO Box 189
Taholah, WA 98587
Tel: 206-276-8211

Colville Fourth of July Powwow
Colville Tribe
PO Box 150
Nespelem, WA 99155
Tel: 509-634-4711

Coeur d'Alene Powwow
Coeur d'Alene Tribal Council
Plummer, ID 83851
Tel: 208-274-3101

Elmo Powwow
Confederated Salish and Kootenai Tribal Council
PO Box 278
Pablo, MT 59855
Tel: 406-675-2700

Toppenish Powwow, Rodeo and Pioneer Fair
Yakima Nation Cultural Center
PO Box 151
Toppenwish, WA 98948
Tel: 509-865-2800

AUGUST
Chief Seattle Days
Suquamish Tribe
PO Box 498
Suquamish, WA 98392
Tel: 206-598-3311

Looking Glass Powwow
Nez Perce Tribe
PO Box 305
Lapwai, ID 83540
Tel: 208-843-2253

Makah Festival
Makah Tribal Council
PO Box 115
Neah Bay, WA 98357
Tel: 206-645-2205

Nesika Illahee Powwow
Confederated Tribes of Siletz Indians of Oregon
PO Box 549
Siletz, OR 97380
Tel: 503-444-2532

Omak Stampede Days
Colville Tribe
PO Box 150
Nespelem, WA 99155
Tel: 509-634-4711

Shoshone-Bannock Indian Festival and Rodeo
Shoshone-Bannock Tribes
PO Box 306
Fort Hall, ID 83203
Tel: 208-238-3700

SEPTEMBER
Puyallup Powwow
Puyallup Tribal Council
2002 E. 28th St
Tacoma, WA 98404
Tel: 206-597-6200

Spokane Indians Labor Day Powwow
Spokane Tribe
PO Box 100
Wellpinit, WA 99040
Tel: 509-258-4581

Yakima Powwow
Yakima Nation Cultural Center
PO Box 151

Toppenish, WA 98948
Tel: 509-865-2800

OCTOBER
Four Nations Powwow
Nez Perce Tribe
PO Box 305
Lapwai, ID 83540
Tel: 208-843-2253

SOUTHWEST

Pueblo dances are held throughout the year.
For a schedule of upcoming events, contact:
Indian Pueblo Cultural Center
2401 12th St NW
Albuquerque, NM 87102
Tel: 505-843-7270

Eight Northern Indian Pueblos Council
PO Box 969
San Juan Pueblo, NM 87566
Tel: 505-852-4265

Hopi Cultural Center
PO Box 67
Second Mesa, AZ 86043
Tel: 602-734-2401

JANUARY
Kachina Dances
Hopi Cultural Center
PO Box 67
Second Mesa, AZ 86043
Tel: 602-734-2401
Kachina dances are held from mid-winter
through summer. Contact cultural center for
details.

San Ildefonso Feast Day
San Ildefonso Pueblo
PO Box 315-A
Santa Fe, NM 87501
Tel: 505-455-2273

FEBRUARY
O'odham Tash Indian Celebration
Tohono O'odham Nation
PO Box 837
Sells, AZ 85634
Tel: 602-383-2221

MARCH
Mul-Chu-Tha Community Fair
Gila River Indian Community

PO Box 97
Sacaton, AZ 85247
Tel: 602-562-3311

San Jose Feast Day
Laguna Pueblo
PO Box 194
Laguna, NM 87026
Tel: 505-552-6654

APRIL
Bear Dance
Uintah and Ouray Tribal Council
PO Box 190
Fort Duchesne, UT 84026
Tel: 801-722-5141

Cocopah Festivities Day
Cocopah Tribal Council
PO Bin G
Somerton, AZ 85350
Tel: 602-627-2102

Holy Week Ceremonies
Pascua Yaqui Tribal Council
7474 S. Camino de Oeste
Tucson, AZ 85746
Tel: 602-883-2838

**Institute of American Indian Arts
Powwow**
1369 Cerillos Rd
Santa Fe, NM 87501
Tel: 505-988-6281

**Native American Student Association
Powwow**
Arizona State University
Tempe, AZ 85287
Tel: 602-965-9011

Spring Roundup All-Indian Rodeo
White Mountain Apache Tribal Council
PO Box 700
Whiteriver, AZ 85941
Tel: 602-338-4346

MAY
Bear Dance
Southern Ute Tribal Council
PO Box 737
Ignacio, CO 81137
Tel: 303-563-4525

San Carlos Tribal Fair
San Carlos Apache Tribe
PO Box 0
San Carlos, AZ 85550
Tel: 602-475-2361

San Felipe Feast Day
San Felipe Pueblo
PO Box A
San Felipe, NM 87001
Tel: 505-867-3381

San Juan Feast Day
San Juan Pueblo
PO Box 1099
San Juan, NM 87566
Tel: 505-852-4400

Santa Cruz Feast Day
Taos Pueblo
PO Box 1846
Taos, NM 87571
Tel: 505-758-8626

JUNE
Bear Dance
Ute Mountain Ute Tribe
General Delivery
Towaoc, CO 81334
Tel: 303-565-3751

Elderfest
White Mountain Apache Tribal Council
PO Box 700
Whiteriver, AZ 85941
Tel: 602-338-4346

San Antonio Feast Day
Sandia Pueblo
PO Box 6008
Bernalillo, NM 87004
Tel: 505-867-3317

San Juan Feast Day
Taos Pueblo
PO Box 1846
Taos, NM 87571
Tel: 505-758-8626

JULY
Little Beaver Rodeo and Powwow
Jicarilla Apache Tribe
PO Box 507
Dulce, NM 87528
Tel: 505-759-3242

Mescalero Festival
Mescalero Apache Tribe
PO Box 176
Mescalero, NM 88340
Tel: 505-671-4495

Navajo Rodeo
Navajo Nation Tourism Office
PO Box 663
Window Rock, AZ 86515
Tel: 602-871-6436

Northern Ute Powwow and Rodeo
Uintah and Ouray Tribal Council
PO Box 190
Fort Duchesne, UT 84026
Tel: 801-722-5141

San Buenaventura Feast Day
Cochiti Pueblo
PO Box 70
Cochiti, NM 87041
Tel: 505-465-2244

Santa Ana Feast Day
Santa Ana Pueblo
Star Rt. Box 37
Bernalillo, NM 87004
Tel: 505-867-3301

Taos Pueblo Powwow
Taos Pueblo
PO Box 1846
Taos, NM 87571
Tel: 505-758-8626

**White Mountain Native American
Festival and Indian Market**
Pinetop-Lakeside Chamber of Commerce
Pinetop-Lakeside, AZ 85935
Tel: 602-367-4290

AUGUST
Intertribal Indian Ceremonial
PO Box 1
Church Rock, NM 87311
Tel: 505-863-3896

Our Lady of Assumption Feast Day
Zia Pueblo
General Delivery
San Ysidro, NM 87053
Tel: 505-867-3304

San Lorenzo Feast Day
Picuris Pueblo

PO Box 127
Penasco, NM 87553
Tel: 505-587-2519

Santa Clara Feast Day
Santa Clara Pueblo
PO Box 580
Espanola, NM 87532
Tel: 505-753-7326
Snake Dance
Hopi Cultural Center
PO Box 67
Second Mesa, AZ 86043
Tel: 602-734-2401

SEPTEMBER
Apache Tribal Fair
White Mountain Apache Tribe
PO Box 700
Whiteriver, AZ 85941
Tel: 602-338-4346

Jicarilla Apache Fair
Jicarilla Apache Tribe
PO Box 507
Dulce, NM 87528
Tel: 505-759-3242

Navajo Nation Fair
Navajo Nation Tourism Office
PO Box 663
Window Rock, AZ 86515
Tel: 602-871-6436

Peach Festival
Havasupai Tribal Office
PO Box 10
Supai, AZ 86435
Tel: 602-448-2961

San Agustin Feast Day
Isleta Pueblo
PO Box 317
Isleta, NM 87022
Tel: 505-869-3111

San Esteban Feast Day
Acoma Pueblo
PO Box 309
Acomita, NM 87034
Tel: 505-552-6604

San Geronimo Feast Day
Taos Pueblo
PO Box 1846

Taos, NM 87571
Tel: 505-758-8626

Southern Ute Fair
Southern Ute Tribal Council
PO Box 737
Ignacio, CO 81137
Tel: 303-563-4525

Stone Lake Fiesta
Jicarilla Apache Tribe
PO Box 507
Dulce, NM 87528
Tel: 505-759-3242

White Mountain Tribal Fair and Rodeo
White Mountain Apache Tribal Council
PO Box 700
Whiteriver, AZ 85941
Tel: 602-338-4346

OCTOBER
Northern Navajo Fair, Shiprock
Navajo Nation Tourism Office
PO Box 663
Window Rock, AZ 86515
Tel: 602-871-6436
San Francisco Feast Day
Ak Chin Indian Community
Rt. 2, Box 27
Maricopa, AZ 85239
Tel: 602-568-2227

San Francisco Feast Day
Nambe Pueblo
PO Box 117-BB
Santa Fe, NM 87501
Tel: 505-455-2036

NOVEMBER
San Diego Feast Day
Jemez Pueblo
PO Box 100
Jemez, NM 87024
Tel: 505-834-7359

San Diego Feast Day
Tesuque Pueblo
Rt. 11, Box 1
Santa Fe, NM 87501
Tel: 505-983-2667

Veteran's Day Rodeo
San Carlos Apache Tribal Council
PO Box 0

San Carlos, AZ 85550
Tel: 602-475-2361

DECEMBER
Our Lady of Guadalupe Feast Day
Jemez Pueblo
PO Box 100
Jemez, NM 87024
Tel: 505-834-7359
Our Lady of Guadalupe Feast Day
Pojoaque Pueblo
Rt. 11, Box 71
Santa Fe, NM 87501
Tel: 505-455-2278

Shalako
Zuni Pueblo
PO Box 339
Zuni, NM 87327
Tel: 505-782-4481

NORTHEAST

MAY
Memorial Day Powwow
Minnesota Chippewa Tribe
PO Box 217
Cass Lake, MN 56633
Tel: 218-335-2252

The Turtle Powwow
Native American Center for the Living Arts
25 Rainbow Mall
Niagara Falls, NY 14303
Tel: 716-284-2427

JUNE
Nett Lake Powwow
Nett Lake Reservation Business Committee
PO Box 16
Nett Lake, MN 55772
Tel: 218-757-3261

White Earth Powwow
White Earth Chippewa Tribe
PO Box 418
White Earth, MN 56591
Tel: 218-983-3285

JULY
Bear River Powwow
Lac du Flambeau Tribal Council
PO Box 67
Lac du Flambeau, WI 54538
Tel: 715-588-3303

Fond du Lac Powwow
Fond du Lac Business Committee
105 University Rd
Cloquet, MN 55720
Tel: 218-879-4593

Honor The Earth Powwow
Lac Courte Oreilles Tribe
Rt. 2, Box 2700
Hayward, WI 54843
Tel: 715-634-8934

Oneida Powwow
Oneida Museum
PO Box 365
Oneida, WI 54155
Tel: 414-869-2768

AUGUST
Ceremonial Day
Pleasant Point Passamaquoddy
PO Box 343
Perry, ME 04667
Tel: 207-853-2551

Grand Portage Rendezvous Days
Grand Portage Chippewa Tribe
PO Box 428
Grand Portage, MN 55605
Tel: 218-476-2279

Land of the Menominee Powwow
Woodland Bowl
Menominee Indian Tribe
PO Box 397
Keshena, WI 54135
Tel: 715-799-5100

Manomin Celebration
Bad River Chippewa Tribal Office
PO Box 39
Odanah, WI 54861
Tel: 715-682-7111

Ni-Mi-Win Celebration
Spirit Mountain
Duluth, MN
Tel: 218-628-2891

SEPTEMBER
Iroquois Indian Festival
Schoharie Museum of the Iroquois
PO Box 158
N. Main St
Schoharie, NY 12157

Tel: 518-234-8319

Labor Day Powwow
Minnesota Chippewa Tribe
PO Box 217
Cass Lake, MN 56633
Tel: 218-335-2252

Mountain Eagle Indian Festival
Hunter Mountain Festivals
PO Box 295
Hunter, NY 12442
Tel: 518-263-4223

Shinnecock Powwow
Shinnecock Reservation
Rt. 27A
Southampton, NY 11968
Tel: 516-283-3776

SOUTHEAST

JUNE
Cherokee Powwow
Eastern Band of Cherokee Indians
PO Box 455
Cherokee, NC 28719
Tel: 704-497-2771

JULY
Choctaw Fair
Choctaw Tribe
PO Box 6010
Philadelphia, MS 39350
Tel: 601-656-5251

NOVEMBER
Poarch Band of Creeks Powwow
Poarch Band of Creeks
Rt. 3, Box 243A
Atmore, AL 36502
Tel: 205-368-9136

DECEMBER
Miccosukee Arts and Crafts Fair
Miccosukee Tribal Council
PO Box 440021
Tamiami Station
Miami, FL 33144
Tel: 305-223-8380

Seminole Fair
Seminole Tribal Council
6073 Sterling Rd
Hollywood, FL 33024

Tel: 305-584-0400

OKLAHOMA

MAY
Oklahoma Indian Heritage Days Celebration
Miami Tribal Office
PO Box 1326
Miami, OK 74355
Tel: 918-540-2890

JUNE
Cheyenne-Arapaho Powwow
Cheyenne-Arapaho Tribe
PO Box 38
Concho, OK 73022
Tel: 405-262-0345

Osage Tribal Ceremonial Dances
Osage Tribal Council
c/o Osage Tribal Agency
Pawhuska, OK 74056
Tel: 918-287-4622

Potawatomi Powwow
Citizen Band of Potawatomi
1901 S. Gordon Cooper Dr.
Shawnee, OK 74801
Tel: 405-275-3121

JULY
Comanche Powwow
Comanche Tribal Office
PO Box 908
Lawton, OK 73502
Tel: 405-247-3444

Kiowa Fourth of July Powwow
Kiowa Tribe
PO Box 369
Carnegie, OK 73015
Tel: 405-654-2300

Otoe-Missouria Powwow
Otoe-Missouria Tribe
Rt. 1, Box 62
Red Rock, OK 74651
Tel: 405-723-4434

Pawnee Powwow
Pawnee Tribe
PO Box 470
Pawnee, OK 74058
Tel: 918-762-3624

Quapaw Powwow
Quapaw Tribe
PO Box 765
Quapaw, OK 74363
Tel: 918-542-1853

Sac and Fox Powwow
Sac and Fox Tribal Office
Rt. 2, Box 246
Stroud, OK 74079
Tel: 918-968-3526

AUGUST
American Indian Exposition
PO Box 908
Anadarko, OK 73005
Tel: 405-247-2733 or 247-6651

Ottawa Powwow
Ottawa Tribe
PO Box 110
Miami, OK 74355
Tel: 918-540-1536

Ponca Indian Fair and Powwow
Ponca Tribe
Rt. 6, Box 2
Ponca City, OK 74601
Tel: 405-762-8104

Wichita Tribal Powwow
Wichita Tribe
PO Box 729
Anadarko, OK 73005
Tel: 405-247-2425

SEPTEMBER
Choctaw Nation Labor Day Festivities
Choctaw Nation of Oklahoma
PO Drawer 1210
Durant, OK 74702
Tel: 405-924-8280

Seminole Nation Days
Seminole Nation
PO Box 1498
Wewoka, OK 74884
Tel: 405-257-6287

OCTOBER
Cherokee Fall Festival
Cherokee Nation of Oklahoma
PO Box 948
Tahlequah, OK 74465
Tel: 918-456-0671

Chickasaw Nation Annual Day
Chickasaw Nation of Oklahoma
PO Box 1548
Ada, OK 74820
Tel: 405-436-2603

Five Civilized Tribes Art Show
Five Civilized Tribes Museum
Agency Hill, Honor Heights Dr.
Muskogee, OK 74401
Tel: 918-683-1701

DECEMBER
Christmas Exhibition of Contemporary Indian Arts and Crafts
Southern Plains Indian Museum
PO Box 749
Anadarko, OK 73005
Tel: 405-247-6221

CALIFORNIA

JANUARY
Annual Native American Film Festival
Southwest Museum
234 Museum Dr.
Highland Park
Los Angeles, CA 90041
Tel: 213-221-2164

MARCH
Agua Caliente Indian Market
Agua Caliente Tribal Council
960 E. Tahquitz Canyon Way #106
Palm Springs, CA 92262
Tel: 619-325-5673

APRIL
San Francisco Annual Powwow
American Indian Studies Dept.
San Francisco State University
1600 Holloway
San Francisco, CA
Tel: 415-338-1111

MAY
Cupa Days
Pala Tribal Office
PO Box 43
Pala, CA 92059
Tel: 619-742-3784

Festival at the Lake
Lake Merritt, Oakland
News of Native California

PO Box 9145
Berkeley, CA 94709
Tel: 415-549-3564

Malki Museum Fiesta and Powwow
11795 Fields Rd
Banning, CA 92220
Tel: 714-849-7289

San Juan Bautista American Indian Art Show
San Juan Bautista Mission
Contact Reyna's Gallerias: Tel: 408-623-2379

Stanford University Powwow
Native American Students Association
PO Box 2990
Stanford, CA 94305
Tel: 415-723-4078

JUNE
Corpus Christi Festival
Pala Tribal Office
PO Box 43
Pala, CA 92059
Tel: 619-742-3784

Indian Day Big Time
Yosemite National Park
PO Box 577
Yosemite, CA 95389
Tel: 209-372-0283

Indian Fair Days
Museum of Man
1350 El Prado
Balboa Park
San Diego, CA 92101
Tel: 619-239-2001

JULY
Gathering Day
Wassama Roundhouse State Historic Park
Ahwahnee, CA
209-822-2332

Hupa Rodeo
Hupa Tribe
PO Box 1245
Hoopa, CA 95546
Tel: 916-625-4110

Kule Loklo Native American Celebration
Point Reyes National Seashore

Kule Loklo Miwok Indian Village
Point Reyes, CA 94956
Tel: 415-663-1092

AUGUST
Sierra Mono Museum Indian Fair
Sierra Mono Museum
PO Box 275
North Fork, CA 93643
Tel: 209-877-2115

SEPTEMBER
California Indian Days
State Indian Museum
2618 K St
Sacramento, CA 95816
Tel: 916-324-0971

Colorado River Tribes Fair and Indian Days
Colorado River Tribal Council
PO Box 23-B
Parker, AZ 85344
Tel: 602-669-9211

San Juan Bautista American Indian Art Show
San Juan Bautista Mission
Contact Reyna's Gallerias: Tel: 408-623-2379

NOVEMBER
American Indian Film Festival
Palace of Fine Arts
San Fancisco, CA
Tel: 415-563-6504

HUNTING & FISHING

Much of Indian Country is pristine territory with abundant wildlife and excellent conditions for hunting and fishing. Restrictions change from one reservation to another. If hunting and fishing are allowed by the tribe, you will most likely need a special tribal permit in addition to a state hunting and/or fishing license. License fees, bag limits and seasons vary. Some tribes, such as the White Mountain Apache and Jicarilla Apache, offer guide services. Others can recommend guides and packers that work in the area. Remember, firearms and hunting are prohibited at national parks and monuments.

INDIAN GAMING

Because of the unique legal status of Indian tribes, legitimate gaming and gambling enterprises may be owned and operated by many tribes. In accordance with the 1988 Indian Gaming Regulatory Act, these gaming operations must be sanctioned by the state and federal governments. The most common type of gaming offered by Indian tribes is bingo, although in some cases casino gambling and parimutuel betting is also allowed. For more information about Indian gaming, contact the Indian Gaming Commission (1850 M St NW, Suite 250, Washington, DC 20036; tel: 202-632-7003) or the Bureau of Indian Affairs Tribal Relations (1849 C St NW, Washington DC 20240; tel: 202-208-7445). Currently, more than 130 tribes run bingo or casino operations. This is a select list of tribes and gaming locations (see tribal listing for complete addresses and telephone numbers):

GREAT PLAINS

Blackfeet Tribe, Browning, MT.
Chippewa-Cree Tribe, Rocky Boys Agency, MT.
Flandreau Santee Sioux, Flandreau, SD.
Northern Cheyenne Tribe, Lame Deer, MT.
Oglala Sioux Tribe, Pine Ridge, SD.
Sisseton-Wahpeton Sioux, Wagner, SD.
Turtle Mountain Band, Belcourt, ND.

NORTHWEST

Confederated Tribes of Siletz Indians, Siletz, OR.
Makah Tribe, Neah Bay, WA.
Muckleshoot Tribe, Auburn, WA.
Puyallup Tribe, Tacoma, WA.
Shoshone-Bannock Tribes, Fort Hall, ID.
Swinomish Tribe, LaConner, WA.
Tulalip Tribe, Marysville, WA.
Umatilla Tribe, Pendleton, OR.

SOUTHWEST

Acoma Pueblo, Acomita, NM.
Cocopah Tribe, Yuma, AZ.
Isleta Pueblo, Isleta, NM.
Pascua Yaqui Tribe, Tucson, AZ.
Quechan Tribe, Yuma, AZ.
Sandia Pueblo, Bernalillo, NM.

San Juan Pueblo, San Juan, NM.
Southern Ute Tribe, Ignacio, CO.
Tesuque Pueblo, Santa Fe, NM.
Tohono O'odham Nation, Tucson, AZ.
Ute Mountain Tribe, Towaoc, CO.
Yavapai-Prescott Tribe, Prescott, AZ.

NORTHEAST

Fond du Lac Chippewa Tribe, Cloquet, MN.
Lac Courte Oreilles Band, Hayward, WI.
Lac du Flambeau Band, Lac du Flambeau, WI.
Mashantucket Pequot Tribe, Ledyard, CT.
Menominee Tribe, Keshena, WI.
Mille Lacs Band, Onamia, MN.
Oneida Nation, Oneida, NY.
Red Cliff Band, Bayfield, WI.
Red Lake Band, Red Lake, MN.
Saginaw Chippewa Tribe, Mt Pleasant, MI.
St Regis Band of Mohawk Indians, Hogansburg, NY.
Seneca Tribe, Salamanca, NY.
Stockbridge-Munsee Tribe, Bowler, WI.
White Earth Chippewa Tribe, White Earth, MN.
Winnebago Tribe, Tomah, WI.

SOUTHEAST

Cherokee Tribe, Cherokee, NC.
Seminole Tribe, Tampa, FL; Big Cypress, FL; Hollywood, FL; Brighton, FL.

OKLAHOMA

Iowa Tribe of Oklahoma, Perkins, OK.
Kaw Tribe, Kaw City, OK.
Otoe-Missouria Tribe, Red Rock, OK.
Quapaw Tribe, Quapaw, OK.
Sac & Fox Tribe, Stroud, OK.
Seminole Tribe, Wewoka, OK.
Seneca-Cayuga Tribe, Grove, OK.
Chickasaw Tribe, Ada, OK; Sulphur, OK.
Creek Tribe, Tulsa, OK; Bristow, OK; Okmulgee, OK.
Choctaw Tribe, Durant, OK.
Absentee-Shawnee Tribe, Shawnee, OK.
Cheyenne-Arapaho Tribe, Watonga, OK.
Citizen Band of Potawatomi, Shawnee, OK.
Kiowa Tribe, Carnegie, OK.
Comanche Tribe, Lawton, OK.
Apache Tribe, Anadarko, OK.

CALIFORNIA

Colusa Rancheria, Colusa, CA.
San Manuel Band, San Bernardino, CA.
Viejas Band, Alpine, CA.
Santa Ynez Band, Santa Ynez, CA.
Barona Band, Lakeside, CA.
Bishop Tribe, Bishop, CA.
Hupa Tribe, Hoopa, CA.
Morongo Band, Banning, CA.

USEFUL ADDRESSES

FEDERALLY RECOGNIZED INDIAN TRIBES

There are over 300 federally recognized Indian tribes in the continental US. Listed below are a selection of tribes of most interest to travelers.

GREAT PLAINS

Arapaho Tribe
PO Box 396
Fort Washakie, WY 82514
Tel: 307-332-6120

Blackfeet Tribe
PO Box 850
Browning, MT 59417
Tel: 406-338-7522

Cheyenne River Sioux Tribe
PO Box 590
Eagle Butte, SD 57625
Tel: 605-964-2542

Chippewa-Cree Indians
Rural Rt. 544
Box Elder, MT 59521
Tel: 406-395-4282

Crow Creek Sioux Tribe
PO Box 50
Fort Thompson, SD 57339
Tel: 605-245-2221

Crow Tribe
PO Box 159
Crow Agency, MT 59022
Tel: 406-638-2601

Devils Lake Sioux Tribe
Sioux Community Center
PO Box 359
Fort Totten, ND 58335
Tel: 701-766-4221

Flandreau Santee Sioux Tribe
Flandreau Field Office
PO Box 283
Flandreau, SD 57028
Tel: 605-997-3891

Fort Belknap Indian Community
Rt. 1, Box 66
Harlem, MT 59526
Tel: 406-353-2205

Fort Berthold Tribe
PO Box 220
New Town, ND 58763
Tel: 701-627-4781

Fort Peck Tribe
PO Box 1027
Poplar, MT 59255
Tel: 406-768-5155

Iowa Tribe of Kansas and Nebraska
Rt. 1, Box 58A
White Cloud, KS 66094
Tel: 913-595-3258

Kickapoo Tribe
PO Box 271
Horton, KS 66349
Tel: 913-486-2131

Lower Brule Sioux Tribe
PO Box 187
Lower Brule, SD 57548
Tel: 605-473-5561

Northern Cheyenne Tribe
PO Box 128
Lame Deer, MT 59043
Tel: 406-477-8283

Oglala Sioux Tribe
PO Box H
Pine Ridge, SD 57770

Tel: 605-867-5821

Omaha Tribe of Nebraska
PO Box 368
Macy, NE 68039
Tel: 402-837-5391

Prairie Band of Potawatomi Indians
Rt. 2, Box 50A
Mayetta, KS 66509
Tel: 913-966-2255

Rosebud Sioux Tribe
PO Box 430
Rosebud, SD 57570
Tel: 605-747-2381

Sac and Fox Tribe of Missouri in Kansas and Nebraska
Rt. 1, Box 60
Reserve, KS 66434
Tel: 913-742-7471

Sac and Fox Tribe of the Mississippi
Rt. 2, Box 56C
Tama, IA 52339
Tel: 515-484-4678 or 484-5358

Santee Sioux Tribe
Rt. 2
Niobrara, NE 68760
Tel: 402-857-3302

Shoshone Tribe
PO Box 217
Fort Washakie, WY 82514
Tel: 307-332-4932

Sisseton-Wahpeton Sioux Tribe
CPO Box 689
Sisseton, SD 57262
Tel: 605-698-3911

Standing Rock Sioux Tribe
PO Box D
Fort Yates, ND 58538
Tel: 701-854-7231

Turtle Mountain Band of Chippewa Indians
PO Box 900
Belcourt, ND 58316
Tel: 701-477-6451

Winnebago Tribe
PO Box 687

Winnebago, NE 68071
Tel: 402-878-2272

Yankton Sioux Tribe
PO Box 248
Marty, SD 57361
Tel: 605-384-3804

NORTHWEST

Chehalis Indian Community
Howanud Rd
Oakville, WA 98568
Tel: 206-273-5911

Coeur d'Alene Tribe
Plummer, ID 83851
Tel: 208-274-3101

Colville Indian Tribe
PO Box 150
Nespelem, WA 99155
Tel: 509-634-4711

Confederated Salish and Kootenai Tribes
PO Box 278
Pablo, MT 59855
Tel: 406-675-2700

Confederated Tribes of Siletz Indians of Oregon
PO Box 549
Siletz, OR 97380
Tel: 503-444-2532

Fort McDermitt Paiute and Shoshone Tribes
PO Box 457
McDermitt, NV 89421
Tel: 702-532-8259

Hoh Tribe
HC 80, Box 917
Forks, WA 98331
Tel: 206-374-6582

Jamestown Klallam Tribe
305 Old Blyn Highway
Sequim, WA 98382
Tel: 206-683-1109

Kalispel Tribe
PO Box 39
Usk, WA 99180
Tel: 509-445-1147

Klamath Tribe
PO Box 436
Chiloquin, OR 97624
Tel: 503-783-2219

Kootenai Tribe
PO Box 1269
Bonners Ferry, ID 83805
Tel: 208-267-3519

Lummi Tribe
2616 Kwina Rd
Bellingham, WA 98226
Tel: 206-734-8180

Makah Indian Tribe
PO Box 115
Neah Bay, WA 98357
Tel: 206-645-2205

Muckleshoot Indian Tribe
39015 172nd St, SE
Auburn, WA 98002
Tel: 206-939-3311

Nez Perce Tribe
PO Box 305
Lapwai, ID 83540
Tel: 208-843-2253

Nisqually Tribe
4820 She-Hah-Num Dr. SE
Olympia, WA 98503
Tel: 206-456-5221

Nooksack Tribe
PO Box 157
Deming, WA 98244
Tel: 206-592-5176

Puyallup Tribe
2002 E. 28th St
Tacoma, WA 98404
Tel: 206-597-6200

Quileute Tribe
PO Box 279
LaPush, WA 98350
Tel: 206-374-6163

Quinault Tribe
PO Box 189
Taholah, WA 98587
Tel: 206-276-8211

Sauk Suiattle Tribe
5318 Chief Brown Lane
Darrington, WA 98241
Tel: 206-435-8366

Shoshone-Bannock Tribes
PO Box 306
Fort Hall, ID 83203
Tel: 208-238-3700

Skokomish Tribe
80 Tribal Center Rd N.
Shelton, WA 98584
Tel: 206-426-4232

Spokane Tribe
PO Box 100
Wellpinit, WA 99040
Tel: 509-258-4581

Squaxin Island Tribe
SE 70, Squaxin Lane
Shelton, WA 98584
Tel: 206-426-9781

Stillaquamish Tribe
3439 Stoluckquamish Lane
Arlington, WA 98223
Tel: 206-652-7362

Suquamish Tribe
PO Box 498
Suquamish, WA 98392
Tel: 206-598-3311

Swinomish Tribe
PO Box 817
LaConner, WA 98257
Tel: 206-466-3163

Tulalip Tribes
6700 Totem Beach Rd
Marysville, WA 98270
Tel: 206-653-4585

Umatilla Tribe
PO Box 638
Pendleton, OR 97801
Tel: 503-276-3165

Upper Skagit Tribe
2284 Community Plaza
Sedro Wooley, WA 98284
Tel: 206-856-5501

Warm Springs Tribe
PO Box C
Warm Springs, OR 97761
Tel: 503-553-1161

Yakima Tribe
PO Box 151
Toppenish, WA 98948
Tel: 509-865-2800

SOUTHWEST

Acoma Pueblo
PO Box 309
Acomita, NM 87034
Tel: 505-552-6604

Ak Chin Indian Community
Rt. 2, Box 27
Maricopa, AZ 85239
Tel: 602-568-2227

Cochiti Pueblo
PO Box 70
Cochiti, NM 87041
Tel: 505-465-2244

Cocopah Tribe
PO Bin G
Somerton, AZ 85350
Tel: 602-627-2102

Colorado River Indian Tribes
Rt. 1, Box 23B
Parker, AZ 85344
Tel: 602-669-9211

Duckwater Shoshone Tribe
PO Box 68
Duckwater, NV 89314
Tel: 702-863-0227

Fort McDowell Mohave-Apache Indian Community
PO Box 17779
Fountain Hills, AZ 85268
Tel: 602-990-0995

Gila River Pima-Maricopa Indian Community
PO Box 97
Sacaton, AZ 85247
Tel: 602-562-3311

Goshute Indians
PO Box 6104
Ibapah, UT 84034
Tel: 801-234-1138

Havasupai Tribe
PO Box 10
Supai, AZ 86435
Tel: 602-448-2961

Hopi Tribe
PO Box 123
Kykotsmovi, AZ 86039
Tel: 602-734-2445

Hualapai Tribe
PO Box 179
Peach Springs, AZ 86434
Tel: 602-769-2216

Isleta Pueblo
PO Box 317
Isleta, NM 87022
Tel: 505-869-3111

Jemez Pueblo
PO Box 100
Jemez, NM 87024
Tel: 505-834-7359

Jicarilla Apache Tribe
PO Box 507
Dulce, NM 87528
Tel: 505-759-3242

Kaibab Band of Paiute Indians
Tribal Affairs Building
HC 65, Box 2
Fredonia, AZ 86022
Tel: 602-643-7245

Laguna Pueblo
PO Box 194
Laguna, NM 87026
Tel: 505-552-6654

Las Vegas Paiute Tribe
1 Paiute Dr.
Las Vegas, NV 89106
Tel: 702-386-3926

Lovelock Paiute Tribe
PO Box 878
Lovelock, NV 89419
Tel: 702-273-7861

Mescalero Apache Tribe
PO Box 176
Mescalero, NM 88340
Tel: 505-671-4495

Nambe Pueblo
PO Box 117-BB
Santa Fe, NM 87501
Tel: 505-455-2036

Navajo Nation
PO Box 308
Window Rock, AZ 86515
Tel: 602-871-6352

Paiute Indian Tribe of Utah
600 North, 100 E. Paiute Dr.
Cedar City, UT 84720
Tel: 801-586-1111

Paiute-Shoshone Tribe
8955 Mission Rd
Fallon, NV 89406
Tel: 702-423-6075

Pascua Yaqui Tribe
7474 S. Camino de Oeste
Tucson, AZ 85746
Tel: 602-578-0227

Picuris Pueblo
PO Box 127
Penasco, NM 87553
Tel: 505-587-2519

Pojoaque Pueblo
Rt. 11, Box 71
Santa Fe, NM 87501
Tel: 505-455-2278

Pyramid Lake Paiute Tribe
PO Box 256
Nixon, NV 89424
Tel: 702-574-0140

Quechan Tribe
PO Box 11352
Yuma, AZ 85364
Tel: 619-572-0213

Salt River Pima-Maricopa Indian Community
Rt. 1, Box 216
Scottsdale, AZ 85256
Tel: 602-941-7277

San Carlos Apache Tribe
PO Box 0
San Carlos, AZ 85550
Tel: 602-475-2361

Sandia Pueblo
PO Box 6008
Bernalillo, NM 87004
Tel: 505-867-3317

San Felipe Pueblo
PO Box A
San Felipe Pueblo, NM 87001
Tel: 505-867-3381

San Ildefonso Pueblo
PO Box 315-A
Santa Fe, NM 87501
Tel: 505-455-2273

San Juan Pueblo
PO Box 1099
San Juan, NM 87566
Tel: 505-852-4400

Santa Ana Pueblo
Star Rt., Box 37
Bernalillo, NM 87004
Tel: 505-867-3301

Santa Clara Pueblo
PO Box 580
Espanola, NM 87532
Tel: 505-753-7326

Santo Domingo Pueblo
PO Box 99
Santo Domingo, NM 87052
Tel: 505-465-2214

Shoshone-Paiute Tribes
PO Box 219
Owyhee, NV 89832
Tel: 702-757-3161

Southern Ute Tribe
PO Box 737
Ignacio, CO 81137
Tel: 303-563-4525

Summit Lake Paiute Tribe
PO Box 1958
Winnemucca, NV 89445
Tel: 702-623-5151

Taos Pueblo
PO Box 1846
Taos, NM 87571
Tel: 505-758-8626

Te-Moak Tribe of Western Shoshone Indians
525 Sunset St
Elko, NV 89801
Tel: 702-738-9251

Tesuque Pueblo
Rt. 11, Box 1
Santa Fe, NM 87501
Tel: 505-983-2667

Tohono O'odham Nation
PO Box 837
Sells, AZ 85634
Tel: 602-383-2221

Tonto Apache Tribe
Tonto Reservation # 30
Payson, AZ 85541
Tel: 602-474-5000

Ute Tribe
PO Box 190
Fort Duchesne, UT 84026
Tel: 801-722-5141

Ute Mountain Tribe
General Delivery
Towaoc, CO 81334
Tel: 303-565-3751

Walker River Paiute Tribe
PO Box 220
Schurz, NV 89427
Tel: 702-773-2306

Washoe Tribe of Nevada
919 Highway 395 S.
Garnerville, NV 89410
Tel: 702-265-4191

White Mountain Apache Tribe
PO Box 700
Whiteriver, AZ 85941
Tel: 602-338-4346

Yavapai-Apache Tribe
PO Box 1188
Camp Verde, AZ 86322
Tel: 602-567-3649

Yavapai-Prescott Tribe
530 E. Merritt St
Prescott, AZ 86301
Tel: 602-445-8790

Ysleta Del Sur Pueblo
PO Box 17579
El Paso, TX 79907
Tel: 915-859-7913

Zia Pueblo
General Delivery
San Ysidro, NM 87053
Tel: 505-867-3304

Zuni Pueblo
PO Box 339
Zuni, NM 87327
Tel: 505-782-4481

NORTHEAST

Bad River Band of the Chippewa Nation
Rt. 39
Odanah, WI 54861
Tel: 715-682-7111

Bay Mills Indian Community
Rt. 1
Brimley, MI 49715
Tel: 906-248-3241

Cayuga Nation
PO Box 11
Versailles, NY 14168
Tel: 716-532-4847

Fond du Lac Chippewa Tribe
105 University Rd
Cloquet, MN 55720
Tel: 218-879-4593

Grand Portage Chippewa Tribe
PO Box 428
Grand Portage, MN 55605
Tel: 218-476-2279

Grand Traverse Band of Ottawa and Chippewa Indians
Rt.1, Box 135
Suttons Bay, MI 49682
Tel: 616-271-3538

**Lac Courte Oreilles Band of
Lake Superior Chippewa Indians**
Rt. 2, Box 2700
Hayward, WI 54843
Tel: 715-634-8934

Lac du Flambeau Band of
Lake Superior Chippewa Indians
PO Box 67
Lac du Flambeau, WI 54538
Tel: 715-588-3303

Lower Sioux Indian Community
Rt. 1, Box 308
Morton, MN 56270
Tel: 507-697-6185

Menominee Indian Tribe
PO Box 397
Keshena, WI 54135
Tel: 715-799-5100

Minnesota Chippewa Tribe
PO Box 217C
Cass Lake, MN 56633
Tel: 218-335-2252

Mashantucket Pequot Tribe
PO Box 160
Ledyard, CT 06339
Tel: 203-536-2681

Narraganset Tribe
PO Box 268
Charleston, RI 02813
Tel: 401-364-1100

Nett Lake Chippewa Tribe
PO Box 16
Nett Lake, MN 55772
Tel: 218-757-3261

Oneida Nation of New York
101 Canal St
Canastota, NY 13032
Tel: 315-697-8251

Oneida Tribe
PO Box 365
Oneida, WI 54155
Tel: 414-869-2768

Onondaga Nation
PO Box 270
Nedrow, NY 13120

Tel: 315-469-8507

Passamaquoddy Tribe
PO Box 301
Princeton, ME 04668
Tel: 207-796-2301

Penobscott Nation
6 River Rd
Old Town, ME 04468
Tel: 207-827-7776

Pleasant Point Passamaquoddy Tribe
PO Box 343
Perry, ME 04667
Tel: 207-853-2551

**Red Cliff Band of Lake Superior
Chippewa Indians**
PO Box 529
Bayfield, WI 54814
Tel: 715-779-5805

Red Lake Band of Chippewa Indians
PO Box 550
Red Lake, MN 56671
Tel: 218-679-3341

Saginaw Chippewa Tribe
7070 E. Broadway Rd
Mt. Pleasant, MI 48858
Tel: 517-772-5700

St Croix Chippewa Tribe
PO Box 287
Hertel, WI 54845
Tel: 715-349-2195

St Regis Band of Mohawk Indians
St Regis Reservation
Hogansburg, NY 13655
Tel: 518-358-2272

Sault Ste Marie Tribe of Chippewa Indians
206 Greenough St
Sault Ste Marie, MI 49783
Tel: 906-635-6050

Seneca Nation
PO Box 321
Salamanca, NY 14779
tel: 716-945-1790

Sokaogon Chippewa Tribe
Rt. 1, Box 625
Crandon, WI 54520
Tel: 715-478-2604

Stockbridge-Munsee Tribe
Rt. 1
Bowler, WI 54416
Tel: 715-793-4111

Tonawanda Band of Senecas
7023 Meadville Rd
Basom, NY 14013
tel: 716-542-9942

Tuscarora Nation
5616 Walmore Rd
Lewiston, NY 14092
tel: 716-297-4990

Upper Sioux Indian Community
PO Box 147
Granite Falls, MN 56241
Tel: 612-564-2360

Wampanoag Tribe of Gay Head
RFD Box 137
Gay Head, MA 02535
Tel: 508-645-9265

White Earth Chippewa Tribe
PO Box 418
White Earth, MN 56591
Tel: 218-983-3285

Wisconsin Winnebago Tribe
127 Main St
Black River Falls, WI 54615
Tel: 715-284-4915

SOUTHEAST

Alabama-Coushatta Tribe of Texas
Rt. 3, Box 640
Livingston, TX 77351
Tel: 409-563-4391

Coushatta Tribe
PO Box 818
Elton, LA 70532
Tel: 318-584-2261

Eastern Band of Cherokee Indians
PO Box 455
Cherokee, NC 28719

Tel: 704-497-2771

Miccosukee Tribe
PO Box 440021
Tamiami Station
Miami, FL 33144
Tel: 305-223-8380

Mississippi Band of Choctaw Indians
PO Box 6010
Philadelphia, MS 39350
Tel: 601-656-5251

Poarch Band of Creek Indians
Rt. 3, Box 243-A
Atmore, AL 36502
Tel: 205-368-9136

Seminole Tribe
6073 Stirling Rd
Hollywood, FL 33024
Tel: 305-584-0400

OKLAHOMA

Absentee-Shawnee Tribe
2025 S. Gordon Cooper Dr.
Shawnee, OK 74801
Tel: 405-275-4030

Apache Tribe of Oklahoma
PO Box 1220
Anadarko, OK 73005
Tel: 405-247-9493

Caddo Indian Tribe
PO Box 487
Binger, OK 73009
Tel: 405-656-2344

Cherokee Nation of Oklahoma
PO Box 948
Tahlequah, OK 74465
Tel: 918-456-0671

Cheyenne-Arapaho Tribe
PO Box 38
Concho, OK 73022
Tel: 405-262-0345

Chickasaw Nation of Oklahoma
PO Box 1548
Ada, OK 74820
Tel: 405-436-2603

Choctaw Nation of Oklahoma
PO Drawer 1210
Durant, OK 74702
Tel: 405-924-8280

Citizen Band of Potawatomi Indian Tribe
1901 S. Gordon Cooper Dr.
Shawnee, OK 74801
Tel: 405-275-3121

Comanche Tribe
PO Box 908
Lawton, OK 73502
Tel: 405-247-3444

Creek Nation of Oklahoma
PO Box 580
Okmulgee, OK 74447
Tel: 918-756-8700

Delaware Indian Tribe
PO Box 825
Anadarko, OK 73005
Tel: 405-247-2448

Fort Sill Apache Tribe
Rt. 2, Box 121
Apache, OK 73006
Tel: 405-588-2298

Iowa Tribe of Oklahoma
Iowa Veterans Hall
PO Box 190
Perkins, OK 74059
Tel: 405-547-2403

Kaw Tribe
PO Drawer 50
Kaw City, OK 74641
Tel: 405-269-2552

Kickapoo Tribe of Oklahoma
PO Box 70
McLoud, OK 74851
405-964-2075

Kiowa Tribe
PO Box 369
Carnegie, OK 73015
Tel: 405-654-2300

Miami Tribe of Oklahoma
PO Box 1326
Miami, OK 74355
Tel: 918-540-2890

Modoc Tribe of Oklahoma
PO Box 939
Miami, OK 74355
Tel: 918-542-1190

Osage Tribe
c/o Osage Tribal Agency
Pawhuska, OK 74056
Tel: 918-287-4622

Otoe-Missouria Tribe
Rt. 1, Box 62
Red Rock, OK 74651
Tel: 405-723-4434

Ottawa Tribe
PO Box 110
Miami, OK 74355
Tel: 918-540-1536

Pawnee Tribe
PO Box 470
Pawnee, OK 74058
Tel: 918-762-3624

Peoria Tribe
PO Box 1527
Miami, OK 74355
Tel: 918-540-2535

Ponca Tribe
Rt. 6, Box 2
Ponca City, OK 74601
Tel: 405-762-8104

Quapaw Tribe
PO Box 765
Quapaw, OK 74363
Tel: 918-542-1853

Sac and Fox Tribe of Oklahoma
Rt. 2, Box 246
Stroud, OK 74079
Tel: 918-968-3526

Seminole Nation of Oklahoma
PO Box 1498
Wewoka, OK 74884
Tel: 405-257-6287

Seneca-Cayuga Tribe of Oklahoma
PO Box 1283
Miami, OK 74355
Tel: 918-542-6609

Tonkawa Tribe
PO Box 70
Tonkawa, OK 74653
Tel: 405-628-2561

United Keetoowah Band of Cherokee
2450 S. Muskogee Ave
Tahlequah, OK 74464
Tel: 918-456-5491

Wichita Tribe
PO Box 729
Anadarko, OK 73005
Tel: 405-247-2425

Wyandotte Tribe of Oklahoma
PO Box 250
Wyandotte, OK 74370
Tel: 918-678-2297

CALIFORNIA

Agua Caliente Band of Cahuilla Indians
960 E. Tahquitz Way #106
Palm Springs, CA 92262
Tel: 619-325-5673

Barona Tribe
1095 Barona Rd
Lakeside, CA 92040
Tel: 619-443-6612 or 443-6613

Benton Paiute Indians
Star Rt. 4, Box 56-A
Benton, CA 93512
Tel: 619-933-2321

Bishop Tribe
PO Box 548
Bishop, CA 93515
Tel: 619-873-3584

Cabazon Band of Cahuilla Mission Indians
84-245 Indio Springs Dr.
Indio, CA 92201
Tel: 619-342-2593

Cahuilla Band of Mission Indians
PO Box 860
Anza, CA 92306
Tel: 714-763-5549

Campo Band of Diegueño Mission Indians
1779 Campo Truck Trail

Campo, CA 91906
Tel: 619-478-9046

Chemehuevi Tribe
PO Box 1976
Chemehuevi Valley, CA 92363
Tel: 619-858-4531

Colusa Rancheria
PO Box 8
Colusa, CA 95932
Tel: 916-458-8231

Cortina Rancheria
PO Box 7470
Citrus Heights, CA 95621
Tel: 916-726-7118

Coyote Valley Band of Pomo Indians
PO Box 39
Redwood Valley, CA 95470
Tel: 707-485-8723

Hupa Tribe
PO Box 1245
Hoopa, CA 95546
Tel: 916-625-4110

Hopland Band of Pomo Indians
PO Box 610
Hopland, CA 95449
Tel: 707-744-1647

Karuk Tribe
PO Box 1016
Happy Camp, CA 96039
Tel: 916-493-5305

La Jolla Band of Luiseño Mission Indians
Star Rt., Box 158
Valley Center, CA 92082
Tel: 619-742-3771

Los Coyotes Band of Cahuilla Mission Indians
PO Box 249
Warner Springs, CA 92086
Tel: 619-782-3269

Manzanita Band of Diegueño Mission Indians
PO Box 1302
Boulevard, CA 92005
Tel: 619-766-4930

Mesa Grande Band of Diegueño Mission Indians
PO Box 270
Santa Ysabel, CA 92070
Tel: 619-782-3835

Morongo Band of Cahuilla Mission Indians
11581 Potrero Rd
Banning, CA 92220
Tel: 714-849-4697

Paiute-Shoshone Indians
1101 S. Main St
Lone Pine, CA 93545
Tel: 619-876-5414

Pala Band of Luiseño Mission Indians
PO Box 43
Pala, CA 92059
Tel: 619-742-3784

Pauma Band of Luiseño Mission Indians
PO Box 86
Pauma Valley, CA 92061
Tel: 619-742-1289

Pit River Indian Tribe
PO Drawer 1570
Burney, CA 96013
Tel: 916-335-5421

Rincon Band of Luiseño Mission Indians
PO Box 68
Valley Center, CA 92082
Tel: 619-749-1051

Round Valley Indians
PO Box 448
Covelo, CA 95428
Tel: 707-983-6126

San Manuel Band of Serrano Mission Indians
5797 N. Victoria Ave
Highland, CA 92346
Tel: 714-864-5050

San Pasqual Band of Diegueño Mission Indians
PO Box 365
Valley Center, CA 92082
Tel: 619-749-3200

Santa Ynez Band of Chumash Mission Indians
PO Box 517
Santa Ynez, CA 93460
Tel: 805-688-7997

Santa Ysabel Band of Diegueño Mission Indians
PO Box 130
Santa Ysabel, CA 92070
Tel: 619-765-0845

Timbi-Sha Shoshone Indian Tribe
PO Box 206
Death Valley, CA 92328
Tel: 619-786-2374

Torres-Martinez Band of Cahuilla Mission Indians
66–725 Martinez Rd
Thermal, CA 92274
Tel: 619-397-0300

Tule River Indian Tribe
PO Box 589
Porterville, CA 93258
Tel: 209-781-4271

Tuolumne Rancheria
PO Box 696
Tuolumne, CA 95379
Tel: 209-928-3475

Viejas Indians
PO Box 908
Alpine, CA 91903
Tel: 619-445-3810

Yurok Indian Tribe
c/o Klamath Field Office
PO Box 789
Klamath, CA 95548
Tel: 707-482-6421

UNRECOGNIZED INDIAN TRIBES

In addition to the more than 300 federally recognized Indian groups, there are about 130 unrecognized tribes. These groups do not receive services from the federal government. However, some of these groups have obtained state recognition and benefits and maintain tribal governments. More information can be obtained regarding unrecognized tribes by contacting the Bureau of

Indian Affairs, 1849 C St NW, Mail Stop 2620, Washington, DC 20240; tel: 202-208-3711

EMBASSIES

Australia: 1601 Massachusetts Ave NW, Washington, DC 20036. Tel: 202-797-3000.
Belgium: 3330 Garfield St NW, Washington, DC 20008. Tel: 202-333-6900.
Canada: 501 Pennsylvania Ave NW, Washington, DC 20001. Tel: 202-682-1740.
Denmark: 3200 Whitehaven St NW, Washington, DC 20008. Tel: 202-234-4300.
France: 4101 Reservoir Rd, Washington, DC 20007. Tel: 202-944-6000.
Germany: 4645 Reservoir Rd NW, Washington, DC 20007. Tel: 202-298-4000.
Great Britain: 3100 Massachusetts Ave NW, Washington, DC 20008. Tel: 202-462-1340.
Greece: 2221 Massachusetts Ave NW, Washington, DC 20008. Tel: 202-667-3168.
India: 2107 Massachusetts Ave NW, Washington, DC 20008. Tel: 202-939-7000.
Israel: 3514 International Dr. NW, Washington, DC 20008. Tel: 202-364-5500.
Italy: 1601 Fuller St NW, Washington, DC 20009. Tel: 202-328-5500.
Japan: 2520 Massachusetts Ave NW, Washington, DC 20008. Tel: 202-234-2266.
Mexico: 1911 Pennsylvania Ave NW, Washington, DC 20006. Tel: 202-728-1600.
The Netherlands: 4200 Linnean Ave NW, Washington, DC 20008. Tel: 202-244-5300.
New Zealand: 37 Observatory Circle, NW, Washington, DC 20008. Tel: 202-328-4800.
Norway: 2720 34th St NW, Washington, DC 20008. Tel: 202-333-6000.
Portugal: 2125 Kalorama Rd NW, Washington, DC 20008. Tel: 202-328-8610.
Singapore: 1824 R St NW, Washington, DC 20009.
South Korea: 2600 Virginia Ave NW, Washington, DC 20037. Tel: 202-939-5600.
Spain: 2700 15th St NW, Washington, DC 20009. Tel: 202-265-0190.
Taiwan: 2300 Kalorama Rd NW, Washington, DC 20008. Tel: 202-483-7200.

IMMIGRATION & CUSTOMS

US Customs
1301 Constitution Ave NW
Washington, DC

Tel: 202-566-8195

US Immigration and Naturalization Service
425 I St
Washington, DC 20536
Tel: 202-633-1900

US Forest Service
201 14th St SW
Washington, DC 20250
Tel: 202-447-3760

US Park Service
1100 Ohio Dr. SW
Washington, DC 20242
Tel: 202-619-7222

TOUR OPERATORS

American Indian Tour and Travel Agency
Daybreak Star Center
PO Box 99100
Seattle, WA 98199-0100
Tel: 206-285-4425

Arizona Bound Tours
5638 E. Thomas
Phoenix, AZ 85018
Tel: 602-994-0580

Crawley's Monument Valley Tours
PO Box 187
Kayenta, AZ 86033
Tel: 602-697-3463

Eight Northern Indian Pueblos Council
PO Box 969
San Juan Pueblo, NM 87566
Tel: 505-852-4265

Goulding's Monument Valley Tours
PO Box 1
Monument Valley, UT 84536
Tel: 801-727-3231

Nava-Hopi Tours
PO Box 339
Flagstaff, AZ 86002
Tel: 800-892-8687

North American Indian Heritage Center
PO Box 275
St Stephens, WY 82524
Tel: 307-856-6688

Singing Water Pottery and Tours
Rt. 1, Box 472-C
Santa Clara Pueblo
Espanola, NM 87532
Tel: 505-753-9663

Further Reading

General History and Culture

Andrist, Ralph. *The Long Death*. New York: Collier Books, 1964.

Brandon, William. *Indians*. Boston: Houghton Mifflin, 1961.

Brown, Dee. *Bury My Heart at Wounded Knee*. New York: Bantam Books, 1971.

Debo, Angie. *History of the Indians of the United States*. Norman: University of Oklahoma, 1970.

Deloria, Vine. *Behind the Trail of Broken Treaties*. New York: Delacorte, 1974.

Deloria, Vine. *Custer Died For Your Sins*. New York: Avon, 1969.

Deloria, Vine. *God Is Red*. New York: Grosset & Dunlop, 1973.

Erdoes, Richard. *Crying For a Dream*. Santa Fe: Bear and Company, 1990.

Fagan, Brian. *The Peopling of Ancient America*. London: Thames and Hudson, 1987.

Highwater, Jamake. *Arts of the Indian Americas*. New York: Harper & Row, 1983.

Highwater, Jamake. *Ritual of the Wind*. New York: Van der Marck, 1984.

Josephy, Alvin. *The Indian Heritage of America*. New York: Knopf, 1968.

Josephy, Alvin. *Patriot Chiefs*. New York: Viking, 1961.

La Farge, Oliver. *A Pictorial History of the American Indian*. New York: Crown, 1974.

Marriott, Alice and Rachlin, Carol. *Peyote*. New York: Signet, 1971.

Mather, Christine. *Native America: Arts, Traditions, and Celebrations*. New York: Crown, 1990.

McLuhan, T.C., ed. *Touch the Earth: A Self-portrait of Indian Existence*. Outerbridge & Dienstfrey, 1971.

McNickle, D'Arcy. *Native American Tribalism*. London: Oxford University Press, 1973.

Nabokov, Peter and Easton, Robert. *Native American Architecture*. New York: Oxford University Press, 1989.

National Geographic Society. *The World of the American Indian*. Washington, D.C.: National Geographic Society, 1974.

Slotkin, J.S. *The Peyote Religion*. Glencoe: Free Press, 1956.

Steiner, Stan. *The New Indians*. New York: Harper & Row, 1968.

Stewart, Omer. *Peyote Religion*. Norman: University of Oklahoma, 1987.

Sturtevant, William, ed. *Handbook of North American Indians*. Washington, D.C.: Smithsonian, 1978.

Tedlock, Dennis and Barbara, eds. *Teachings From the American Earth*. New York: Liveright, 1975.

Underhill, Ruth. *Red Man's Religion*. Chicago: University of Chicago Press, 1965.

Walker Art Center. *American Indian Art: Form and Function*. New York: Dutton, 1972.

Weatherford, Jack. *Indian Givers*. New York: Crown, 1988.

Regional

Barrett, S.M. *Geronimo: His Own Story*. New York: Dutton, 1970.

Brown, Joseph Epes. *The Sacred Pipe*. New York: Penguin, 1971.

Debo, Angie. *Geronimo: The Man, His Time, His Place*. Norman: University of Oklahoma, 1976.

Eargle, Dolan. *The Earth Is Our Mother: A Guide to the Indians of California*. San Francisco: Tress Company Press, 1986.

Ferguson, Erna. *Dancing Gods*. Albuquerque: University of New Mexico, 1931.

Gifford, E. & Block, G., eds. *California Indian Nights*. Lincoln: University of Nebraska Press, 1930.

Gilbert, Bil. *God Gave Us This Country*. New York: Atheneum, 1989.

Hyde, George. *Red Cloud's Folk*. Norman: University of Oklahoma, 1937.

Kroeber, Theodora. *Ishi*. Berkeley: University of California Press, 1961.

Locke, Raymond. *Book of the Navajo*. Los Angeles: Mankind Publishing, 1976.

Momaday, N. Scott. *The Names: A Memoir*. Tucson: University of Arizona Press, 1976.

Marriott, Alice. *Maria: the Potter of San Ildefonso*. Norman: University of Oklahoma Press, 1948.

Matthiessen, Peter. *Indian Country*. New York: Viking, 1984.

Matthiessen, Peter. *In the Spirit of Crazy Horse*. New York: Viking, 1983.

Mays, Buddy. *Indian Villages of the Southwest*. San Francisco: Chronicle, 1985.

Neihardt, John. *Black Elk Speaks*. Lincoln: University of Nebraska, 1961.

Opler, Morris. *An Apache Life-way*. Chicago: University of Chicago Press, 1941.

Sandoz, Marie. *Crazy Horse: The Strange Man of the Oglalas*. New York: Knopf, 1942.

Spivey, Richard. *Maria*. Flagstaff: Northland, 1978.

Vestal, Stanley. *Sitting Bull: Champion of the Sioux*. Norman: University of Oklahoma, 1957.

Waters, Frank. *Book of the Hopi*. New York: Penguin Books, 1963.

Waters, Frank. *Masked Gods*. Athens: Swallow Press, 1950.

Fiction and Poetry

Erdrich, Louise. *Love Medicine*. New York: Holt, Rinehart and Winston, 1984.

Other novels by Erdrich: *Beet Queen*, *Tracks*.

Allen, Paula Gunn. *Spider Woman's Granddaughters: Traditional Tales and Contemporary Writings by Native American Women*. Boston: Beacon Press, 1989.

Harjo, Joy. *She Had Some Horses*. New York: Thunder's Mouth Press, 1983.

Other collections of poetry: *In Mad Love and War*.

Highwater, Jamake, ed. *Words in Blood*. New York: Meridian, 1984.

Short fiction, poems and stories by Native Americans.

Hillerman, Tony. *Skinwalkers*. New York: Perennial Library, 1986.

Hillerman is the author of a popular series of mystery novels featuring Navajo policemen. Other titles include: *Dark Wind*, *Dance Hall of the Dead*, *The Blessing Way*, *Talking God* and *Coyote Waits*.

Momaday, N. Scott. *House Made of Dawn*. New York: Harper and Row, 1966.

Other novels: *The Way To Rainy Mountain*, *The Gourd Dancer*.

Ortiz, Simon. *From Sand Creek*. New York: Thunder's Mouth Press, 1981.

Other poetry collections: *A Good Journey* and *Going for the Rain*.

Silko, Leslie Marmon. *Ceremony*. New York: Penguin, 1986.

Other novels: *Storyteller*.

Storm, Hyemeyohsts. *Seven Arrows*. New York: Harper & Row, 1972.

A poetic exploration of Northern Cheyenne history and spirituality, part narrative, part poetry, part philosophy. A unique and moving work.

Welch, James. *Fool's Crow*. New York: Penguin, 1987.

Other novels: *The Indian Lawyer*, *Winter in the Blood*.

ART/PHOTO CREDITS

Photography by

134, 136, 137, 139, 151, 163	**Richard Baldes**
168, 171	**Kenny Blackbird**
262, 265, 267, 268/269, 270	**Steve Bruno**
328, 330, 332	**Lee Brumbaugh**
77	**Joseph Cavaretta**
335	**Dolan Eargle**
101, 104, 284	**John Gattuso**
260/261, 263	**George Hardeen**
103, 235, 245, 290	**Alan Manley**
202, 205, 206, 207	**Larry Mayer**
296/297, 300, 301, 303, 304	**Minnesota Tourism**
28/29, 37, 38, 305, 324	**National Museum of American Art, Smithsonian Institution**
32/33, 127, 331, 333, 334	**National Park Service**
277, 278	**Stewart Nicholas**
31, 68, 248, 253, 282	**Mark Nohl, New Mexico Economic & Tourism Department**
310	**North Carolina Division of Trade & Tourism**
3, 18/19, 20/21, 27, 30, 52, 54, 55, 59, 60, 61, 63, 66, 67, 70/71, 74, 75, 76, 84, 85, 87, 92, 95, 96/97, 98, 102, 106/ 107, 108/109, 141L, 144/145, 185, 192/193, 209, 210/211, 215, 222, 225, 226, 230, 232, 233, 234, 236/237, 249, 251, 257, 279	**Monty Roessel**
100	**Tom Root**
Cover, 9, 14/15, 16/17, 22, 23, 24, 25, 26, 36, 64, 65, 70/71, 72, 78/79, 80, 81, 82, 83, 86, 88/89, 90, 93, 105, 110/ 111, 112/113, 132/133, 138, 140, 141R, 142, 146, 147, 152, 155, 156, 157, 158/159, 160, 162, 172/173, 176, 177, 178, 179, 180, 181, 182, 183, 184, 194, 196, 197, 198, 199, 200/201, 212, 213, 214, 216, 217, 218, 219, 223, 227, 228, 229, 231, 238, 239, 240, 241L, 241R, 243, 244, 246/247, 250, 252, 254, 255, 256L, 256R 258, 264, 272, 274, 275, 280, 286, 291, 298, 302, 306/307, 308, 311, 312, 313, 314, 315, 316/317, 318, 321, 322, 323, 326/327, 336	**John Running**
34, 35, 39, 40, 41, 42, 43, 44, 45, 46, 47, 48, 49, 50/51, 53, 56/57, 58, 69, 125, 131, 135, 143, 149, 150, 166, 170, 187, 189, 195, 204, 259, 266, 271, 273, 283, 299, 309, 319, 325	**Smithsonian Institution, National Anthropological Archives**
120, 121, 122, 124, 126, 128, 129, 130	**South Dakota Tourism**
94, 203, 208	**Spiker Communications**
287, 288, 289, 292/293	**Sandra Tatum**
169	**Travel Montana**
190	**Washington State Tourism Division**
276	**Vennie White**
186, 188	**Jan Wigen**

Maps **Berndtson & Berndtson**

Illustrations **Klaus Geisler**

Visual Consultant **V. Barl**

INDEX

APA INSIGHT GUIDES

ARE Going Places:

Asia & Pacific
East Asia
South Asia
South East Asian Wildlife
South East Asia
★Marine Life
Australia
Great Barrier Reef
Melbourne
★★Sydney
★Bhutan
Burma/Myanmar
China
Beijing
India
Calcutta
Delhi, Jaipur, Agra
India's Western Himalaya
Indian Wildlife
★New Delhi
Rajasthan
South India
Indonesia
★★Bali
★Bali Bird Walks
Java
★Jakarta
★Yogyakarta
Korea
Japan
Tokyo
Malaysia
★Kuala Lumpur
★Malacca
★Penang
★★Nepal
Kathmandu
Kathmandu Bikes & Hikes
New Zealand
Pakistan
Philippines
★Sikkim
★★Singapore
Sri Lanka
Taiwan

Thailand
★★Bangkok
★Chiang Mai
★Phuket
★Tibet
Turkey
★★Istanbul
Turkish Coast
★Turquoise Coast
Vietnam

Africa
East African Wildlife
South Africa
Egypt
Cairo
The Nile
Israel
Jerusalem
Kenya
Morocco
Namibia
The Gambia & Senegal
Tunisia
Yemen

Europe
Austria
★★Vienna
Belgium
Brussels
Channel Islands
Continental Europe
Cyprus
Czechoslovakia
★★Prague
Denmark
Eastern Europe
Finland
France
★★Alsace
★★Brittany
★★Cote d'Azur
★★Loire Valley
★★Paris

Provence
Germany
★★Berlin
Cologne
Düsseldorf
Frankfurt
Hamburg
★★Munich
The Rhine
Great Britain
Edinburg
Glasgow
★★Ireland
★★London
Oxford
Scotland
Wales
Greece
★★Athens
★★Crete
★Rhodes
Greek Islands
Hungary
★★Budapest
Iceland
Italy
Florence
★★Rome
★★Sardinia
★★Tuscany
Umbria
★★Venice
Netherlands
Amsterdam
Norway
Poland
Portugal
★★Lisbon
Madeira
Spain
★★Barcelona
★Costa Blanca
★Costa Brava
★Costa del Sol/Marbella
Catalonia

Gran Canaria
★Ibiza
Madrid
Mallorca & Ibiza
★Mallorca
★Seville
Southern Spain
Tenerife
Sweden
Switzerland
(Ex) USSR
Moscow
St. Petersburg
Waterways of Europe
Yugoslavia
★Yugoslavia's Adriatic
Coast

The Americas
Bermuda
Canada
Montreal
Caribbean
Bahamas
Barbados
Jamaica
Trinidad & Tobago
Puerto Rico
Costa Rica
Mexico
Mexico City
South America
Argentina
Amazon Wildlife
Brazil
Buenos Aires
Chile
Ecuador
Peru
Rio

USA/Crossing America
Alaska
American Southwest
Boston
California
Chicago
Florida
Hawaii
Los Angeles
Miami
Native America
New England
New Orleans
★★New York City
New York State
Northern California
Pacific Northwest
★★San Francisco
Southern California
Texas
The Rockies
Washington D.C.

★★Also available as
Insight Pocket Guide
★Available as Insight
Pocket Guide only

INSIGHT POCKET GUIDES

SEE Y'ALL SOON!

See You Soon! In USA

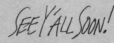